SHUTTING DOWN THE NATIONAL DREAM

SHUTTING DOWN THE NATIONAL DREAM

A.V. ROE AND THE TRAGEDY OF THE
AVRO ARROW

GREIG STEWART

McGRAW-HILL RYERSON LIMITED
Toronto Montreal

SHUTTING DOWN THE NATIONAL DREAM

Copyright © 1988 by Greig Stewart

First published in 1988 by
McGraw-Hill Ryerson Limited
330 Progress Avenue
Scarborough, Ontario   M1P 2Z5

Care has been taken to trace the ownership of any copyright material contained in this text. The publishers welcome any information that will enable them to rectify, in subsequent editions, any incorrect or omitted reference or credit.

1 2 3 4 5 6 7 8 9 0 D 7 6 5 4 3 2 1 0 9 8

Canadian Cataloguing in Publication Data

Stewart, Greig
  Shutting down the national dream

ISBN 0-07-549675-5

1. Avro Arrow (Turbojet fighter plane). 2. A. V. Roe Canada Limited. 3. Aircraft industry – Canada. 4. Canada – Politics and government – 1957–1963.* I. Title.

TL685.3.S83 1988   338.4'76237464'0971   C88-094383-1

"High Flight" by John Gillespie Magee, Jr., is quoted from *The New Treasury of War Poetry: Poems of the Second World War,* edited by George Herbert Clarke (New York: Literary Classics Incorporated, 1943.)

Book design: Kirk Stephens

Printed and bound in Canada

—————

This one is for
Margaret Jeannie McGregor,
Robert G. Stewart,
the 14,528 employees
of A. V. Roe Canada who lost more
than just their jobs
that cold Friday afternoon in 1959,
and Marlène

CONTENTS

ACKNOWLEDGEMENTS

Through interviews, historical research, private papers, and company correspondence, I have sought the story of A. V. Roe Canada. The threads that run through the story are people; some were there throughout the entire life of the company, others were there at the beginning or at the end, but all took part in or witnessed many of the key events that make up the A. V. Roe Canada story.

I would especially like to thank Paul Dilworth, the first general manager of A. V. Roe's gas turbine division (which later became Orenda Engines); James C. Floyd, who designed the C-102 Jetliner and later became vice-president engineering of Avro Aircraft; and the late Fred T. Smye, first employee of A. V. Roe Canada who later became president of Avro Aircraft and a director of A. V. Roe Canada. To them I will always be indebted for giving so freely not only of their time, but of their personal papers, diaries, and thoughts as well.

In the case of the late Crawford Gordon, Jr., stories and recollections of his activities were drawn from friends, associates, and immediate family.

Special thanks go to Professor James Eayrs for his unpublished paper on the story of the Arrow from the government/Chiefs of Staff Committee side of things; to Desmond M. Chorley for John Frost's views of the CF-100 from his unpublished manuscript, "The Clunk: Canada's World Beating All-Weather Jet Fighter;" and to Robert R. Robinson, author of *Scrap Arrow,* who watched this book seed and grow and whose cheerful encouragement never waned. To the staff in the "morgue" of the *Globe and Mail* who patiently put up with my research crusade through their archives, thank you also.

I would also like to thank the many former employees of A. V. Roe Canada, the members of the RCAF, those at Trans Canada Air Lines, and the "just plain interested folk" who gave of their time, hearts, and minds in order that this story might be told. They include Ron Adey, Ernie Alderton, Ray Atkin, Lloyd Attridge, Jim Bain, Mrs. Ken Barnes, Winnett Boyd, Elizabeth Buchanin, Air Marshal Hugh Campbell, Gloria Collinson, Mike Cooper-Slipper, Joe Cribar, Waclaw Czerwinski, S. D. Davies, Des Earl, Air Vice Marshal John Easton, Wing Commander Ray Foottit, John Frost, Professor John Gellner, Mary Gordon, Dianna Gordon, Crawford Gordon III, Geoff Grossmith, Guest Hake, John D. Harbron, Stan Harper, Hubert Harris, Paul Hellyer, Ernie Hemphill, Jack Hilton, Jim Hornick, General A. C. (Chester) Hull, Bob Johnson, Harry Keast, J. N. (Pat) Kelly, Sam Lax, Professor James Laxer, Hugh Mackenzie, Larry Milberry, Jack Millie, David Moran, Joe Morley, Betty Moore, Ron Nunney, Ron Page, John Painter, John C. Pallett, Mario Pesando, W. D. (Dave) Roberts, George Robertson, Don Rogers, Squadron Leader Joe Schultz, Kay Shaw, Dorothy Carswell Smye, Randy Smye, Tim Smye, John Tory, Jr., Joe Turner, W. A. (Bill) Waterton, Murray Willer, Elwy Yost, and Janusz Zurakowski. The only individual who repeatedly refused any assistance whatsoever on this story was John George Diefenbaker.

On a personal note I'd like to thank Celeste and Amanda, Dunner, Father Mike, Hans and Emma, Connie Hodges, John Thomas Lloyd, Lizzie Renwick, Dr. Joan, Pat Orbill, Mary Catherine, Hurricane Mike, Cheryl Elizabeth, Different Dan, Valerie, Dr. Bob, and Wise Jim for being there during the darker moments, and Dina Wells and Sandy Suckly for typing the manuscript.

For the loan of photographs I am indebted to Jim Floyd, Jack Hilton, and Ron Nunney. The cover image is taken from Robert Curry's fine painting of the Avro Arrow (courtesy Keith Kennedy).

For reading the page proofs and making many helpful critical comments and corrections of facts and spellings of names, I gratefully acknowledge the assistance of Desmond M. Chorley, Paul Dilworth, James Eayrs, Jim Floyd, Larry Milberry, Mario Pesando, and Janusz Zurakowski.

Finally, to Glen Ellis of McGraw-Hill Ryerson for his faith in this project, and to my editor, Andrea Gallagher Ellis, who brought the story to life, my sincerest appreciation.

FOREWORD

In the life of every nation there are efforts and achievements worthy of documentation. Such is the story of A.V. Roe Canada, a chapter of Canadian aviation history I was proud to be a part of. Greig Stewart's work sets the story of the Avro Arrow in its historical, political, and international context. Through interviews with many of those involved with the company and its aircraft, he offers a representative cross-section of perspectives, and demonstrates how frequently personality struggles directed the course of events.

The story of A.V. Roe's Avro Arrow has a sad ending: the cancellation of an aircraft that, for many Canadians, had become the national dream. On February 20, 1959, it was with disbelief that we heard of the announcement, in Parliament, by Prime Minister John George Diefenbaker that the Arrow program would be terminated.

I can still see the faces of the people, the thousands of men and women who had contributed to the design, development, and production of the Arrow. Their dream of providing Canada's defence with the best fighter plane in the world, and the jobs they had been so proud of, had suddenly disappeared.

Less than two months later, the five Arrows already test flown were cut up for scrap, and all components, drawings, photographs, and reports relating to the aircraft were destroyed on government instruction. Since then, many people have wondered how it could have been possible for so many years of hard work and so much success to be ruined.

Why did the government take this action? Personal animosity of the Prime Minister towards Avro management? Rivalry among branches of the armed forces? The influence of a competing American aircraft industry? The cost of the aircraft? Or perhaps government inexperience in understanding the problems and costs of research and development in modern industry.

Whatever the reasons for it, the brutal termination of the Arrow was a devastating blow to our technological potential. Even before the installation of its ultimate (Iroquois) engines, the Arrow was probably the most advanced interceptor in the world. Its cancellation resulted in the loss, in many cases to other countries, of the technological brain trust that created her and damaged our confidence in ourselves. It was almost as if our spirit as a nation died.

Contrary to some of the expert opinion of that time, the Arrow was far from being the last of its line and kind. Former Chief of the General Staff, General Guy Simonds, was proven incorrect in his assertions that the fighter-interceptor was obsolete for defence purposes. Since the cancellation of the Arrow, Canada has purchased many aircraft of this type and intends to use them for years to come.

The Arrow was very similar in specifications and performance to the latest and most capable Soviet interceptor, the MIG-31, in service since 1983. The number of strategic bombers in service in the Soviet Union is currently in excess of 1,000.

The outstanding performance of the Arrow can best be appreciated through speed comparisons with other aircraft. The Arrow was about 750 mph faster than the first Canadian jet interceptor, the CF-100 (its maiden flight preceding the Arrow's by eight years). Thirty years ago the Arrow was flying faster than today's most advanced Canadian fighter, the CF-18, which we purchase from the United States. The Soviet Union now supplies over twenty countries with aircraft that have a maximum speed of twice the speed of sound (the same class as the Arrow). Our service aircraft, including the CF-18, have not yet reached this speed.

About thirty years have gone by since the days of the glory and destruction of the Arrow, but the memory of that time has not disappeared. At Avro and Orenda reunions many hundreds still gather to talk about the good times—and the sad time.

Governments and torches can destroy an aircraft, but they cannot destroy hope, and aspiration, and the majesty of the questing spirit. In the hearts of the people, the dream lives on.

—Janusz Zurakowski

Oh, I have slipped the surly bonds of earth,
And danced the skies on laughter-silvered wings;
Sunward I've climbed and joined the tumbling mirth
Of sun-split clouds — and done a hundred things
You have not dreamed of — wheeled and soared and swung
High in the sunlit silence. Hov'ring there,
I've chased the shouting wind along and flung
My eager craft through footless halls of air.
Up, up the long delirious, burning blue
I've topped the wind-swept heights with easy grace,
Where never lark, or even eagle, flew;
And, while with silent, lifting mind I've trod
The high untrespassed sanctity of space,
Put out my hand, and touched the face of God.

John Gillespie Magee, Jr.

PROLOGUE

Just about every Saturday afternoon, soon after the bars open, in legion halls, hotels, and taverns scattered across Canada, men with a common past gather for a weekly ritual. Many are retired, most are grey or greying, all are over fifty—men whose fingers remember the touch of a draftsman's pencil, whose ears still ring with the long-ago sound of cutting metal and the machine-gun clatter of rivet guns, who still look up at the sound of a high flying aircraft—men who were seduced by the romance of flight.

When the first round of drinks is cleared away, the conversation drifts from stories of kids and grand-kids and vacations and families to a time, their time, not so long ago, when these men and thousands like them had jets in their eyes.

These are the men of A. V. Roe Canada, the one-time post-war aircraft conglomerate which, in fourteen short, precocious years, almost single-handedly turned the aviation world on its ear. Working at A. V. Roe Canada and its two subsidiaries, Avro Aircraft and Orenda Engines, was the time of their lives. They designed and produced aircraft and engines that, even by today's standards, were top shelf—the CF-100, the Jetliner, the Orenda, the Iroquois, the Arrow . . .

1

By the third round, the air is thick with memory. Small, commonplace events that took place thirty years ago in the offices of Orenda or the assembly bays of Avro are recalled as though they happened only yesterday.

As the past draws nearer, the main event comes into focus. It is a bleak Friday morning, the twentieth of February, 1959. To a man, they can tell you, with astonishing clarity, like those of us who remember the Kennedy assassination, exactly where they were, precisely what they were doing, the day they shot the Arrow down . . .

The aircraft known as the CF-105 Avro Arrow was cancelled by John Diefenbaker's Conservative government on February 20, 1959, and three years later the industrial giant known as A. V. Roe Canada disappeared from the aviation scene. Not only did the company design, build, and produce from scratch Canada's first jet engines and aircraft; the design and development personnel, the engineers, the men of vision, were described by General Lauris Norstad of NATO as "just about the best team anywhere."

During its short life, the company gave birth to a giant aircraft and gas-turbine complex spread over some 400 acres and having a manufacturing area of over 2,000,000 square feet by 1958. Avro Aircraft and Orenda Engines were only two of the many companies that allowed A. V. Roe Canada, by 1957, to call itself the third largest corporation in Canada.

This is more than just a story of aircraft and engines and corporate acquisitions; it is a story of people. Avro and Orenda were more than just employers in the 1950s, they were *the* places to work. There was a special "esprit-de-corps" among Avro and Orenda personnel that kept employee absenteeism low and lateness almost non-existent. Virtually everyone, from assembly bay workers to accountants to maintenance men, felt good about what they were doing. They felt, at the time at least, that they were making a contribution to Canada.

People who visited Avro and Orenda in the Arrow days described the atmosphere as "magic." "There was a camaraderie, a dedication, a sort of bond among those people that was almost tangible," reflected one writer. "They were so proud of that airplane, and of the inescapable fact that they were producing something that was the best in the whole bloody world. You could sense it the minute you walked in the place."

There were casualties that extended far beyond the broken bits of CF-100's and Jetliners and Arrows scattered throughout the country in junkyards, museums, and basement recreation rooms. The real casualties of this story were the 14,000 men and women who lost their jobs and in many cases their future as well.

Since the cancellation of the Arrow in 1959, Canadians have become obsessed with what happened at Malton and elevated it to the status of legend. In many ways the legend is larger than life. Hardly a month passes without some news publication running a story on the Arrow or the Jetliner or "Black Friday." Several books and countless feature articles have been written on the company and its planes, to say nothing of the numerous films and radio documentaries.

A. V. Roe Canada was founded in 1945 when Hawker-Siddeley Aircraft in England bought out the wartime crown corporation Victory Aircraft on generous terms from the Canadian government, in the person of C. D. Howe. The English company had been impressed with the achievement of Victory Aircraft in building their Lancaster under licence during the war, and the Canadian government was anxious to develop an indigenous aircraft industry under British guidance.

In the beginning the company was to develop a jet fighter for the RCAF and a jet transport for Trans-Canada Air Lines (another crown corporation). The jet transport was delayed because of a change in engines which necessitated redesign, and by the time it flew, TCA had turned to other sources. The jet fighter was subject to grave design flaws which were not dealt with before it was rushed into production, and the first shipment of 10 aircraft was returned by the RCAF.

By this time it was 1951; if senior members of the Liberal cabinet had really understood how bad things were, they might well have shut the entire operation down then. As it was they sent in a trouble-shooter, hand-picked by C. D. Howe, in an attempt to salvage their huge investment in the CF-100 jet fighter. Crawford Gordon took control in 1951 and A. V. Roe Canada was reborn.

Under Gordon, the company began to make a name for itself and A. V. Roe Canada executives quickly became the bulls in the china shop of Canadian business, a brash, cocky band of brothers who had trouble following the rules.

Most of the company executives were products of a wartime Canada, some of them "dollar-a-year" men who skipped military service and went to Ottawa to be tutored by the legendary and indomitable C. D. Howe in his Department of Munitions and Supply. Young, most of them college educated and eager, with Howe they learned a basic economic lesson which would follow them into senior positions with corporations in the post-war years and stay with them the rest of their corporate lives. It is this: that when Canada spends money in Canada to design, develop, and manufacture high-technology products like aircraft, the unit cost of such items is not of overriding importance. The money is spent in Canada to provide jobs for Canadian workers who in turn pay Canadian taxes and buy goods and services, helping to strengthen other Canadian companies and the economy as a whole. Design, research, and development are investments in the future, raising the level of Canadian technology and lowering our reliance on foreign technology and expertise.

Toronto's three dailies—the *Star*, the *Telegram*, and the *Globe and Mail*—all had full-time aviation reporters in the 1950s. And much to the chagrin of companies like de Havilland and Canadair, in the late fifties the only aviation news really worth covering was what was happening with the Arrow at A. V. Roe Canada. Indeed, between 1957 and 1959, not a day passed without at least one story on A. V. Roe in the first few pages of one of the major dailies.

Apart from the tenacity of the *Globe*'s aviation writer James Hornick, what was missing were the real stories—stories of alcohol abuse and nervous breakdowns that took their toll on key executives and design people; of cliques and power struggles within the company that inhibited the flow of vital information; of corners cut; of basic design flaws surfacing long after aircraft had been ordered into production; and of lives lost because someone who should have known better, didn't. At A. V. Roe Canada, patience and caution sometimes seemed to take second place to getting the engines and the aircraft into the air as soon as was humanly possible.

It has often been said that the oil behind the wheels of A. V. Roe Canada was bourbon, and that company executives were little more than a bunch of canny political cowboys, free-wheeling and free-spending, who managed to herd the imagination of an entire nation into truly believing the company motto: The Next Big Step.

A. V. Roe Canada was the child of C. D. Howe and a long-entrenched Liberal administration. By 1957, after twenty-two years of Liberal rule, the government had become arrogant, self-serving, and admittedly out of touch with the Canadian people. When Diefenbaker and the Conservatives were elected, scapegoats were sought, and the prime target was C. D. Howe.

Howe had come into the government in 1935 on his own terms, and during the Second World War was given a mandate as Minister of Munitions and Supplies that made him the most powerful man in the country. He continued to enjoy this power almost undiminished as long as the Liberals remained in office. He had a "let them howl" attitude to all opposition, whether public or political, and he passed this attitude on to the younger men who tutored under him, some of whom formed the top management of A. V. Roe Canada.

By the late fifties the men who ran A. V. Roe had "fallen victim to their own unbridled enthusiasm, their supreme conviction that no assignment, no matter how challenging, was beyond their capabilities." They were arrogant, overconfident, belligerent even, when dealing with the Diefenbaker administration, and in the end, it was this more than anything that cost them it all.

In the course of researching the material for this book and in conducting the many interviews that give it life, it struck me that this could be called a love story, a love story between men and engines and aircraft. In the quiet way they remember, and in the way their eyes occasionally mist up when they recall a special moment during those days at Malton, these men seem haunted by a past they didn't have a chance to finish. It is painful to recall what was obviously the time of their lives, but it is even more painful living with the unfulfillable desire to get another crack at it and this time to get it right. A chance, regrettably, lost to time. It's the "might have beens" that still hurt and that touch with profound sadness virtually every person I interviewed who was there.

In the late afternoon darkness of the Legion Hall, another Saturday afternoon comes to an end much sooner than the men sitting around the table would like. These men with a common past find comfort in each other's company, and though the stories have all been told before, they will all be told again. The love affair continues.

1

THE BUSINESS
OF WAR

This story begins as it one day would end, with an airplane. In the beginning it was the Lancaster, in the end, the Arrow.

It might not have begun at all had not a tired, face-worn Englishman named Roy Hardy Dobson decided to take a working holiday to Canada in the late wartime summer of 1943. Dobson was typical of so many British production managers of the time, an up-from-the-workbench, never-forget-where-you-come-from type, hardened by the events of the previous quarter century—the General Strike, the First World War, the Great Depression, and now the Second World War. Rough-spoken and ebullient, he had risen to become managing director of A. V. Roe and Company in Manchester, part of the massive British Hawker-Siddeley aircraft conglomerate responsible for such well-known airplanes as the Anson, the Hurricane, the Tempest, the Whitley, and most recently a converted Manchester heavy bomber everyone called the Lancaster.

Since January, 1942, the Victory Aircraft Company in Malton, Ontario, had been tooling up to produce Dobson's Lancaster under licence. For over a year now stories had been drifting across the Atlantic to England:

this Canadian company claimed they could build a Lancaster in six days (beating the best British effort to date by a full two days); they could turn the Lancaster out at the rate of one a day; and they could build a better plane as well.

The war, now in its fourth year, had taken its toll on Dobson, aging him well beyond his fifty-two years. He needed a change, and the outrageous boast of Victory Aircraft gave him all the excuse he needed. In company with friend and fellow director Frank Spriggs, Dobson crossed the Atlantic by Ferry Command, hoping to be at Malton for the roll-out of the first Canadian-built Lancaster. As it happened, they were two weeks late. "Oh lumme," said Dobson upon arriving at Malton, "I didn't expect the buggers to produce their first plane until next year!"

Canada has never been a nation of war. Our heroes are more likely to be found in politics, the arts, or sports, than in the military. We are the only nuclear-capable nation in the world that has chosen on principle not to develop nuclear weaponry. Our prime ministers have yet to seek election on their war records, and our statesmen have always insisted, even in wartime, on maintaining strict control over all military decisions and actions.

A considerable Canadian military establishment had come into being during the First World War and the Department of National Defence (DND) was formed more to organize the armed forces with economy and efficiency than for the defence of Canada. The National Defence Act was passed on January 1, 1923, despite opposition from military brass who feared that it would mean not only less money allocated for military appropriations, but that competition for those limited dollars would reduce Canada's air, sea, and land forces to little more than bickering sisters. They were right.

This "sibling rivalry" prompted Prime Minister Mackenzie King to establish the Joint Staff Committee (JSC) comprised of representatives of the three branches of the military. The committee would make "collective" decisions to be presented to the cabinet for consideration. The JSC, later known as the Chiefs of Staff Committee (CSC), was formed in 1927.

It comes as no surprise, then, that when the Liberal government of Mackenzie King began exploring the possibility of a re-armament program for the sadly neglected armed forces in the late 1930s, it did so quietly, cautiously, and with as little fanfare as possible. Stores of military equipment and supplies were at an all-time low. The militia, air corps, and navy were understaffed and underequipped, the munitions industry rudimentary.

The decision to take those first tentative steps at re-arming was a bitter pill to swallow. Still painfully fresh in the memory of the country was Canada's involvement in the Great War: 400,000 Canadian young men in uniform, 60,000 dead. Since Armistice, Canada had retreated from anything military like animals running from a forest fire: blindly and quickly. "The Ottawa authorities may as well realize," said an editorial at the time, "first as last, that Canada is not going to stand for the wholesale expenditure of large sums of money for military and naval purposes. The people of this country do not propose to submit to the God of Militarism."

When it came to the military, austerity and bare sustenance were the orders of the day. Any monies made available for the maintenance of the armed forces, a little over $13 million in 1933/34, was barely enough to keep the men in uniform, let alone close to combat readiness. A deep-rooted reluctance to spend money on military preparedness in time of peace was intensified by the public feeling that anyone seeking a career in the armed forces was obviously too lazy to earn a real living. To Canadians, war was a state of emergency, to be dealt with only when war was declared and not a moment sooner.

Compounding the problem for Mackenzie King were his own feelings. He had always been suspicious of military leaders, generals in particular: surely they withheld vital information from him and planned secret military projects without his knowledge or consent. He was certain of it. "Is it not for the civil arm of the government to lay down the scheme of policy and liabilities," he would argue, "and then for the military to submit plans accordingly?" No, Mackenzie King was not going to submit to the God of Militarism.

During those dark, money-scarce, military appropriation years just prior to the Second World War, Mackenzie King decided that the cabinet should have access to the military decisions of the Joint Staff Committee. The possibility of a military strong enough to overpower a civilian government was a very real concern to him. The result was the formation of the Cabinet Defence Committee (CDC) made up of the Prime Minister as chairman, the Minister of National Defence, the Minister of Finance, and the Minister of Justice.

Nowhere was the austerity felt more keenly than in the Royal Canadian Air Force. The militia at least had guns. Money spent on both civil and military aviation for 1933/34, for instance, was only $1.75 million compared to $5.23 million the previous year. As for military readiness, the picture was even more disturbing. In October, 1933, the RCAF's Assistant Senior Air Officer, Group Captain G. O. Johnson, had prepared a report on the minimum aircraft requirements for the country in peacetime. Johnson indicated that Canada would require a total of 70 aircraft of which 46 would be "front line" and 24 "second line." At the time the RCAF could muster barely 19 aircraft, all of the "second line" category. Even as late as 1939, on the very eve of war, the air force consisted of a paltry 4,061 officers and airmen flying a total of 270 assorted airworthy craft of which only 40 were suitable for combat.

Political opinion was divided. On one side were those who certainly didn't want a repeat of the First World War experience—many Canadian companies had made huge, highly suspicious profits turning out sometimes less than first-rate material. The infamous Canadian-made Ross rifle was one such example. Used by the Canadian First Division in Flanders in 1914, the rifle was found to jam up in combat, and the men discarded the weapon in the field for the more reliable British-made Lee Enfield .303.

On the other side, however, were Meighen, Bennett, Manion, Drew, and others who were convinced that war in Europe was inevitable and that Canada should be ready to come to the aid of Britain and France. The Prime Minister did not agree: "The present danger . . ." he said, "is minor in degree and second hand in origin." Mackenzie King had come away from a visit with Hitler in 1935 convinced that Germany had no intention of war.

Although defence spending more than doubled between 1935 and 1939, it was still comparatively modest at $35 million. The Prime Minister had no intention of sending a large expeditionary force overseas; he felt a smaller force in the air would be more economical and effective. Even after the war began, Canada's main contribution was intended to be war production and the training of Canadian airmen through the British Commonwealth Air Training Plan (BCATP). In December, 1939, Mackenzie King signed the BCATP agreement which called for 48,000 Canadian recruits over three years. (Of the 131,000 graduates of the BCATP, over half were Canadian.)

Then came Dunkirk in June of 1940 and in a matter of a few weeks, the world was suddenly a different place. The Wermacht might be marching down Whitehall by Christmas. Great Britain who, up until that point, had been Canada's main source of military hardware— same weapons, same uniforms, same equipment—was suddenly in the reverse position of looking to Canada as a source of supply. Before the last Allied soldier was off the beach at Dunkirk, Britain had already placed an order in Canada for small arms, shells, Bren guns, and troop carriers. But the Canadian warehouse was empty.

"It is obvious," wrote a Canadian government official, "that we have no Canadian sources of supply adequate for the present situation." He went on to suggest that Canada and Britain could not totally rely on American sources of supply, that the only wise move was to have all of the necessary equipment produced in Canada.

The Prime Minister had little choice. Time had run out. The country still had an army of only 4,000 soldiers, a navy of only 17 ships, an air combat force of only 40 planes, and was now being called upon to be Britain's wartime lifeline. Mackenzie King wanted to avoid conscription, so he opted for all-out support of setting up a defence industry. The job of organizing the war industry fell to the transportation minister, a shrewd, American-born academic-turned-businessman, Clarence Decatur Howe. Howe

was very different from the old Wasp elites that ruled Toronto and Montreal, whose members were British in their orientation, turning towards Government House, the Crown, and the Empire for guidance. Howe was middle class, self-made, a tough, American get-up-and-go engineering type. The dollar-a-year men who came to aid in the war effort had grown up with Hollywood movies, the first generation to do so. They were in love with the American style of easy-going brashness, the "get things done without a lot of stuffy nonsense" attitude that Howe so perfectly epitomized. . . .

Born at Waltham, Mass., in 1886, Howe graduated from MIT in 1907 and stayed on as an engineering instructor for a few months until his professor recommended both him and a fellow graduate for a full-fledged lectureship at Dalhousie University. They tossed a coin to see who would apply, and Howe won. After five years in Halifax, he moved to the Lakehead as chief engineer with the Board of Grain Commissioners and three years later established his own engineering firm. During the next decade and a half, Howe built grain storage facilities worth $125 million at harbours from Canada to Argentina, including the Port Arthur Saskatchewan Pool Seven, the largest grain elevator in the world. . . .

He now began to move into the highest circles of the Liberal Party, which had been temporarily put out of office by R.B. Bennett in 1930. One of his friends was Norman Lambert, . . . the party's national organizer. During the winter of 1933, Lambert invited Howe to dine at the Chateau Laurier with Vincent Massey, then president of the National Liberal Federation. Convinced by the two men that he should stand for the Port Arthur seat in the next election, Howe set one condition: that if elected, he would immediately be taken into the Cabinet. Mackenzie King promptly invited him to Laurier House and enthusiastically endorsed both his candidacy and the pledge of a portfolio.

Mackenzie King returned as Prime Minister in 1935 and Howe won the Port Arthur seat by a comfortable margin. On the strength of his engineering background, Howe was appointed Minister of Railways and Canals.

John Deutsch, who was probably the most remarkable and certainly the most practical of the great Ottawa mandarins, watched Howe operate at close hand for more than two decades. "The fact is," says Deutsch, "that CD didn't know a policy when he saw one. He knew how to run a railroad, how to make the thing go—but *why* you had a railroad, that is a question he did not ask. He never had any decisive input in general policy matters. Someone responsible told him, 'This is what we need,' and he went and did it. He was an operating executive—one of the greatest this country has ever had."

Howe rejected the original proposal that Canada's war industry be organized under the Department of National Defence, favouring an entirely new organization set up along the lines of private industry. Accordingly, the Department of Munitions and Supply was formed on April 9, 1940, and Howe became its first and only minister. The new department's sole purpose and function was to "develop aircraft, naval and land vehicle production facilities, not to mention additional facilities for munitions and a variety of other equipment" and the minister responsible was authorized to "mobilize, control, restrict or regulate . . . in his absolute discretion, any branch of trade or industry in Canada or any munitions of war or supplies." For Howe, the position was ideal. Of particular interest was the idea of using the new department to set up crown corporations, something he became noted for.

> Crown corporations provided both the kind of legal entity to which businessmen were accustomed and a degree of bureaucratic decentralization no government department could attain, yet their directors were chosen by the minister in charge, their accounts were vetted by the Auditor-General, and the issued capital shares were held by the government.

As far as Howe was concerned, this was the way to get the Canadian war effort off the ground.

But even a man of C. D. Howe's stature would need help. He found it, one thousand strong, in business and industry from Halifax to Victoria, men he recruited to come to Ottawa for the duration, well-known, experienced businessmen, many of whom came for a "dollar-a-year" and the prestige of becoming part of the exclusive group known only as "Howe's Boys." To understand the character of A. V. Roe Canada, one first has to understand the character of these men who served under Howe at Munitions and Supply. They were one and the same.

Howe wanted men "who knew how to run a business, and who combined common sense and determination with an absolute refusal to be cowed. There were plenty of men in their late thirties or forties, just over military age," many in the higher echelons of business—J. P. Bickell, R. P. Bell, J. B. Carswell, E. P. Taylor, Crawford Gordon, Jr., H. R. MacMillan—the future who's who of Canadian business. To a man, Howe was their mentor.

For many of the dollar-a-year men, World War II was to be the most creative season of their professional lives. Their innovative talents flourished as they learned to extend the boundaries of their self-reliance, to manage the world at large without having to copy or feel inferior to the British or the Americans. . . .

[Howe] taught them an important insight: that knowledge is power. In first reviving, then operating, a diverse economy flung across an unlikely hunk of geography, Howe's protégés deliberately set out to learn where all the important pieces were; who counted and who didn't; how to deal with each other, with cabinet ministers, and with the political system. . . . [They forged a] network of connections and interconnections between business and government. . . . When the dollar-a-year men fanned out at the close of the World War II to run the nation they had helped to create, the attitudes, the working methods, and business ethic they took with them determined the country's economic and political course for the next three decades. . . .

The dollar a year men who spent the war in Ottawa considered themselves grossly overworked, but what came out of their mutual experience was a great sense of comradeship: a terrific knotting together of people making common cause and, above all, the fact that they really got to *know* each other. [They reached] a consensus about the kind of country they wanted after the war. . . . They began to exchange confidences, to sponsor one another for club memberships, to share perceptions and ambitions. It was an enduring trust, and even though the business Establishment has many strains within it, no badge of honour carries more prestige than the phrase: "I put in time under CD."

Howe's combination clicked. The record of Munitions and Supply is astounding, even by today's standards. Through the twenty-eight crown corporations it controlled, and a number of other company conversions, Canada's defence production grew so quickly that, by 1943, Canada stood fourth among the Allied nations in industrial output, overshadowed only by the United States, Russia, and Britain.

In 1940, a rivulet of war supplies had trickled from sources immediately available; 1941 had been a year of planning, of construction, of plant conversions to war products, of output slowly rising. By 1943, war-related industries were employing 1.1 million men and women with another million in the armed forces. The GNP had leapt from $5 billion in 1939 to an astounding $12 billion. Munitions and Supply's annual budget totalled $1.365 billion.

The Canadian aircraft industry, by 1944, had produced almost 11,000 aircraft of various types. The shipyards had launched and fitted 232 cargo vessels and 356 ships of war. The automotive plants had delivered more than 500,000 units of mechanical transport plus an additional 31,000 armoured vehicles. Heavy guns for the army and navy, including barrels, carriages, and mountings, had been completed to number 83,000. In all its previous history, Canada had never turned out even one piece of heavy artillery. "Never again," said Howe in 1943, "will there be any doubt that Canada can manufacture anything that can be manufactured elsewhere." That "anything" most certainly included aircraft.

2

BATTLESHIPS
OF THE AIR

Malton, August, 1943. Champagne and cheers were an easy mix that warm summer day in Malton, Ontario, when Mrs. C. G. Power, the wife of Canada's air defence minister, smacked a bottle of champagne against the front landing gear of the very first Lancaster bomber to roll off a Canadian assembly line. "Outstanding piece of work," remarked a British government official present for the ceremony. The Toronto *Globe and Mail* called it the "world's best bomber," an "armoured battleship of the air."

C. D. Howe was there too, as Minister of Munitions and Supply, and very, very pleased. It had been a mere fourteen months since this crown corporation of his called Victory Aircraft had begun tooling up for the big bomber amidst a nagging doubt, even among Howe's cabinet colleagues, as to whether Canadian industry had the know-how to take on a task as great as that of building an advanced, state-of-the-art aircraft like the Lancaster. It took 8,000 workers at Victory Aircraft to prove everyone wrong.

"I am now able," beamed Howe to the throngs of joyous aircraft workers and dignitaries assembled, "to cable Mr. Churchill that the first edition of his birthday present is on the way."

The roll-out of that first plane was largely for ceremonial purposes; inside, the plane was a mess. A former foreman at Victory Aircraft on the Lancaster recalls what happened after the ceremony:

The first Lancaster we made was never completed here in Toronto. The electrical system was just a shambles—wires hanging all over the place all through the plane—but there was the ceremony for the departure of this aircraft for England. The plane took off and got as far as Dorval; we knew when the plane got to England the electrical system would be finished but I was called into the General Manager's office and told: "I want you to get to Montreal and don't leave the job until you get that plane outta there and finished."

—Jack Hilton

The first edition of Churchill's birthday present was followed by one a day for the next 430 days.

Prior to 1940 and the formation of the Department of Munitions and Supply, Canada's aircraft industry consisted of perhaps sixteen firms, employed barely 4,000 people, occupied a floor space of less than 500,000 square feet, and turned out not quite forty different types of aircraft per year. Some of the earliest "heavier-than-air" machines seen in the British Empire, however, were designed by the Aerial Experiment Association established in Halifax in 1907 by Alexander Graham Bell.

Development accelerated during the First World War when the newly formed Imperial Munitions Board set up a company called Canadian Aeroplanes to build training aircraft for the fledgling Canadian Royal Flying Corps unit. The first non-government-controlled aircraft company in Canada was Curtiss Aeroplanes and Motors (1916), which manufactured under licence over 3,000 Curtiss Jenny bi-planes and a number of flying boats for the Americans. Both Curtiss and the Imperial Munitions Board shut down after the First World War and aircraft production in Canada came to an abrupt halt. Although there was considerable aeronautical activity after the war, most of it revolved around the use of surplus war aircraft, of which there was a considerable amount.

In 1923, one of the first decisions made by the new Department of National Defence was to order eight single-engine amphibian flying boats for aerial surveying in Manitoba. Significantly, the Canadian Air Corps' director of technical services, Air Commodore E. W. Stedman, insisted that the planes be "home-built." This never-heard-before stipulation was important from a nationalistic point of view: it was the first time an aircraft would be constructed to meet specifically Canadian needs and conditions. The aircraft was the Viking, and Canadian Vickers of Montreal got the contract.

In the 1930s, Canadian aircraft production meant the production of airframes only; all engines were imported, usually from Britain or the United States. One type of airframe might be "married" to many different types of engines depending on what power plants (engines) were available at the time of assembly.

There was no such thing as a Canadian-designed-and-built airplane until Robert Noorduyn's Norseman, which was a bush plane, in 1935; it was followed by Elsie MacGill's Maple Leaf Trainer which took to the air in October, 1939, but was never put into production. The first wholly Canadian engine in production was the Orenda which test-bedded in 1950 but didn't fly in production aircraft until 1951. All airframes built in Canada in the 1930s were produced under licence from aircraft manufacturers in the United States and Britain and, in many cases, were unsuitable for Canadian needs. "The Brits especially had quite a colonial attitude to us when it came to aircraft," recalls Jim Hornick, who spent most of the fifties and sixties covering the aircraft business in Canada for Toronto's *Globe and Mail*.

All our early contracts to build aircraft largely came from outside the country, mostly from Britain . . . . The Brits would licence us to produce planes that were so obsolete they couldn't be sold to any buyer except our own government. Consequently, we had to buy them and turn them over to our airforce who really had no choice but to take them.

—*Jim Hornick*

After the First World War British aircraft firms began to take more than a passing interest in Canada. Many of the world's leading aircraft manufacturers set up branches, companies, or agencies in Canada, and by 1939 the list of aircraft firms both foreign and Canadian included Armstrong-Siddeley in Ottawa, Boeing Aircraft in Vancouver, Canadian Car and Foundry in Fort William, Canadian Pratt & Whitney in Montreal, Canadian Vickers in Montreal, Consolidated Aircraft in Ottawa, Cub Aircraft in Hamilton, de Havilland Aircraft in Toronto, Fairchild Aircraft in Montreal, Fleet Aircraft in Fort Erie, MacDonald Brothers Aircraft in Winnipeg, National Steel Car in Malton, Noorduyn Aircraft in Montreal, Ottawa Car Manufacturing in Ottawa, Reid Aircraft (later Curtiss-Reid) in Montreal, and Wright Aeronautical in Montreal.

The reason for all this activity was obvious: "Recognition is being given to the vulnerable position of Great Britain," wrote a British aviation correspondent working in Canada at the time,

and plans are being laid for the material expansion of manufacturing facilities across the Atlantic . . . where requirements of the last fifteen years have created the foundation on which a great industry can be established. It is desirable that aircraft for British defence and to supplement British production should be built far from the actual theatre of war. Canada is the logical empire centre from which supplies could be acquired.

Not all the Canadian firms began as aircraft manufacturers; one of these was National Steel Car, a rolling stock operation based in Hamilton which produced freight cars, buses, and automobiles. Its president, Robert J. Magor, was a dynamic, visionary man who saw great opportunities in the budding defence industry. In the late winter of 1938, Magor bought 6 acres of hayfield on the northeast corner of what was then Toronto's new airport near the hamlet of Malton. In April ground was broken for a small, semi-detached building containing an office, a very small assembly bay, and a paint and fabric shop, a total of 50,000 square feet. The key to this new operation was Toronto Airport's allowing the use of its runways which ran adjacent to the company. And all this with no contracts to build aircraft yet on the books.

At that time there were few people in Canada knowledgeable about aircraft manufacturing. There was, however, a nucleus of enthusiastic young men, Canadian, British, and American, some just out of university, with the ink on their engineering degrees still wet, who wanted to be on the leading edge of what was then still a new science: aviation. National Steel Car and Robert Magor gave them this chance.

The first National Steel Car, Aircraft Division, contract, negotiated in England by Magor himself, was for a batch of gull-winged Westland Lysander army co-operation planes for the RCAF and the Indian government. The first Lysander came off the line in 1939, and, before its paint was dry, Magor secured another contract to build eighty Hampden bomber centre sections and outer wings.

In 1941, while the Hampden program was still going on, the company started on a contract to build Ansons for the British Commonwealth Air Training Plan. For this particular task, the Canadian government had formed Federal Aircraft, a crown corporation responsible for the issue of contracts and co-ordinating the Anson program. National Steel Car became one of three major suppliers of Ansons, completing more than 700 in just over two years. The work involved building about 50 per cent of the airframe, including the fuselage, and assembling the whole aircraft. Ansons were assembled in Bay 1, Hampden wings in Bay 2, and Lysanders in Bay 3.

By 1942, its last year of operation, the company had grown to a 400,000-square-foot plant containing offices, a detail and administration building, and three assembly bays. Personnel had risen from about 500 in 1938 to nearly 4,000. The plant ran two shifts a day and everyone had a work quota.

During its short, four-year life, National Steel Car, Aircraft Division had a total production output of 238 Lysanders, 80 Hampden wing sections, 119 Yorks (assembled), 26 Harvards, 17 British-type Ansons, and 736 Canadian Ansons.

But behind the statistics lies another story, the story of the people that made the company go, and no one who remembers National Steel Car can forget its general manager, Dave Boyd.

Nicknamed the Great White Father by the employees, Boyd was a demanding manager who nevertheless became loyally attached to the company and its employees, especially the men on the floor—those more comfortable in overalls than ties. Originally from Montreal, Boyd studied engineering at McGill and, upon graduation in 1927, became assistant works manager with Dominion Bridge. From there he went to the aircraft division of Canadian Car and Foundry at Fort William and was closely associated with the remarkable success of the Hurricane fighter program in the early days of the Second World War. Anyone who worked for Dave Boyd loved him, and for good reason.

We were encouraged to think, to come up with ideas that would make the job easier or less costly, and to be original.

—Joe Cribar

But what people remember most are Boyd's daily and nightly walks through the plant, in his shirt sleeves, and his knowing practically everyone, supervisors and maintenance men alike, on a first-name basis. It was not uncommon for Boyd to dip into his own pocket between paydays to help someone.

He was the type of guy that made that plant go. He would constantly ask, "How are things going?" And if there were any problems, he would call you directly, never go through your supervisor.

—Ken Molson

He swore like a trooper. I remember once he got a letter from the Depart-
ment of Defence Production, a two-page letter with all kinds of stuff in
it and he just took a big black pen and wrote spherical objects all over it;
in other words, "BALLS!" and mailed it back. This was typical of Boyd.

—Ron Adey

Magor hired Dave Boyd in the summer of 1941 because National
Steel Car was in trouble. Although there were plenty of orders on the
books, and more in the works, the Malton operation had, in the eyes
of some people in Ottawa, become extravagant and inefficient. Part of
the problem was the plant's failure to achieve any degree of autonomy
from the Hamilton head office. Although Magor was company president, the Malton plant reported directly to and operated under R. S.
Hart. Hart had never been in favour of Magor's getting into the aircraft
business and did what he could to make things difficult for the aircraft
division, so much so that many of Malton's senior people had resigned.

Boyd eagerly jumped into the position of general manager but for
all his enthusiasm, he too was soon at loggerheads with Hart. The
unexpected death of Robert Magor in the summer of 1942 forced a
showdown. Gathering all the company supervisory personnel in his
office one afternoon, Boyd and his assistant, L. F. McCaul, took a
desperate last stand. They drafted a telegram to C. D. Howe which
strongly advised that he make National Steel Car a crown corporation
if he wanted the company to produce any more airplanes.

Howe moved more quickly than anyone had expected. Wartime
doesn't allow much time for reflection. The word went out from Howe's
office to Boyd to get those thirty-five so-and-so's who signed the telegram into the board room at the Malton plant. Many of the men
thought it meant immediate dismissal, and some had already lined up
other jobs.

All of a sudden, the big doors down at the end of the room opened and
in walks J. P. Bickell, the Canadian millionaire who says, "As of this
moment, this company has been expropriated by His Majesty's govern-
ment. I am now the chairman of the board; there's your general manager,"
pointing to Dave Boyd. "That's all I have to say. Now, get on with the
job!" Then Boyd, who'd been quiet up to that point says, "Well you've
heard what the score is. There's the new boss and we're now called Victory
Aircraft."

—Ron Adey

The date was November 5, 1942.

In many ways, Roy Dobson was not unlike the aircraft his company produced: powerful, sturdy, reliable, a force to be reckoned with. An English bulldog type, Dobson was already close to legend in his own country when he stepped off the plane in Montreal with Frank Spriggs that September day in 1943. Ruddy-faced and blustery, accustomed to making friends or enemies just about every time he opened his mouth, Dobson hailed from Yorkshire, the northern English county where some of the toughest businessmen in the world have been bred. Around the aircraft factories in Manchester, he was known as a "real bloody character." His language was so colourful at times, that even some labour unions refused to negotiate with him unless he cleaned it up.

Dobson was born in the village of Horsforth, not far from Manchester, on September 27, 1891. At the age of seventeen, just five years after the Wright Brothers' first flight, he joined an engineering firm in Manchester as an apprentice. At twenty-three, he was already doing well as a salesman/engineer for woodworking machines and crude oil engines.

Then one day a friend in Manchester mentioned he had started working for a fellow named Alliot Verdon Roe. Just fourteen years older than Dobson, Roe had already entered the history books when he became the first Englishman to fly in a British-designed, British-powered bi-plane on June 8, 1908. He had gone into business as A. V. Roe and Company to design and construct aircraft, starting with a small office in Manchester in 1914. The First World War and an increase in orders from the war department necessitated moving to larger facilities at nearby Newton-Heath as well as the town of Hamble on the south coast for the testing of seaplanes.

"Oh lumme," Dobson said, "you don't want to get mixed up with that lot. They're crazy."

"They're not crazy," replied his friend, "and what's more, you should work for them, too." Dobson reconsidered.

The following Monday I went down and presented my card at the sales window because I didn't want to stand in the line-up of fellows waiting to get jobs. When old A. V. (he wasn't old then, of course), said he didn't want any woodworking machines or engines, I said, "Well, as a matter of fact, I'm not selling anything but myself. I want a job as a fitter."

—*Roy Dobson*

Dobson started with A. V. Roe and Company not as a fitter but as a draftsman, and from 1914 to 1919 he did every job in the place, alternating between the workshops, which he loved, and the white collar jobs, which he hated.

By 1916 Roe was producing its first multi-engined aircraft and Dobson, or "Dobbie," as he was nicknamed, was put in charge of Roe's experimental department which had been set up to design a trainer for the Royal Flying Corps and what later became the famous Avro 504 series of aircraft. Soon after the war Dobson "put on the white collar for good," becoming works manager at A. V. Roe's Newton-Heath plant, a position he would hold until 1934.

Dobson worked directly for Roe for only fourteen years. In 1928, Roe sold his interest in the company to take controlling interest in S. E. Saunders, renamed Saunders-Roe; he remained its president until his death in 1959, the same year another company bearing his name, A. V. Roe Canada, would lose its Arrow.

Control of A. V. Roe and Company now passed to the Armstrong-Siddeley Development Company, headed by John D. Siddeley, who also had controlling interest in Armstrong-Whitworth Aircraft.

Consolidation within the British aviation industry began in July, 1935, with the formation of a public company, Hawker-Siddeley Aircraft, which took over Hawker Aircraft, its subsidiary Gloster Aircraft, and the controlling interest in Armstrong-Whitworth Aircraft, A. V. Roe and Company, and a non-aircraft operation, Armstrong-Siddeley Motors. This public company became the Hawker-Siddeley Group on June 18, 1948.

When Dobson took over the Newton-Heath plant as works manager in 1919, he inherited a large facility manned with only a skeleton staff. The company, built on the strength of First World War aircraft contracts, now lay empty and idle. Drawing on his previous experience as a salesman, Dobson made trips to London twice a week in an attempt to hustle contracts while his small staff back at the plant kept busy making everything from billiard tables to baby's high chairs and ventilation fans.

In 1929, the plant started making car and truck bodies. Story has it that Sir William Letts, the company's new managing director, felt that making airplanes was a waste of time. To him, cars were the vehicles of the future, so he sold off all the aircraft machinery. On hearing this, Dobson now a fifteen-year veteran of the aircraft industry, marched into Letts' office and said "Sir, our factory is going to make aircraft whether you like it or not!"

Dobson took the next train to London and did some fast talking. He returned convinced he was about to get a government contract to build aircraft, although he had nothing official. He demanded £9,000 from Lett's to buy back the necessary equipment at auction. Letts refused. But Dobson purchased the equipment on his own security and had his aircraft team install it after hours. Within a few days, the Air Ministry ordered a fleet of training aircraft from A. V. Roe and Company, and Dobson was summoned to Letts' office.

"I suppose we'll have to buy that machinery you wanted," lamented Letts.

"That's right," gloated Dobson, "and what's more, you'll have to buy it from me and it'll cost you a 10 per cent commission."

One could argue that Roy Dobson's gruff, blustery public personality dated from this time. In the 1930s the aircraft industry was far from flourishing and competition for contracts was stiff. Dobson's edge was to guarantee fast delivery, and he jumped all over his staff and workers to keep to the tight production schedules. "I've just been down to the works and given them all a bloody good do," he would often say. "That woke them up. That'll keep them on their toes till I get back."

Dobson would go to any lengths to get a contract, but he also followed a certain non-negotiable set of rules. He would never stipulate the delivery date on the unit cost. He would agree to terms on a cost-plus basis and ask the customer to pay for part of the development costs of the project if possible. He would never put an untried engine into an untried airframe; one of the two had to be proven and reliable before he would marry it with the other. Those who worked for him had to follow these rules or feel his wrath.

His rough manner notwithstanding, Dobson was a man of immense personal charm. He could make a woman in overalls feel like a queen and command the loyalty as well as the respect of those who worked for him.

It was at least partially due to this charm and salesmanship that the British Air Ministry awarded A. V. Roe and Company a substantial contract in 1933 to design and build a coastal reconnaissance aircraft which later became the Anson. More pilots learned to fly in the Anson under the British Commonwealth Air Training Plan than all other aircraft put together. Known as "unbreakable Annie, this plane was produced in such numbers that it made a fortune for the company and facilitated Dobson's climb to the position of general manager in 1934, director in 1936, and, ultimately, managing director in 1941.

Between 1919 when he became works manager, and 1945 when he founded A. V. Roe Canada, Dobson was directly responsible for dozens of aircraft projects. Undoubtedly the most important of these was the Lancaster bomber, which, without Dobson's stubbornness, might never have been built.

Shortly before the Second World War, A. V. Roe and Company entered the heavy bomber field with the design for the Type 679 Manchester in response to a British Air Ministry specification (P13/36) for an aircraft of "advanced conception with internal bomb storage and two new

Rolls-Royce Vulture engines." Originally, two Handley Page H.P. 56's and two Manchester prototypes were to be built, but the former was put aside because of the shortage of Vulture engines.

The design of the Manchester fell to Roy Chadwick, chief designer at A. V. Roe and Company since 1919. Dobson and Chadwick were very close; they'd "come up together fighting all the way," and to some, the two were like brothers. Chadwick was responsible for Avro's famous rotary engine 504 Series, as well as for the design of the Anson, the company's most famous aircraft to date.

In July, 1939, the Manchester Type 679 prototype, powered by two Vulture engines, took to the air with the finesse of an elephant with wings. Dobson and Chadwick were devastated. The engines failed to develop the expected power—the catapult take-off—which the Air Ministry had so dearly hoped for. Chadwick attempted to reduce the weight of the plane, but impatience in the Air Ministry threatened to cancel the entire project. For a while, it seemed that A. V. Roe and Company's first attempt at a heavy bomber was to be its last.

In a major design departure, however, Chadwick decided that what the plane needed was not a drop in weight, but two more engines. Four Rolls-Royce Merlins, the same engines used in fighter planes, would give the Manchester at least 30 per cent more power on take-off. Chadwick drew up a four-Merlin-engine conversion of the plane, at the same time adding a new undercarriage and a few other modifications. Early performance calculations showed spectacular results.

Dobson took the new design to the Air Ministry—since it didn't meet the original specifications it had to receive authorization. The Air Ministry, however, failed to share the enthusiasm of Dobson and Chadwick, partly because of the already huge investment they had made in developing the Vulture engine. Authorization for the four-engine bomber was denied. Furthermore, Dobson was instructed to continue with development of the Manchester until another bomber, the Halifax, built by a rival company, was ready as a replacement.

Furious, Dobson appealed directly to Lord Beaverbrook, then Minister of Aircraft Production.

"It is not a frivolous request," he said. "I want four engines."

"Well, you can dig for them," was Beaverbrook's response. Although sympathetic, he refused to reverse the decision of the Air Ministry.

Undaunted, Dobson called on Rolls-Royce before returning to Manchester, and begged Lord Hives, the managing director, to "lend" him four Merlin engines, the engines reserved for the Hurricane and Spitfire. Hives agreed, and Dobson got his engines.

During the spring and summer of 1940, what started out as the Manchester evolved into the Lancaster, and in July Dobson brazenly invited the Air Ministry to watch the new plane go through its initial test flights. Impressed as they were, the very next morning, a wrathful Beaverbrook was on the phone to Dobson.

"What's this four-engined bomber we hear you've suddenly produced?"

"It's the one you wouldn't give me the engines for," replied Dobson.

"Then where did you get the engines?"

"I dug for them."

Within a few days, the Air Ministry officially requested one of the Manchester bombers for tests. But Dobson himself was not completely satisfied with the design. He was looking for a plane that could be manufactured and repaired with greater ease, that was light in weight, and "overpowered" to be able to carry heavy bomb loads.

"How much time have we got?" asked Chadwick.

"None," was Dobson's reply, so he stalled the Air Ministry as best he could while Chadwick moved all the engineering and drafting departments into the hangar. They worked day and night, sawing off everything that wasn't necessary, re-drawing, and re-designing some of the plane's systems for easier maintenance. Dobson and Chadwick stormed about the place cheering everyone on.

Then, on January 9, 1941, Dobson delivered prototype Lancaster BT408 to the Royal Air Force, having accomplished in months what normally took three years. Air Ministry officials were speechless, not only at the spectacular performance of this new Lancaster which, on a flat run, could outfly the famous Hurricane, but also at the audacity of Dobson, who had deliberately ignored their instructions and delivered an airplane they hadn't ordered. In wartime, this was tantamount to treason. A once-secret report on the Lancaster concluded with this statement: "Although we must admit that the bomber has a remarkable performance, we cannot but deplore the methods by which it was obtained."

The Manchester, as Chadwick had predicted, continued to be plagued by engine problems throughout its trials, production, and brief, two-year operational service with the RAF.

The Lancaster became the workhorse of the RAF and was the only Allied aircraft capable of carrying the huge 22,000-pound blockbuster bombs of the war's ultimate phase. Sir Arthur Harris, Chief of Bomber Command from 1942 to 1945, called the Lancaster "the greatest single factor in winning the war."

Malton, mid-November, 1942. Within days of National Steel Car's becoming Victory Aircraft, the pieces were already beginning to fall into place. C. D. Howe wasted no time in recruiting people, most of them already part of his organization, to run the operation.

On the recommendation of his Director General of Aircraft Production, Ralph Bell, Howe made his first call to John Paris ("J.P.") Bickell, the wealthy mining magnate and close friend of Lord Beaverbrook, asking him to come over as Victory's president and chairman of the board. Bickell was a businessman's businessman. Born in the hamlet of Molesworth, Ontario, and educated at St. Andrew's College, by the time he was twenty-four, he had already started his own brokerage firm and held an interest in McIntyre-Porcupine Mines, a company he would eventually control.

In the early days of the Second World War, Bickell was the Canadian representative for Lord Beaverbrook's British Ministry of Aircraft Production and played a key role in establishing the famous wartime Ferry Command, ("the aircraft is very noisy and earplugs or cotton wool are an advantage") the famous trans-Atlantic air-ferry service.

Bickell didn't hesitate for a moment and he and Bell recruited Victory Aircraft's first board of directors which included G. H. Logan, Donald McCaskill, F. C. Fox, and W. Kasper Fraser. The management team was now complete: Dave Boyd reported to Bickell and the board who in turn reported to C. D. Howe.

Far removed from the world of Bickell and Howe were over 8,000 men and women, working three eight-hour shifts a day, most for less than a dollar an hour, who were proud to call themselves Victory Aircraft employees and who had their own stories to tell about the company. The average wage at Victory Aircraft during the peak war years was fifty-eight dollars a week. There were no coffee breaks, but each assembly bay had a small canteen in every corner. During lunch, and after each shift ended, the company operated a dance hall on the second floor of the "details" building.

Not privy to board politics and boardroom decisions, the ordinary employees remember another Victory Aircraft, things to do with the day-to-day, and the free spirit and daring of the test pilots. They recall when Victory built apartments near the plant to house some of the 2,300 women employees, many of whom had to travel great distances, sometimes in the middle of the night, to get to work. There are stories of the "gals" smuggling in some of the young pilots stationed at Malton with the British Commonwealth Air Training Plan. They all remember the great snowstorm of 1944 when nothing moved to and from the plant for three days.

By the end of 1943, the floor space of the plant had surpassed 1,000,000 square feet. The number of employees had expanded from about 1,000 in 1940 to 4,500 in 1943, and around 9,600 in mid-1944.

Meanwhile in Ottawa, C. D. Howe, now known as the "Minister of Everything," was dealing out crown corporations with the ease of a Mississippi gambler dealing cards, especially in the aircraft manufacturing sector. At the peak of wartime production in 1944, Canada had over forty-five aircraft companies, in operation twenty-four hours a day and employing over 80,000 workers, and had turned out over 16,000 planes for the war effort.

The Canadian companies produced aircraft at a faster rate than their British or American counterparts. De Havilland built Ansons and Mosquitoes at a rate of 80 per month; Boeing made over 50 Catalina seaplanes per month; Canadian Car and Fairchild between them produced Helldivers and Hurricanes at a rate of 123 per month; and Victory Aircraft, which had become the third largest company in North America in pounds per aircraft per day, turned out a Lancaster a day.

Yet, for all the attention Victory Aircraft received over its ability to produce the Lancaster bomber, the company almost didn't get the chance to build it. National Steel Car was under contract to build the Martin B-26 Marauder. A team of six draftsmen and engineers, Jack Hilton, Laurie Marchant, Tom Shaw, Bob Johnson, Chris Wilson, and Vic Simmons, spent close to a month in Baltimore, Maryland, at the Martin plant in the summer of 1941, to learn all they could about the still-secret bomber.

As was the custom in the business at the time, each man was assigned a section of the plane to study, with the intent of preparing the tools and drawings to build it. The Martin had its problems—"no damn good" one of the men recalls. Because the Americans had wanted a high-speed bomber, the design coupled an undersized wing with a new, unproven Wright engine. The plane tended to land too quickly and had been involved in a series of accidents. In fact, while in Baltimore, the Canadians saw a B-26 blow up, killing pilot and crew— not the kind of thing to generate enthusiasm for the project. Just the same, the six-man team completed their study of the Marauder and the Malton plant started tooling up for its production, only to have the project suddenly cancelled.

In the summer of 1941, E. P. Taylor had been appointed chairman of the British Supply Council in Washington, D.C., which was set up by Whitehall to arrange for the production of British war materials under licence in friendly countries. Upon returning from his first visit to England in his new capacity, Taylor informed a meeting in Washington attended by C. D. Howe and Ralph Bell that his most important mission was to arrange for the production of the Lancaster in North America. As this was an impossibility as far as the United States was concerned—American companies would only build American planes— the challenge was thrown to Canada. It was eagerly accepted by Howe and Bell who committed National Steel Car to produce thirty of the big planes per month, one a day, providing the British would guarantee the supply of Martin B-26's for the RCAF from the United States.

National Steel Car, soon to become Victory Aircraft, took the same team of men who had begun work on the Martin and reassigned them to the Lancaster project. A liaison office was set up at A. V. Roe and Company in Manchester to ship over all the drawings and technical information on the Lancaster. Walter Duncan and Murray Willer ran the office.

Our job was to take prints of all the drawings and ship the negatives to Canada to be made back into prints. The idea, from the very beginning, was to build as much of the plane as possible, including accessories, in Canada.

—*Murray Willer*

An actual service Lancaster was flown from Manchester as a "visual" prototype. Not everyone was confident that the company could build the big plane, and to some, its arrival was interpreted almost as a form of intimidation, a chance for Canada's "greenhorn" aircraft people to "all gaze in wonder at this marvellous airplane we were going to build." Jack Hilton, the man in charge of its final assembly, recalls thinking when he first saw the Lancaster, "My God, how are we gonna build something that big!"

How, indeed. The Lancaster is designed around the portion of the aircraft formed by the bomb bay roof, the wing centre section, and the undercarriage. The floor is long to accommodate large bomb loads and is slung from the spars of the wing centre section so that the two frames form the fore and aft and transverse limbs of the cross-shaped chassis which, in turn, is the backbone of the entire aircraft. Each wing is nearly as long as the fuselage. The plane consists of 55,000 separate parts and requires more than half a million different manufacturing operations. Big plane. Big problems.

Victory Aircraft's final assembly bay was not wide enough to accommodate a complete Lancaster, so the decision was made to produce the aircraft in three main sections (fuselage, wings, and tail), marry these sections in the hangar, and then roll the aircraft out onto the tarmac to add the wing tips. To streamline production, the engine shop, tire shop, propeller shop, radio shop, paint shop, and the final assembly were all brought under one foreman.

Sheer size was not the only problem. The Lancaster was designed to British specifications, using British equipment and accessories. It was necessary to re-engineer the plane to American materials, standards, and equipment which were used generally in Canadian industry. The Canadian Lancaster was therefore a little different from its British counterpart. All Canadian-made Lancasters were designated Mark X and were equipped with American-made Packard-Merlin engines, as opposed to Rolls-Royce Merlins. There were all kinds of differences in the electrical systems, the instruments, and the communication systems. But the only striking visible difference was the aircraft's brightly painted finish. British Lancasters were painted with a much duller finish to avoid being picked up by searchlights at night.

Of the 430 Lancasters produced by Victory Aircraft, only one was lost over the Atlantic during delivery, the result of an improperly installed bracket in the fuel-control system. All in all, the Canadian-built Lancaster was a good product, better in some ways than the British version. The British, for instance, couldn't build an aileron, a critical part of an aircraft, to fit the Lancaster properly. The Canadians did and the design was used on all future British Lancasters.

When the first Canadian-made Lancaster arrived in Manchester, many at A. V. Roe and Company felt it was the best-equipped aircraft they had ever seen. The chief inspector, Sandy Jack, told his inspection supervisors: "Look fellows, if you want to see how a plane should be built, go out and take a look at this Lancaster."

To keep tabs on Lancaster production at Malton, A. V. Roe and Company set up an "engineering liaison office" at the Victory plant. The office was run by Alf Sewart, an engineer with A. V. Roe, who arrived just as Victory was unwrapping the blueprints to begin Lancaster production.

In his official capacity Sewart was to assist in clearing up any engineering problems associated with the bomber, and to monitor the Lancaster program for the British Air Ministry. But everybody knew him as Dobson's man.

Sewart was not technically responsible to Dave Boyd and continually irritated him by spending time in the shops, acting as if he, and not Boyd, were running the show. The men liked him well enough however, and he had his own way of encouraging them. "I was talking with Churchill just the other day and Winnie said to tell you Canadian fellows 'Good job!' "

Sewart liked what he saw at Victory and took every opportunity to let Dobson know about it. Dobson heard the same tales from Willer and Duncan in the A. V. Roe liaison office at Malton—Canadian Lancaster production was way ahead of schedule; Canadian engineers had improved the plane; the Canadian Lancaster was a better-built plane; the Canadians were building it faster. Dobson had to see for himself, and as the first Canadian-built Lancaster prepared to roll off the line months ahead of schedule, he headed for Canada. He found all the stories more than true.

> *It opened my eyes, I'll tell you. If these so-and-so's can do this during a war, what can't they do after. One thing this country would need is an aircraft industry of its own: design and development, not just assembling somebody else's stuff. And yet, it seemed to me that it might be lacking the finer engineering developments and things like aircraft engines and so on. And I couldn't possibly imagine a nation with this sort of potential carrying on without demanding, not just asking or thinking about, but demanding, its own aircraft, its own aircraft industry, its own engine industry, and indeed, a lot of other industries, too. But, of course, I was an aircraft man at the time and I said: "All right, that's my field. I'm going to have a go at it."*
>
> —Roy Dobson

Making no bones about the fact he knew "absolutely nothing about Canada," Dobson set out to meet the people who would help him establish his "little empire in Canada."

Ralph Bell, Canada's Director of Aircraft Production, arranged for Dobson to meet with the key people at Victory Aircraft and to get a first-hand, if brief, look at Canada's aircraft production facilities.

Dobson renewed his acquaintance with J. P. Bickell, Victory's chairman of the board, whom he'd known from Ferry Command days, and met John Tory, the company's legal man, for the first time.

John Tory, unlike many men in public life at the time, shunned publicity and "made a point of avoiding it whenever possible," something which he felt allowed him the freedom to manoeuvre, to work behind the scenes unhindered. He was a successful, forty-year-old Toronto lawyer, a graduate of Osgoode Hall and Harvard (class of '28), and founder of the law firms of J. S. D. Tory and Associates and the prestigious Tory, Miller, Thomson, Hicks, Arnold and Sedgewick. Having connections with both the provincial and federal Conservative parties, Tory held directorships in many large corporations. In 1944, he became a board member of Victory Aircraft.

Tory would provide much of the legal wizardry that allowed A. V. Roe Canada to grow from a one-product company to the third largest corporation in Canada in a mere twelve years. Dobson would seek Tory's counsel and advice ever after. "No financial or legal decision was made," recalls one company insider, "without first clearing it with John."

Then Dobson met someone who did not have the corporate credentials of a J. P. Bickell, nor the legal mind of a John Tory, nor the managerial expertise of a Dave Boyd, but who would prove to be "absolutely invaluable" to him. Barely twenty-seven years old, the assistant to Ralph Bell had been assigned to take Dobson and Spriggs on a tour of the aircraft companies. The young man's name was Frederick Timothy Smye.

3

TAKEOVER

There is a story about a man who had two sons, one an optimist and one a pessimist. He decided one Christmas to put them to a test. He set a gleaming fire engine under the tree for the pessimist and a box of horse manure for the optimist. When he came downstairs Christmas morning, he found the pessimist sitting morosely beside the fire engine expressing fears that the wheels wouldn't stay on. Meanwhile, from out in the yard, he heard whistling and singing. He went out to discover the other child searching the grounds with the explanation that "with all the shit around here, there must be a pony!" Such was Fred Smye, always looking for the pony and making everyone around him believe there was one.

Although most of his adult life was spent in or around airplanes, Smye was not an aircraft man in the same sense as Dobson or Chadwick. He admits himself that when he first got involved in the aircraft business, he knew "bugger all about planes," but what he lacked in raw technical knowledge, he more than made up in intelligence, a full-of-ginger type of enthusiasm and, most of all, optimism.

Smye was a young man on the go and in a hurry. He hustled his way into his own business by the time he was twenty, was general

31

manager of Avro Aircraft before he was thirty and vice-president of A. V. Roe Canada before he was forty.

Born in Hamilton, Ontario, on August 6, 1916, the only child of an ex-Liberal cabinet minister, Frederick Thomas Smye, and Maude Linfoot, Smye attended Trinity College School and toyed with the idea of becoming a lawyer, or perhaps a journalist. But his father died when Smye was fourteen, and his mother wanted him nearby.

She wanted me to stay close by and go to McMaster [in Hamilton], but I thought it was a waste of time, so I went into the printing-advertising business and worked for a full year for nothing.

—Fred Smye

In 1939 Smye married Dorothy Jean Carswell, whom he had known for years. She was the daughter of J. B. Carswell, the president of the Canadian Construction Association and a good friend of C. D. Howe.

At the time Smye was involved in a lawsuit over his new milk carton business. He and two others had formed a company to produce "paper milk bottles" but sales were slow because some American carton producers had distribution and marketing rights in Canada. Smye took them to court over their patent rights, won the case, and his Pergo Containers became the first company to introduce and control paper milk cartons in Canada.

When Canada entered the war in 1939, Smye looked for a kind of role that would keep him out of uniform. He approached his father-in-law about a possible job in the wartime government. Carswell spoke to Howe, who was in the process of putting together his Department of Munitions and Supply. Smye was hired and sent to New York in June, 1940, to work in the Munitions and Supply office there. Ralph Bell visited the New York office one day and Smye told him of some strange dealings.

I smelled a rat in the British Purchasing Commission and I told Bell so. "Boy, you better be right," was Bell's only reply. I was, and as a result, saved the government some money and embarrassment and from that point, Bell and I hit it off pretty well.

—Fred Smye

After only a month with Munitions and Supply, Smye became Bell's personal representative in New York. From then on, he worked solely on aircraft procurement for the Canadian government. For someone who admittedly didn't know one end of an airplane from another, he did very well.

Although he was number one with Ralph Bell, I could never understand how they could have a man in that position with very little technical capability. I remember him asking me once a couple of questions about the Pratt & Whitney engine. "What do you know about Pesgo pumps?" he would ask, "how are they designed and where do they go?" All from a guy who was supposed to know about aircraft. I do recall, though, he was a very good writer; he could compose an honest letter in those days, but I think, probably, everyone was honest then.

—*Joe Morley*

In those New York days he made a lot of contacts, both in the United States and Canada, contacts which would be remembered later with A. V. Roe Canada. In December Smye was reassigned to Ottawa for six months. The following May, Bell went to England and ordered Smye to hold the fort in Ottawa in his absence. "You just sit in my chair and do my job," he said. Smye was now Bell's executive assistant; he had just turned twenty-six.

In the late 1930s, Theodore Anderton was a young Canadian draftsman working in the stress office at A. V. Roe and Company's Chadderton operation. To anyone who'd listen, Anderton would pass the time telling stories of his homeland—he was "almost as besotted with Canada as he was with airplanes." Sitting at the next drafting table was a young English draftsman by the name of James Charles Floyd. At first, to young Floyd, Anderton's stories of Canada were amusing and mildly interesting. Canada was simply that big country on the other side of the Atlantic, full of Indians from the pages of *Dandy* and *Topper*, a place the Queen and King liked to visit on occasion.

Over time, however, Floyd became entranced by Anderton's stories. He even considered, in moments late at night, actually "going over." But this was 1939, the eve of war, and any such ideas were eclipsed by the immediate and pressing events of the next six years.

The world of aircraft design in 1939 was an arena where the competitors all strove for one thing: to see *their* planes in the air. Aircraft designers walked with a swagger and talked in a tone that set them apart from ordinary mortals. Each was motivated by the mission that he might build for one pound of weight what any of his fellows could do for two. But Jim Floyd was different. In place of the arrogant swagger and tone and the overriding competitive ego common in the profession was a soft heart and a gentle manner.

Floyd was born in Manchester, England, on October 20, 1914, just a few days before his soldier/father left for Flanders. Living close to the Barton airfield at Ringway, his curiosity was aroused early to the wonder of powered flight.

While he was in high school, A. V. Roe and Company started a program in which bright youngsters were selected through auditions to train with the company as apprentices. Competition was fierce, but Floyd's uncle was a friend of Roy Dobson, then works manager with Roe. He went to see Dobson about Floyd's joining the company. "All right," barked Dobson to the mild-mannered fifteen-year-old, "but I don't know you from here on. You join the scheme, you're on your own entirely". It was January 1930.

For four or five years, Floyd drifted through the plant doing all manner of jobs. When the company sponsored a competition among the apprentices for an opportunity to study engineering at university. Floyd did well and entered the Manchester College of Technology, working four days a week at the plant and going to school the rest of the time.

Upon graduation, he joined the design office at Hawker Aircraft, then located at Kingston-upon-Thames, "the ultimate place that all young engineers wanted to go," and assisted in the design of the Hawker Hotspur, a variation of the famous Hurricane fighter. In the summer of 1937, he returned to A. V. Roe and Company to work in the design office under Roy Chadwick, who was then working on the Anson.

I did the tailplane and quite a lot of the systems and then when we did the Manchester, I did the tailplane again (I became an "expert" on tail-planes). Chadwick came around when I was drawing a very nice tailplane with square tips and he said, "That's not what I want. I want something that looks like an egg. Now take an egg and make it like that and see how it goes." So, we had an elongated egg that eventually became the tail of the Lancaster.

—Jim Floyd

In the spring of 1938, Floyd got another new boss, Stuart Davies, a Londoner whose nickname "Cock" might have been short for Cockney, or cocky. Either way, he had a unique way of using the English language; in short, he gave new meaning to the word profanity.

Davies had also worked at Hawker as project engineer on the Hurricane and the Henly. He was recruited by Dobson primarily because Chadwick needed an assistant, and was given the title of assistant chief designer.

Davies was quick to make his presence felt; he did some forward thinking, analysed what the company should be doing and developed a ten-year plan. Chadwick assigned Jim Floyd to work as Davies' assistant, primarily because he thought Floyd would "suit" the man. To the gentlemanly, mild-mannered Floyd, those first few days in Davies' company were difficult ones.

Davies was a task master and I was his slave. Every sentence had a four-letter word. Should anything go wrong, I had to get used to his descriptive comments on my birth.

—Jim Floyd

In time, Floyd would learn that, coming from Davies, "bastard" was almost a term of endearment. Floyd soon came to recognize that Davies was a genius and to this day he has deep respect for Davies' capabilities and engineering know-how.

By 1939, A. V. Roe and Company had moved to Chadderton and the Manchester-to-Lancaster conversion and redesign was well underway. Jim Floyd now moved to the stress office in Chadderton to work under Chadwick on the York bomber.

It was there he would meet two people who would have a profound effect on his life. The first was Irene whom he married in July, 1940. The second was the Canadian, Theodore Anderton.

In Ottawa, Fred Smye was languishing as executive assistant to Ralph Bell. He longed for action, any activity that would put excitement back in his life. Most of his duties consisted of visiting aircraft companies, filling in for Bell, or acting as tour guide to visiting dignitaries.

When Dobson and Spriggs first arrived in Canada in September, 1943, as representatives of Hawker-Siddeley, Ralph Bell invited them to Ottawa, but not before assigning Smye the job of showing them any aircraft plant they wished to see. Bell recalls that Smye was keen to have Hawker-Siddeley financially involved in Canada. It wasn't long after Smye took Dobson and Spriggs down to visit the operation in Malton that Bell, Smye, Bickell, and Tory, seeing something in the blustery Englishman, all agreed that Dobson should talk to the one that counted, C. D. Howe.

Dobson and Howe were of similar physical stature and temperament. Both liked the occasional cigar and brandy, and in disposition were hard nosed and gruff in equal measure. To each, a handshake was good, a deal, and better than a contract. Their first encounter was what is known in the business world as an "easy" meeting. They discussed in a general way the possibility of Hawker-Siddeley's further involvement in the Canadian aircraft industry. When Dobson left for England, he said to Fred Smye, "I'll be back."

Sensing opportunity, Smye resigned as Bell's executive assistant and joined the crown corporation Federal Aircraft in Montreal as assistant general manager. Better learn as much as he could about airplanes, he thought, it may come in handy.

Early in 1944 Howe called Colin Gibson, Canada's Minister of National Defence for Air, and made an appointment for Dobson. At the meeting, as well, was the Chief of the Canadian Air Staff, Robert Leckie. Discussion centred around the post-war aircraft industry in Canada, specifically whether Canada should design her own aircraft for her own air force and have the industry in place to support the concept. Leckie, personally, was in favor, having pushed for this idea since before the war, but he really didn't see how all this could come about. He had a lot to learn about Roy Dobson.

In February, 1944, J. P. Bickell locked horns with C. D. Howe over the selection of a Victory board member. To Bickell, the episode started as another in a long line of labour difficulties that had plagued the company since January of the previous year. To Howe, it was a bid for power on Bickell's part.

Under the crown corporation scheme, all companies were required to have at least one representative from the company union on the board of directors. Since Victory was the only one of the twenty-eight crown companies that had no labour representation on the board, the company had had three near strikes in ten months. Canada could ill afford this sort of situation in a company vital to the war effort. Howe had written to Bickell some weeks before, suggesting he conform to crown company policy and get that union man on the board. Bickell refused; although technically responsible to Howe, *he* was chairman and president of the company, and *he* would decide who sat on the board. "Just being stubborn," said the *Toronto Star*, commenting on Bickell's stand, and went on to add that labour troubles at Victory would be few and far between if the company appointed a labour man. Bickell would hear nothing of it and, on February 1, 1944, he and his four directors resigned.

Howe reacted with characteristic speed, commandeering V. W. (Bill) Scully, another of his dollar-a-year men currently heading up the crown corporation War Supplies, to step in and take over. Scully was a no-nonsense, dark, and powerfully built Irishman who made a quick and indelible impression.

We were all sitting in the cafeteria the day he started. He walked in, walked up to the front of the room and said, "I had the feeling when I came in here you were all taking a good look at me and thinking, now what sort of son-of-a-bitch is he? Well, I'm gonna stand up on this chair and have a look at you and figure out just what kind of sons-of-bitches you are!"

—Ernie Alderton

Howe and Scully put together a new board of directors which included a representative from the Machinists Union.

Throughout the fall of 1944 and into 1945, Roy Dobson stayed in touch with both Bickell and Howe. Bickell and Dobson had become great friends, and Dobson would often stay at Bickell's estate in Port Credit on his subsequent visits to Canada.

Bickell was the senior man, the elder statesman to Dobson. It's true Bickell respected Dobson when it came to building aircraft, but not when it came to finance and economics.

—Fred Smye

With Howe, the situation was a little different. Although Dobson valued and asked for Howe's advice often, Howe looked upon Dobson as someone he could do business with. And a lot of that had to do with the way Howe liked to do business. "He was irritable and impatient with the cautious ways of Canadians," writes Peter Newman. "He felt that they hung back, had little zest, demanded assurance of a big return on their money before they'd start anything. The boys with the risk money . . . theirs was the language he understood." If any deal to take over Victory Aircraft was to be made, it would be Dobson and Howe that would make it.

Meanwhile, at Federal Aircraft in Montreal, most of Fred Smye's time was taken up with helping the company wind down their aircraft production program and writing lots of memos to C. D. Howe about the possibilities for post-war aircraft production in Canada. After all, Smye would soon be in need of a job.

Dobson had become a regular visitor to Canada and occasionally he would drop in to see Smye in Montreal on his way out. He had taken a special liking to "Freddie" and liked to pass the hours over scotch talking about the future and what great faith he had in Canada. It was one such visit in June, 1945, that changed Smye's life forever. Dobson had taken Smye to dinner, and over liqueurs and cigars, told Smye of the discussions he'd been having with Howe about taking over Victory Aircraft.

Just days before, a breakthrough of sorts had been reached. With John Tory overseeing the legal side of things, Dobson and Howe, in a corner of Howe's office, had worked out the first draft of the takeover on the back of a Players cigarette package. The deal was a simple one: Hawker-Siddeley would take over the Victory operation on a sort of rent/purchase basis. "We were to pay half our profits in rent," recalled Dobson later. "But, no profits, no rent."

"This'll be the biggest and best piece of Hawker-Siddeley," Dobson said to a wide-eyed Smye. In fact, he added, he was on his way back to England to present the deal to the Hawker-Siddeley board of directors. And that wasn't all.

On Bickell's advice, Dobson had come to Montreal to offer Fred Smye a job. With all this going back and forth between England and Canada, Dobson needed, as he had with Alf Sewart, a man in Canada, and he wanted that man to be Fred Smye.

Smye readily accepted and when Dobson arrived back in England in early July, the first thing he did was get on the phone to Bill Scully, just six months into the running of Victory Aircraft. "I've hired this guy so put him on the payroll," said Dobson; but when Smye arrived in Malton in August, 1945, the reception was less than warm. "I'll put you on the payroll," said Scully reluctantly, "but it's only a loan. If this deal goes flop, I want my money back."

Meanwhile, the Victory plant was gearing down. What began as an initial layoff of 800 the previous January, had, by midsummer of 1945, left only 5,000 men and women on the floor from the wartime high of 10,000. And it was just the beginning.

In Toronto, the CCF were alarmed at the situation at Victory and other wartime plants; when they got wind of the Dobson-Howe takeover negotiations, they protested to Howe that selling the Victory plant would only cost more jobs. The Toronto District Labour Council echoed this fear but expressed the hope that once the war with Japan ended, all the men would be hired back when the new owners took over.

In Ottawa, the first of a string of hopeful announcements regarding the future of the plant, appropriately timed to soften the blow of layoffs, proclaimed Victory would soon be producing a new bomber called the Lincoln, which was similar to the well-known American Superfortress. Workers at the plant, on hearing the news, weren't overly excited. "It's a grand ship," said one, "but it might be scrapped." It was; Victory made just one and a few pieces for others.

Before long, more announcements. Victory would soon begin work on two more aircraft, the York and a commercial aircraft, a favourite of Dobson's, called the Tudor. The York went the same way as the Lincoln: only one was produced. The Tudor didn't make it beyond the blueprint, at least not in Canada.

For Dobson, the months between January and December, 1945, were frustrating. Although no formal agreement had been worked out with

Howe for the takeover of Victory, Dobson fully expected the deal to go through once the war ended. He needed to start lining up contracts, any contracts, to give the company a foundation from which to build, and to keep the doubters on the Hawker-Siddeley board—and there were many—off his heels. Combat aircraft were no longer in demand with the war ending. The first contract should be for a transport and the first buyer, if any, would logically be either Trans-Canada Air Lines (TCA) or the RCAF. And, if either of them were to be sold on the idea of buying a new airplane, the man to do the convincing would be Roy Dobson himself. A knock at TCA's door came first.

In an address to the House of Commons two years before, Mackenzie King had said:

> Trans Canada Airlines will continue to be the instrument of the government in maintaining all transcontinental air transport services and in operating services across international boundary lines and outside Canada. The government will encourage the company to obtain modern aircraft, which will keep present services up to modern standards and will expand these services to the fullest extent that post-war conditions permit.

Encouraged by the Prime Minister's comments and, more recently, by rumours he had picked up in England—that TCA was actively looking for an inter-city replacement for the DC-3 and a trans-Atlantic aircraft "with the idea of having the airplane designed in Canada for their use"—Dobson introduced Hawker-Siddeley's newest commercial venture: the Tudor. Since January, Dobson had been looking at developing a commercial series from the now-famous Lancaster, a series that would include the Lancastrian, the York, and the Tudor.

H. J. Symington, the president of TCA, listened politely to Dobson but made absolutely no commitment on the Tudors. When the meeting was reported to Howe, however, the reaction was a little different. On July 24, Howe called a press conference in Ottawa and, much to the chagrin of TCA and Symington, announced his intention to sell Victory Aircraft to Hawker-Siddeley on the condition that the new company "manufacture large passenger transport planes after the war with the view to meeting competition for world airline traffic." Howe didn't say what the planes would be, or who they would be for, but for Dobson, back in England at the time of the announcement, the answer was obvious. After all, TCA was another crown corporation, and C. D. Howe was still running the show.

Dobson immediately cabled Dave Boyd at the Victory plant to come up with a scheme to convert the ill-fated Lincolns into Tudors. Since the Tudor was basically a transport plane with Lincoln wings, surely it wouldn't take the fellows at Victory long to throw a few aircraft together; they could easily, he wrote to Symington, "get a dozen delivered before the end of the year." But Symington was still uncommitted. Dobson had mistaken Howe's comments and enthusiasm as a sure thing, a deal. He was wrong. And it wouldn't be the last time.

Next Dobson went to the RCAF. In the closing days of the Second World War, one man was emerging who, more and more, personified everything that was the RCAF; that man was Robert Leckie, now an Air Marshal and Chief of Air Staff. For years Leckie had fought for an independent air force for Canada, and, as early as the 1930s, argued, along with many other prominent air force men, that the RCAF should have aircraft suited to Canadian needs, built and designed in Canada. Leckie was also chairman of the CSC, the committee that decides for the armed forces who gets what, when, and for how much. Leckie had never abandoned his desire for an up-to-date, independent air force nor his belief that the aircraft should be Canadian-made. Surely, thought Dobson, hiding his disappointment with TCA, Leckie will want the Tudor. But Leckie was not without his own problems that summer of 1945.

Although Leckie was certainly more sympathetic than Symington, by this time the RCAF was the third largest air force in the world in terms of men and equipment. Granted, most of the planes were of either American or British design and manufacture; still, there were thousands of them, enough to equip a post-war air force for years.

Leckie was under pressure from the government to demilitarize as quickly as possible after the cessation of hostilities with Japan. Canada would quickly return to being an unmilitary country after the war.

Converting the Tudor to the RCAF's needs, supposing they were in the market for a transport aircraft, would mean financing for development. No, said Leckie to Dobson, if the RCAF were in a position to buy *any* new aircraft, it would probably be a pure military plane, a trainer or a fighter, something small scale and politically acceptable in terms of cost.

Although disappointed in his attempt to introduce the Tudor to Canada, Dobson was by no means out. The war would soon be over. Things were sure to look up.

For Dave Boyd, Victory Aircraft's popular general manager, the end came sadly and quickly. When rumours of the impending takeover first reached the plant, Boyd had hoped there might be a role for him in the new company, but with the hiring of Fred Smye in August, that hope vanished. The week after VJ-Day, Howe notified Boyd through Bill Scully that his services were no longer required.

Boyd was devastated. Although he had been at Malton for only four years, they were dramatic, exciting years for him and the 10,000 men and women who worked under him. The friendships and loyalties were strong, and severing them was painful.

We had heard production was going to slow down, and we'd already started to build Lincolns. Then the message came through the plant we were finished; everyone was to be laid off. So Boyd got everyone in the shops together in one of the assembly bays and with tears in his eyes made a farewell speech that said we were in shutdown, everyone was finished, including himself, and the one's they wanted would be rehired because we were now going to become part of a company, a company called A. V. Roe, and I never saw Dave Boyd again.

—Jack Hilton

Boyd eventually went on to become works manager at the John Inglis Company in Toronto until 1951 when he joined Rolls-Royce in Montreal. But to everyone who worked for him at Malton he is remembered as the guy who snatched National Steel Car from R. S. Hart to help create the company called Victory Aircraft.

Fred Smye, now on board as Dobson's "first" employee, was worried, now that the Tudor scheme had petered out.

Things did not look all that bright. It was a low point, probably the lowest we would ever face as a company.

—Fred Smye

On Smye's suggestion, Dobson talked to Victor Drury, president of Canadian Car and Foundry, one of the largest industrial organizations in the country at the time. During the war, they had built Hurricane fighters and manufactured artillery shells, and they had a large machine shop and foundry operation.

Drury was prepared to offer Dobson a deal that "would exchange facilities, capacity and cash for the ideas and technical know-how of the Hawker-Siddeley operation." Dobson turned him down flat. As far as he was concerned, the handshake and the scratch on the back of the cigarette package were still good. Still, the same question met Dobson at every turn: Why drag yourself and your successful company into a venture at a time when everyone else was bailing out?

Dobson was attempting the impossible, and yet he was determined to continue to the extent of disregarding the future consideration that his career was at stake, both here and in Britain. He had everything to lose and he knew this. Everyone thought Dobson was just plain crazy.

—Fred Smye

"You know Freddie," Dobson would say on occasion, "I used to dream of a little empire in Canada." And it appeared he was damned if he wasn't going to give his all to see it happen.

One can only imagine the pressure on Dobson that summer and fall of 1945. From a business point of view, he was doing everything wrong. On one hand, there was the "deal" riding on a handshake. Up to now he had no prospective Canadian takers for what was Hawker-Siddeley's most promising project, the Tudor. Victory Aircraft was laying off hundreds of people a week and had no contracts whatsoever on the books. In England the Hawker-Siddeley board took a dim view of the venture and were not entirely sold on the idea. One board member in particular—"he and Dobson used to row like crazy"—was totally opposed to the idea and persistently organized opposition to the plan from other board members.

With assets exceeding $146 million, with a wartime production effort of $2.233 billion in aircraft, and with $42 million in actual currency on hand, Hawker-Siddeley was certainly not going to jeopardize any of its holdings—to say nothing of its prestige—so that Roy Dobson could go off half-cocked to Canada to buy a defunct company at a time when such production space was a dime a dozen in England.

The only one still urging the deal was C. D. Howe. Not only would it provide an excellent opportunity to unload over 3,000,000 square feet of excess industrial space, but it would give the Canadian aircraft industry the backing of the Hawker-Siddeley organization. Added to this was the possibility of disposing of other air-industry-related crown corporations, notably Turbo Research, where attempts were being made to develop a Canadian jet engine. "Prospects for aircraft production in Canada," Howe continued to preach, "are encouraging."

As encouraging as he may have been in public and to the press, his last meeting with Dobson—mid August, 1945—before the deal was signed was a different story. Howe knew the outcome of Dobson's meetings with Symington, Leckie, and Drury, and greeted him with "Well Roy, I suppose you're here because you want out." Howe then offered to forget the whole thing, but Dobson insisted he was in and staying.

"No," said Dobson, "I don't want out."

"Well you've got more guts than brains."

Within a few short weeks after VJ-Day, only 3,000 people remained in the entire Canadian aircraft business which, just a few months before, had employed 80,000. Victory Aircraft was now laying off at a rate of 500 per week.

Since his first visit to Canada in 1943 Dobson had kept up a steady stream of cables and letters to Canada. There was never any doubt that he would be back and that a deal was imminent. But after his August meeting with Howe communication suddenly stopped. No visits, no cables, no letters, no phone calls; nothing. Smye hadn't heard from him, and Scully and Howe couldn't get in touch with him either. For some reason, he wasn't replying to their letters or cables.

Smye was concerned, not least for himself. He was still on Victory's payroll, but the work force had shrunk to barely 300. By late September, his concern turned to worry. Did Dobson want out? He flew to England to see Dobson.

"What's all the flap about for Christ's sake?" Dobson bellowed. "I'm busy over here. I made a deal with the government of Canada. You tell those dummies to keep their shirts on and I'll be over as soon as I can."

Maybe Dobson thought the Canadians should cool their heels for a while. If they didn't want his Tudor, what *did* they want? Or maybe he was truly busy with the adjustment to post-war conditions in Manchester. In any event his silence had unnerved the Canadian government; they wanted some reassurance. Howe told Smye to bring back some Hawker-Siddeley people as a show of Dobson's good faith.

Smye returned to Canada with Joe Lindsay, the chief designer with Armstrong Siddeley Gas Turbines; W. G. Carter, the chief designer with Gloster Aircraft, and W. W. W. Downing from the same company; and Stuart "Cock" Davies, then chief designer of the Yeadon Division at A. V. Roe in Yorkshire.

"This should keep those Canadian buggers happy," mumbled Dobson to Davies. "And make sure Freddie doesn't make any promises for me till I get over." Dobson promised to follow in a few days.

Smye quartered Dobson's people at the King Edward Hotel in Toronto, and over the next two weeks the five men hatched ideas that would lead to the first three big projects of the new company: a fighter, a jetliner, and a jet engine. Downing, Carter, and Lindsay met with some RCAF and gas-turbine (jet-engine) people in Ottawa, while Davies met with the remaining Victory Aircraft engineers. While the Tudor business was pretty well dead, Davies and some of the Malton engineers had come up with an idea for another aircraft, a four-engine turbo civil transport, and wanted a chance to talk to TCA about it.

Smye didn't know it at the time, but Davies was in Canada for another reason, as well. The Hawker-Siddeley board, still skeptical over Dobson's plan, had asked Davies to report on the Victory operation.

Smye also had a job to do. He prepared for Dobson his recommendations on just what portion of the massive Victory operation Dobson should take. The administration building to house an engineering department and just one assembly bay should do it, he thought.

When Dobson arrived, he read the report and the two immediately went to Ottawa to see Howe.

They took rooms at the Chateau Laurier, and Dobson then went off alone to see Howe.

He had in his little black briefcase my recommendations, and when he returned to the room, he threw his briefcase on the bed and said, "Well, Freddie, we've taken the whole bloody thing!"

—Fred Smye

The "whole bloody thing" turned out to be 1,000,000 square feet of plant, including all the buildings, all the assembly bays, all the tools, machines, and personnel, as well as the waterworks and other municipal services in the village of Malton. Dobson announced to the press:

For a period, the Canadian company will be a design, research and development affair with no aircraft being produced. We are putting into Canada a team of designers. I do not expect there is much we shall need to get from here (England) except technical guidance. We have not gone into Canada as a money-making organization; we have gone in to spread development of the science of aeronautics and to give Canada a basic industry which, in our opinion, she badly needs. Canada will become the aircraft production centre of the British Empire within ten years.

The contract was essentially the same deal that Dobson and Howe had shaken hands on six months earlier. It called for operating the plant on a rent/purchase kind of arrangement with a separate clause should any profits be made. Dobson would get the entire operation for $2.5 million but would not be obliged to pay the $2.5 million up front, just be covered for it. And he wouldn't have to pay a cent in rent unless and until the company started to make money. In return for this financial generosity, Howe imposed a few conditions to the deal, namely, that the new company be a Canadian effort; that the company get into design and development, and not be merely an assembly-type operation; that Hawker-Siddeley agree to take and train

Canadians in up-to-date design, development, and research; and that the company have a Canadian president and board with a resident chairman in Britain. "The whole plan," said Howe, when it came his turn to meet the press, "is very satisfying from the standpoint of Canada."

The date of the agreement was November 2, 1945, to take effect one month to the day later. The new company would be called, appropriately enough, A. V. Roe Canada.

4

A GATHER
OF AERONAUTICAL MEN

It was December, 1945, eighteen months since Jim Floyd had left the Chadderton plant and the Lancaster program to work at Yeadon where a completely new engineering and design office had been set up to look at post-war commercial projects.

Stuart Davies was heading up the new office as chief designer. The first thing he did, recalls Floyd, was "grab me by the scruff of the neck and say, 'You're going to be my chief project engineer.' "

For close to a year, Dobson had been keen on the company getting into the civil aviation business, right at the ground floor, as soon as the war was over. He had learned from his failure to sell the Tudor that a different kind of plane was called for, and the new design office was exploring other possibilities. For Floyd, it meant working on a number of design projects at the same time, including putting metal wings on the Anson; and ten, twelve, and twenty-four seat turbo prop (700 Series) commercial aircraft.

With Davies back and forth to Canada a lot during the fall and winter of 1945/46, Floyd hardly saw him and was left pretty much on his own. During this time, an offer to join Chrislea Aircraft—for three times the salary—came up and he jumped at it. But he would wait until Davies returned from Canada.

At Malton, the 300 or so Victory employees left at the plant awaited the inevitable. Dave Boyd was no longer there, nor were the familiar wartime noises associated with making planes: cutting metal, rivet guns, and engine revs. Office staff cleaned up files and paper work, maintenance and power house staff cleaned floors. What technical and engineering people that remained sketched idly away on blueprint paper designing additions to their homes and cottages.

The three huge assembly bays were deserted save for hundreds of pieces of Lancasters, Lincolns, and Yorks stacked up against the walls or hung from the ceiling like meat in a butcher shop. Outside on the tarmac, finished Lancasters, their wings clipped, hid under the snow.

Roy Dobson had a few details to take care of before the deal with Howe could go through.

Up front he needed money for incorporation of A. V. Roe Canada as a new company, a credit guarantee for the agreed purchase price of close to $2.5 million, and some short-term contracts for work to pay his 300 or so workers until the big-money contracts arrived. Foreign exchange restrictions at the time prevented money from leaving Britain so Dobson had to obtain the necessary credit guarantee in Canada. He didn't have far to look.

One evening in early December, 1945, Dobson was discussing the takeover financing with Bickell. "I must go on," he said to Bickell, "but I can't do it without money; two and a half million dollars of it."

"It's lying on the bar in front of you Dobbie; pick it up."

"No Jack, this is a gamble and I don't gamble with my friend's money. But, you can guarantee an overdraft for me."

"It's done," said Bickell. He was a director with the Canadian Imperial Bank of Commerce, and guaranteeing an overdraft for the amount in question proved easy for Bickell.

The story goes that the bank's directors at first balked at the idea of covering the chit for an Englishman they didn't know, in order to purchase a company that didn't yet exist. At some point during the crucial board meeting, Bickell decided that the bickering about the overdraft had gone far enough. He took the floor and delivered an ultimatum: "I'll give you guys ten minutes to grant the overdraft. And if you don't, I'll grant it myself and resign from this joint." The overdraft was granted. And the $1,200 incorporation fee for Dobson's company came from Bickell's own pocket.

On Friday, November 3, 1945, Victory Aircraft closed its doors for the last time. Supervisors instructed some 150 or so personnel to "stay close to the phone" over the weekend. On the following Monday, 2 people showed up for work. By the end of the week, 136 had been called back, and by mid-January, about 350.

Among those 350 were Murray Willer (National Steel Car, 1940) who since 1941 had been the one responsible for sending over from Manchester all the engineering drawings for the Lancaster; Joe Turner (National Steel Car, 1938), cost accountant, who had been largely responsible for all government accounts; Don Rogers (National Steel Car, 1942), the only remaining test pilot; Ken Molson (National Steel Car, 1938), whose wartime job had been to correct engineering problems with the Lancaster; Bob Johnson (National Steel Car, 1940), who during his years at Malton would work for seven different aircraft companies, yet never leave the one site; Joe Cribar (National Steel Car, 1941), foreman, sheet metal worker on the Lancaster; Ernie Alderton (National Steel Car, 1939) metal worker, who took over the experimental department, and later the personnel department; Ron Adey (National Steel Car, 1939), administrator, production control manager, who went to the experimental department; Mario Pesando (National Steel Car, 1942), aeronautical engineer, who joined as a flight test engineer; Earle Brownridge (Victory Aircraft, 1943), standards inspector, who would eventually end up running the engine division; Jack Hilton (National Steel Car, 1938), production, was general foreman of the Lancaster production program at Victory; and Jack Millie (National Steel Car, 1940), draftsman/aeronautical engineer, was one of the few Canadian-born aircraft designers at the new company.

Most of the 350 had come to Malton back in the days of National Steel Car and Robert Magor's Lysander factory; others had joined Victory Aircraft during the war. All knew each other and were now back working for A. V. Roe Canada. They would form the nucleus of what would become the most famous company in Canadian history. But this was still the winter of 1945/46, and A. V. Roe Canada was as yet a simple operation with only four main departments: sales and service, engineering, manufacturing, and finance.

With most of his financial problems behind him, Dobson could now turn his attention to recruiting a board of directors, men of his own choice who could bring his new company through those first critical years. He asked Bickell to be chairman of the board, ironically the same position he had held with Victory Aircraft a year and a half before. There were no surprises in his selection of the company's first directors, either. They included John Tory, who drew up the company's first constitution; T. O. M. "Tom" Sopwith, the great British aviator and Dobson's pal; and Frank Spriggs, who had accompanied Dobson on that first fateful trip to Canada in 1943. Fred Smye was offered the position of assistant general manager, and was to be responsible for the sales, service, and contracts end of things as well.

Now came the job of looking for number one, a president and general manager. Dobson wanted someone with aircraft production experience; someone well respected in the industry; a Canadian, and most of all, someone highly visible. He did not want Bill Scully, Victory

Aircraft's most recent president who had since returned to private business.

Because Scully never had a piece of paper on his desk whenever Dobson went to seek him, Dobson never believed he was an aircraft man and would never have hired him.

—Fred Smye

Ralph Bell suggested Walter Deisher, the general manager of Fleet Aircraft in Fort Erie, Ontario. Fleet, like Victory, had an impressive wartime record, producing American-designed Cornell trainers faster and cheaper than three equally large plants in the United States. Deisher was a short, stubby, quiet, unassuming man with a grey toothbrush moustache. Famous for his twice-a-day strolls through the Fleet plant, and for giving his department heads full authority to run their own show, critics of Deisher would later say he lacked the ability and the desire to lead.

I walked out of his office lots of times believing he was crazy. He'd sit there for an hour and discuss things and you'd go away believing he'd made a firm decision. Then, fifteen minutes later, he'd change his mind.

—Ron Adey

Deisher was a Virginia-born Canadian who had emigrated to Canada in 1913 when he was twenty-four. Although most of his pre-war background lay in the automotive industry—he had raced cars in the 1930s and loved big automobiles—one of his most treasured souvenirs was his pilot's card signed by Orville Wright.

What Dobson saw in Deisher was the aircraft man he was looking for and hired him just after Christmas, 1945. Although Fred Smye technically reported to Deisher, it was soon apparent that he, and not Deisher, was running the show.

It is common when senior executives move from one company to another to bring staff with them. Deisher brought several men with him including Andrew Caggie, who found his way under Fred Smye's skin. Smye was always a supporter of anyone who worked for him; Deisher's people didn't work for him and it showed.

Caggie was supposed to be our great production czar. We'd have a meeting and you'd look around and the guy was falling asleep, literally falling asleep. It began as a joke but it started eating into the morale of our own guys . . . . They were nothing more than a group of incompetent dumb-

bells, except maybe Hollingshead the financial guy. They knew as much about building airplanes as my foot did. We had our problems and most of them were related to those donkeys.

—*Fred Smye*

In the beginning the company that would one day build the Arrow took contracts to make forms for plastic hairbrushes and fenders for Wilson trucks, to design and test oil burners, and to make the occasional part for Cockshutt tractors. Then came the first contracts to overhaul, repair, and store all types of surplus aircraft flown in from all across the country. Sea Furies, Harvards, Dakotas, Mitchells, and Hudsons, and, of course, Lancasters.

We had to empty the gas tanks, take the wings off and store the fuselages, wings, and engines in bays 1 and 2.

—*Jack Hilton.*

Just about the time all the Lancasters had been dismantled and stored, the RCAF asked if they could be converted. As a result, the Lancaster Conversion Program was set up and fifty-seven planes were converted into photo reconnaissance aircraft for the RCAF and commercial transports, called Lancastrians, for TCA. Twenty other contracts followed to convert Mitchells, Sea Furies, Venturas, and Dakotas. Although piece-meal at times, the conversion programs paid the wages and continued as late as 1950. One employee in the gas turbine division had flown Lancasters during the war; one in particular was "his" plane. He was reduced to tears one day when his old plane, "Daisy," was brought in for conversion.

Five long years, I've waited for news about Daisy, and here she is.

—*Jim Mulholland*

For this early "government work" as it was called, the company received progress payments, awarded monthly through C. D. Howe's new Department of Reconstruction and Supply, for work done the previous month. Some work, some payment; no work, no payment. Because of the rent/purchase arrangement, it made sense for the government to give A. V. Roe as much work as possible—the money would be turned back as rent or put towards the purchase price. Either way, it was good business.

Joe Turner handled most of the company finances from the outset. He had been a Victory Aircraft cost accountant in 1945, keeping track of costs that would satisfy the government accountants; Smye and Dobson were both impressed with him, and he eventually became vice-president of finance in 1955. A. V. Roe Canada, from the day it began, operated on a "cost-plus" basis:

How the cost plus 5 per cent scheme worked was, once a target price for a contract was agreed to with the Crown, and if there was a cost overrun, the Crown would reimburse you for a percentage of the overrun. If your costs were less than the target, you would share the profit with the Crown. The maximum rate of cost plus was 5 per cent, or on overhaul contracts, cost plus 10 per cent. The Department of Defence Production used to tell me that de Havilland's poured money down the drain compared with the way we operated; their costs were very, very high.

—Joe Turner

This method allowed A. V. Roe Canada to start making a profit very early in the game, in its second year, in fact. The final payment on the Malton facility was made by August, 1948. Dobson's gamble was paying off.

With most of the plant busy converting Lancasters and Mitchells and making tractor parts, little attention was given to a small group of a dozen engineers hidden away in the engineering department. The group, all of them Canadian, worked unofficially under Stuart Davies, in what was unofficially known as the "initial projects office," on unofficial projects.

Davies came to Canada often during the fall and winter of 1945/46; much of his time was spent at this initial projects office talking with Bryan Wood who was struggling with Dobson's Tudor II effort, or with Jack Millie, one of the few Canadians in the plant with a degree in aeronautical engineering, who was working on a design for a single-seat fighter—but it was strictly speculative.

There was myself and a couple of draftsmen. We had one guy looking after stress, another looking after aerodynamics, and I was trying to tie it all together, that is, getting down on paper something the other guys could work with and something we could submit to the government as a proposal. We were not working on any response to any Operational Requirement for the RCAF. We had heard somewhere the air force wanted an airplane and we were trying to come up with something.

—Jack Millie

Davies would also drop in to see Wilhelm Ulric Shaw, "Woo" to everyone who knew him, who had been chief engineer at both National Steel Car and Victory Aircraft. Most of his previous experience had been with small bush aircraft, mostly structural work.

In early 1942, during the British Commonwealth Air Training Plan days, the RCAF had issued a proposal for what they called an "aircrew trainer." Six companies were invited to bid on the project, including National Steel Car, Noorduyn, Fleet, Fairchild, de Havilland, and Ottawa Car. The RCAF then short-listed the proposals and asked National Steel Car, Noorduyn, and Fairchild to resubmit around a second specification in April, 1943. All three had become more heavily involved in war production, and the project was less of a priority than the year before. Nonetheless, Shaw was appointed project engineer on the scheme, and a small group of draftsmen curtained off part of Assembly Bay 3 and went to work.

Given the nickname "Shaw's Trainer," the plane was to be designed with two seats and two engines, and would have been roughly the size of a DC-3. Shaw relied on Alf Sewart, Dobson's liaison man at the plant, for advice on the project, and even did some test analysis on the project in England. The plane, however, didn't get much beyond the paper stage, even though Shaw was still toying with it in 1946 when it was finally abandoned.

The problem with the project was the RCAF had done two things. Not only did they specify the power plant they wanted (Pratt & Whitney engines) but they also specified all the equipment they wanted on board so, consequently, they had anyone who was working on the project trapped. From then on, however, whenever the RCAF issued a specification, all they did was to tell the manufacturer what they wanted done and that's it; that way, the engineers can go and make the best possible airplane powered in the best possible way.

—Ken Molson

It is unlikely anyone would have batted an eye if A. V. Roe Canada had stayed in the tractor parts, oil furnace, and aircraft conversion business. Creating employment for 350 people in a brand new company in early post-war Canada was accomplishment enough in itself. For Roy Dobson, however, the work had just begun. With the financing and the board of directors in place and Walter Deisher on board, Dobson turned his attention to the commitment he had made to Howe: to put a team of designers into Canada.

Stuart Davies and Fred Smye were to recruit these technical people with only one instruction from Dobson: "Think Future." For Davies, the task really came down to who Roy Chadwick could spare from Manchester. Smye's job was a little tougher, finding what few Canadians there were with an aeronautical background who might be persuaded to join A. V. Roe Canada.

Davies and Smye were as different as night and day, not only in their backgrounds, but in their views of what was necessary for the new company to survive as well. Davies set out to find himself a chief designer; Smye, on the other hand, set out to find himself a salesman, someone he knew and could trust. The job went to a wartime friend from his Ralph Bell days, Joe Morley.

A gregarious, bespectacled, prematurely balding man, Morley held a degree in engineering from the University of Toronto and had worked for Pratt & Whitney in Connecticut before the war. In 1941, when the Canadian government issued a decree that all Canadians with professional standing were to register back home, Morley returned to Canada where Fred Smye hired him as a co-ordinator of aircraft equipment in Ottawa as one of Ralph Bell's staff. Morley's job in Ottawa involved setting up subcontracts for various aircraft companies and suppliers; companies like Fleet, de Havilland, and of course, Victory Aircraft.

In January, 1946, Smye hired Morley as sales and service manager. Although his background was in the technical and engineering areas, he was quick to learn sales, marketing, and public relations—to such a degree people thought he had done it all his life. As his assistant, Morley recruited Murray Willer who had been with National Steel Car since 1940 and had been Victory's liaison person on the Lancaster. Willer and Morley formed the new company's sales and service department. They had to sell whatever the company was able to produce, to whoever would buy it.

Stuart Davies set out to find a chief engineer for A. V. Roe Canada; someone with years of experience, someone to set the tone at the new company, a conservative, a man to keep to the tried and true of engineering principles rather than one who would fly off in new directions. This was no time for experimenting. He wanted a doer, not a visionary. He chose Edgar Atkin, a stocky, middle-aged Briton who was "intensely practical behind his horn-rimmed glasses."

In many ways, Edgar Atkin was like his new boss Walter Deisher. He was quiet, almost secretive, and kept his cards pretty close to his chest. He made few friends, so few, in fact, that the people at Malton called him "the Lone Ranger."

He had been assistant chief designer at A. V. Roe Manchester for twelve years. Jim Floyd, his co-worker, called him "the best mathematician I ever met." Before the war, Atkin had been chief technician for Boulton-Paul Aircraft and, from 1939 to 1945, an assistant designer on the Manchester and the Lancaster.

He was a very different man, very quiet and capable, but reluctant to divulge anything, especially to management.

—*Ron Adey*

I think he always resented Smye as a young whippersnapper. A number of times Atkin went behind Smye's back and corresponded directly with Dobson and Dobson would come back at Smye with, "What the bloody hell are you doing over there!"

—*Joe Morley*

Soon after his arrival in Canada in December, 1945, Atkin's name was added to Fred Smye's list of undesirables, right below that of Walter Deisher. And, it stayed there for all his days with the company.

Technically, he was well qualified, but no leader, no manager, and that's what we needed.

—*Fred Smye*

Atkin's arrival signalled the beginning of what came to be known as "the British Airlift," a steady stream of technical people recruited in England over the next fourteen years to work at A. V. Roe Canada.

Around this same time Smye went to see Bob Noorduyn. Noorduyn Aircraft was not adjusting well to post-war conditions, and some of their staff might be welcome at A. V. Roe Canada.

Bob Noorduyn was a friend of mine, and he knew his company was going down the drain. "Whatever you do," he told me, "hire my boy Chamberlin." In those days, Chamberlin was a big, gawky kid, hard to talk to, and he couldn't make himself understood—in normal language, anyway. But, if Noorduyn had faith in him, he must be good. So, when Atkin arrived in December of 1945, I told him, "This guy's your chief aerodynamicist."

—*Fred Smye*

James Arthur "Jim" Chamberlin was difficult, the typical absent-minded professor, and regarded by those who knew and worked for him as one of the most brilliant men in his field. Born in Kamloops in 1916, Chamberlin received his education at the University of Toronto and the Imperial College of Science and Technology in London, England, before serving as chief engineer for the Clark-Ruse Aircraft Company in Dartmouth, Nova Scotia. From there, he supervised project work for the RCAF with Howe's Federal Aircraft operation in Montreal before joining Noorduyn Aircraft in the same city at war's end.

He was an unusual man, but probably the smartest technical man in the organization. He couldn't have cared less about administrative details, management, or a project that was finished. What was done was done, so let's forget it. All he did care about was the project he was currently involved with, perhaps the one following it, and a good shot of his favourite Hudson's Bay rum.

—Ron Adey

Davies and Smye had now finished the first phase of their recruiting. Here was a gather of aeronautical men that would design Canada's first jet fighter and first jet airliner.

5

GETTING OFF
THE GROUND

Canada in 1945 was an entire generation removed from the Canada of 1939. Although the country had emerged from the war with unprecedented military and industrial strength, the government's immediate and instinctive reaction was much the same as it had been in the days following the First World War: retreat to the relative safety of our borders and reduce military forces to the bare minimum.

Canadian troops had been abroad for six long years, and, although more than a million men and women had been in uniform between 1940 and 1945, fewer than 35,000 remained so by 1948. Defence expenditures, a whopping $3 billion in 1944/45, had dropped to $195 million by 1947. Moreover, those traditional Canadian defence assumptions, so prevalent under Mackenzie King in the late 1930s, were reasserted under the post-war Mackenzie King. The Canadian military, once marching the streets from Caen to Singapore, had been reduced to defending Canadian territory and the strategic sea approaches.

There was never any doubt about whose set of post-war rules Canada would follow. There was little resistance among Canada's political leaders in "accepting the American view of international relations in the post-war world." This "American view" had two basic themes. First, there was the general threat of communism—ideological, economic, and political. Second, there was the communist military threat. The United States had little trouble convincing Canada that the Soviet Union was "capable and willing to spread her brand of communism through direct military means" and that Canada could help prevent it. "We saw the world as ours to defend," said Henry Kissinger.

Canada willingly undertook to assist in the collective preservation of peace through the United Nations and NATO, but was vague when it came to defining the commitment in hard military terms during the early post-war years. Such was not the case for the United States. The unprecedented swiftness of post-war political and technological developments, when combined with appropriate doses of anti-Soviet rhetoric and paranoia—a spy, a report, and an airshow—would make any military ventures that much easier for the public to swallow.

The spy was Igor Gouzenko. On September 6, 1945, the Prime Minister was informed that Gouzenko, a cypher clerk with the Soviet Embassy in Ottawa, had presented Canadian officials with documented evidence of an extensive Russian espionage system operating in Canada and the United States. The revelations were a source of great private concern for Mackenzie King. He wrote in his diary, "If there is another war, it will come against America by way of Canada from Russia." President Truman was more blunt. "Unless Russia is faced with an iron fist and strong language, another war is in the making. Only one language do they understand: How many divisions have you? I am tired of babying the Soviets."

The report was released May 23, 1946. The product of the Working Committee on Post Hostilities Problems, it was entitled *The Post War Canadian Defence Relationship with the United States: General Considerations.* The committee had operated under the auspices of the Permanent Joint Board on Defence of 1940 whose members included American and Canadian military personnel; the senior Canadian officer on the board was Air Vice Marshal Wilfred Austin Curtis.

The objective of the committee was to identify strategic security problems and the necessary military defensive responses to those problems. The Americans on the committee operated under the assumption that the major threat to the security of North America lay in the possibility of a massive Soviet air strike on the North American industrial heartland, coming from across the Canadian Arctic. Air deterrent must therefore, they felt, be the principal defence priority. The committee estimated that by 1950 the Soviet Union would have the capability to launch a massive conventional and nuclear air strike against North America from across the Pole. To counter the threat, the immediate construction of an extensive and integrated Canadian-American air defence system should be the number one priority for continental security.

Startling though the report's predictions were, Mackenzie King and some of the Canadian military chiefs, particularly Bob Leckie, Chief of Air Staff, had strong reservations. Leckie was particularly concerned that only American intelligence estimates were used in preparing the report and was not convinced that any future war with Russia would start with a polar air strike. If war was to come, reasoned Leckie, it would begin in Europe with ground and air forces, and any attack on North America would be a small operation designed to divert Allied military resources and personnel from the European continent.

Mackenzie King, as anti-military as ever, shied away from giving the impression of openly supporting or participating in any active joint defence effort with the United States; it would be this above all else that would provoke Soviet response. He truly believed that Canada should "be the link that would keep the other two powers united."

Accordingly, when the Joint Planning Committee submitted their recommendations to the Cabinet that summer of 1946, they were shelved. And quickly. President Truman was furious, having believed every-thing in the report, and immediately "summoned" Mackenzie King to Washington to discuss future military co-operation between the two countries. Mackenzie King was sympathetic to his good neighbour the United States, but he remained unmoved and returned to Ottawa as uncommitted as ever.

The air show was the Tushino Moscow Air Show of August, 1947. Similar to the traditional Russian May Day parade, the air show allowed the West the opportunity to get a look at the latest in Soviet aircraft. The Tushino show of 1947 was full of surprises.

Leading the "fly-past" were three four-engined heavy bombers, sim-ilar to the Boeing B-29 Superfortress. Called the Tupolev TU-4, the Russian bomber, of course, was a copy, but if as good as the B-29, would enable the Russians to reach many North American industrial centres.

Even more alarming was the first appearance of the Llyushin IL-22 bomber powered by four TR-1 jet engines. Although still in the pro-totype stage, the sight of the plane created a lasting impression on the western military attachés who had been invited to watch. A Sukhoi SU-9 twin jet fighter and a Tupolev TU-77 twin jet assault bomber also made their debuts that day. These were Russian versions of the late Second World War German jet aircraft and, while fairly limited in capability, they were nonetheless jet aircraft.

In this air show, the Russians had succeeded in heightening the paranoia level in the West more than any John Foster Dulles speech could ever do. And nowhere was it felt to a greater degree than in Ottawa. "It was the most serious situation that we could have possibly imagined," wrote Mackenzie King, "altogether beyond anything I had hitherto thought possible. In a word, it came down to this: there may be another war."

Canada and the United States rushed to find an answer to "stopping the armed bomber" and concluded this could only be done by using a combination of radar and interceptor fighter aircraft. "There is no way of making a continent of seven million square miles impregnable with a kind of Maginot Line," said Brooke Claxton, Canada's defence minister. The radar would track and identify incoming Russian aircraft and the fighters would scramble from air bases across Canada to intercept and destroy.

Putting the radar aspect of the defence scheme together would be easy; that had been done before. Vampires and Mustangs were acquired from the RAF as "interim aircraft," but the RCAF now had indisputable grounds for demanding jet aircraft built to its own specifications.

What we needed was a different type of aircraft; an aircraft which could operate over the vast distances of our country at all hours of the night and day and in all weather. That meant long range, easy take-off, short landing, full instrumentation and navigation, and the capacity to carry the fuel and equipment, the arms and the ammunition to destroy any invader. Such an aircraft didn't exist anywhere and, moreover, so far as we could learn, none was even planned, still less on a drawing board.

—*A/M Wilf Curtis*

"There was no plane in existence," echoed C. D. Howe, "that could be used in the defence of our northern systems." It seemed the country had but one choice: to build one.

A brief two hour meeting in Ottawa in September of 1945 set the course of A. V. Roe Canada for years to come. In attendance were senior RCAF personnel, some people from Turbo Research representing the National Research Council (NRC), and the visitors from Hawker-Siddeley that Fred Smye had literally dragged away from Roy Dobson to reassure the Canadian government and C. D. Howe that Dobson wasn't getting cold feet on the Victory Aircraft deal.

The RCAF people were A/V/M A. L. James (in the chair), A/V/M Wilf Curtis, and A/V/M John Easton; from the NRC and Turbo Research were three engineers, Ken Tupper, Paul Dilworth, and Winnett Boyd.

Dobson's people included W. G. Carter, W. W. W. Downing, and Joe Lindsay.

The meeting had been arranged by Smye to give his British guests some reason for optimism on the future of aircraft development in Canada and to allow the Canadians present, then on the leading edge of that development, "an opportunity to pick the British brains."

James opened the meeting with a presentation of the RCAF's first operational requirement for a home-built aircraft, issued proudly some nine months before, Air-7-1-Issue 1. It called for a single-engine fighter—a small one to be sure, piloted by a crew of one and to fly at subsonic speed—and an engine to go with it.

Three of my old university classmates were kingpins in British engine development, and I used to go over to Britain and thought I'd gained a pretty good understanding of how the things worked and what could go wrong. So, we looked at all the different things that were on the drawing boards in different places, but no matter how much looking we did, nobody had any engines.

So, we sat down and wrote an operational requirement based on the defence plan, the plan that focused on air defence, and we looked at an appropriate engine to meet our defence requirements and we figured a 5,000-pound-thrust axial flow engine would do it.

—A/V/M John Easton

Downing was "horrified" that the RCAF wanted a single-engine fighter—and an engine of only 5,000 pounds thrust. Such an aircraft and engine might be acceptable in Great Britain where there were many airfields and distances between them were short, but never for Canada where the airfields were comparatively few and distances between them were great. No, said Downing, Canada would be better off with a two-crew, twin-engine aircraft. Even the latest aircraft being developed in Britain, the Gloster Meteor, had two engines. And as for the engines, they should have at least 6,500 pounds thrust each. Turning to the NRC people, he advised them to "design the best engine you can that will fit within an engine nacelle of 32 inches."

Now this was a pretty tall order. A pretty tall order, indeed.

—Winnett Boyd

While Downing and company were in Ottawa, Smye and Davies journeyed to Montreal to meet with H. J. Symington of TCA. Symington had resisted Dobson's attempts to sell him the Tudor, and although the airline's aging domestic DC-3 fleet was being phased out, TCA's engineers were not convinced that the Tudor was the replacement aircraft they wanted.

Present at the meeting was Jim Bain, a young, Scottish-born TCA engineer. Bain had been involved in commercial aviation in Britain since 1931 and had come to Canada and joined TCA in 1938 soon after its formation. In 1945, he was TCA's superintendent of engineering and maintenance and was on loan to Canadair on the North Star project.

Unlike Symington, Bain was somewhat familiar with the Victory operation, having negotiated with Victory during the war about converting York aircraft to commercial transport for TCA's post-war Atlantic runs. Bain came away from those negotiations convinced that Victory's enthusiasm for the project far outdistanced their engineering capabilities, and turned elsewhere for the contract. If Smye and Davies were to have any hope of success with TCA, they had first to convince Jim Bain.

The meeting was inconclusive. Smye, Davies, and Bain agreed to keep in touch since TCA had not finalized its post-war commercial requirements. But Davies, from his personal experience in civil transport, "guessed" that TCA might require a four-engine aircraft that would hold thirty passengers. He advised Jack Millie and his team at Malton in the initial projects office to adapt some of the Tudor information to help him with his drawings.

It was now December, and Roy Dobson had taken over the Victory Aircraft plant "lock, stock, and barrel." A. V. Roe Canada was now a company, a company with no contracts.

The RCAF took the advice of the British aircraft designers to heart. The specification for the fighter would be changed to more realistically serve the needs of Canada. But, as far as Curtis was concerned, it still had to be built in Canada.

Wilf Curtis joined the Canadian army in the First World War, but in 1916 at the age of twenty-three he transferred to the Royal Naval Air Service in Britain after receiving his pilot's licence from the Curtiss Aviation School (established in Toronto in 1915). He was credited with shooting down thirteen enemy aircraft and was decorated with the Distinguished Service Cross and Bar.

After the war he turned to civilian life—there was no Canadian air force at the time—and in 1923 successfully established the W. A. Curtis Insurance Company which today is still run by his descendants. He was a founding member in 1928 of the Toronto Flying Club, the first association of its kind in Canada. He joined the RCAF in 1932 after eight years as an officer in the Toronto Scottish Regiment, and assisted in the formation of the 110th City of Toronto RCAF Reserve Squadron, becoming a wing commander in 1938.

In the first months of the Second World War, Curtis was in charge of a committee to select airport sites in Ontario for the British Commonwealth Air Training Plan. He then went to Ottawa as commanding officer of the training school at Uplands, and in 1941 to England as Deputy Commander-in-Chief RCAF Overseas.

Following the war, he became senior officer on the Permanent Joint Board on Defence and was appointed Chief of Air Staff in 1947, succeeding Robert Leckie, another champion of made-in-Canada aircraft.

His uncompromising stand that the new fighter be built in Canada could be traced back to 1942. The Japanese were poised in the Aleutian Islands for a possible sweep down Canada's West Coast. The RCAF home defences were desperately short of aircraft should any such attack occur. Canadian squadrons at home were operating with second or third line aircraft or fretting on the ground with no aircraft at all. As Deputy Commander-in-Chief of the RCAF in England, Curtis had to appear before an aircraft allotment conference of non-Canadians in England to plead for Hurricanes that had been built at Fort William, Ontario, by Canadians, and justify Canada's need for the aircraft. He lost the argument and the planes he wanted were sent to Russia.

Maybe they did need the planes more than we did, I don't know. But I do know that we needed them very badly. And I realized right then, walking out of that meeting and feeling every inch a failure, that until we didn't have to tip our hats to anyone to get aircraft when we needed them, we'd never have the air force a first rate nation really deserves.

—A/M Wilf Curtis

In those days, air specifications were drafted by RCAF Operational Requirements' staff, usually with some assistance from the Defence Research Board (DRB). The proposals were then considered by the Air Council, five senior officers at RCAF headquarters. The officers approved any submission before passing it on to the Chiefs of Staff Committee.

The chairman of the CSC was then responsible for ensuring that the proposal received a critical and thorough examination and that its priority in relation to other projects and to the overall defence plan was established. In order to ensure that all aspects of the proposal were carefully screened, it was customary to invite the Secretary to the Cabinet (who briefed the Prime Minister), the Under Secretary for External Affairs (who advised on the political aspects), the Deputy Minister of Defence Production (who advised on the problems of purchase or production), and a representative of the Treasury (to monitor the costs).

This process not only allowed for scrutiny at every level, but allowed officials of other interested departments to become familiar with the proposal and to brief their respective ministers prior to a meeting of the Cabinet Defence Committee (CDC).

When and if the Chiefs of Staff reached an agreement, a draft submission to the CDC was drawn up and discussed with the Prime Minister. If he was satisfied, the submission was signed and forwarded to the CDC. On occasion, the Prime Minister would defer approval, pending informal discussions with the CDC, other ministers, or some of his colleagues.

The Chiefs of Staff and deputy ministers from relevant ministries were usually invited to CDC meetings. Members of the government could then question the Chiefs of Staff on the submission, have technical and tactical matters explained, and informally "size up" their military advisers. On many occasions, CSC proposals were turned down or delayed by the CDC for what could only be termed "political" reasons.

Wilf Curtis was adamant that this would not happen with the fighter. The feeling on the CSC however, was far from unanimous. The committee chairman, General Charles Foulkes of the Army, was perhaps the most skeptical of Curtis and his motives. Granted, a solid air defence was one thing, but the idea of designing and manufacturing an aircraft was quite another. Canadian industry's attempt to design and manufacture a tank during the Second World War had met with failure. Foulkes was on record as doubting whether Canada was capable of the much more exacting feat of turning out an up-to-date fighter. Other members of the CSC were concerned that if the project were approved, and if at some point it began to look impracticable, it might be difficult to abandon or cancel the project. Those who shared this concern might well have said "I told you so" more than once to Wilf Curtis.

But Curtis stood his ground and won the right to submit his proposal to the CDC, and eventually to the cabinet itself, a proposal which would one day end up as the CF-100. While Curtis took on the responsibility of politically piloting the fighter through the CSC, James and Easton headed an RCAF planning team, which included A/V/M H. M. Carscallen, A/V/M W. R. MacBrien, and A/C P. A. Gilchrist. Collectively, they re-wrote the original fighter proposal as Air-7-1-Issue 2. It said in part:

The aeroplane shall be powered by two gas turbine jet propulsion engines and shall provide for a crew of two. It shall be of all metal construction with a pressurized cabin . . . . The aeroplane shall be designed for satisfactory operation over an ambient air temperature range of −57°C to +45°C . . . . The range in still air with built in fuel tankage at maximum gross weight shall be sufficient to permit the following operation: Taxi and run-up 4 minutes, takeoff 1 minute at takeoff RPM, climb to 40,000 feet, cruise to a radius of action of 650 nautical miles, combat 15 minutes at 490 knots at 40,000 feet, return cruise 650 nautical miles, descent 10 minutes from 40,000 feet, approach 7 minutes idling RPM. The operational ceiling shall not be less than 50,000 feet . . . . The sea level rate of climb shall not be less than 10,000 feet per minute . . . . The maximum true air speed in level flight at 40,000 feet altitude shall not be less than 490 knots (.85 Mach).

First we had to look at the specification for the best bombers in the world, how high they could fly, and how fast. Then we asked for a fighter which would fly higher, and fly faster. It became obvious that if our air force was to have the kind of aircraft our planners said it needed, then we would have to design it ourselves. That is precisely how the CF-100 was born.

—A/M Wilf Curtis

Stuart Davies had picked up a folder of drawings from Jack Millie in Malton and was on his way to Montreal to meet with Fred Smye before heading back to Manchester. Dobson, Downing, Carter, and Lindsay had already left weeks before. Although Smye was now working in Malton, he maintained his apartment in Montreal on Dufferin Road (dubbed "Aircraft Row" because almost everyone who lived on the street either worked for TCA or was a Ferry pilot).

It was about two o'clock in the morning, and Davies had Millie's drawings spread out on the floor of my apartment. Jim Bain lived right across the street from me and I knew he'd be arriving any moment from England so I had my eye out for him. Davies and I wanted Bain to get a look at the work our Malton guys had done before Davies returned to England. When Bain eventually showed up, I remembered Davies stretching the plans out and Bain saying, "Forget it. Any airplane that TCA's going to buy is going to be a straight jet airplane. Period."

—Fred Smye

Davies didn't know what Bain was talking about. Jim Bain picks up the story.

It all started because Rolls-Royce had never had one of their engines in a civil airplane and were delighted by TCA putting Rolls engines into our North Stars. They were regular Merlin engines with a special gear ratio for the propeller, mind you, but the engine, itself, was basic Merlin.

Because we were a civil airline and because Rolls wanted to get into civil aviation, Lord Hives, he was E. H. Hives then, called me into his office one day when I was in England. "You know," he told me, "we have a new jet engine we have developed with what we call an axial-flow turbine. At the minute we are confident it's going to be very successful." And he said that although the engine was still on the SECRET list, because we had been a good customer, he was confident we could get permission from the government to install it in a civil aircraft if we wanted to build a civil aircraft around a couple of them. This was the whole thing: he was so enamoured of us because we had put a Rolls engine in a civil aircraft and it put them into commercial aviation.

I told Hives I didn't know a damn thing about axial flow engines, but if they would go over it and explain it, I would go back and talk to the folks back home.

—Jim Bain

The engine Bain had seen was known as the AJ-65, the famous Avon engine. The Avon was Rolls-Royce's first axial flow turbojet to go into large-scale production and was intended to replace the Nene, primarily in the military field. The 65 was for 6,500 pounds thrust; with afterburner it reached 17,000 pounds thrust in its Mark III Series. "If you want us to have an airplane," said Bain to Smye and Davies that early December morning in Montreal, "it's got to have that engine in it."

In his office at Yeadon, Jim Floyd reluctantly awaited Davies' return from Canada. When he arrived in Yeadon Davies was full of enthusiasm over the prospect of a jet-powered civil transport, the takeover of Victory Aircraft, and the future of Malton in general. He rushed into Jim Floyd's office and dumped Jack Millie's plans on his desk, muttering his usual, "Here's their ideas—make them into an airplane."

But Jim Floyd had other ideas. The time had come to tell Davies that he was leaving the company to become chief engineer at Chrislea Aircraft.

"You're bloody mad! You're crazy!" Davies shouted. He was not about to lose Jim Floyd, not now. He told Floyd everything that had happened. This TCA project could be Jim Floyd's airplane. Young engineers, or any engineers for that matter, don't get too many chances in life to work on a brand new airplane from the ground up and carry it through. "Your future lies in Canada, Jim."

When Jim Bain left Fred Smye's apartment that December morning, the first person he went to see was Symington at TCA.

Symington said he wasn't prepared to make any decision regarding the use of jet engines because it involved the Canadian government and we'd better go up and see C. D. Howe. Howe said, "Find out more about the engine. Find out what's involved; find out what kind of airplane is needed". . . So I did.

I went to Jack Dyment, Clayton Glenn, and Fred Ades [TCA engineers] and it was a question of them looking at what we would require as a domestic airplane. We had enough detail on the Avon to be able to work out what the airplane would look like. It was a matter of coming up with a specification for an airplane they thought would fit the power plants that we knew were going to be available.

It just happened that the type of airplane that was going to be necessary was a thirty seater type for trans-continental and domestic service but not for flying across the Atlantic. We did know what we wanted in a domestic airplane; the size, the range, and so on. It just so happened that with building an airplane that size, the two engines just fit in beautifully . . . .

Just to see if we were off base at all, we went down to the States and showed Eddie Rickenbacker, then head of American Airlines, the proposed airplane and asked, "If we were going to build this airplane in Canada, would you be interested?". . . Rickenbacker was a blunt man and when I went back the next day, the answer I got was, "Build an airplane like that and I'll buy twenty of them."

—*Jim Bain*

Meanwhile, Jim Floyd was putting together what he thought the TCA airplane should look like. Using Jack Millie's drawings as a base to work from, within fifteen days he had come up with three possibilities. Two of these were "basically the same aircraft; the difference lay in the fact that one was powered by two jet, and the other by four gas turbine engines with propellers."

While Floyd put together his proposals for TCA, Davies further investigated the Avon. He spent a lot of time with Ray Dorey, an engineer at Rolls-Royce, and became "more and more convinced of the advantages of a straight jet installation." It was Dorey and Davies, according to Fred Smye, who finally sold Dobson on the idea. If Dobson was indeed convinced, it was quite a turn-around for him. It broke one of his basic rules—never put an untried engine in an untried aircraft.

But, if there was any degree of hesitancy about the project during those first weeks of 1946, neither TCA nor A. V. Roe Canada showed it. That the Avon, the engine that would power the new aircraft, was still on the SECRET list and was, basically, a military engine, appeared to pose no great problem. Lord Hives, head of Rolls-Royce, repeatedly assured both A. V. Roe Canada and TCA that the engine would be fully certified for use in civilian aircraft by the time the jet transport was in service.

At the end of December, 1945, Davies had sent Symington a preliminary study of jet transport he had prepared, and on February 1 he forwarded Jim Floyd's proposal brochure entitled "Thirty-six Seater Transport Aircraft for Trans Canada Airlines." Under the title were the words "prepared by A. V. Roe Canada Ltd., Malton, Ontario," although Jim Floyd had only just left England.

He agreed to go to Canada to talk to TCA, firm up the jet transport requirements, and stay there as long as it took to start the ball rolling. Floyd told his wife they would be in Canada for about a year. They stayed for fourteen.

I set off from England with a feasibility study on possible configurations of jet transports tucked under my arm on the last day of January, 1946. My trans-Atlantic flight was in a TCA Lancastrian, a converted Lancaster bomber. We had a stop of two days in the Azores because of a burst tire on landing to re-fuel; a day's wait in Montreal for a flight to Toronto in a DC-3; a diversion of that flight to North Bay because of bad weather at Malton; a night on a bench in a drug store in North Bay. And then we took an early morning train to Toronto, arriving in a snowstorm.

—Jim Floyd

Floyd arrived in Malton four days after leaving England. In 1979 he would fly London-to-New York on the Concorde, this time in just under four hours.

At Malton, Fred Smye couldn't wait to meet the man who would give him a plane he could sell to TCA. He saw Floyd as the new company's door to the future.

My first recollections of Jim Floyd was seeing this little red-headed guy in sandals, a wonderful little red-headed guy.

—Fred Smye

He was one of the nicest guys you'd ever want to meet. Too big a heart, maybe; he couldn't hurt anybody. He was one of those people who was always able to put things in their right perspective.

—Ron Adey

Floyd agreed to come to Canada to work for the princely sum of $6,000 a year. Any reservations he might have had as to whether he could survive on such a salary were put to rest when his friend Lyle Crowe told him: "Don't worry Jim — you can live like a king in Canada for $6,000."

Smye and Morley now turned to the business of working out an agreement with Jim Bain and Jack Dyment to produce the civil transport. On March 5, Smye wrote a lengthy letter to TCA. It reviewed the status of the new company, A. V. Roe Canada, talked a little about the proposed aircraft, and discussed, if not prematurely, some contract information. The next day he sent TCA the second proposal, a result of the most recent meetings with Bain and Dyment.

The second brochure was entitled "Thirty Seater Transport Aircraft for Trans Canada Airlines." It differed from the first brochure in that the four-engine turbo prop version aircraft had been dropped, and the design now proposed thirty, as opposed to thirty-six, seats, coming closer to TCA's original specification. On the TCA side of the design team were Jim Bain (although most of his time was spent at Canadair on the North Star), Clayton Glenn, Jack Dyment, and Fred Ades. On the A. V. Roe Canada side was Jim Floyd, busily assembling a team of engineers.

Floyd's meeting with TCA came about finally in early April in Winnipeg. He took along two engineers, Mario Pesando and Norman Ring. TCA sent Dyment, Hugh Reid, and Jack Grisdale. They were there to talk about a thirty-seat aircraft that would cruise at about 425 mph, have a range of 1,200 nautical miles, operate at 30,000 feet, and be suitable for most domestic routes. It would be powered by the Avon (or any other engine that could produce a 6,500-pound thrust).

> *TCA wanted an aircraft that could fly from coast to coast, stop at all the major cities and still beat the North Star, the DC-4, across the continent. This, unfortunately, was our undoing, but, nonetheless, they wrote the spec. It was government funded. So we optimized the aircraft to fly a stage length in the order of 400 to 500 miles as we would go from Victoria to Vancouver to Lethbridge to Saskatoon to Winnipeg, Thunder Bay, Toronto, Ottawa, Montreal, and all the way across. In doing so, we were still able to beat the non-stop, one-stop North Star going across the country.*
>
> *Now, this was TCA's interpretation of the market at the time. As things developed, they began to realize that people would want to fly farther . . . . They brought the stage length from 400 miles to 1,100 miles; they needed an aircraft that would fly a little further, carry more people and fly faster.*
>
> —Mario Pesando

They had their own specs, and we told them what could be done and what couldn't, and by a process of elimination we then got down to a joint specification which we eventually called the C-102.

We got along famously, and at the end of the meeting, Jack Dyment said, "Well, we should have a celebration because it looks like we're really off to the races." We came away from the meeting very optimistic.

—*Jim Floyd*

Floyd was not alone in his thinking. Jack Dyment had just completed a comparison of Floyd's thirty-seater design with another proposal, the Martin 303, and concluded that A. V. Roe Canada would be able to produce an airplane to TCA's satisfaction. Clayton Glenn echoed the sentiment, but admitted that it was an "ambitious project." He added, "If an airplane was to be purchased on looks alone, the C-102 would be a winner."

At the same time, by December, 1946, the revised specification for the RCAF's jet fighter had been completed. In October, a contract had been signed between A. V. Roe Canada and the Canadian government to construct two prototype airframes and one static test airframe.

The difficulties were great. However, it was decided to give A. V. Roe Limited the job of designing an aircraft and the engine to enable it to do the job. The decision was made on my advice and I have never regretted it.

—*A/M Wilf Curtis*

In February, company president Walter Deisher announced to the Malton Businessman's Association:

We have a contract to supply the government with jet-propelled fighters which will be as fast or faster than the Gloster Meteor. Our products will be on par with the best in England and the U.S. We are going to build aircraft designed to suit Canadian conditions. Canada has always built the other fellow's product; now we are going to have aircraft that are Canadian from the drawing boards to the stars.

By May, 1947, a general design was agreed upon between A. V. Roe and the RCAF, and detailed design work commenced. Stan Harper, assistant to chief engineer Edgar Atkin, came up with the idea of starting all company projects at the number 100 and then adding a

"C" (Canada) to avoid confusing A. V. Roe Canada's projects with any in Britain or the United States. The fighter was originally designated C-100, Shaw's trainer C-101, and the Jetliner C-102. Later, the C-100 was changed to XC-100 for a short time, the "X" signifying experimental. The RCAF set up their own designation system based on the American system of using "F" as a prefix on their fighters; Canada used "CF" (Canadian Fighter). Thus, when it entered squadron use, the XC-100 was designated the CF-100.

Atkin decided to stay as close to conventional design as possible for the XC-100 in an attempt to shorten the length of time usually needed to get an aircraft from design to flight. In pure engineering terms, this meant the aircraft would have straight wings, not swept wings then being experimented with in the United States, nor the delta-shape of the newest British designs. "Except for the jet engines near the fuselage," writes Larry Milberry, "the airplane had a basic World War II look to it."

In an unpublished work on the XC-100, writer Desmond M. Chorley concludes that Atkin and his engineers "derived the aeroplane's aerodynamic features from a study of the best available English, American and German data. And it always looked, felt and performed that way . . . always hinting it was an aircraft of Germanic rather than Canadian lineage." Mario Pesando, one of the engineers on the jet transport project, took it one step further when he said the XC-100 looked exactly like a German V-2 rocket if you removed the wings and substituted a rocket for the aircraft's high tail.

While Floyd met with the TCA engineers in Winnipeg, Fred Smye was drafting a contract between A. V. Roe and TCA for the jet transport airliner. First and foremost, he thought, the terms and conditions must be presented in such a way that TCA couldn't refuse them.

First, the aircraft was to be basically the one outlined in Floyd's second brochure. Second, the aircraft would be delivered within thirty months. Third, the cost would be $350,000 per plane and TCA would take a minimum order of fifty aircraft. Fourth, TCA would start making monthly progress payments three months after the company started work on the plane, and last, because this was a Canadian effort, Smye would guarantee that A. V. Roe and Company in England would not start to produce the same aircraft for at least three years.

Smye did not consult Dobson on the terms. He knew well enough by now that the old man would go bananas if he learned that Smye had stipulated both a delivery date and a price per aircraft up front. Dobson would never, ever, commit to a fixed price or delivery date, especially on new aircraft, until well along in the development. In designing a new airplane, there are just too many unknowns.

Following Floyd's Winnipeg meeting, and with optimism in the air, Smye drafted his five conditions into a "letter of intent" between A. V. Roe Canada and TCA. He sent it to Symington on April 5, and it was returned to him signed on April 9, 1946.

Although the letter and conditions read as though they were written by TCA, it was, in fact, Smye's letter, Smye's conditions. It might look like Fred Smye was cutting his own throat. Even the most experienced of aircraft companies, let alone one barely five months old, would be running a great risk in promising delivery of a brand new aircraft, within thirty months, at a fixed price. "The very thought of a fixed price," writes author Jim Dow,

> was enough to set off a flurry of chain-smoking among Avro exec-
> utives. Estimating the development cost of complex technology
> involved a good deal of elaborate guesswork. Maybe the govern-
> ment could accept contracts on a cost-plus basis, but the airline
> was in no position to give Avro a blank cheque.

Smye's reasons were obvious. A. V. Roe needed the jetliner project if they were going to stay in business. It was too early for an outright contract, and he wanted to secure a commitment from TCA. The letter of intent was a ploy he had picked up when he had worked with Ralph Bell, putting together contracts for the Department of Munitions and Supply during the war. The letter would buy him time—the time he needed in order to get a real contract out of TCA.

Symington had sent a copy of the letter of intent to his "boss" C. D. Howe in Ottawa who passed it on to financial consultant F. H. Brown for scrutiny. It is interesting to note that, in his commentary, Brown refers to the document both as a draft and as a proposal:

> This draft letter covers the situation adequately and [I] have only
> the following minor suggestions.
>   I would suggest that the proposed Letter of Intention should
> carry our usual clause stating that it only sets out the agreement
> in principle and that the formal contract will carry general terms
> and conditions in form satisfactory to our lawyers not inconsistent
> with the broad meaning of the Letter of Intention. No doubt TCA
> have a number of general conditions to insert, particularly as regards
> continuous inspection of materials, quality of workmanship, test-
> ing, warranty, insurance, maintenance of secrecy, etc. If TCA have
> no general conditions, I would suggest that their lawyers examine
> our standard form and select such terms as appear applicable.

Our Letters of Intention usually make provision also for the eventuality of cancellation, but I presume that no question of arbitrary cancellation enters into a case of this kind—TCA can cancel for non-fulfillment of contract but not otherwise.

No doubt TCA would provide for a clause in the contract under which the cost estimates for purposes of progress payments would be checked either by the company's auditors or by the Treasury Cost Accountants. Otherwise, TCA might find, as we have on occasion, that the company's estimates of cost have been too high, and that the contractor has had the use of substantial amounts of our funds.

On April 10, Symington notified all his senior staff that he had signed a letter of intent with A. V. Roe. He added, interestingly, "I think it most important that this matter be kept entirely secret as long as possible. No reference should be made to it in your monthly reports."

Then, on April 14, congratulations to Symington from C. D. Howe:

I have studied the technical data which you have furnished me. I feel that TCA is justified in placing a contract in the form outlined by your draft letter of intent. It would seem desirable to hope that Canada may produce and fly the first jet engine transport plane, which would be a real feather in our cap. In addition to providing TCA with modern equipment of a type suitable for its operation, the new plane, if successful, will relieve the government of Canada of rebuilding runways at its principal airports. In addition, the building of the plane will provide stimulus to our aircraft industry and employment for Canadian workmen skilled in this type of production . . . . I congratulate you and your officers in the initiative that has been displayed in working out this design.

Jim Bain was working with Canadair on the North Star program for much of this time, but was much more excited at the prospect of Canada's first jet airliner. He knew that the letter of intent had been signed and was happy that TCA and A. V. Roe were at last in collaboration. One evening in mid-April, Bain returned home to his Montreal apartment to find a letter from Fred Smye. It said in part:

I don't think I want to thank you so much as I want to express my admiration. I know, Jim, that the airplane we are going to build is *your* airplane and, had it not been for your vision, courage and determination, we would not be proceeding with the job. You have the brains and the engineering ability and, while other people also possess these attributes, perhaps in lesser degree, what most of them lack is the foresight and resolution to stand behind their convictions.

For Fred Smye and A. V. Roe Canada, the letter of intent was only the first step in a thousand-mile journey, but at least it had the signature of the president of TCA on it. For all intents and purposes, A. V. Roe was in business.

6

JETS IN THEIR EYES

Howe used to say of the Canadian economy that it "always needed one great project to keep it functioning properly. That did not mean the thousand and one small projects that postwar planners once envisaged, but something mammoth, something national in scope." Whether that project was the result of foreign investment or not, if it brought benefits to Canada, it was okay with him. "You will always find me glad to extend a helping hand," he wrote to Dobson when the final arrangements of the takeover of Victory Aircraft had been set. He added, "the transaction will be all the more satisfactory should it lead to your settling in Canada. We welcome your type of citizen."

In the three years since their first encounter, Roy Dobson and C. D. Howe had come to know each other pretty well. Dobson's efforts with the Lancaster during the war had brought him knighthood in 1945, while Howe continued at the hub of Canada's economic machinery. Dobson admired Howe's ability to make decisions and to delegate, and shared with him an impatience with the trivial. He often reflected that the two of them would have made ideal business partners. Some would say that the only things distinguishing the two men were geography and accent.

74

One evening in April, 1946, Dobson and Howe were dining together at the Chateau Laurier in Ottawa where Dobson was staying. Howe seemed a little more preoccupied than usual. At length he mentioned to Dobson that, after nearly three years of promising results and work, Canada might, regrettably, have to get out of the jet engine business. Jet engine business? Dobson's eyes widened as they did every time he was caught a little off guard. He had been well aware of his own country's efforts since 1928 to design and build a workable gas turbine engine, largely through the work of Frank Whittle, but he had no idea that Canada was also active in the field. How in heaven's name, he thought, could this country possibly be involved in the jet engine business when Canada had not made even one successful inroad into the aircraft piston engine business? Canada's entire wartime aircraft production program had relied entirely on importing engines from the United States and Britain. Dobson definitely wanted to know more about this Canadian jet engine business. And Howe was glad he did— his department had been hoping for months to interest private enterprise in the project.

It all began, said Howe, back in 1942 when he and Ralph Bell made one of their frequent wartime trips to the Munitions and Supply office in London, England. It was during that visit that the RAF brought them up to date on British experiments with turbojet engines, work due largely to Frank Whittle's theories on jet propulsion. The British officials asked Howe whether Canada would be at all interested in assisting them; perhaps Canada could send a research team over from the NRC to get the inside story. Howe like the idea: he thought that Canada "might well attempt to pioneer in jet propulsion."

When Bell and Howe returned to Canada, Bell reported what he had learned to Canada's Air Council. The council immediately set up a committee to deal with all questions related to jet propulsion. At its first meeting on October 29, 1942, the committee decided to send a research team to England, and in a matter of weeks a four-man team was recruited. C. A. Banks, Canada's senior representative in the London office of the Department of Munitions and Supply, would liaise with the British government. A/V/M E. W. Stedman, chairman of the committee, was named to the team in an ex-officio capacity because it was thought that the RCAF should have at least token presence. Two research engineers from the NRC, Paul Dilworth and Ken Tupper, would form the nucleus of the team, carrying out the technical research in the field.

The research team's tasks were to study and report on the history and the present state of development of jet propulsion in England; to recommend how Canada could contribute to the development of jet propulsion engines; to indicate the necessary facilities, machinery, staff, and cost involved for a program of research in Canada; and to detail the organization, facilities, and machinery required for the manufacture of jet propulsion engines.

By far, the most enthusiastic member of the research team was Paul Dilworth. He was a quiet-spoken, easy-going man, moving and thinking like the young Gary Cooper in one of those old movies—the ones where he doesn't say too much but you know he's there and you feel good about it.

Dilworth completed a degree in mechanical engineering at the University of Toronto in 1939. His love of engines went back to his boyhood when he was always tinkering with the engines on his parent's motorboats at their Muskoka cottage. But it was having family friends like Frank Trethewey and Phil Garratt that turned his interest to aircraft and the engines that made them fly. Trethewey helped to establish de Havilland in Canada in 1928 and was a member of its first board of directors; Garratt, a First World War fighter pilot and a test pilot for de Havilland in the thirties, became a member of the board as well as general manager of de Havilland Canada in 1935.

Dilworth was still an undergraduate when it first occurred to him that Canada should get into the design, development, and manufacture of aeroengines. He tried to interest American engine manufacturers like Pratt & Whitney and Jacobs in the idea, but had no success. In fact, Pratt & Whitney told him that Canada wasn't nearly ready to enter the high-tech world of engine development.

Soon after graduating he secured employment in the engine lab of the NRC where he worked on aeroengine research and the design of new engine test facilities. He had been with the NRC three years when he was seconded by C. D. Howe to be a member of the jet engine research team to be sent to England.

Dilworth and Tupper would spend close to five months in England, visiting aircraft factories, interviewing RAF officials and British aircraft engine designers and engineers, and making hundreds of pages of notes. There were, at the time, five jet engines under development in Britain: Power Jets and Rolls-Royce's W2B, de Havilland's H.1; Metro Vickers's F-2, Armstrong-Siddeley's A.S.X., and Rolls-Royce's S.T. (Derwent 1). Dilworth and Tupper were able to see first-hand what was being done in developing these engines and to visit many subsidiary companies. Dilworth observed that British jet propulsion engines had a very high rate of fuel consumption; it was a very serious problem to which no solution had yet been found. He commented that a very co-operative relationship existed between the British government, the RAF, and the private jet engine companies with respect to jet engine development. He also noted that most of the jet engine development work was being carried out by young men; most of the older men tended to be "unenthusiastic about jet propulsion engines" and quite content to work on improving piston engines.

Even before their research was completed, Tupper and Dilworth realized that now was the time for Canada to get into the jet engine business. It was a priceless opportunity to get involved from the ground up. All that remained was to convince Banks, the RCAF, and the Canadian government. They accomplished this in their joint report, which came to be known as the Banks Report.

The Air Council was particularly interested in three of the recommendations made by the Banks Report. The first was the creation of a winter testing establishment in Canada for the purpose of testing jet engines under low temperature conditions such as would be encountered at high altitude. This recommendation resulted in the creation of the Winnipeg Test Establishment created at Stevenson Field. Ground was broken on September 15, 1943, and the buildings were occupied and running the first British test engine on January 4, 1944. This first British engine and a quantity of vital instruments and test equipment had been secretly flown from Britain to Canada by U.S. Army Air Transport late in December.

The second recommendation was for the design, construction, and eventual operation of a compressor test plant. The site chosen for this was Nobel, Ontario. There was a CIL plant in Nobel that had been set up in 1940 to produce explosives, and, although it was pretty well falling apart by war's end, it was chosen for some very practical reasons.

It had a substantial steam plant with turbo generators, and we needed a large, high-speed device to drive the test compressors. As well, the plant was becoming available as wartime surplus property. The combination of all of these factors met what we wanted.

—Paul Dilworth

The third recommendation was that if Canada was to get into the jet engine business, research played an important part, and some sort of research facility should therefore be established somewhere in Canada. To undertake that research, a cadre of Canadian engineers should be sent to Britain to "go to school" on British engine development. This concept became known as the "100 men," although there were only thirty or forty who actually went.

In a letter to Banks, Tupper recommended that the manufacture of jet propulsion engines in Canada "could probably best be started by building in Canada under licence one or more of the successful British types. This would provide a starting point for production and further development."

The Air Council, the Canadian government, and the NRC acted quickly on setting up the Winnipeg Test Establishment, the compressor work at Nobel, and the "100 men" proposal. For the time being, however, they judged it premature to set up an independent jet engine research establishment. That would have to wait.

While Winnipeg and Nobel were being set up, the NRC was busily recruiting engineers and fitters from across Canada—the "100 men" to send to England to study British jet engine work. Among them was Winnett Boyd, one of Fred Smye's classmates from Trinity College School. Boyd was brilliant, and his habitual smile was deceiving, for it could mask his brilliance as well as his furious temper.

Boyd had studied mechanical engineering at the University of Toronto, graduating first in his class with the second highest grades in the history of the university (95 per cent). He missed being nominated for Rhodes scholar because of "engaging in a rather lively argument with the examining board." He then went to do post-graduate work at M.I.T. on a staff scholarship, but withdrew in 1940 because of the war. He returned to Canada and joined the Aluminum Company of Canada. In the summer of 1943, he obtained a leave of absence from Alcan to join the Royal Canadian Navy as a sub-lieutenant.

When I was in the Navy, I heard that the NRC was seeking people to go to England to work on a secret project. I couldn't resist the temptation to write to Ken Tupper and he replied that it was an aircraft project. I went to Ottawa to see him and he mentioned it had something to do with a new type of aircraft propulsion and I said, "Well, it's either got to be a rocket or a gas turbine." Tupper said they'd like to have me, so I got a leave of absence from the Navy and went to England in the fall of 1943.

—Winnett Boyd

For the first couple of months in England he worked pretty much on his own; then he was joined by another engineer, Doug Knowles. Boyd and Knowles made their headquarters at Whittle's company, Power Jets.

Some of the "100 men" returned to Winnipeg in December, 1943, to work at the cold-weather test establishment and formed the backbone of trained staff which operated the station during that and subsequent winters. Others, including Boyd and Knowles, returned later to work on the design of a compressor test facility and jet engine designs at a facility in Leaside in Toronto, which was set up on the recommendation made by Tupper and Dilworth in the Banks Report.

This facility was called Turbo Research, and was designed to be roughly the equivalent of Power Jets, which had been nationalized by the British government. Turbo Research was charged with carrying out research and development related to gas turbine engines.

Some people may not know this, but Turbo was set up to cover not only jet engines for aircraft, but gas turbines for such things as locomotives, as well.

—Paul Dilworth

Set up as another of Howe's crown corporations, Turbo's shareholders consisted of seven people, each of whom owned one share, except for Howe himself, who owned twenty-five shares. The other shareholders were W. E. Philips, Brigadier F. C. Wallace, C. A. Banks, H. J. Carmichael, A/V/M A. L. James, and J. H. Parkin. The cold weather test station at Stevenson Field was turned over to Turbo. Ken Tupper was named the chief engineer at Turbo Research, while Paul Dilworth, shuttling back and forth to England at the time, was asked to take over the cold weather test station. F. C. Wallace was to be general manager.

The first activity of the new company was to recruit, train, and organize the engineering staff. A number of the engineers and draftsmen that were hired were sent for further training to England at Power Jets and a few other British firms. The RCAF also sent a number of officers over to take courses of instruction. Some of them later took up employment with Turbo Research when they left the air force.

By the autumn of 1944, Winnett Boyd was busy on the design of a major compressor test-rig facility for jet engine development.

I prepared a very extensive and complete specification for a jet engine compressor and combustion system test plant. The approach was rather novel and horrified most people at the time, but the soundness of the approach was confirmed by the fact that several such test plants, notably that of the Bristol Aeroplane Co., have subsequently been made on the same fundamental basis. It was at this time that Ken Tupper made one of his frequent trips to Ottawa and on his return said that the government had decided we were spending too much money and that we really should get down to the business of actually designing a jet engine—even if just to show the taxpayers that we were actually doing something. So he said to me, "Winn, you design the engine."

—Winnett Boyd

Progress was understandably slow during the spring and summer of 1945 because of the "greenness" of the Turbo design team and because the country's jet engine requirements were by no means settled.

I struggled with that engine's design all through the spring, summer, and early autumn. However, I did conceive two designs on paper: an engine with a centrifugal compressor I called the TR-1 (Turbo Research no. 1), and another with an axial compressor I called the TR-2.

—Winnett Boyd

In those days, there were, basically, two types of gas turbine engines— the centrifugal type and the axial type. All of Frank Whittle's work had been on centrifugal compressors. Whittle preferred centrifugal compressors because they were better understood at the time and simpler. Boyd chose an axial compressor because it showed a better potential for the future.

I submitted these proposals to a team of three people, one of whom was Air Marshal Stedman, and they decided on the axial compressor. The Air Force didn't really know that was going on in the jet engine field and had very few people who had insight into how the things worked. Detailing work did commence on a design known as the TR-3, but it was crude, to say the least, and I was delighted when the opporunity came in the autumn to abandon it. For the record, it might be worth noting that the TR-3 was designed for 4,200 pounds thrust and was 40 inches in diameter.

—Winnett Boyd

Then came Boyd's attendance at the fateful Downing-Carter-Lindsay/ James-Easton-Curtis meeting in Ottawa in September, 1945. Undaunted by what he had heard about coming up with an engine to fit an engine nacelle of not more than 32 inches, he started working, and by Christmas, 1945, the general arrangement of the TR-4 was established. There is a marked family resemblance between it and the later Orenda.

By this time, however, the possibility existed that Winnett Boyd's engine designs might never leave the paper they were sketched on. The wartime Department of Munitions and Supply was now the Department of Reconstruction, and it was their job to dispose of all wartime industrial plants, including crown corporations, as quickly as possible. One of them slated to go was Turbo Research. The director general of the Department of Reconstruction, Crawford Gordon, reported to Howe on the status of Turbo Research in November, 1945:

It is my understanding that Turbo Research have proposed a five-year program for the manufacture and development of prototype jet engines and that this program will cost some eight million. It is also my understanding that Turbo Research was formed to (a) develop and manufacture jet engines for aircraft and (b) provide the nucleus for a new industry in Canada, presuming the "Jet principle" could be adapted for peacetime use. Following my discussions in the last two weeks, I cannot help but feel that these two objects cannot be attained under the present plan of operating a Crown Company working solely on aircraft jet engines.

As I see it, the jet engine will be used in many fields, i. e. locomotives, stationary power units, ship propulsion units, aircraft engines and possibly for the automotive industry. . . .

We never developed an aircraft industry in Canada during the war mainly, I believe, because we could not keep pace with the United States and Great Britain, and because constant changes in design, etc. would have made our costs prohibitive for the quantity of engines our aircraft industry would have absorbed. Similarly, I cannot see how Canada can hope to establish an aircraft jet engine industry to compete in the world markets. Therefore, I would conclude that the only logical step would be to turn the development and manufacture of aircraft jet engines over to some group such as A. V. Roe and Company which company, I believe, is interested in building units for the RCAF and possibly for their own aircraft . . . .

To sum up, if A. V. Roe is able to bring a group into Canada to work on aircraft jet engines, I feel Turbo Research should be disbanded, A. V. Roe & Company and the National Research Council absorbing the majority of the skilled personnel . . . . Industry, itself, would enter the manufacturing field as soon as the jet turbine became a commercial product.

Four days later Howe replied to Gordon, saying that he agreed with the idea of turning Turbo over to a private company and was "anxious to have the project located at Malton, providing we can interest A. V. Roe & Company."

Although Howe was aware that A. V. Roe Canada might be a leading candidate to take over Turbo Research, he told Dobson that he was concerned the company might be taking on too much at one time with both a commercial airliner and a fighter possibly in the works.

"So there really isn't anybody," he told Dobson that April evening in 1946 over dinner, "who has the guts to take it on."

"I have," said Dobson.

"You!" exclaimed Howe, tongue in cheek. "Your plate is full now. Besides what do you know about engines?"

"Not much," said Dobson, "but they've always been one of my little hobbies."

As for the cold weather test station at Winnipeg, by January, 1946, it was considered no longer useful. In a letter to V. W. Scully (who for the previous six months had been running Victory Aircraft and was now Howe's second in command in the Department of Reconstruction) Turbo's general manager, F. C. Wallace, recommended that the station be closed down.

> The amount of work done during three winters of operation has been much less than originally anticipated and the value of that work is considered by our technical men to be small in relation to its cost . . . . It is recommended that the NRC be asked whether they wish to have the physical facilities of the Cold Weather Test Station at Winnipeg transferred to them.

The first time I told Howe and Scully we wanted to take over Turbo, they told me to hold my horses. They both wanted an established company to take it on. So they put out proposals to Pratt & Whitney, Rolls-Royce, and Bristol with the condition that any and all technical data in the hands of these existing companies would be made available to the Canadian companies. The first to fold was Pratt & Whitney. The next to go was Rolls-Royce who cracked, "Tell the Canadians they can put a maple leaf sticker on the Avon if that'll make them happy."

So that left Bristol and ourselves. Bristol sent a team to look things over. When they went back to England, I followed them. We had a meeting in T. O. M. Sopwith's office and the Bristol team said right off the bat that Canada wouldn't know how to even manufacture an engine, let alone design one, so count them out.

That left us. I immediately phoned Scully from London and told him about the meeting and I said I was on my way back to Canada to pick up the contract.

In the meantime, Dobson went to the Ministry of Aircraft Production and met with Sir Archibald Rowlands, the Deputy Minister and said he wanted him to authorize Armstrong-Siddeley and Bristol to provide us with all their data so when we took over Turbo we would have all the latest tech data available to us from England. We got the permission. Turbo was ours.

—Fred Smye

For most of the eighty-five or so survivors who made up Turbo Research and the test facility at Nobel, the impending move to Malton and A. V. Roe was welcome news. Winnett Boyd was relieved for now his engine designs might become reality. Walter Deisher wrote to Paul Dilworth:

> The Canadian Government has honoured this Company by entrusting to us the responsibility of carrying on the design, development and production of the Gas Turbine Engine on which Turbo Research Limited has been working for some time.
>
> Probably one of the most important factors in the government's decision to favour our Company was the fact that, from the outset, our policy and that of our associate companies in England, has been to establish in Canada an aircraft and gas turbine engine design and development organization which will create and produce airplanes and engines for the Canadian and world markets . . . .
>
> Our initial task is to carry out the development of the gas turbine aircraft engine for the jet fighter for the RCAF. From this starting point, it is our intention to continue the development of aircraft engines, and, in addition, all forms of gas turbine power plants for varied industrial application . . . .
>
> We are very pleased to welcome Turbo Research Limited personnel to the Avro Canada family, and we hope that you will be agreeable to joining us in our undertaking.

Turbo Research became A. V. Roe Canada's gas turbine division with Paul Dilworth as manager and chief engineer. All Turbo personnel accepted A. V. Roe's offer with the exception of Ken Tupper, who wanted to return to the NRC, and Wally McBride, Turbo's chief aerodynamicist, who could not reach an agreement with Fred Smye on the terms of employment.

> *McBride wrote me a five page letter outlining his conditions to work for A. V. Roe and one of them was that he would hold all the patents to everything. So I wrote him a one liner back, No Thanks! When Boyd and Dilworth came, they didn't know anything about this, so I told them, "Sorry, but he ain't coming." And they said, "We can't do the engine without him." And I said, "Well, you better because he ain't gonna work for this company."*
>
> —*Fred Smye*

The other key people in the gas turbine division were: R. L. Whitelaw, chief experimental engineer, Winnett Boyd, chief designer, W. C. Barlow, chief draftsman, J. Gould, executive engineer, Doug Knowles, chief development engineer (Knowles was also responsible for the Nobel operation), J. A. Marcouiller, works superintendent, and F. M. Staines, chief inspector.

Although the deal was made to take Turbo in May, the actual moving of men and equipment didn't happen until June. And what a June it was, hottest in memory, people said. The operation was set up on the second floor of the "details building." A few partitions were knocked out, but there were no blinds on the windows and no air conditioning and the place was like a furnace that first summer.

Paul Dilworth spent his first few days at Malton setting up the organization and making sure his staff had facilities. Basically, the gas turbine organization would be made up of two major divisions: the manufacturing division comprising all shop, tool design, and planning personnel, and manufacturing equipment; and the engineering division comprising all design, experimental, laboratory, inspection, and test personnel.

The physical facilities with which work was carried on fell into three main groups. First, there was the experimental shop comprising a major portion of the former Victory Aircraft machine shop. Second, there was the laboratory facilities comprised of a mechanical test laboratory for testing engine components, a fuel system component test laboratory for testing and developing fuel system components, an aerodynamic laboratory, an instrument laboratory, and a test engine laboratory. Third, there was the plant at Nobel near Parry Sound used for testing and developing compressors, turbines, and combustion chambers.

Not everyone was looking forward to Fred Smye's first encounter with Winnett Boyd. Although they had been at school together, neither had made a particular impression on the other. Since then, although each had heard of the activities of the other through mutual acquaintances, they had not met.

> *I had heard about this guy, Boyd, this dictator who everyone was scared stiff of and when I went out to Turbo to ask them to join A. V. Roe, I walk in the door and the first person I see is this Winn Boyd. "Christ," I say, "are you the guy that's this terrible Boyd?" And he says, "Don't worry, I've heard some terrible things about you, too."*
>
> —Fred Smye

Fred Smye took a keen early interest in A. V. Roe's new gas turbine division probably because he felt it was filled with young, eager men like himself. Although he knew even less about jet engines than he did about aircraft, having Jim Floyd in charge of the jet transport project on the aircraft side allowed him to spend time with this new group.

Being a student of bureaucracy, Smye was famous for cutting through government red tape and getting results rather quickly, usually because of his relationship with C. D. Howe.

Soon after Turbo had joined A. V. Roe Canada, the deal that Dobson had negoitated with Bristol for their technical jet engine data ran into a snag. For security reasons, Bristol had been funnelling the data through the NRC, a step which sometimes took months. In a business where results are needed almost daily, this could be catastrophic. Then, one day Paul Dilworth complained so loudly that Smye went to see Howe to find out what could be done about this "monkey business at the NRC." Howe then phoned Jack Mackenzie, head of the NRC, and said, "Freddie Smye's got a little problem here so I want you to talk to him."

So I went over and told him the story. He brought in J. H. Parkin and he said, "Mr. Smye is missing a few reports," and as soon as he mentioned Howe, Parkin started to shake. It seems Parkin had been sending some of the reports from Bristol back to England by surface mail, questioning whether the material should be made available to A. V. Roe.

He explained this to Mackenzie who turned about six shades of red and asked how many of the reports had been returned. It turned out to be many.

This was one of the things we had to put up with occasionally—the technical jealousy of Parkin and his guys in NRC. They felt that if anybody was going to develop airplanes and engines, it should be them. Well, the missing reports started to show up at Malton the very next day.

—Fred Smye

Finding a competent aerodynamicist to replace Wally McBride was the number one priority for Paul Dilworth. In the meantime, Winnett Boyd had to make a decision on the TR-4 design.

It was wisely decided, as an exercise for all concerned, to carry the design through to completion and to manufacture six sets of parts from which three engines and a test compressor could be built.

—Winnett Boyd

The situation was complicated, however, by having no aerodynamicist; pleading his case to Dilworth, Boyd got permission to go to England in July, 1946, to find the right man for the job. It didn't take him long.

I first went to Hawker-Siddeley in St. James Square and then to Power Jets—which had been partially disbanded at the time—and I narrowed

my search down to two men and then to Keast. I saw him, made him an
offer, and he accepted.

—Winnett Boyd

In 1942, Harry Keast, engineer, was unemployed when he received
an offer from Power Jets, but he wasn't particularly enthusiastic about
it. Many of the experts thought that all that would come out of Frank
Whittle's work was better super-chargers for piston engines. No one
ever expected his engine to do anything.

*At the time, all reports about Whittle and his work were that his engines
were stupid and ridiculous, that he had limited assistance, but that he
had some novel ideas on centrifugal compressors—engines working on
pressure ratios of 4:1 instead of the usual 2:1.*

*Needless to say, I joined up and by the end of the war, we had gone as
far as we could with our main engine at the time—the W2-700—which,
eventually, got us 2,200 pounds thrust.*

*Whittle's position was that his company, Power Jets, was under the
Official Secrets Act, and although he had a few individuals who had
invested money, he couldn't go out and sell stock on the market. So
naturally he had to be supported by the government.*

*When the end of the war came, all the aircraft industry was closing
down and the government felt they couldn't have Power Jets in competition
with private industry, so they invited us all to become civil servants. We
asked if we would be designing new engines and the answer was that that
was the role of private enterprise; we would be doing mostly research
work.*

*Most of us were pretty disgusted because Power Jets just sort of fell
apart and there didn't seem to be a place for us in the established aircraft
industry. For a while, I worked at English Electric in Rugby which was
working on the idea that gas turbines might be a good idea for marine
propulsion, when one of my old friends, still at Power Jets, told me a
fellow named Winnett Boyd was looking for someone to do aerodynamic
design in Canada on aircraft engines.*

*Boyd was very optimistic and I knew it was being backed by A. V. Roe
Manchester. But what intrigued me was Boyd's interest in an axial-flow
engine. The axial engine was still a thing of the future. I'd heard of a
group at RAE [Royal Aeronautical Establishment] that did some work
on axial flows and this group had proved conclusively to themselves that
an axial flow compressor could only reach a pressure ratio of 2:1 and then
they heard a Swiss company had reached 3:1 and even 4:1. We centrifugal
people had already done this with a centrifugal compressor.*

*To Boyd, the axial was a better proposition. I had gained some experience
on axial flow engines through a close friendship with A. D. Haswell, the
axial man in England. He had published some papers but he also had a
lot of information he hadn't published which he let me have.*

Although Dobson still had to approve their offer of my salary, and although he gave me just one day to hand in my notice, all this was secondary to the fact that I was getting the chance to work on a brand new engine.

—*Harry Keast*

Harry Keast arrived in Canada on August 8, 1946, with the promise of the title of chief aerodynamicist reporting directly to Paul Dilworth, although initially Keast found himself reporting to D. G. Sheppard, the chief experimental engineer.

To Dilworth, Keast was a "goldmine of a find." He was quickly put to work on Boyd's TR-4, his first piece of work expected on Dilworth's desk by September 15.

The TR-4, like the TR-3, was an axial-flow engine designed for a relatively modest performance of 2,600 pounds thrust at take-off and a maximum speed of 10,000 rpm. The engine itself consisted of a nine-stage compressor, a single-stage turbine, and six straight-through combustion chambers. Fortunately for Keast, he was able to incorporate some of Haswell's principles in the TR-4 design. Research and development on the TR-4 and a second engine, the TR-5, continued for almost two years. Early in 1948 they were ready to be built and tested, and by then Winnett Boyd had given them names.

It was during an evening of conversation with a friend of mine in Leaside that I first thought of identifying my engines. Up until that time, we just had a letter and number designation for them and during this conversation one evening, we deplored the American way of doing things, of just identifying engines and airplanes with numbers like B-29 and X-15 and so on. We liked the British way of doing things, like giving their engines and airplanes a bit of personality with names like Hawker Hurricane, Supermarine Spitfire, Rolls-Royce Merlin and Bristol Pegasus. We concluded between ourselves that what we ought to do in Canada was to give our engine a name, also. Eventually the name Chinook came up. The chinook, as you know, is the name given by the Westerners to a warm wind blowing across the mountains. And, certainly, a jet engine spews out a certain amount of warm wind. It was a nice name, Chinook. Two syllables, identifiable with Canada. That was it.

—*Winnett Boyd*

7

STORM CLOUDS
GATHERING

By October, 1946, detailed design work on the Jetliner was proceeding at a fairly rapid rate. Jim Floyd was now officially chief project officer on the jet transport and reported to the chief engineer, Edgar Atkin. Since the aircraft was revolutionary, to say the least, Floyd opted to stay as close as possible to the conventional and proven.

> There wasn't a teething ring for the Jetliner per se, but if you've worked on airplanes all your life, you learn something new about every airplane you've ever worked on. We learned something from the Tudor fuselage— the structure on the Jetliner was very similar to the Tudor. None of the airplanes I had ever worked on, however, had a high tail. This was done on the Jetliner to stop the downwash from the jets. We weren't worried about the temperature of the jets as we were about the downwash.
>
> —Jim Floyd

With both a fighter and jet transport on the drawing boards, the company was busily recruiting engineers, who "were arriving so fast we didn't know what to do with them," recalls Floyd. And costs were starting to pile up. By December, TCA had not yet finalized their specification for the jet transport and had not forwarded one progress payment to help pay for the mock-up and developmental work going on at a rapid pace. Smye and Dobson took the matter to Bain at TCA, who appealed to Symington on behalf of A. V. Roe Canada.

Lack of our specification prevents the signing of a formal contract and makes the Avro company's position a difficult one to handle. They are working very hard on the engineering investigation and mock-up of the project and are receiving from us no progress payments. I am advised by Mr. Smye that approximately $100,000 has already been spent, all of which has been borrowed from the banks at a high rate of interest . . . . I feel that because our specification cannot be completed for some time yet and because the Avro company is making exceptionally rapid and satisfactory progress with the project, some form of progress payments should be now made to them.

Despite Bain's appeal, no money came from TCA to finance the project. Even more troublesome to Smye was the concern that he might not be able to live up to the conditions in the letter of intent (April 9, 1946). Development costs had well exceeded $150,000 by this time, and there was no contract yet in place. Part of the problem, of course, was that the engine designated for the jet transport was the Rolls-Royce AJ-65 Avon; it was a military engine and therefore subject to strict secrecy conditions. This circumstance made it difficult to interest any other airline in the plane.

On December 6, he met with Symington, president of TCA, to advise him that increases in the costs of materials and labour and a possible increase in the price of the Avon engines made it unlikely that the price quoted in the letter of intent could be met. Smye was pinning his hopes on TCA's taking thirty airplanes, the required break-even number. If they did, and with any luck at all, perhaps he could sell them for $350,000 per copy. He would write in a follow-up letter dated February 12, 1947:

We find it difficult to deal with certain aspects of the problem, in view of the fact that we do not know how many airplanes you propose to buy, although a quantity of thirty has been mentioned on various occasions. We would appreciate it very much, indeed, if you could indicate to us the quantity on which our proposal should be based.

On February 24, Symington replied; it was more a lecture on the aircraft business than a letter.

It is still premature to discuss the total quantity we require of these aircraft . . . . The building of C-102 by your company is a commercial venture which must be based on your own estimates of the total market for the type. If your studies show a production quantity of one hundred is required to meet the prices of competitive types, you must be prepared to build and sell one hundred aircraft, regardless of the quantity ordered by TCA . . . . My letter to you of April 5, 1946, still stands as the basis of the contract I am prepared to negotiate with your company; however, I require from you a fixed price per aircraft regardless of the total quantity which will ultimately be purchased by Trans Canada Air Lines.

If you have sufficient faith in your ability to build this advanced type, you will not try to cover your costs completely in a TCA order. If you do not have such faith in the C-102, then it will be better for all concerned that the project be abandoned immediately.

Abandoned! The word literally jumped from the page and stunned Smye. Were the cracks beginning to show? Smye and Joe Morley sat down and prepared a revised Jetliner price list which was sent to Symington on March 6. If TCA bought thirty aircraft, the price per aircraft amounted to $484,000. For seventy-five aircraft, the price would be $350,000 per plane. For twenty aircraft, the price jumped to $588,000 per copy.

For Symington the situation was rapidly getting out of hand. When C. D. Howe was briefed, he wasted no time in letting Symington know what he thought of the situation. The letter of intent he said, was clear and binding in its terms and would commit TCA for expenditures already made. The engine for the C-102 was still on the secret list, he said, and there was no indication when it would be released. Further, he said, it was now quite evident that the cost of the limited number of planes which TCA would require would be wholly excessive, with tooling costs added.

He suggested that TCA cancel the letter of intent and release A. V. Roe from the secrecy provisions in the hope that they may be able to interest other users and thus build up a demand sufficiently large to absorb cost of tooling. In the meantime they should all wait to discuss the situation with Roy Dobson, who was expected to visit Canada early in April.

But it was not so simple to cancel the letter of intent upon further consideration, "particularly," said Howe the following week,

as it is in the exact form used by the Department of Munitions and Supply during the war period. Pretty likely since Smye, an ex-Munitions and Supply employee wrote it. I suggest that you place a stop order on the work as far as the interest of TCA is concerned pending a conference with Dobson.

Symington acted on Howe's advice and on March 12 ordered A. V. Roe Canada to stop work on the C-102 until the whole affair could be clarified with Dobson. Fred Smye now turned Symington's earlier words to his own account, saying that they couldn't just suspend the project for a month—what were they supposed to do with the staff? Unless they decided to abandon the project altogether, A. V. Roe would carry on.

On April 8, with Dobson due to arrive any day, Symington wrote a brief note to Howe; he had been in touch with Rolls-Royce, the makers of the AJ-65 engine, the proposed power plant for the C-102.

> Mr. Hives of Rolls-Royce . . . told me it will be years before it [the AJ-65 Avon] is perfected and it is going to cost a great deal of money. He says it is quite impossible for commercial airlines to foster these things and that it must be a military proposition.

This was the end of the line for TCA. They were out of the project. But A. V. Roe Canada had gone too far to turn back now, and they knew just how to get to C. D. Howe.

On the eleventh, Roy Dobson arrived in Canada and met with Howe, Symington, Smye, and Deisher to discuss the future, if any, of the C-102 program and to clear the air on the project. Howe made it clear to them that work on the jet passenger must stop. But when he was fully apprised of the situation at A. V. Roe, he backed up a little.

Dobson pleaded with Howe to give the project more time. Perhaps he even threatened a little. Following the meeting Howe wrote to Symington, "It may be desirable to continue work on the passenger plane for a short period."

Within two weeks of the meeting Dobson had forwarded a proposal to Howe. In two long pages, he outlined his rationale for continuing the project to build two prototypes. Approximately 200 people, he informed Howe, were engaged on the C-102 project, involving a monthly expenditure of 50,000 man hours, but the program was planned to employ 500 production workers and require 90,000 man hours per month by January, 1948.

The two prototypes would first be tried with Rolls-Royce Nene engines, but, and it is interesting to note, the prototype schedule was based on the receipt of the Avon AJ-65 engines in October, 1948. The prototypes would be ready for delivery in July, 1949.

To meet the production target, Dobson offered to finance the difference temporarily, provided that Howe would cover the costs to that date and provide the material and equipment for the two prototypes, as well as guarantee a production order "at an appropriate time." If Howe agreed to the proposal, Dobson estimated that the first production aircraft could be delivered as soon as June, 1950, almost two years after the date specified by TCA in its letter of intent.

Would Howe go for it? He wanted time to think about it. "You may expect my advice," he wrote to a nervous Symington, "in due course." The candle keeping the C-102 alive, it seemed, still flickered.

"In due course" Howe wrote to Symington. It was uncharacteristic of Howe to reverse a decision on anything, but when he realized that abandonment of the C-102 might mean the end of all his plans for the Canadian aircraft industry, he authorized funding of $1.5 million from the Department of Reconstruction for the immediate continuation of the project. His explanation to Symington was that "development work of that type is not possible for commercial airlines as far as financing is concerned."

We were pushing ahead with the design of the aircraft and had cut a substantial amount of hardware for the prototype when, in the late spring of 1947, we received an urgent cable from the UK to say that Rolls-Royce had decided they were pushing engine technology a little too fast on the AJ-65 engine development and would not now be able to supply a certified civil version of that engine until some two to three years after we needed it.

—Jim Floyd

The Avon had such a terrible compressor design. It was a ten-stage design but the first four stages in the compressor were so mismatched that Rolls-Royce ran the engine on the first four stages until they were able to match up all eight.

Now Rolls had all the money it needed and the Avon was the result of RR putting a helluva lot of push on to save what everyone knew was a rotten engine.

—Harry Keast

Gas Turbine was consulted on the Jetliner, and we very strongly recommended not to proceed with the development of the Jetliner around the Avon engine. We felt it was in too early a stage of development—it was an axial engine and we hadn't had too much success with axials up to that time. We felt if we were going into commercial production of a Jetliner, we better get a damn reliable engine in it.

—Paul Dilworth

Originally, Dobson and A/V/M Smith had wanted to put a General Electric engine in the XC-100 and I was dead against it, as was Wilf Curtis. Well, I ended up going to England and to Rolls to see Lord Hives, and I entered into an agreement with him that he would provide the AJ-65 for use in the XF-100 at a reduced thrust of 6,000 pounds (the engine was expected to produce 6,500 pounds thrust) and a guaranteed weight, price and delivery. Hives and I signed a contract and I took it to Dobson and he was real mad. I thought it was the right thing to do. The GE engine was a 5,000-pound thrust engine and probably wouldn't have got the XF-100 off the ground.

Well, it was on that same trip, during a stroll through his rose garden, that Hives told me we couldn't have the AJ-65 for the Jetliner. He explained that it didn't have any experience and it should have military time before commercial . . . .

I then went to see Ray Dorey at RR's flight test place at Hucknall and he showed me all the stuff they had concocted using four Derwent engines and they thought it would still be a good airplane with four Derwents. I came back with the data, gave it to Jimmy [Floyd], and that was that.

—Fred Smye

The CF-100 was originally designed around the Orenda and the intention right from the start was to power it with the Orenda. The Avon was in there as a hedge for two reasons. We didn't think the Orenda would be ready as soon as the Avon, and there was the question of confidence in our team to be able to both develop and produce a first-line military jet engine without any prior background or experience.

—Paul Dilworth

Two things surface when one talks about the power plants for the CF-100. One is the fact that the interim engine, the Avon, was the same engine that was unavailable for the other company project, the Jetliner. Second, the company was breaking one of Dobson's basic rules of aircraft designing, facing the possibility of marrying an untried engine, the Orenda, in an untried aircraft, the CF-100.

The first six or eight aircraft were supposed to be powered by the Avon and the others with the Orenda. Eventually, this was cut back to the first three.

—Paul Dilworth

By the early spring of 1947, the RCAF's jet fighter, the XC-100, was at the wooden mock-up stage. For security reasons, the mock-up was built behind a big canvas curtain. The purpose of the mock-up was to determine cockpit configurations, and it was necessary to consult with air force Operational Requirements staff.

There were five RCAF liaison officers right in the plant. They were part of a newly formed XC-100 planning team and included Carscallen, James, MacBrien, Easton, and Gilchrist—the same five responsible for rewriting the original aircraft specification. The key A. V. Roe people on the project were Jack Millie and Jim Chamberlin. "Throughout this period," writes Larry Milberry,

> the RCAF were busily defining and clarifying the requirements for the new fighter. Air Force HQ was preoccupied with getting the aircraft built as specified and getting such vital components as radar, fire control, and weapons selected and ordered for delivery to meet deadlines. Simultaneously, it was organizing a major training program to place the CF-100 in service initially on an operational training basis, then as an operational fighter. All this activity made for hectic times, but each step along the way was carefully planned and timed to produce the best results.

As the design of the CF-100 progressed and air force interest in the project intensified, and with the C-102 program on his plate as well, Edgar Atkin realized that he needed someone to take charge of the CF-100 project. He found that someone in John Frost.

Joining de Havilland Aircraft Company in England in 1942, John Frost became one of the senior members of the Hatfield design team, and probably its youngest. He eventually became project engineer responsible for the DH-108. On June 14, 1947, he arrived at Malton to inherit the eighteen-month-old XC-100 as project engineer.

There were many reasons for emigrating to Canada in the post-war years. For Frost the crucial accommodation shortage meant that his wife was living with her mother in the north of England while he worked at Hatfield in the south, near London. But Frost's move to Canada might have had more to do with recent events at de Havilland in England and his involvement on the DH-108 than with anything else.

> *The Comet jet airliner was being designed with heavily backward swept wings and no tailplane. Sir Geoffrey called me to his office and asked me if I could convert a Vampire jet fighter into this configuration in eight months. It was imperative that they should have a free flying model for the Comet to justify this layout, and to check its stability.*
>
> *I think we had a team of eight to ten draftsmen and engineers. And we completed the job in just under eight months.*
>
> *Three were built. Masterful pilot, Geoffrey de Havilland, Jr., test flew the prototype and found it so fast that the company prepared for an official*

attack on the world's speed record. On September 21, 1946, while he was practising, the DH-108 went out of control at high Mach number, at or near the speed of sound, due to the instability of its tailless configuration, and disintegrated. He was killed.

—*John Frost*

If ever there were two men destined not to get along, it was John Frost and Jim Chamberlin. There were defenders on both sides. As difficult as he was to deal with, people would agree Chamberlin was very seldom wrong. Frost was more the negotiator, always willing to discuss anything at any time. Frost was always a perfect gentleman whereas Chamberlin was more in the line of a mad scientist. Their association on the jet fighter project was one long feud.

The mock-up of the XC-100, which had been constructed from plywood and paper, awaited Frost's arrival. Behind the canvas curtain was a disappointingly crude structure.

I was very shocked when I was shown this and found it hard to take seriously. It made me wonder at the wisdom of going all the way to take on something that looked so monstrous. You must remember, the aircraft I had just left, the DH-108, which was rightly nicknamed the Swallow, was one of the prettiest little aircraft ever built.

—*John Frost*

In attempting to meet the RCAF specifications Chamberlin and Millie had placed the engines close to the fuselage. This would provide the aircraft with the minimum rolling inertia and minimum time to roll. The fuselage itself was square with rounded corners.

There was nothing for it but to try and see what could be done to clean up the concept. I had no quarrel with the engines close or alongside the fuselage. I did think the wing should have been swept back to delay the drag rise, and wasted no time in giving the fuselage a circular section and a better fineness ratio. Also, we set about considering the design from a structural point of view; nothing had been done towards this at that state.

The wing was a two-spar arrangement. The main spar, with a joint either side of the fuselage, was arranged in such a way that it passed just behind the engine, with the jet pipe passing over the upper boom. In those days, this went straight across from one side of the fuselage to the other, generally parallel to the lower boom across the fuselage.

This greatly reduced the frontal area of the aircraft, since the bottom of the engine was now level with the bottom of the wing, and not sitting on top of it as previously.

The design was shaping up. The aircraft had an evil, eager look about it, and with its relatively small wing and long thin fuselage, gave the impression of speed.

—*John Frost*

With the design now proceeding at a great rate, Frost's team was boosted to twenty draftsmen, six or eight stress men, six to eight in aerodynamics, and perhaps eight in the lofting department. Jim Booth, who had come over with Frost from de Havilland in England, became chief stress engineer.

I had come up with an arrangement which looked much as the CF-100 looks today, but with considerable wing sweep. Results were considered sufficiently satisfactory for the straight wing that I was not allowed to proceed with the swept wing version. Edgar Atkin was, perhaps, wisely conservative; swept wing aircraft were still quite a new departure and the RCAF was becoming most impatient that its fighter design was not proceeding at a rate it had expected.

—*John Frost*

The anxious RCAF sent an engineering officer, Wing Commander H. R. (Ray) Foottit, to the Malton plant to find out just what was going on, a year having slid by since the contract was let.

Foottit had served with the RCAF during the war, but had left prior to war's end to take a job as an aeronautical engineer with the Ryan Aeronautical Company in Southern California. Returning to the RCAF in 1946 in design and development, Foottit was one of the few air force people who was a practising aeronautical engineer, with experience in both the commercial and industrial sides of the aircraft industry. His instructions were to recommend cancellation of the contract if he wasn't satisfied with what he saw. The report he turned in, however, was favourable. But just.

Basically, my job was to keep the air force in touch with what was happening and to approve all the different changes, anything the company was doing in the way of specifications. I think Edgar Atkin was kind of reticent to discuss anything with the air force unless he really had to. I don't believe he held anything back, it just wasn't his nature to go and talk about something that was going on in the engineering side. If there were major changes, I was supposed to know about them. But, generally, my overall impression was that they had a goddamned good engineering department.

—*W/C Ray Foottit*

The task now facing Jim Floyd and his group, to re-engineer the jet transport to take four Rolls-Royce Derwent engines instead of two Avons, was not a formidable one. The Derwent fuel consumption was higher, resulting in a weight increase for comparable range, but there were also advantages: the Derwent was a well-proven, reliable engine, and with four engines the plane would be safer in the event of engine failure. Floyd had always been against using the Avon because it was untried.

As opposed to the newer, untried, axial-flow Avon, the Derwent had a centrifugal compressor. The engine, derived almost directly from the original Whittle development engines, was based on a prototype developed by Whittle's Power Jets in 1942. Rolls-Royce took over the design and developed it into the Derwent. The engine had a 3,000-pound thrust.

One of the interesting persistent stories surrounding the unavailability of the Avons for the C-102 is a strange one. For Jim Bain, who had started the whole project in motion in December, 1945, the retraction of the Avon was a bitter disappointment. He insists to this day it was Roy Dobson himself who put pressure on Hives and Rolls-Royce to withdraw the use of the Avons.

The contract for the C-102 placed considerable financial responsibility on Avro's shoulder. This is the way Sir Roy Dobson tried to play it safe by building the Jetliner with four centrifugal compressor engines rather than the C-102 with two axial flow RR Avons. He didn't like the idea of using an undeveloped, untested engine . . . . Dobson went to the Air Ministry in England and by some means got them to withdraw the right to use the Avons . . . .

He wanted a safe journey; a venturesome bold step was not for him. He lost for Canada the Avro C-102, an aircraft which could have made Canada the leader in the aircraft production industry . . . . When one considers the outstanding success of the Avon engine and the reduced fuel consumption made possible by the axial flow compressor, it is clear that the C-102 could have had huge potential; a potential thrown away by Sir Roy Dobson.

—*Jim Bain*

Jim Floyd questions this, recalling that the air was "suitably blue with our thoughts on Rolls-Royce" over the Avon decision, and Fred Smye winces when he remembers Dobson's reaction to the decision: "There's your friend Hives for you," he said. "Rolls-Royce—they'll screw you every time!"

The change from two to four engines did, however, necessitate design changes.

We had to completely redesign the centre section of the aircraft, but as the redesign progressed, it became obvious that there were many advantages in the four-engine layout which allowed the landing gear to be tucked very neatly in the twin nacelles between the engines, resulting in probably the shortest and simplest undercarriage ever seen on any transport . . . . The nacelle arrangement we finally designed would have made it much easier to fit better and more economical engines as these came along.

—*Jim Floyd*

That the engines were half the thrust of the Avons was of little concern to Floyd. What was bothersome, however, was a 13 per cent increase in fuel consumption which would affect operating costs of the plane and some concern that the redesign of parts of the aircraft might delay getting it into production, two items which would put a further strain on the already stringent conditions in the delicate TCA/ A. V. Roe letter of intent.

But even more ominous was the fact that the aircraft was no longer the C-102, the aircraft brought to life in the Winnipeg meeting of April, 1946. The summer of 1947 was long and hectic.

The four-engined redesign, coupled with the on-off slow down situation, resulted in considerable delay in the program, but by the end of September, 1947, we had carried out sufficient engineering analysis on the redesign to be able to show that the Derwent version would meet the TCA specification by a reasonable margin, despite the higher fuel consumption of the Derwents and the resulting increase in the gross weight of the aircraft.

—*Jim Floyd*

Floyd's proposal for the redesigned four-engine jet transport was sent to C. D. Howe, who now had to decide whether to proceed beyond the prototype stage. He wrote to Symington: "Please have your engineers examine the proposed specification and advise me whether it is one the government should support, having in mind your own needs for equipment for the next few years." The TCA investigation team was headed by Jim Bain, and it would be five months before a full report was made.

The revised design and performance data were sent to TCA in October for their engineering approval only, which Howe had requested in view of the government's contract with Avro to complete the prototypes. He wanted some assurance from TCA that at least, technically, they considered that the aircraft met the original requirement and that the C-102 would be suitable for operation on TCA's routes or, indeed, any airlines.

—Jim Floyd

By the end of October, A. V. Roe Canada set about to clear up a couple of loose ends, namely the C-102 prototype contract with the Department of Reconstruction, and what to do about TCA's letter of intent. "Following my interview with Mr. Howe and Mr. Scully last week in Ottawa," wrote Dobson to Symington,

the final contract for the C-102 Transport has now come through and it has been signed and returned to Ottawa today.

Under this contract, we are constructing two prototype C-102 aircraft, each fitted with four RR Derwent Turbines, and I am sure it will turn out to be a first class serviceable aircraft, particularly suitable for Canadian operation, and it may also be found suitable in many other spheres . . . . Mr. Scully did mention to me the fact that you were a little uneasy about the Letter of Intent which you sent to A. V. Roe Canada Ltd. some time ago, and I should like to take this opportunity of clearing your mind on that score, as, whatever the circumstances may have been, this contract [with the government] over-rides anything that may have gone before . . . . I still hope that on my visit to Canada, I may have the pleasure, and privilege, of meeting you and talking with you, merely for friendship's sake.

Friendship's sake was all it would be, for H. J. Symington had been succeeded as president of TCA by Gordon McGregor.

On February 25, 1948, the Jim Bain/TCA assessment of the C-102 was complete. It was the last step out the door for TCA. The C-102 was found "to be deficient on several grounds." With the higher fuel consumption of the Derwents estimated to be 23 per cent greater than the Avon configuration, an increase in fuel costs could quickly erase the marginal profitability of the jet transport. Moreover, the slow installation of instrument landing systems at Canadian airports meant the C-102 would have to carry more fuel reserves than had been anticipated in 1946. The combination, it was felt, sharply limited the commercial feasibility of the aircraft.

Apparently ignoring the instruction to avoid suggesting that A. V. Roe amend its specifications, the TCA engineers proposed several changes to make the aircraft more attractive for airline operation. Modification of the wing would help bring the capability of the C-102 up to a speed of 500 mph and a range sufficient to carry a payload of 8,000 pounds from Toronto to Winnipeg against a 50-mph headwind. It was Floyd's turn to be indignant. In almost every category of analysis, TCA brazenly suggested performance improvements far beyond what they had originally specified.

> TCA had used the higher fuel consumption of the Derwents over their specified AJ-65's as a strike against Avro, and to my knowledge, they never admitted their own monumental error in demanding that the AJ-65 be used to power their aircraft. There could never have been a C-102 with AJ-65 engines in the time scale specified, but Avro had no alternative but to go along with their demands, and as it turned out later, Avro also had no alternative but to put in the Derwents, at least in the prototypes. TCA also knew that the aircraft had been designed to take the more economical new technology engines when these became available.
>
> I could only assume that the TCA recommendation that the cruising speed be increased to 500 mph was a final attempt to shake off any hope that either Avro or Howe might have had of TCA ever taking the C-102 seriously. . . .
>
> Our emphasis was on the simplicity, safety and the stringent take-off and landing requirements specified by TCA, and we felt that the 200 mph increase in speed offered by the C-102 over most contemporary aircraft was a very substantial step forward.

On April 19, 1948, a meeting attended by Smye and Atkin of Avro and W. F. English and Jack Dyment, both of TCA, was held in the office of TCA's new president, Gordon McGregor. McGregor reaffirmed that TCA was not prepared to accept a commitment to purchase the jet transport. On May 4, Smye wrote to Rod McLean, Howe's executive assistant, explaining that A. V. Roe was going to approach airlines in the United States. Howe knew the president of Eastern Airlines, Eddie Rickenbacker, and offered Smye an introduction.

Within a month, Smye was in New York to see the airline president and he reported to Howe on June 7 that Rickenbacker was very interested. This initial optimism was soon extinguished, however, as it was discovered that both Rickenbacker and the president of Amercian Airlines, C. R. Smith, didn't think the jet engine was yet practical for civilian use. Thus, on much the same grounds as TCA had done, American and Eastern Airlines turned A. V. Roe away.

Although Smye still had no buyer for the C-102, an additional authorization of $2 million from the Canadian government carried the project into 1949. This gave A. V. Roe time to explore other avenues that could lead to the American market. G. T. Baker, the president of National Airlines and a former USAF general, thought the C-102 might give his young company a competitive advantage over the older, more cautious airlines on his main route between New York and Miami. He later recalled his reaction to his engineer's assessment of the plane. "I send two of my most conservative people up to Canada for a couple of days to look at the C-102 jetliner and they come back stark raving mad with enthusiasm for it." National Airlines assessment of the jetliner led to negotiations with A. V. Roe for the purchase of as many as ten aircraft. It began to look as though the C-102 was finally going to take off.

8

STEALING THE THUNDER

In January, 1948, John Frost made a trip to England to discuss engine installations with Rolls-Royce. Although the CF-100 was being tailored to carry A. V. Roe Canada's own Orenda engines as power plants, the XC-100 prototypes 18101 and 18102 were to fly with Rolls-Royce's Avons. While in England, Frost also looked in at Fairey Aviation, the suppliers of the power boosters; Martin Baker, the makers of the ejection seats; and Dowty, the undercarriage company.

Construction of the prototype was well advanced, and it was ready for wind tunnel tests by the time Frost left for England. When Frost first came to the design, the engines had been placed so that they projected forward beyond the wings, the rationale being ease of repair and replacement, but in that position the engines invaded the crew's field of vision and placed the centre of gravity too far forward. Frost had moved the engines back and down slightly into the wing; the wings, engine nacelles, and fuselage were now much more smoothly integrated. In a front elevation drawing the two engines and the fuselage looked like three circles side by side, the one in the centre larger, and the centres on a line in the horizontal plane.

We had arranged the structure and equipment so that everything fitted together beautifully—particularly difficult in a fighter since everything depends on obtaining minimum frontal area, together with the optimum fineness ratio.

On the XC-100, the engines were on either side of the fuselage, just ahead of the wing. This made for a very broad fuselage in plain view just ahead of the wing—that is, the two engines and fuselage all side by side. This large plan area would obviously contribute to the total lift of the aircraft. To satisfy stability, there is a fixed relationship between the position of the centre of total lift on an aircraft, and the centre of gravity.

—John Frost

The wind tunnel tests, carried out while Frost was in England, showed the centre of lift too far forward, so Chamberlin, in Frost's absence but with the approval of chief engineer Edgar Atkin, decided to move the engines back to increase the area of the undersurface just behind the wings and thus move the centre of lift back. The engines themselves tapered from front to back, and, to maintain their position in the horizontal plane, it was necessary to dip into the upper boom of the main spar. The main spar ran from side to side of the main body of the aircraft, forming a rigid platform for the two engines and the fuselage; the wings were fitted to the main spar on the outside of the engine nacelles. With the engines moved back, the upper boom of the main spar was now curved down and around to accommodate the taper of the engines. This introduced an undesirable degree of flexibility into the main spar that seriously weakened the wing joint (although this was not fully apparent until much later); to counter the flexibility caused by the dip, reinforcement plates were added to the upper boom of the main spar.

Now this was a very wrong decision. Suddenly the aircraft got a main spar that carried all the load but very much weakened it. If it had to be done, it should have been done at a much earlier stage.

—Waclaw Czerwinski

Wind tunnel results from the first XC-100 model had been computed and analysed and, in my absence, had been interpreted to mean that this plan area of fuselage and engine nacelle ahead of the wing had pulled the resultant lift of the total machine too far forward with respect to the centre of gravity, and that under these conditions satisfactory stability for the aircraft was in some doubt.

There were obviously only two things to do if this situation really existed: one was to move the centre of lift back in some way, and the other to move the centre of gravity forward.

It had been decided to move the engines backwards by about a foot to reduce the forward overhang of the nacelles ahead of the wings. On my return, when I was told of this decision, I was horrified and explained that it just could not be done, since to move the engines back would mean that they would foul the aircraft's main spar. I was assured that my assertion about the spar had been looked into and was told that if the depth of the spar was reduced in this area by bending the top boom down towards the lower, the rearward shift of the engines could be accommodated.

The problem of reducing the spar depth locally, and bending the upper boom, must have cost at least an extra 200 pounds structure weight, and led to serious deflection problems which the aircraft ran into later, and never should have.

The ridiculous thing about it was that by moving the engines back, you certainly moved the centre of lift back by a small amount, but the weight of the engines being moved aft also moved the centre of gravity back as well—in the wrong direction—and it was doubtful whether the final result altered matters at all.

This was even more unfortunate since when the Orenda engines were installed on the third aircraft, the addition of the de-icing cowling on the front of the engine intake extended the nacelle the foot forward again that the engines had been moved back! And the aircraft always flew well with no stability troubles.

Whether all this was due to a misinterpretation of wind tunnel results, or an assumption that the centre of gravity was further aft than it really was, will probably never be known.

I found it a very hard thing to do, since it was against any logical reasoning I could produce. I was terribly upset but having put up the best argument I could to have the decision changed, with no success, I decided I had better do my best to make it work.

Luckily, apart from this, the rest of the design was good . . . . After this upset, we settled down again and finished the prototype design.

—John Frost

By the time Frost returned to Canada, the changes to the prototype had already been made. His objections were not taken seriously by Chamberlin and were overridden by Edgar Atkin. They felt that Frost had miscalculated the centre of lift and, although Frost himself was not convinced of this, enough time had already been wasted. There was considerable pressure coming down through management from the government and the RCAF to get on with the project, and a lot remained to be done before the first prototype was finished and ready for pre-flight testing late in 1949.

Security and secrecy around the design of the XC-100 was naturally tight, but occasionally unauthorized personnel got a glance of what was taking shape behind the canvas curtain at the end of assembly bay 3. While Jim Hornick's articles in the *Globe and Mail* touched an occasional nerve with company executives, nothing caused quite the furor as the piece that appeared in the November 8, 1948, edition of the American publication *Aviation Week*.

Entitled "Details on Canada's Jet Fighter," and carrying an embarrassingly accurate artist's impression of the XC-100, the article stated: "The British have no all-weather fighter and the combination of speed, range, adaptability and firepower may prove an important factor in the ordering of this airplane for mass production." It made mention of John Frost as the designer, and went on to discuss the fuselage, the wings and tail, the armament, the power plants, the landing gear, and the applications—all with an eye to accuracy.

A. V. Roe was embarrassed and the RCAF was furious. An RCMP investigation was called to see if the Official Secrets Act had been violated; but it was discovered that a reporter from *Aviation Week* had toured the plant the previous month and, while he was denied a look at the aircraft itself, he was given, apparently with company blessing, free access to documents and pictures and interviewed some of the staff. "Not entirely accurate," fumbled company officials. A company employee was dismissed as a result of the inquiry. Military security, it seemed, was an unfamiliar thing to Canadians.

In the early hours of St. Patrick's Day, March 17, 1948, the Chinook engine had its first run. First run to an engine man is like first flight to an aircraft man, the opportunity to see if the stuff you did on paper really works. The "official" run of the Chinook was scheduled for March 24, but, because "the future of the entire company hung on that little engine," it was wisely decided to run it unofficially a few days before just to make sure the thing worked. The engine's designer, Winnett Boyd, apparently knew nothing about the unofficial test.

> *It is interesting to recount that we weren't even permitted the luxury of quietly trying the engine in private before putting it on display . . . . The people who were paying the shot for this were the RCAF and the people in the Department of Reconstruction and Supply . . . . They said they wanted to be on hand, and said, "None of this first sneak try." . . . It would have been much more hazardous for us had we tried the engine in secret and them not been aware of it.*
>
> *—Winnett Boyd*

Maybe so, but not everyone was as confident as Winnett Boyd that the engine would run. Could Fred Smye have secretly authorized the

March 17 run and made sure somehow that Boyd never found out? A memo to "All Personnel Concerned" outlined the day's program for the first official run of the Chinook. Of particular interest is a point under item 12 of the memo: "All personnel are to refrain, if possible, from mentioning that the engine has run previously."

The Chinook ran at two-thirty in the morning. J. L. Mackenzie and J. H. Parkin from the NRC and myself flew down to watch it. If anything had gone wrong, it would have jeopardized the entire program. Technician Fred Staines, on a signal from J. L. Brisley, head of the test section, pushed the starting button at a little after two-thirty in the morning. The engine worked and the crew prepared themselves for the official run on March 24.

—*A/V/M John Easton*

C. D. Howe was present for this one as was Bill Scully, A. L. James, Wilf Curtis, and Brooke Claxton, Minister of Defence. At 11:47 A. M. the button was once again pushed and the engine started.

The thing started up in a matter of thirty or forty seconds. The other engines of that era used to have great long flames coming out of the jet pipe. Our test house was arranged so that we had a window looking out on the engine and another window that looked outside where the jet pipe came out of the test cell, and I was at the window that looked at the jet pipe. If the thing wasn't going, if the compressor and turbine weren't matched properly, we'd get a whole lot of flame and she'd be overheated and the turbine wouldn't be developing the power to accelerate the compressor, so I was watching that, and there wasn't a lick of flame.

I had complete confidence that the thing would run . . . . Now there were others who weren't as familiar with the design as I was, who had no basis for the confidence that I had, but of course, all they could do was go by the precedent that usually engines didn't work all that well the first time you pressed the starting button.

We approached the design here in Canada in a very different way than the British approach. The study of efficiency in a jet engine lends itself to mathematical analysis. So, you can design a gas turbine from scratch and expect it to run reasonably well. And since most of the English designers had come from the "old school"—the old piston engine school— they tended to design their jet engines the same way they designed their piston engines. We designed from the first principle, whereas the English carried on with the approach they had always taken with piston engines.

—*Winnett Boyd*

"Jets are ideal for Arctic operations," commented Air Vice Marshal James when the test run was over. "They are easily started; there are

no propellers to worry about. We are certainly thrilled at its performance today." For that matter, so was A. V. Roe. Prior to the first run
of the Chinook, Smye had held daily meetings to ensure there were
no last-minute snags, and in the final few days before the run he
himself was rushing around, picking up parts and delivering them to
help get the engine off on time. "If we failed," recalls Smye, "we might
lose the contract for the big one." The "big one" was the Orenda.

It was no secret that each year when the federal budget was drawn
up, A. V. Roe had faced the prospect that unless they could demonstrate progress on their design and development work, government
subsidies would be cut off. It was a little more than mere coincidence,
then, that the Chinook ran a bare two weeks before the end of the
government's fiscal year.

*Designing aircraft is more glamourous than designing engines but when
you get right down to it, the first cutting of metal at A. V. Roe, the first
success the company had, was with the Chinook.*

*This small band of some forty young Canadian engineers undertook to
design the . . . most powerful power plant ever designed by man . . . .
The point is, that the small group of enthusiastic amateurs at Malton,
beat both Rolls-Royce and General Electric in accomplishing basic specification performance of their engines.*

—Fred Smye

*The Chinook was well on its way and the Orenda was just in our minds.
We then had to think of a "family" of names that could be used for
subsequent engines . . . . I went down to the Royal Ontario Museum,
which has a particularly good exhibit of Indian artifacts. I don't know
exactly when the idea of using mythical Indian figures occurred to me,
but it did, and especially the names of the spirits that are supposed to
have, and to endow people and things with, great powers. So, I came
across the names Orenda, Manitou, and Wakunda. The one I rather
fancied was that of a god of the Iroquois, Orenda. It had three syllables,
but it made an attractive combination with Avro—Avro Orenda. I went
back to Malton, into the drafting office, and without asking anyone, said,
"Along with TR-5, from now on, in parenthesis, put the name Orenda."
And it stuck.*

—Winnett Boyd

The Orenda, as far as A. V. Roe was concerned, was indeed the
"big one." Similar in design to the Chinook, the Orenda was expected
to achieve a take-off thrust of 6,500 pounds at 7,000 rpm. On February
10, 1949, it had its first test run adjacent to a viewing room crowded

with government officials and RCAF officers. This was A. V. Roe's first major project to reach this stage and it was common, yet unspoken, knowledge that the personal reputations of both the company and its gas turbine engineers were on the line that day. "You could hear the knees knocking for half a mile," recalled Fred Smye, afterwards.

The thing that was most disturbing about the first run of the Orenda was that we weren't allowed to light it up until all the dignitaries had assembled. We were permitted to "motor" the engine and make sure it spun around, and I went to the back and put my hand in the jet pipe and felt a good strong breeze coming out of the jet pipe so I knew the compressor was pushing some air through. We were allowed to match the ten fuel injectors outside the engines, and we were allowed to test the ignition system for spark.

We had lunch and we were walking over to the test cell and Smye says to me, "Is that god-damned compressor of yours gonna work, Harry?" And I just showed him my fingers crossed.

—Harry Keast

But when the button was pushed, the Orenda sprang to life to begin the story of one of the most successful turbojet engines ever made. "The engine is so good," wrote Jim Hornick in the *Globe and Mail*, "that it caused Canadian Defence Department officials to delay their negotiations with the Americans for F-86 fighters."

Knowles, Dilworth, Boyd and myself were actually inside the test cell when it first lit up. It was a horrible experience because when it first lit up, there was a solid yellow flame out through the nozzle and I was concerned about how long one turbine would last with the flame—the engine then accelerated very rapidly—I believe it must have been spectacular if you were outside the cell.

—Harry Keast

The Orenda was always a somewhat hotter starter than the Chinook. The first time on the test stand it ran for about 30 hours. Then it was stripped and inspected, and since it was in perfect condition, it was reassembled, put back on the stand, and run for 70 hours. During this run, it exceeded its design thrust of 6,500 pounds by 200 pounds. After the above test, the Orenda was again inspected, and since it was still in perfect condition, it was reassembled . . . .

The Orenda ran for 784 hours without being taken off the test stand or having any major repairs made to it. The combustion chamber liners were changed at the 300- and 600-hour marks, and I believe one fuel pump had to be replaced. It should be remarked that, in achieving these results, the Orenda was not "babied" in any way. It consistently gave 6,500 pounds thrust at take-off speed and completed (unofficially) the 150-hour type tests and 50-hour special category tests of Canada, the U.S., and Great Britain.

—Winnett Boyd

Boyd would look at the thrust meter and say, "Look at that thrust!" And I'd say, "Yeah, but look at that jet pipe temperature." It was almost like over-revving an automobile—you can get all the thrust you want for a short period of time before the blades burn off.

—Harry Keast

Today, the first Chinook engine sits quietly in a museum in Brampton, Ontario. As for that first Orenda, fate would provide it with a much less glamorous end. In the summer of 1949, one of Orenda no. 1's test-bed engineers entered the test cell while the engine was running. He was wearing a very loose lab coat, and in one of his pockets was a packet of Schick injector razor blades. The engineer got too close to the engine's air intake and the coat was sucked right into the compressor. When the package of blades hit the whirling blades of the compressor, there came a grinding explosion and Orenda No. 1 came noisily to a halt, never to run again.

Early development running of the Orenda continued through 1949 and early 1950. However, the early success of the engine caught A. V. Roe's gas turbine engineers completely off guard since they suddenly realized that they had a flyable engine with nothing to fly it in.

Boyd wanted to put the engine in an F-86 Sabre right away. This was not to be, however. The engine must first be flown on a test bed. A Lancaster Mark X was quickly modified to take two Orendas in the outboard nacelles. The Lancaster test bed with the two Orendas and two of its own Packard-Merlins flew for the first time on July 13, 1950.

Test-bedding the Orenda in a Lancaster was done on Dobson's insistence, because he felt it had to be tested on a flying test bed before cleared for flight. We had to do it in something and the Lanc was a logical choice. Neither Winn nor myself thought this a necessary step before flying it in the Sabre, but Sir Roy said this was how it had to be.

—Paul Dilworth

The RCAF made arrangements with the USAF to have North American Aviation modify an F-86 Sabre to take an Orenda so that it could be test flown at Muroc, California. The first flight of the special F-86 was made on October 5, 1950. Later, an American pilot in an Orenda Sabre flew from Minneapolis to Toronto in one hour, and A. V. Roe's Mike Cooper-Slipper flew one from Toronto to Montreal at 665 mph.

"I have flown four different engines in jet airplanes," said American test pilot Jacqueline Cochrane, "and of the four, the Orenda, in my opinion, is far smoother and finer in every way than the other three, which included one British and two American." She backed her judgment by going on to break five world speed records in an Orenda-powered Sabre.

These would provide good arguments when it came to getting government approval to produce the Orenda in quantity. After all, the project and the funds thus far were for "development" purposes only. In the summer of 1950 Fred Smye made a special trip to Ottawa to see C. D. Howe.

All of the first aircraft engines were built in the aircraft machine shop. We had to line up a lot of machinery to build the Orenda—put it into production. Dobson and Howe were both against me setting up a separate engine shop so we built the first ones in the aircraft machine shop.

Production meant more space and machinery and a fair amount of set-up money involved, so I went to Ottawa with A/V/M Smith and Frank Trethewey to see Howe, who was going to give me a letter of authority to purchase this necessary equipment.

After introductions, C.D. hands me the letter and I said to him, "I want to make sure, Mr. Howe, you understand what this is all about." He said, "I understand, Freddie." And I said, "This is all for production equipment to build the new Orenda." He grabbed the letter out of my hands and said, "I had no idea!" He went on about the history of aviation and how there was a lot of engines taken to the point of the Orenda, and how the Orenda was a good engine and had demonstrated its performance, but it had a long way to go before it went into production.

Well, I was there an hour, but he eventually gave in and I made a bet with him, "I'll bet you ten dollars the Orenda gets into production," and he said, "You're on!" During the Arrow debates, he referred to this story and the risks but what he failed to say was, he lost the bet.

—*Fred Smye*

On June 20, 1951, the first flight of a CF-100 powered by Orenda engines took place, and on October 17, 1951, Roe delivered the first production CF-100, equipped with Orendas, to the RCAF, the first of many hundreds.

In February, 1949, word began to filter over from Britain that de Havilland was also working on a jet transport, a four-engine, long-range aircraft they called the Comet. At first, the company showed but minor interest in the de Havilland project until Jim Hornick, the *Globe and Mail*'s aviation writer and Avro-watcher, saw the opportunity to arouse publicity for the project by giving the story an interesting angle. "The race is on between Canada and Britain," he wrote with a certain amount of glee. "Britain may be way ahead of the United States, but if Canada was to gain the upper hand with the Avro C-102 Jetliner, the Malton company would receive world-wide respect."

I played up the race between the two companies to the hilt, because the story of the Jetliner, as I saw it, was the story of the first jet transport aircraft to fly. If Avro beat de Havilland's, they would corner the world market.

—*Jim Hornick*

Stories of a potential race aside, at Malton, Jim Floyd and his group were much more concerned with just getting the aircraft into the air. Hornick's headlines persisted. "The race is purely for reasons of prestige," "British aviation experts predict the Comet will be the first." Hornick knew Fred Smye well enough by this time to realize he was not an admirer of de Havilland; he frequently referred to them as a "matchbox factory." Smye would not be able to resist, Hornick reckoned, the chance to out-do de Havilland; the unofficial word soon went out from Smye's office to Jim Floyd and the men in the shops: beat the Comet.

Smye decided to pay us a five-hundred-dollar incentive if we got the airplane out by a certain date. Then Stan Wilson—he worked in the standards department at the time—told him not to be such a cheapskate. And Fred said to me, "Ernie, if you get that plane out by a certain date, I'll pay you five thousand!

—*Ernie Alderton*

It was exciting. We, with our friends at de Havilland's . . . obviously knew what was happening . . . . We knew the approximate date they expected to fly . . . . We would've liked to have flown the Jetliner before them, but our main consideration was getting a no-risk program because it was our first airplane . . . . If anything had gone wrong on that airplane, we'd have been dead and, therefore, the no risk was the important thing rather than the race.

—*Jim Floyd*

We could have flown the aircraft long before we did but there were a lot of things we wanted to get under our belt from a safety point of view. We could have taken risks and flown the aircraft a month, even two months before. There was one occasion when we'd run the engines out on the tarmac and the guys were running it at maximum rpm when suddenly there was a loud explosion—POP! POP! and all the nacelle skins had been sucked in—the cooling system had failed. Things like that set the program back ten days.

—Ernie Alderton

If we'd taken a risk and not done that test, we would've flown two weeks ahead of the Comet. But we felt we just had to run those engines to get all the data, all the information we wanted from them prior to flights.

—Jim Floyd

As soon as Fred Smye had that letter of intent, the mock-up on the Jetliner began. We were going six, seven days a week, and three nights. Floyd must have been there fifteen hours a day, and those rare times he wasn't, he gave us his home phone number and said, "Call me and I'll come in. I don't care when, call me and I'll come in."

—Bob Johnson

The engine cooling system was only one problem; there were others: hydraulics, undercarriage, crooked windows—all minor enough in themselves, but each a factor in postponing the first flight. The calls from Fred Smye's office down to the shop were almost irritating in their frequency: "Is today the day? Can we get her up today?"

Jim Floyd's face was a road map of exhaustion. The effort to beat the de Havilland Comet into the air was taking its toll on the young designer. While the *Globe and Mail* reported work on the Jetliner was "accelerating," Floyd was putting in seven days a week. The Jetliner was being assembled during the day, all tests on the aircraft were being carried on overnight, and Floyd had to be there for all of it. When he could, he would nap on a cot in the plant hospital. Although, he recalls, his working hours at the time weren't all that unusual: it was a ritual he was locked into for two years.

Other people worked until midnight or later without caring whether anyone else knew about it. It wasn't only my airplane, it belonged to everyone who worked on it. I've worked on a few airplanes and I've never seen such an emotional involvement of everyone concerned. They were going to make it fly and make it a good one. Everyone, just everyone, seemed besotted by it.

We were all conditioned during the war to spending as much time as possible in the plant. When I came here, I expected to spend a lot of time in the plant because it was a new challenge. Everybody was so dedicated— Bob Johnson, Eric Peckam, Mario Pesando—so dedicated. I never really felt all that tired . . . . It was the happiest time of my life.

—Jim Floyd

On July 25, 1949, the Jetliner was ready for final inspection. Taxiing trials had just begun when de Havilland's Comet hopped a few feet off the runway, making history as the first jet airliner in the world to take to the air. "The race is over," screamed the *Globe and Mail*, "and Canada lost."

The decision when and if to fly was made collectively by the inspection department, the engineering department, and the pilot. But in the end, it's the pilot himself who decides everything is ready to go. As he would do with the CF-100 prototype, Dobson sent over one of his experienced test pilots, a heavy-aircraft pilot named Jimmy Orrell, to fly the Jetliner.

Orrell was a British Empire bi-plane pilot. He had flown airplanes to the Middle East and had been with Avro in England for a few years. I flew with him in Lancasters over there before we got our first one. Went over again in 1948—they had a jet conversion of the Tudor, and I flew with him in that. The understanding was he would do the first few hours of flying in the Jetliner, and I would fly with him and take over after that.

—Don Rogers

Within days of the Comet's first flight, Orrell was pleased enough with the Jetliner's taxiing trials to discuss with Floyd the possibility of duplicating the short hop of the Comet. The sooner the better. They had lost the jet race, but a close second would greatly restore the spirits of everyone.

Even though faced with the obstacle of a short runway and soaring temperatures, Floyd approved having a go at it. The temperature on the tarmac topped 103 degrees Fahrenheit—Mario Pesando thought the runway was better suited to frying eggs than testing aircraft. To complicate things even more, the main runway at Malton Airport was being rebuilt, and the only runway available for the Jetliner trial might be too short. It was estimated that the aircraft would need at least 3,000 feet of runway to accomplish the short hop.

Orrell took the aircraft to the threshold of the runway, opened the throttles on the four Derwents, and accelerated smoothly to take-off speed. At 90 mph the nose wheel lifted off the ground and the Jetliner was poised for take-off, when Orrell decided that the remaining distance was insufficient to achieve take-off and still enable him to stop in the remainder of the runway. The short runway and the high temperature were too much for the plane. When Orrell closed the throttles and pressed on the brakes, all four main tires blew. Damage was light, however, and the very next day the exercise was attempted again. After more taxi runs, Orrell tried once more to get the Jetliner into the air, but there wasn't enough runway. This time, as all hands from the factory watched, two tires blew when the brakes had to go on again.

The idea of a short hop was abandoned. Orrell decided that the only way to get the plane into the air was to "take her up, all the way." He could get double the runway space by taking the plane up and coming back to land. Floyd agreed, and called Fred Smye, then vacationing in Muskoka, to get his approval. TCA officials were invited.

We were asked to go down to witness the flight of the aircraft. We didn't go down with any idea of re-investigating it as being the right airplane. We knew damn well we weren't going to buy it.

—Jim Bain

It was August 10, a Wednesday, just after lunch. Jim Floyd was the heart of an anxious, almost silent group of spectators who watched as the Jetliner finally left the ground. A. V. Roe's first aircraft, Jim Floyd's plane, was airborne.

Orrell quickly took the aircraft to 500 feet and tested the controls. They were fine. He then took her to 8,000 feet. "Everything feels wonderful," he radioed. In the co-pilot's seat was Don Rogers. Bill Baker was the navigator/technician. The airplane flew for about an hour until a 35-mph crosswind came up. Orrell brought her down easily, and found she handled beautifully, even on the short runway. It was a mere two weeks after the Comet had first flown in England. In the control tower, amidst the boisterous whooping and cheering, Jim Floyd wept for joy.

The very next day, Fred Smye paid Ernie Alderton his five thousand dollars.

Within days of the Jetliner's first flight, Jim Floyd was hunched over the microphone in the control tower with the look on his face like a man watching his house on fire. The Jetliner was in the air, again, but this time there was trouble; the main undercarriage gear had jammed closed, and although the nose wheel was down, the hydraulic fluid was used up. For over an hour, Baker had been manually trying to crank the main wheels down without success. In fact, he pulled so hard on the manual lever mechanism that he'd dislocated his shoulder, compounding Orrell's difficulty. Word spread quickly through the plant. The Jetliner was in trouble.

The word was the gear wouldn't come down. I never came so close to being sick to my stomach.

—*Jack Millie*

Workers left their machines and ran outside; foremen and supervisors who had tried to stop people gave up and followed. Because Orrell had to keep the plane in the air to burn as much fuel as possible, Toronto radio stations had enough time to pick up the story, and before long people were lining the airport fence. Traffic along Dixon Road was bumper to bumper and still they kept coming. Up in the Jetliner's cockpit, co-pilot Rogers was too busy to be sick or frightened.

I remember the crowds of people most of all. The first flight occurred during the plant [summer] shut-down but on this flight, most everyone was back. Before long, management and the troops were lined along the runway fence . . . . As co-pilot, I was doing the radio work with the tower. I don't recall any great strange feelings that day. There was some suggestion by the airport manager that we dump the airplane in Lake Ontario . . . . Now, when you land an airplane on water, it does a lot of damage . . . . I think the airport manager was more concerned about us digging up his airport than anything else.

—*Don Rogers*

It was then they decided to belly-land the plane—no main wheels.

I don't think we really expected any disaster. Lots of airplanes do belly landings. The aircraft was quite light in weight, so light in fact, we could hardly get it to slow down enough, to landing speed—it would just float and float because with the gear up the wing was so close to the ground, it created a ground cushion, and we had to make three or four attempts at it.

—*Don Rogers*

Orrell buzzed the field. The front wheel was down. He went once to have a look. Then he made two more runs, but he was going too fast and too high to land. The pilot faced a new problem. He had a new ship, did not know how it would behave. The flaps were not down to stop her. On the fourth run, Orrell brought the plane down. The plane was floating and would not edge in properly, but he did a great job. He came in on the grass just north of the east-west runway. He did not have much room because the new north-south runway had made the ground rough. There was a cloud of smoke and dust. She bounced a little twice and skidded 1,500 feet and stopped 50 feet short of the highway fence where a crowd of people were waiting.

—eye witness

Smye was in Ottawa at a meeting and when he heard the Jetliner was on its belly, he "damned near died." For Don Rogers, it was nothing more than a routine belly-landing; for Jim Floyd, it added a good number of years to his life and a good number of grey hairs to his head.

It showed us another side of the safety of an aircraft which had no propellers to get in the way in an emergency like this.

—Jim Floyd

The airplane suffered the least for the experience. Damage was light— four bent tail pipes and caved-in plating at the rear of the fuselage. The Jetliner was in the air again in six weeks.

The C-102 now went through flight testing and routine analysis, and work was progressing on the second prototype. It was time to market the plane.

Our sales/marketing budget was miniscule compared to Boeing, Douglas or even de Havilland. We had only one outside sales office at LaGuardia Airport in New York manned by the very capable Dixon Speas.

—Joe Morley

Dixon Speas, a graduate of M.I.T., had also attended the Boeing School of Aeronautics. He joined American Airlines in 1940, and in 1944 was cited as one of the ten outstanding men in the aircraft industry in the United States. He fell in love with the Avro Jetliner.

What we lacked in "bucks," we made up for in total effort. We had the backing of the best technical team, an excellent flight test department, knowledgeable marketing people and comparative management. Policy- wise, I had established very early that we should not try to cover the waterfront, but concentrate on our national airline, TCA, and those Amer-

ican carriers that had made a marked contribution in the air transportation field and who were not adverse to buying "first-offs."

—Joe Morley

With TCA now largely out of the picture, Morley turned his sights to the United States. But with next to nil in promotion money, what could be done to interest potential buyers? The answer: demonstration flights. Let the buyer get a look at the product first hand. The publicity stunts, garish at times, were designed to get headlines. And they did just that.

If we had tried to sell U. S. airlines on paper, they could always come back to the bad reports of TCA on the airliner. So what we had to do was demonstrate the aircraft—let them sit in it, let their pilots fly it, let them analyse it to the nth degree and decide themselves whether they could use this aircraft for their own routes . . . . I make no excuse for the fact we took this line . . . . This was the only market left.

—Jim Floyd

"The Jetliner's flight program went unbelievably well," wrote Jim Floyd for *Canadian Aviation*'s fiftieth anniversary issue.

Airline flight times were halved by the Jetliner on all inter-city flights all over the U.S. and Canada. Many U.S. airline executives were aboard on these flights and without exception were enthusiastic about the aircraft.

It was clear that Avro still regarded TCA's endorsement of the Jetliner as vital to its sales effort. Long after the airline had pulled out of the program, each time it agreed to co-operate—usually at Howe's insistence—in the development of the C-102, there would be a flurry of press releases from A. V. Roe implying that TCA intended to buy the aircraft. Roy Dobson put the case quite clearly in a letter to C. D. Howe on March 29, 1950:

I think we have a market for the C-102, providing it gets started off right . . . . If TCA use the C-102, it will sell in the States and elsewhere. If TCA do not use it, then it will not get the hall mark of approval of its own Government Airline, and that will take a lot of arguing away.

On one flight in April, 1950, one of the VIP's was a reluctant Gordon McGregor of TCA, ordered on the flight by C. D. Howe to give the impression that TCA was at least morally behind the project. "McGregor will be on that first flight to New York," Howe had written to Dobson. "I have given strict instructions that no member of TCA is to knock the plane or its performance." He concluded with the interesting footnote: "I am backing the proposal that TCA buy five C-102's for use in its triangular run, Toronto–New York–Montreal–Toronto."

"We could not well be too discouraging," wrote Gordon McGregor of the experience years later,

> since the government had an interest in the project, and was anxious to foster aircraft design and manufacture in Canada, and although it was unsuitable for TCA, the possibility had to be allowed, of a limited market among other carriers. These were wooed by Avro in a series of sales promotion flights, on one of which I was talked into being a passenger . . . on April 18, 1950.
>
> As a publicity stunt, they sent along a peace pipe, which (contrary to all airport regulations) was to be lighted and puffed once or twice on the ramp beside the aircraft, the theory being that the pipe would still be going when the aircraft arrived in New York, stressing the short duration of the flight. Sure enough, the pipe was still going on arrival, and many press photographs bear witness to this fact, although I would not bet a great deal that the pipe did not receive some surreptitious encouragement en route.

The following day, a New York newspaper printed a picture of the Jetliner flying over the city. The accompanying caption read: "This should give our nation a good healthful kick in its placidity. The fact that our massive but under-populated good neighbor to the north has a mechanical product that licks anything of ours is just what the doctor ordered for our over-developed ego. The Canadian plane's feat accelerates a process already begun in this nation—a realization that Uncle Sam has no monopoly on genius."

Not everyone at A. V. Roe thought it was wise to continue pressuring TCA to buy the Jetliner. Jim Floyd thought it was a "ridiculous imposition" on the airline.

> *I knew that we had a really first-class aircraft, with an excellent potential, and I felt that if TCA now had no interest in the Jetliner, we should leave the poor sods alone.*
>
> *—Jim Floyd*

Joe Morley received literally hundreds of invitations to demonstrate the Jetliner during 1950 and 1951 but selected only those opportunities that would afford the maximum exposure for the plane and its crew.

He made sure that no major American airline missed the opportunity to get a look at the Jetliner. With Don Rogers at the controls, the plane started on a tour that rivals those taken by a modern-day Pontiff: Toronto to Chicago in ninety-one minutes; New York to Toronto in sixty-seven minutes; Winnipeg to Toronto in two hours and thirty-three minutes; Toronto to Tampa in just under three hours; Miami to New York in two hours, thirty-six and a half minutes.

The C-102 Jetliner did more for the Canadian aviation industry in those flights than any aircraft before or since, with headlines in Los Angeles, New York, Miami, and points between. An editorial reprinted in many American newspapers commenting on the first Toronto to New York jet air-mail flight on April 18, 1950, grumbled, "and where are we? On the drawing boards." And the influential magazine *Air Trails* wailed: "What happened to the great American aircraft industry?. . . In the race to get a jetliner into the air, Canada won, hands down . . . . Our hat's off to the Canadians."

But, with all the hoopla, did the company actually sell any Jetliners?

We did get a letter of intent from Ted Baker, president of National Airlines, for four aircraft and an option for a further six. There was no question in my mind about Baker's seriousness. I had just completed an extended trip with him to the U.K. where we had met with Rolls-Royce to discuss and get assurances on Derwent jet overhauls in Miami. The letter had the usual conditions—firm price, a guarantee of performance, and a U.S. certificate of airworthiness.

We had lined the contract up on a cost-plus basis with no obligations, and this drove him [Dobson] bananas. No deal! Sir Roy would not allow us to make this decision in Canada. This lack of confidence was the straw that broke the camel's back.

—*Joe Morley*

That, and the coming of the Korean War. An important part of Canada's foreign policy in the post-war years was the support of the United Nations Charter. In 1950, Canada held seats on both the Security Council and the Economic and Social Council. With the invasion of South Korea in June, 1950, Canada, keen to show support for the Charter, responded to the UN's appeal for military aid. All three branches of the armed forces contributed to the effort, and the RCAF was more anxious than ever to have its new jet interceptor, the CF-100.

Delays in the CF-100 program had caused C. D. Howe to demand that Avro clean up its act and get the fighter into production at all costs. If that meant stopping work on the Jetliner, then so be it. "I trust," he wrote to Fred Smye in December, 1950, "that you have stopped work on the second prototype and cleared this work out of the shop, so that all your effort, for the time being, can be devoted to the production of the CF-100 and the Orenda engine."

To Dixon Speas, Howe was more succinct. "Mr. Speas," he said impatiently, "have you ever heard of a company that's got too much on its plate? Well, that's Avro!" On February 5, 1951, Fred Smye issued a directive to discontinue all promotion of the Jetliner as a commercial transport.

9

THE QUICK AND
THE DEAD

If a man be judged on appearance alone, Bill Waterton was the ideal test pilot: slicked down, close-cropped hair, parted ever so straightly to one side, predictable handle-bar moustache decorating a square, dark-eyed face resting atop a 6-foot frame that never moved except in a swagger. Nothing appeared out of place.

One has little trouble imagining Waterton, with an air base his stage, downing that last drop of tea before scurrying up the wing of his Spitfire, white scarf blowing majestically in the wind, to chase away Messerschmitts with a good bit of stiff upper lip derring-do.

Those who met Bill Waterton for the first time would swear he was British, and he himself did nothing to disabuse them of this impression, but in fact he was born and raised in Camrose, Alberta, and distinguished himself during the war as a squadron leader with the RAF. During the war, he had amassed plenty of jet time on the Meteor and gained quite a reputation as a test pilot of the famous plane.

Since the Meteor was manufactured by Gloster Aircraft, one of the Hawker-Siddeley Group's companies, Waterton was well acquainted with Sir Roy Dobson. One night at a company party in Dorchester during the winter of 1948/49, Dobson cornered Waterton over a drink:

"How'd you like to go to Canada and fly this new airplane A. V. Roe Canada is producing for us?"

Waterton thought the old boy was joking when he replied with, "Sure, I suppose I'm as big a sucker as the next guy."

He told me that the Canadians were keen, eager to get on with it, and the most ignorant lot you'll find anywhere.

—Bill Waterton

But along with the enthusiasm, there was a gentle warning for Waterton. It seems that after the war, Waterton had applied to the RCAF and was turned down. Some of the top RCAF brass knew about it and felt it wouldn't look good to have a pilot that didn't qualify for the RCAF to now be given the responsibility of test flying Canada's new fighter. "Under no circumstances," Dobson told Waterton, "are you to ever say you were turned down. Wilf Curtis has been on to me and he's afraid you're going to let that out."

When word reached A. V. Roe Canada that the pilot who would test the XC-100 was not one of their own, reaction was mixed. "There was the inevitable sourness and snarling over my being chosen for the job," writes Waterton.

But the reason was simply that I was by far the most experienced jet pilot in the Group at that time. I had flown hundreds of hours in jets, single and twin-engined, and knew the Rolls-Royce Avons fitted initially in the CF-100. . . . An additional factor may well have been a political one: to boost national pride by enabling the Group (Hawker-Siddeley Group) to say that Canada's first completely home produced jet fighter was initially flown by a Canadian born pilot.

Don Rogers and Mike Cooper-Slipper, A. V. Roe's own test pilots, were in the process of receiving jet training on the Vampire. And Rogers was preparing to take over the pilot duties with the Avro Jetliner. "It was no skin off my nose that Waterton was here," recalls Rogers. "I was quite happy to have a qualified pilot." The feeling was reciprocal. Calling Don Rogers "one of the best handlers of aircraft he ever met," Waterton paid him the ultimate pilot's compliment by saying he "had a nice pair of hands."

Mike Cooper-Slipper, A. V. Roe's other test pilot, recalls a much different feeling about Waterton's coming in. "He acted as if he was a white knight here to show the Canadians how to fly their own plane."

In the fall of 1949 Waterton began his study of the CF-100.

I didn't even know what the CF-100 looked like at this point, so Dobson got me to meet some of the sub-contractors on the thing. I looked at some drawings and studied its aerodynamics . . . .

And so I flew to Canada in December, 1949, the country I had left eleven years before . . . . At Toronto's Malton aerodrome, I was met by Don Rogers and Edgar Atkin, at the time, Avro Canada's Chief Engineer . . . . Within an hour I was in the hangar looking over my new charge.

I liked the new plane—although she was by no means ready for me. She was a big plane, her twin engines close into the fuselage—exactly as I had wanted Gloster's to do with the Meteor. The CF-100 had a decidedly Germanic appearance.

While the CF-100 was being prepared for flight, I busied myself learning all I could about her—structure, controls, electrics, hydraulics, fuel system, pneumatics, and so on. I studied wind tunnel reports, calculations of expected performance and aerodynamic behaviour.

The prototype would soon be ready to fly, and John Frost wanted it to look good. He chatted with Dick Smallman-Tew, who had a reputation for being artistic in a practical way.

"What colour should we paint the fighter, that will be both distinctive and different?" Frost asked him.

"If you had an expensive automobile, like a Rolls-Royce, what colour would it be?"

"Black, probably."

"That's right. Only because it's long and thin and wicked looking, give it a white lightning flash to show it off."

Smallman-Tew had a scale model of the fighter painted that way.

It looked good, so that's the way the two prototype aircraft were painted.

—*John Frost*

In the early weeks of 1950, in preparation for his first flight on the CF-100, Waterton went up several times with A. V. Roe test pilots Don Rogers and Mike Cooper-Slipper to familiarize himself with the layout at Malton and the surrounding countryside as well as the location of other airfields.

I ground-ran the CF-100's engines, worked her hydraulics, and called for one or two changes in cockpit layout. To my delight, . . . the alterations were made expeditiously and without argument. I liaised amiably with the civil airport's flying control staff and the RCAF personnel involved in the project.

I had no personal doubts about the CF-100's success. She looked right and seemed right. There would certainly be troubles, but teething problems are common to all aircraft. It was clear that I would have to "sell" the 'plane as well as fly her, for the critics and weak-of-faith would not understand the ramifications of experimental work with its inevitable setbacks. There was pressure to get the aircraft in the air before the end of 1949, but it could not be done. Faces dropped, and morale was low. When I saw the aircraft at the beginning of December, I doubted whether she'd be ready in four months. But this was Toronto, not Gloucestershire, and on the evening of January 17, 1950, I commenced taxiing trials.

For John Frost, the situation had now reached the same pitch that Jim Floyd had faced with his Jetliner five months earlier. Frost would follow the taxiing aircraft in a car, watching through binoculars. During the high-speed taxiing test, with the nose off the ground, he caught one minor item which could have been troublesome. The nose wheel door, which opened backward towards the tail, was trying to close. He had calculated that the natural push of air would hold the door open, but the airflow was, instead, sucking it shut, so that in the air, the nose wheel would be trying to come up against a partially closed door. Right then and there Frost and Atkin sketched on the back of an envelope the changes that would be necessary to make the door lock open until the nose wheel came up. It wouldn't be the first impromptu redesign session the aircraft would go through.

We literally designed and redesigned parts of that plane many times on whatever scrap of paper happened to be handy right on the spot.

—Geoff Grossmith

I formed a deep respect for Avro Canada's aerodynamicist [Jim Chamberlin]. Unlike some others of the breed, he would tell me what I could expect from the plane—and was invariably right . . . . [John Frost was] very much the keen English public school boy type. Here was another delightful contrast to England, where I was never able to find a designer with spare time enough to fly in his own creation . . . .
    The taxiing trials on 18101 [as the first XC-100 was numbered] went off better than those of any prototype I handled. I beat up the runways, down wind, into wind, and across wind, at increasing speeds, stopping only for examination of the brakes or to allow an airliner to take-off or land. Then I tested control effectiveness at near take-off speeds. I could position the nose where I wished,

and the elevators were O.K. The rudder was satisfactory, and the pressure on the stick told me the ailerons were responding. The brake plates glowed red in the gathering dusk, due to stopping at high speed. After one sortie of about 55 minutes, I was satisfied—most unusual for me. There were some minor adjustments to be made, and a thorough inspection was needed, for I had deliberately bounced the plane over rough ground to "shake things up." But all in all, 18101 seemed an excellent job of work.

Nothing in the aircraft business matches the day when the aircraft makes its first flight, the day when all the "safe" testing ends and the "unknowns" begin. The culmination of everyone's plans, hopes, and fears all come together the moment a prototype aircraft leaves the ground. The first flight of the CF-100, was no exception.

January 19 was cold and bright, the wind blowing almost straight down the runway: ideal conditions for a maiden flight. The hangar was an agitated, nervous, excited, confident confusion of activity as final inspections and checks were made . . . . I was feeling a bit twitchy, wondering if I'd remembered everything and knowing that, despite satisfactory ground trials, the plane's performance in the air was still an enigmatic question mark.

All the employees of A. V. Roe and Malton Airport left their work and went out to watch the first CF-100 take off. The RCAF, government officials, and the press were there en masse, and the highway was jammed with parked cars.

Acceleration was tremendous, and in less than 500 yards, we lifted cleanly from the runway. I throttled back, and at 140 knots, climbed to 500 feet . . . . I gently braked the wheels and pressed the up button to raise the undercarriage. But, as on all my first flights in prototypes, part of the machinery had gone wrong—the button did not want to be pressed home.

I was in the control tower. The gear wouldn't retract and there was too much float. And all I could hear was Waterton yelling, "Settle you old sod! Settle!"

—Jack Millie

On that type of undercarriage installation, an electrical ground lock was fitted. When the weight of the plane was on its legs, to prevent the pilot accidentally raising the undercarriage, a switch was fitted which required forty pounds pressure to work—as against a three to five pound pressure when the plane was airborne. When the aircraft took to the air, this safety switch should have been automatically released. To override the switch was to ignore that something was wrong. This, I knew, had been done on another aeroplane, resulting in a belly landing. So, I left things as they were.

I flew 18101 for forty minutes at up to 5,000 feet and 180 knots, testing airbrakes, flaps, controls, turning, and getting the "feel" of the aircraft's general flying qualities. There was nothing to worry about: she seemed a sound design . . . . I came in on a straight approach. The plane was as steady as a rock, and touched down at about 100 miles an hour within the first 150 yards of runway. We stopped with smooth ease within 600 yards of the start of the runway. For a first flight, I was well satisfied.

We were all a little disappointed at first flight because we all wanted to see more, but with the undercarriage not retracting, Waterton was restricted as to what he could do.

—Jack Millie

The brass, sweating it out on the ground, is always rather pathetic at such times, looking at you with spaniel-eyes, pleading to be told the best, terrified they'll hear the worst.

They were all standing around with their mouths open waiting to hear the good news. "Well," I said calmly, "it flies."

Roy Dobson came over to Canada at the end of January to see the CF-100 in flight. Waterton, taking the plane up for only the third time, decided to treat Dobson to a performance.

Like dogs, 'planes usually bark before they bite; like horses, they twitch before they kick or buck; like many boxers, they telegraph their punches. This is transmitted in many ways and a test pilot must learn to recognize even subtle variations in feel, sound, vibration and smell. Not only recognize them, but must know how to act, for it is truer of experimental flying than of anything else to say that there are only two kinds of people: the quick and the dead . . . .

We ran into trouble. Quite simply, I "bent" the aeroplane . . . . I did a mild beat-up. Nothing elaborate, just high and low speed flying, with rolls and tight turns.

Bob Johnson was a member of the ground crew that day as a somewhat shaken Waterton brought the fighter back to the airfield.

Bill lands the aircraft and says to my foreman, Eric Peckam, "You better have a look around the cowlings, something went off with one hell of a bang up there." All the cowlings were pulled away, all stripped, which meant the wings had flexed too much. So Eric said, "Just push them up so nobody can see them and keep the people as far away as possible!"

—*Bob Johnson*

The plane was carefully examined. It was quite obvious that the dip in the main spar was the root of the wing's flexing. After this, the plane was allowed only gentle handling while Frost tried to figure out how to solve the problem. Although not panicking, he was concerned enough to go along with Waterton on the aircraft's eighth flight.

What I feared was happening—the centre section spar with the bends in the top boom made it locally very shallow and, therefore, more flexible at this point than the rest of the wing. This was also the point of highest bending, so that local deflections were large.

It wasn't a question of strength, just deflection; the spar was deflecting upwards under load, and the fairing of the nacelle to which it was attached, being relatively stiff, could not get out of the way. The result was the fairing had to buckle. All prototype aircraft have some problems come to light during test flying, but this worried me, considerably.

—*John Frost*

Putting right the cause of the CF-100's "bending" progressed slowly, for the firm did not want to take risks. The second prototype, 18102, was almost ready for its first test flight, so the first two production models (18103, 18104), were stripped down in the experimental department and studied. The conclusion was that more reinforcing should be done on the main spar.

Apart from this, the aircraft was behaving well, and at the company, there was a tendency to pretend that the buckles were of no consequence, since it was evident that only secondary structure was in trouble—the strength of the main load-carrying members was not in doubt. I was not nearly so complacent.

—*John Frost*

Reinforcement of the main spar was done by adding more doubler plates to the upper boom, and although this increased the weight, it seemed to Waterton to have the desired effect.

When she was back in the air, the CF-100 gave every promise of a fine top performance. Rates of climb, level speeds and Mach numbers seemed to be above expectations. Without elaborate tests and equipment, our figures had to await confirmation, but the plane would fly rings round an escorting Vampire, despite the best efforts of that aircraft. The CF-100's qualities showed during a trip to Washington in May . . . .

The purpose of the flight to Washington was to show the plane to the Americans . . . . I felt privately that if the Americans were sufficiently interested, they could have come to Canada instead of Avro's taking the plane to Washington. I suspected, further, that the Yanks did not propose buying anyway, but wanted to sample the Canadian fighter's features and performance for themselves . . . .

The Americans were, I thought, rather offhand to the Canadian Air Force Chiefs. My blood boiled to see the way they were treated as second-rate, poor relations and the Canadians unfortunately lacked that air of down-the-nose patronage with which the seediest, down-at-heel Englishman can successfully squelch that type of ostentatious boor . . . .

I aligned the plane along the runway—one the Americans did not use for jets because they considered it too short. But the CF-100 did not need a long take-off, and made them duck as it screamed over their heads to start a performance with which no American plane of its class could hope to compete.

But how impressed were the Americans afterwards when they went over the plane with a fine tooth comb? They weren't buying.

During the demonstration, the mid-rib section between the wings and the tail cracked. When the test pilot brought the plane down, he was so shaken that he refused to fly the plane home. So the compay had the plane brought back under canvas on the back of a railway flat car.

—Geoff Grossmith

By July, 1950, the second prototype was finished and ready to fly. After Waterton tested it out, he took up F/L Bruce Warren, an RCAF test pilot whose later involvement with 18102 will never be forgotten.

No story about Waterton and the CF-100 would be complete without recounting the time he almost landed the aircraft with its wheels up. "They had changed around the cockpit sequence," recalls Waterton.

The flap controls had been altered in the cockpit and as I came in, I was concentrating so hard on getting the changed procedure right, that I neglected to lower my wheels. This would have meant a belly landing . . . .

Fortunately, one of the company radio trucks was out on the runway that day with radio operator Jack Cuddy on board. When he saw the aircraft coming in, he screamed into the mike, "Bill, Bill! Pull her up! Pull her up!"

I looked like a real shit. Ex-Avro people are always bringing that story up.

—Bill Waterton

Following the American demonstration, Waterton took the fighter to an air show in Toronto later in the year, but it continued to have problems at the wing-to-spar joint even after the extra reinforcing.

While pulling up into the vertical climb of a loop, I heard a violent crack: a sharp thunderclap of sound clearly audible above the engine and wind noise. Something had gone—but what? I smartly rolled out at the top of the loop, ready to head for open spaces and bale out. Nothing drastic seemed to have occurred, however, for the plane flew on without further trouble. But I had the wind up and wasn't taking chances. I cut short the display and came in. The crack, we discovered, had been caused by the rupture of metal: the skin of the wing and centre section had, again, split— and this time worse than ever.

Like a cold, bitter winter, Bill Waterton had been around for too long. As dedicated as he was to the aircraft itself, there were many people anxious to see him go. Bob Johnson and test pilot Mike Cooper-Slipper felt that Waterton was far too protective of the flawed aircraft, like an anxious parent of a disabled child, reluctant to let anyone else near it, and that this slowed up development.

Waterton put the CF-100 program back six months. And when we finally got the plane away from him, we found an awful lot wrong with it.

—Mike Cooper-Slipper

We did not treat him in the lofty manner which he thought he should enjoy. He was a prima donna and got under our skin a little.

—Fred Smye

On February 7, 1951, Waterton shook John Frost's hand, climbed on a plane in the middle of the night, and returned to England. Other than Frost, nobody from A. V. Roe went to the airport to see him off.

And, like the dashing hero leaving behind a broken heart, Waterton left behind a broken airplane.

By December, 1949, people started to notice a change in Winnett Boyd. They would ask him questions, and he wouldn't, or couldn't, answer. He himself would admit that he wasn't concentrating. By December, 1949, Boyd was suffering from mental illness.

According to some estimates, 25 per cent of all Canadians, at one time or another, suffer bouts of mental depression, instability, or fatigue—moments when the ability to absorb strain is overwhelmed by too much of it. This was true of Winn Boyd that cold winter of 1949/50. In February, Paul Dilworth ordered him to take a vacation.

> *Boyd took an extended vacation and came back in reasonably good shape. In his absence, we had separated the design activity from the development activity, and we were attempting to get more effective engineering activity. I wanted him to head up the design of new and advanced projects and leave the bulwark of the developmental design to someone else and transfer the development test responsibility to Doug Knowles.*
>
> *—Paul Dilworth*

In other words, take some of the pressure off Boyd. The difficulty was, however, that Dilworth was almost in as bad shape as Boyd. Here they were, two men desperately trying to hold on, and basically in no shape to do so. People wondered who would be the first to go, Boyd or Dilworth. It was Boyd. Boyd's temper was the stuff of legends at A. V. Roe, especially near the end. Joe Turner recalls a time in Boyd's office where he found him throwing furniture and books all over the place simply because a part he had ordered for one of his engines hadn't yet arrived.

> *Before the engines ran, very few people had anything to do with us. I was free to work as I pleased. . . . I made all the decisions. After the engines ran, it was a whole new ball game.*
>
> *—Winnett Boyd*

In the autumn of 1950, Boyd was attempting to purchase an afterburner for the Orenda from a company in the United States. In the past, this was a relatively easy thing to do; he phoned the company, put in the order, got the part, and paid the bill. But in Boyd's "leave of absence," the company had hired a purchasing agent who turned out to be one of the fools Boyd didn't suffer. He refused Boyd's request and all hell broke loose.

Boyd was the smartest guy on the whole property. He designed those engines by himself, but when it got around to making them, everyone in the shop said they couldn't deal with him.

I sweated over the decision for days. Finally one day I went down to the plant and called Winn over and said, "Winn, I've got to fire you because it's either you or everybody else, and I've got no choice.

—Fred Smye

Smye said to me, just before I left, "Winn, we're going to publicize your work as A. V. Roe accomplishments and your name will be removed from everything as far as we're concerned." And from that day, I was never invited to any company milestone occasions.

—Winnett Boyd

Then, we had a board meeting. I wanted to arrange a very generous settlement, and proposed it. Bickell raised blue murder. I said, "Well, Mr. Bickell, if it hadn't been for that one man, you wouldn't be sitting there talking about the subject. He's the key to this whole company, that one man."

—Fred Smye

Boyd got his settlement. He left December 24, 1950.

Although Winnett Boyd had left A. V. Roe at the end of 1950, he remained in contact with the gas turbine division. He was naturally interested in the progress on the engines.

The Orenda, like the Chinook, had its normal allotment of development problems. The first three experimental engines ran for a total of nearly 2,000 hours with little more than a few modest modifications. But the first close-to-production Orenda came off its test bed with a cracked ninth-stage compressor blade. In the experimental engines, there had been trouble with the seventh-and eighth-stage blades, but never the ninth. There are nearly 2,000 blades in the Orenda, and the blades are the most intricate part of a turbojet. The blades are subject to specifications finer than those of a watch part, and a variation of even a thousandth of an inch in one blade can affect performance.

After Boyd left, I heard a lot of the problems. There were problems with blade vibration, and we had to get someone in from Hawker-Siddeley on this. We went through umpteen changes to solve blade vibration, cracking, and fatigue.

One of the earlier problems we had was when we were waiting for the Orenda to clear flight test in an F-86 Sabre at Edwards Air Force Base in California. A stubb shaft on a turbine came off when they tried to lift the disc in the shop—the big turbine disc with all of its blades had been cracked and we began to doubt the whole forging process that went into them.

—Paul Dilworth

I was quite disturbed about the Orenda because it was a higher pressure ratio, and also I'd deviated from some of Haswell's recommendatons and I realized we could have trouble here . . . . I was disturbed by the single-stage turbine. It was over-worked. After issuing the data to the drawing office, I immediately designed a two-stage turbine for the Orenda. I knew I could never sell this idea to Boyd. He used to always say that a two-stage turbine was much too complicated.

—Harry Keast

Avro's test pilots had some early concerns about the engines as well. Mike Cooper-Slipper, flying the Lancaster test bed, concluded that the Orenda as it then stood was far too difficult to handle above 15,000 feet, and doubted it would be used in combat aircraft. Don Rogers felt the same way after flying the Lancaster test bed in the Toronto Flying Club airshow—the plane would not be satisfactory in combat aircraft.

The early Orendas did not have a very efficient flow control unit on them. The pilot had to very carefully adjust the fuel control with the throttle and if you were just a little fast, you would over-fuel the engine and have what is called a compressor stall where you get vibrations and shaking.

—Don Rogers

The "performance" of an aircraft refers to how high and how fast it can fly whereas performance in jet engines means thrust—the number of pounds of boost the engine produces at maximum rpm. Although the Orenda, like the Rolls-Royce Avon, was designed to produce 6,500 pounds thrust, many of the pre-production versions, although able to sustain long, uninterrupted runs, failed to reach that level. It was this point, the argument over whether they did or did not achieve a consistent 6,500-pound thrust, that made enemies of Winnett Boyd and Harry Keast.

Harry was the most likeable guy; we got along beautifully. But Harry was guilty of distorting the facts about the performance of the Orenda in the early days.

An advertisment appeared for A. V. Roe/Orenda Engines which pointed out that originally the Orenda only developed 5,500 pounds thrust and by a great development effort on behalf of the company and its engineers, they got it up to 6,500 pounds thrust. This was because they were talking about the first production engines and how they had to struggle to get the production engines back to the performance we had achieved with the development engines.

So I wrote to Harry and said, Harry, this advertisment is misleading. You know as well as I do that the first Orenda produced almost 6,700 pounds thrust . . . the first Orenda was the best one we ever had.

—Winnett Boyd

No way, no way. I crossed swords with Boyd on this. The Orenda specification was originally 5,500 pounds thrust. The RCAF wanted 6,500 pounds based on the Avon, but this was before I was on the scene. The principals in the company thought this was a very high target and lowered it to 5,500 pounds . . . with an increase to 6,500 by development.

—Harry Keast

Harry wrote back a letter to me that said, in effect, I must have been mistaken, that this really didn't happen at all. I'll never speak to him again. To me this was complete intellectual dishonesty.

—Winnett Boyd

Winn assuredly deserves credit as the prime architect for the Orenda design, and for a very great proportion of its detail. This, I feel, has earned him unchallengeable right to credit for the major role in that engine's design, structure, mechanical, thermodynamic and, to a degree, aerodynamic design.

Harry, however, was the quiet genius to whom major credit is due for the engine's basic aerodynamic design—both compressor and two-stage turbine—and for its evolutionary or developmental thermodynamic performance.

Doug Knowles directed the development program. It was he and his team who sweated out all the many bugs in the original design . . . [and] turned the Orenda from a truly great basic design into a fully operational and reliable fighter aircraft engine—the very best of its time.

—Paul Dilworth

On April 5, 1951, the CF-100 took its first lives. Prototype 18102 was lost in a crash near London, Ontario, killing the plane's pilot and observer.

After Bill Waterton had returned to England in February, the RCAF, in an attempt to get closer to the program, loaned the company a number of pilots. One of them was a young flight lieutenant named Bruce Warren who had been up with Waterton in the second prototype. Warren had been a Spitfire pilot during the war and was a recent graduate of the Empire Test Pilots' School. His observer that April day was Robert Ostrander from A. V. Roe's flight test department.

On the day of the crash, the aircraft had been involved in a high-speed flight test. The idea was to take the plane to 36,000 feet, check in over Kingston, do a high speed run to Malton, check in again, do another high speed run to London, check in once more, then return to Malton. A simple test under most circumstances.

They checked in at Kingston all right, and he checked in over Malton and that was the last report we got. We knew he had plenty of fuel and that if his radio had gone out, then they'd head for home. But nothing showed up. Then we got a call from Trans-Canada Air Lines that one of their pilots had seen a black aircraft in an almost vertical dive heading for the ground.

Well, then we got in touch with the OPP [Ontario Provincial Police] in London who told us they had had some calls from people saying they'd seen a plane crash and it was then we knew it was one of ours.

—Bob Johnson

When we realized the plane was overdue we had a real quick meeting, and Wally Parish, who was the chief inspector, and I went down to London, nearly losing our own lives taking off in an air force plane. When we arrived we went to search the area and found this field where it had plowed in. It was almost unbelievable, the size of the crater where the airplane hit. I would think that it would be almost a hundred feet in diameter. They found pieces of the engines three and four hundred feet away.

—Ernie Alderton

It had landed in a bog, almost vertical, and what had exploded out was hanging in the trees around the crater. The main aircraft had gone right into the bog and the only thing sticking out was the tail. Our idea was to get cranes there and pull the thing out but by the time we got the cranes there, the plane had sunk out of sight.

—Bob Johnson

The crater was there but we couldn't see the airplane, so we brought in a local contractor with a steam shovel to dig. We found a right hand and a left hand and we had to prove to the coroner there were two people in that airplane. Finally, about a couple of days later we found another hand.

—*Ernie Alderton*

Jim Floyd was called in from Malton to identify one of the hands with a ring on it. It proved to be that of the observer, Robert Ostrander.

When we started down for the airplane, we finally found the tail but we didn't dig any further; too much quicksand, so we had to abandon it.

—*Ernie Alderton*

The RCAF immediately started an inquiry into the crash and put together an investigation team that included employees of A. V. Roe, people from Rolls-Royce, suppliers of the Avon engine, and from Dowty, who had manufactured the hydraulics. The investigation went on for months with no conclusion.

Then, one day, one of the air force investigators was sitting at Bruce Warren's desk, and he's talking on the phone and pulling the desk drawer out and sorting through there and he found this little tube. The tube was one inch long and about an eighth of an inch in diameter with a little hole through it, and he stopped what he was doing and said, "What in the world is this?"

Well, his final conclusion was that it was a piece out of Warren's oxygen mask. Somebody had seen the pilot cleaning his own mask that day as he was talking on the phone. And the investigator came to the conclusion that Warren had left this piece off his mask.

—*Ernie Alderton*

We think Warren must have passed out. Ostrander may have been all right, but he couldn't do anything because in the prototypes, you could only jettison the canopy from the front seat, so we never did really find out whether the observer was conscious in the dive or not.

—*Bob Johnson*

Regardless, the company felt it had its culprit—lack of oxygen. S/L Joe Schultz, a flight lieutenant at the time, would become one of the first three RCAF pilots to fly the CF-100 when it went into squadron use. For twelve years, he was head of Flight Safety for the RCAF.

There was no malfunction in the aircraft that I know of. If the pilot had suffered anoxia by leaving out a part of his mask, this would have affected him and not the observer . . . . This is still very sensitive to some people.

—*S/L Joe Schultz*

The late summer and early fall of 1951 were turning out to be the most difficult of times for the young company. The strain was evident in the eyes of Fred Smye. Working seven days a week, usually from seven-thirty in the morning till at least eight o'clock at night, A. V. Roe's assistant general manager was looking more and more every day like he would go the way of Winnett Boyd. His 6-foot-plus frame, often stooped with weariness, seemed to be everywhere, in and out of offices, on the tarmac, always there to solve a problem, put out a fire, or run an errand.

Walter Deisher seldom left his office, becoming more and more incommunicative. J. P. Bickell, the company's popular board chairman, had died in New York August 22. Winnett Boyd, one of their best and brightest, had been gone for six months, leaving a void they were having trouble filling. Paul Dilworth, although valiantly struggling to run the gas turbine division, was still not fully recovered from his breakdown. Edgar Atkin, John Frost, and Jim Chamberlin were still at odds struggling with the design and weight problems on the CF-100 which was already three months behind in delivery to the RCAF.

At night, Smye would lie awake for hours, his mind stewing over the Jetliner he couldn't sell, C. D. Howe's growing impatience with the CF-100 program, and Walter Deisher's self-imposed isolation. During the darker moments, Smye would get out of bed in the middle of the night, drive from his home in Oakville to the plant, and stand for hours in one of the Orenda test cells. Listening to the engine run gave him some degree of comfort.

I had thirteen loyal people working for me, and every one of them knew we weren't doing well as a company.

—*Fred Smye*

But by summer's end, 1951, Smye came to the realization that if he didn't take some action, and soon, his beloved company might soon disintegrate around him. He had to do something about Walter Deisher, and most of the managers at A. V. Roe were rapidly coming to the same conclusion: Walter Deisher had to go. Paul Dilworth sums up the feeling at the time:

Right from the start we had misgivings about Walter. The man never really knew what he was doing. And because Smye didn't have a clear executive position—more like Dobson's right-hand-man—this made it even more awkward for Deisher. He'd done a good job at Fleet [Aircraft] but it was a different game at Malton.

—*Paul Dilworth*

Finally, on October 11, 1951: "Manager of Avro Reported Quitting," said the headlines in the Montreal *Gazette*, "as a result of internal strife, political interference and government indecision." Officially, Deisher was leaving because of "ill-health" but for all intents and purposes, according to Jim Hornick, Walter Deisher was simply bought off. "The idea was that he and his wife would go to Mexico until the furor over his dismissal had died down. That way, he would be unavailable to all press people."

Part of this so-called "buy-off" involved Deisher's house, Briarcrest, an impressive Tudor-style mansion near Malton. The company bought the house and used it to accommodate visiting dignitaries, and for meetings. "In the end," said his secretary, "all Walter really cared about was his big car, his big house, and his electric train set."

The job of running A. V. Roe was really too much for poor Walter. He really knew bugger-all about airplanes . . . . He was from the bi-plane era, for God's sake. Just how bad he was for us will never be known.

—*Fred Smye*

But what to do about a replacement. Dobson had to be careful not to make the same mistake again, especially now. He had to find someone who would put Howe at his ease and restore his confidence in the company, someone Howe could trust, someone definitely Canadian, familiar with aircraft production in Canada, and who, in Smye's words, "would buy us insurance in the future."

"What about Fred Smye?" asked Dobson.

"If you put Smye in charge," replied Howe, "you'll kill him."

"Well, who do you have in mind?"

"Crawford Gordon of Defence Production."

10

REBIRTH: THE COMING OF CRAWFORD GORDON

The argument persists whether he was one of the greatest industrialists and business minds this country has produced or whether he was nothing more than a canny political cowboy who herded the imagination of an entire country into his corral of schemes and money-making junkets. Unfortunately, because of his short life, and because he did things in half the time it took everyone else, the jury is still out. One thing is certain—anyone who ever had anything to do with Crawford Gordon, men and women alike, never forgot him. They either hated him or they loved him.

Gordon was a very blunt, fuck-you, sort of person. Arrogant as hell in his operation of A. V. Roe. Unfortunately, he had no sense of self-preservation.

—Jim Hornick

He was a lot like E. P. Taylor, impatient and impetuous.

—Fred Smye

Like Fred Smye, Gordon was another of "Howe's boys," a Munitions and Supply man during the war. Born in Winnipeg on December 26, 1914, Gordon was the son of an executive with the Canadian Imperial Bank of Commerce; his mother was a survivor of the *Titanic*, having lost her father and brother on the ill-fated voyage. When his father opened the first Commerce branch in Jamaica, Crawford lived there for six years before moving to England and then to Toronto. To all his boyhood pals, he was known as Pik, short for pickaninny, probably a leftover from his Jamaican days.

He attended Appleby College in Oakville and took a B.Sc. at McGill University in Montreal, graduating inconspicuously in the class of 1936. In November of that year, he met Mary Tearney.

He wouldn't leave me alone. From the first time we met, he wouldn't let up on me. He was so, so irresistible . . . . I liked his style.

—*Mary Gordon*

His irresistibility would become his trademark. Gordon was anything but handsome, yet there was a certain charm. Fred Smye's secretary, Betty Moore, walked into Gordon's office unannounced one day and found Gordon and a young woman "in the most compromising of positions" on top of Gordon's desk.

A male could never understand this kind of charm but it just about dropped the pants off every lady he met.

—*Jim Hornick*

Gordon proposed to Mary Tearney after a two-week courtship and they were married in September, 1937. Already, it seemed, Crawford Gordon was a young man in a hurry. Just before the wedding, Canadian General Electric offered Gordon a job in their auditing department at a monthly salary of $125.

I was on special assignment for awhile. Then I went to the head office in Schenectady for a two-year training course. When I came back to Canada, I was put on the internal auditing staff. That embraced a lot of jobs: market research, production costs and profits.

—*Crawford Gordon, Jr.*

When war broke out, Gordon asked General Electric to lend him to the Canadian government, specifically to C. D. Howe and his newly created Department of Munitions and Supply.

Crawford worshipped C. D. Howe and wanted more than anything the chance to work for him.

—Mary Gordon

There were always pictures of Howe and Louis St. Laurent in the house. When Howe died, my father went into mourning for a week. He was the only man my father ever revered.

—Crawford Gordon III

One day, Gordon got a telephone call from Ottawa, and for the duration of the war, worked with the Department of Munitions and Supply as director general of organization and assistant co-ordinator of defence production.

Working with Howe in this relatively senior position was an ideal "teething ring" for Gordon; he was able to get an inside look at Canadian industry and witness first-hand wartime shortages "caused by our reliance on others for the basics of our aircraft and other industries."

At war's end, Gordon stayed on with Howe for another year as director general of industrial reconversion in the peacetime Department of Reconstruction, where he was involved with the problems of companies converting from wartime to peacetime production. Early in 1947, he returned once again to private business as president of the English Electric Company and executive vice-president of the parent John Inglis Company.

On Gordon's departure from government, Howe wrote that Gordon had been a "tower of strength" to him and recommended him for the Order of the British Empire which he received in 1946.

In 1949, Canada joined NATO and with this new association came the responsibilities of maintaining and equipping an up-to-date armed force. But Canada's armed forces in 1949 were in a state of neglect similar to that of 1939—undermanned and underequipped. Barely fifty thousand service personnel were spread throughout the army, navy, and air force, standing on guard with equipment ten years old.

To refurbish the forces and honour the NATO commitment, C. D. Howe initiated the creation of the Department of Defence Production (DDP) in 1950.

Basically, the DDP was made up of three branches: materials, production, and purchasing. Each was to have its own co-ordinator responsible to Howe. For his production co-ordinator, Howe wanted Crawford Gordon. "Am organizing new defence production department," he cabled to Gordon in England on February 5, 1951, "and most anxious to obtain your services as Director of Production." On March 15, 1951 Gordon accepted.

"Gordon is a hard-hitting blunt businessman," said *Saturday Night* magazine on hearing of the appointment. "He's getting a little thin on top, his face is rugged, but still youthful and full of vigour. He looks no more than his thirty-eight years. Everything about him suggests the phrase: No Fooling."

Gordon suddenly found himself responsible for a three-year, $5-billion defence budget allotment divided among eight areas: defence construction, small industries, electronics, mechanical transport, machine tools, guns and ammunition, shipbuilding, and aircraft. Gordon's first objective was the production of home-based military aircraft and the problems with Canada's aircraft companies.

Because of the government's investment in the CF-100 program, A. V. Roe Canada was the priority. Initially, the DDP had asked for the CF-100's to be delivered at the rate of five per month. With the advent of the Korean War the figure was upped to twenty-five per month. As for the Orenda power plant, the original twenty-per-month request had been upped to a hundred.

A. V. Roe Canada was so far behind in its deliveries that if the Korean War had begun in 1953 instead of 1950, the company might have been on target. Management problems, aircraft redesign problems, engine production problems, resources committed to the unsellable Jetliner, and the simple fact that A. V. Roe's expertise was primarily design and development and not production, had seriously undermined Howe's early enthusiasm for the company.

By summer's end, 1951, Crawford Gordon in his new position was looking at A. V. Roe in a way not unlike "the farmer who kept a family cow on which he lavished considerable care and attention. The farmer, oddly enough, kept accounts, and his affection for the cow dwindled somewhat when he found that her milk was *costing him* 75 cents a quart." A. V. Roe needed a take-charge person, someone who could turn it all around.

In the beginning, Dobson was lukewarm to the idea of having Crawford Gordon come in. Gordon had been "rough as hell" on him over the CF-100. Nonetheless, a deal was struck—Gordon's salary would be $35,000; in addition, the company would take over the mortgage on his Forest Hill home in Toronto. Fred Smye, for his part, was happy to have someone, finally, that Howe approved of.

"Arms Production Chief Takes Over Job at AVRO," proclaimed the *Globe and Mail* (October 12, 1951). "He will take charge of the Avro organization on Monday, a year almost to the day since the company received its first substantial defence contract, one calling for 124 aircraft for the RCAF. Since then, not one has been delivered."

"My job at A. V. Roe," said Gordon when his appointment became official, "will be to organize, deputize and supervise. For nearly six years we've been designing, planning, testing and carrying on intricate research. We've achieved very ambitious objectives: two Canadian jet engines, a Jetliner, a Canadian jet fighter. The next step will be to produce them in quantity."

Within days Gordon moved to take control. On November 2 he called Dilworth and Smye into his office to discuss reorganizing the company, and on November 8 he ordered a halt to the building of the second C-102 prototype and the closing of the New York sales office which had opened eighteen months earlier to promote American sales of the Jetliner.

Pressure was on to get the 100 and the Orenda out. There was one company and one management for the whole thing and it was my opinion that to take the Jetliner and put it into production with all the other things, we'd screw up the whole works.

—Fred Smye

Dobson had founded the company on the record of its wartime activity; that's where, in Gordon's opinion, its future lay—with military aircraft.

Gordon brought with him his secretary of six years. Like many women who crossed Gordon's path, she was very much in love with her boss. They had been having an affair for years.

On October 17, 1951, A. V. Roe Canada, with a sigh of relief, delivered the first production versions of the CF-100, Mk. 2, to the RCAF in a ceremony at Rockcliffe in Ottawa. It had taken the company five years to bring the plane from paper to delivery and no one was more pleased than C. D. Howe. "This aircraft, " he beamed, "is a notable Canadian achievement marking as it does a new milestone in Canada's industrial progress . . . a triumph of skill and ingenuity . . . . I am satisfied that Canada will lead all countries in the production of this type of aircraft."

"Five years is a short time for any country to produce from the planning stage to production a modern fighter aircraft," echoed A/M

Wilf Curtis, head of the RCAF since 1947. "Avro can be justly proud of its achievements."

"I don't believe the public at large has any appreciation of the difficulty of producing an aircraft and an engine at the same time," added A/V/M McGill.

The public would soon know just how difficult for, just one month later, the RCAF would return all ten aircraft to A. V. Roe for what the company called "structural modifications." These modifications, while thought to be minor at first, really necessitated an entire redesign of the aircraft; a redesign, said one engineer, of the magnitude of "taking all the bones out of a chicken, altering some of them, then putting them all back in."

The original contract between the government and A. V. Roe Canada for the CF-100 called for the company to produce 400 aircraft, and this had been upped to 718 complete aircraft and 738 spare engines. This did not include the ten pre-production aircraft. The 718 planes were estimated by A. V. Roe to cost (cost plus 5 per cent) $360,000 per airframe and $60,000 per engine for a unit cost per copy of $420,000. With spare parts, publications, flight and maintenance manuals, tools, and other items, the entire CF-100 project would cost the Canadian government $544,500,000. Other estimates by writers Jim Hornick and Desmond M. Chorley put the cost of the plane at $700,000 and $1,000,000.

The idea was to produce twelve pre-production CF-100's—the original two black prototypes which were called Mk.1's, one Mk.2 single-control; four dual-controlled Mk.2's to assist in pilot training, four dual-controlled Mk.3 pre-delivery aircraft, and one hand-built, modified Mk.4.

Officially, the CF-100 was known as the Canuck. While nobody at A. V. Roe questioned the obvious patriotic connotations of the name, many felt it an unoriginal label for what they considered to be a revolutionary aircraft. John Frost wanted it to be called the Thunderbird. Because no one at A. V. Roe took to the name Canuck, everyone simply called it "the 100."

To this day, many ex-A. V. Roe personnel thought company president Walter Deisher had something to do with it since he had come from Fleet Aircraft, home of the famous Fleet Canuck trainer, but this wasn't so.

It was A/V/M Wilf Curtis that came up with the name. When I asked him why he told me he had named it after the Curtiss JN-4, the Canuck.

—*Jim Hornick*

The first Mark 2 flew on June 20, 1951, powered by company-built Orenda engines. A good number of these early aircraft were delivered to the RCAF's Central Experimental and Proving Establishment (CEPE) in Ottawa for testing, even prior to the official hand-over in October. Two of CEPE's pilots, Paul Hartman and E. L. "Shan" Baudoux, had flown the CF-100 a year before under the reluctant tutelage of Bill Waterton. The press was full of praise for Canada's new fighter at this point.

Canada is the bright spot in the North Atlantic Treaty picture. Next to this country, the Dominion will be the largest producer of aircraft for the NATO countries in the immediate future. Avro Canada's CF-100 all-weather fighter likely is the equal of anything on this side of the border and sometime this year should get into large scale production.

The Canuck is designed primarily for Canadian conditions. It is as versatile and invaluable in modern conditions as the Mosquito was in the last war. If we had enough Canucks, the air experts would be content to rely on them entirely for the defence of Canada.

At CEPE, the engineers and pilots predictably enough were running into the usual snags and problems found in pre-production aircraft. Nothing out of the ordinary occurred until one day, test aircraft 18104 landed after a routine test flight showing worse than ever the same skin wrinkling problems at the junction of the wing and the engine nacelle that had first been discovered when Waterton tested the aircraft. The continuous assurances of Edgar Atkins's engineering department that this problem had been cured were obviously incorrect.

The RCAF took no chances, however, and returned all the aircraft to Malton; A. V. Roe promised to have them back in working order within six months. Although an attempt was made to return them to Malton as quietly as possible, word soon reached C. D. Howe in Ottawa and he was furious. "This letter is to advise you," he would write to the company in November, 1951,

that all work in connection with new development is to be suspended, at least until the problems involved in the production of airframes and engines now on order have been resolved and deliveries are being made at a satisfactory rate. Personnel and facilities that are now engaged in new development work should be directed to the redesign of the engines and airframes now on order to improve machine ability or to overcome other production problems.

Members of the Opposition, sensing some political gains to be made over the CF-100 situation, invited reporter Jim Hornick, who was critical of A. V. Roe over the CF-100, to an off-the-record private meeting. Hornick had been indirectly associated with the CF-100 project almost from its inception. His daily work required that he keep informed, to the utmost degree possible for an interested layman, about all aspects of Canadian aviation activity. This led, inevitably, to the cultivation of close relationships with many of the key figures involved in striving to transform the trouble-ridden, experimental CF-100 into a production-line commodity.

Early in 1952 I was approached by two members of the Progressive Conservative Party, then sitting in Opposition in Ottawa, and asked to render a confidential, considered and detailed opinion of affairs on the Avro Plant. In common with other members of their Party, these men were becoming increasingly alarmed by the Liberal Government's seemingly prodigal support of a program which had yet to deliver a single, urgently needed operational aircraft.

A few months later, after I had indicated that my research had enabled me to form some fairly definite impressions, I was invited to Ottawa to discuss those impressions. In a private conference room at Rideau Club, across Wellington street from the House of Commons, I met members of the Conservatives' "shadow Cabinet." Presiding was George Drew, then the Party's national leader. Grouped along the table were perhaps a dozen others. They included Major General George R. Pearkes, Howard Green, Gordon Churchill, Douglas Harkness and James M. Macdonnell.

—*Jim Hornick*

Not long after the meeting, Douglas Harkness got to his feet in the House. "When the CF-100 was first test flown in January, 1950, over two years ago," he argued,

and when the first production orders were given in June, 1950, nearly two years ago, on each occasion there was a great deal of fanfare by the government. The impression was given to everyone in the country that the best long-range fighter in the world would start rolling off the assembly lines and going into service with RCAF squadrons almost immediately. That was nearly two years ago; today the RCAF has none of these CF-100 fighters. Last October, again with great publicity and great fanfare, one CF-100 was turned over to the RCAF. A few weeks later, it was taken back to Malton where it was manufactured and it is still there. The story is that it is undergoing minor changes and so on . . . . It would seem quite apparent that that machine should never have been turned over to the RCAF, and that if it was turned over, it should have been turned over for test purposes only, and without a whole lot of publicity leading people to believe that these great fighters, and I believe that they are great fighters, were rolling off the assembly line in great numbers, and that we were perfectly safe behind their cover . . . . We are not getting these aircraft and engines which we were led to expect two years ago, that we would be getting them in quantity, in fact, we were told that our squadrons would be equipped with them now. I do not think that there is any doubt that the government made a bad miscalculation in connection with these aircraft.

Fred Smye tried to deflect the daily criticisms C. D. Howe was receiving by defending his company's record. This aircraft, he pointed out, had taken some thirty-seven months from drawing board to delivery, and while some modifications might be necessary, that still bettered the British time by one month and the average American time by seven months. (Smye, however, did not take into consideration that Jack Millie had actually started work on the aircraft in the summer of 1945. This would increase the company's time from thirty-seven months to seventy-five months.)

"If there is no satisfactory solution of the present difficulties in sight within the next two or three weeks," Howe would write to the company in January of 1952, "we will have to consider abandoning the project. I am determined that if we can't get production as planned, we will get some other producer." Impatient as he was at the situation, Howe never really did know how bad things were with the CF-100 and A. V. Roe. "If we had told Howe," said Fred Smye years later, "he would have scrapped the CF-100 and the engine for sure." What bothered Howe more than anything was that he had gambled millions on inexperience, and now he couldn't do much about it.

Soon after Gordon's appointment, Edgar Atkin, number two on Fred Smye's hit list, was scheduled to go to England to meet with Hawker-Siddeley officials about possible solutions to fix the CF-100. Smye mistrusted Atkin, and he convinced Gordon that he and Joe Morley should follow Atkin to England, "to keep an eye on him."

Atkin's big failure was he was too stingy with information about how engineering was getting along. They would have gross mistakes . . . not mistakes as such, but the end result of their efforts was a dead loss . . . redesign after redesign would take place and they'd be months behind schedule and management was not told a thing. Atkin would not divulge anything to management, and this was really where the falling out between Smye and Atkin happened.

—Ron Adey

He couldn't see any time for us at all. He thought we [test pilots] were out to get him. He didn't think we were any more than a piece of hangar garbage. I remember three of us got together once and ganged up on him over the centre-spar thing in his office. We didn't like him and we wanted him to know it.

—Mike Cooper-Slipper

The day after their arrival in Manchester, Smye and Morley met with Jack Green, the key shop man at Hawker-Siddeley. They pulled no punches in talking of their feelings for Atkin and Deisher and the way A. V. Roe Canada was being run. A little later on, Green casually mentioned this conversation to Roy Dobson.

He [Dobson] couldn't understand why were were over here, and thought it ridiculous we couldn't solve our own technical problems by ourselves . . . . The real problem with the CF-100 was myself and my Canadian friends in the RCAF who were trying to torpedo Edgar Atkin.

I was shocked. I kept telling Dobson that I couldn't handle the situation at Malton any longer. We had to reorganize as a company. He disagreed and right there and then I decided to resign when I returned to Canada.

Well, Dobson didn't believe me, and when I returned to Canada, I walked into Crawford's office and said, "It's all yours, boy; I'm through!" And I told him that Dobson had blamed me for the CF-100 problems and said that I had engineered them with the air force as an attack against Atkin, and that I was fed up.

After Crawford had calmed me down, I told him I would stay on as head of the aircraft division provided neither himself nor Dobson would stick their nose in it, that it's all mine, no interference whatsoever. Until Gordon had gotten there, I had been putting all my time on the engine side because of Deisher and his donkeys running the aircraft side.

So, then I asked Gordon to take over the engine business—I was still executive vice-president of the company—and once he agreed, and I got his assurance of no interference, I said, "Phone Atkin and remove him, and phone Frost and remove him." Atkin because I didn't trust him, and Frost because of the "integrity of the design."

—Fred Smye

John Frost stayed with A. V. Roe Canada, and not long afterward set up a special projects section to develop the ground-cushion concept which resulted in the Avrocar. Atkin was temporarily given the title of "technical advisor" to Crawford Gordon. He formally resigned in August, 1952, when he joined Grumman Aircraft in New York.

It was no secret Fred Smye's real love was Jim Floyd's Jetliner. But despite his hope the Jetliner might one day sell, Smye knew full well that the company's life blood, its cash crop, its key to survival, lay with the CF-100.

Having lost complete faith in Edgar Atkin, Smye now turned to the only person he could truly rely on who also had the expertise, experience, and straightforwardness to give him the answers he needed on the CF-100—Stuart Davies at A. V. Roe in Manchester.

Without telling Dobson the full story, Smye asked to "borrow" Davies for a time to review the CF-100 program and provide some objective recommendations. When Davies arrived in Malton in late October, one of the CF-100's had already been returned from CEPE and was sitting in a hangar. Joe Schultz was the air force pilot who brought the plane home.

> *When I landed it at Malton, it was an interesting sight; rivets and things were hanging on to the bottom of the wings through the cracks. Engine nacelles scratched because the wings flexed. Engine bullits bent thirty degrees. Quite a mess.*

> *—S/L Joe Schultz*

It took only about two weeks for Davies to go over the aircraft. According to Smye, Davies recommended that they "burn it." "Burn what?" asked Smye. "Burn the plane, every bloody part of it. It's understressed. We haven't got time to build a new one, so go to Howe and tell him you can build Northrop Scorpions under licence."

Davies might as well have torn out Smye's heart. Gathering what was left of his composure, Smye quietly thanked Davies for his efforts but refused his recommendation.

> *I could not believe him. It would have been the end of the philosophy upon which the company was started and built. I felt there must be a better answer.*

> *—Fred Smye*

Smye's next move was to put Jim Floyd in charge of "fixing" the CF-100. Floyd immediately formed a "blitz group," putting one of his Manchester colleagues, Bob Lindley ("a wonderful trouble-shooter"), in charge. Lindley had worked on the York and the Tudor and, more recently, had been with Canadair. Later he would gain fame as the "guts of the Arrow program."

Lindley was another great ego; he was loud, sometimes abrasive, and had a voice that could cut cardboard. "You know what's wrong with you," he would shout on occasion, "you don't know how to toe the bloody line!"

Shortly after his transfer to the CF-100, Floyd remembers being introduced to C. D. Howe as the new works manager.

Fred Smye mentioned that I was the chief designer on the Jetliner. Howe turned to me and said, "I suggest that you forget that airplane and put your energy into getting the CF-100's out." I said nothing but my thoughts would have turned the room blue! This was the only time that I had ever met Howe, despite his tremendous influence throughout the course of the Jetliner project, and as I drove home that night, I couldn't help thinking how ironic it was that, after a dedicated team had worked their hearts out on the project for over five years, and produced that world-beating aircraft, all he could say was "forget it"—but then I never did understand politicians.

—Jim Floyd

To deal with the CF-100's faulty main spar, Lindley organized a team that became known as the "fix" section of the blitz group. To head this team, Lindley recruited Waclaw Czerwinski. Czerwinski had been involved with the Polish aircraft industry since 1933. He came to Canada in 1941 and worked as a project engineer on de Havilland's Mosquito project until 1946, when Edgar Atkin hired him for the Jetliner stress office. It was there that Lindley found him. Czerwinski would be the one to find the relatively simple solution to the CF-100's flexing wings.

Bob Lindley appointed me to the job because Atkin's position was very shaken by the discovery that the CF-100 was no good. We had always thought that the explosion Bill Waterton heard on his test flights was something starting to fail in the main spar.

—Waclaw Czerwinski

A thorough investigation of the CF-100's flexible spar then took place, and though it was now impossible to make it much stiffer, some more weight by the way of heavier top and bottom booms was added, together with a pin joint where the cowling arch was attached to the top boom of the spar. So, although the main spar was not prevented from flexing, due to the flexible pin joint the cowling could now flex with it.

—*John Frost*

I think the answer came in a plastic model of the structure centre section. It was messing around with that that provided the answer.

—*Guest Hake*

The spar work didn't take very long—about six weeks—but I did much more because there were other problems with the CF-100.

—*Waclaw Czerwinski*

These "other problems" were alluded to in an A. V. Roe report prepared for the RCAF:

The centre section spare rib failure on aircraft 18104 necessitated a certain amount of re-engineering to this particular component and the testing of specimens in order to clear this engineering as it pertained not only to the Mk.3 but to the first ten aircraft, as well. At the same time, a complete but rapid review was made on all of the structure, and it was found to be deficient in varying degrees in other components throughout the aircraft.

Stuart Davies' conclusion that the aircraft was understressed was starting to ring truer than ever. The aircraft, concluded Lindley and Floyd, would have to go through a major redesign.

I was under tremendous pressure over this. I was working all hours on the aircraft. Fred Smye was down just about every day during this time. The air force was aware that something wrong was going on but they were not aware of how the repair was being made. At the time, everyone was pessimistic. We all became very good at keeping secrets.

—*Waclaw Czerwinski*

Years later, Fred Smye claimed more than 4,300 changes were made in the CF-100 during this period. Jim Floyd puts the figure closer to 34,000. All in all, the fix took more than eight months from redesign of the aircraft to resumption of production. And then, there was the extra weight.

This must have cost another four hundred pounds. Four hundred pounds on the bare structure weight was a terrible penalty for the poor old bird to carry around all its life. How much better it could have been, if only this silly mistake had never been made.

—*John Frost*

For John Frost, the father of the aircraft, the situation was becoming unbearable. While as chief engineer Edgar Atkin was held mainly responsible for the centre spar, recalls Frost's friend Des Earl, a lot of the fingers were pointing to Frost himself.

Frost certainly felt he wasn't to blame. He tried his best to change it [the design], but Chamberlin wouldn't agree to moving the engine position [again], and Atkin made the decision that the design was too far along to make a change.

—*Des Earl*

In a company desperately looking for scapegoats over the CF-100, Frost and Chamberlin became prime targets. Fred Smye wanted to fire Frost because of his role in compromising "the integrity of the design," but it was probably Roy Dobson that stayed his hand.

For some years, Frost had been interested in vertical take-off vehicles; his desk was loaded with different models, and in 1950 he had interested the United States military in the concept. There was a distinct possibility that the Americans would provide funds for research and development if A. V. Roe would provide support and working space. Smye ended up agreeing to sponsor Frost in this endeavour.

Chamberlin, too, was moved aside but not entirely out of sight. It had become quite apparent by this time that few people could work with Jim Chamberlin, let alone understand him. *Nobody* could really work with Chamberlin. Jim Floyd recalls: "I would never have fired Jim Chamberlin . . . never." So the deal was to have him set up as a sort of oracle/genius, to whom anyone, no matter what they were working on, could go for advice. In this way, Chamberlin could still be a participant.

By the end of December, 1951, less than three months after Crawford Gordon had taken over A. V. Roe, the organization was already feeling the effects of his presence. Deisher was gone. Frost was totally out of the CF-100 project and now on his own in "special projects." Smye headed up the aircraft division, and Paul Dilworth the gas turbine division. Jim Floyd had replaced Edgar Atkin as chief engineer.

In January, 1952, Ron Adey, an engineer, was appointed as Gordon's assistant "to help him get oriented with the details of the organization without him running around himself." In the fall of 1951, Smye had drawn up a new structural plan for A. V. Roe in consultation with Price-Waterhouse. Adey now worked with Gordon in trying to implement some of the corporate and organizational recommendations outlined in Smye's study.

By the end of January, Gordon had compiled a list of essentials and priorities, not only for the CF-100, but for the future as well. The list reflected his tutelage under Howe and addressed both industrial techniques and human relations. The company was to be restructured. Because aircraft and engines were separate products with potentially separate markets and problems, Gordon wanted them to remain in separate divisions.

He concentrated on the organization of these new divisions, as he called them, and upgraded people to positions of responsibility where they could work with a minimum of interference, giving them appropriate titles and encouraging them to high objectives through various incentives. In a speech to the Canada Club he outlined his philosophy.

I cannot stress too strongly the necessity for understanding that the internal friction which is apparent in any large organization of capable executives, can only be kept to a minimum if there is complete understanding and application of the organization structure and authority. What is meant by "Management Teamwork" and how is it achieved? My definition is taken from the "Three Musketeers: "One for all and all for one." You may ask how this happy state of affairs is brought about? I believe by attention and action to ensure (1) proper organization, (2) appointment of well qualified personnel to key positions, (3) clear-cut definition of duties and responsibilities, (4) proper delegation of authority, and (5) aggressive internal communications programs to ensure that all employees are aware of policies and plan of the company . . . .

Our company had been using the functional type organization which, while appropriate when we were wholly occupied in development work, was completely inadequate as soon as the government inaugurated a Defence Program and ordered production . . . .

An organization cannot be a one-man operation and succeed. Accordingly, it is necessary for me to segregate my authority and pass it on to members of the organization by way of specific assignments, with titles indicating responsibility; the authority definitely delegated to the position and the responsibility which must go with that authority.

At A. V. Roe Canada, we believe that a company functions best when every employee, from the Chairman of the Board to sweeper, understands his part in the mission of the company; and further understands fully how and when his part is to be played and what he is to accomplish. No person or organization can amount to much unless he or it sets an ultimate goal. And the best way to achieve this goal in a big organization, we think, is to make it clear and obvious to all just what the goal is and keep everyone up to date on the tactics employed from time to time to achieve that goal.

With a new organization came new faces. For industrial relations, Gordon brought in his pal Bill Dickie from John Inglis. In October, 1952, Gordon hired Harvey Smith, a production executive from Kaiser in Detroit, as director of manufacturing. He arrived on the scene with the finesse of a donkey running through a cornfield. Smith liked to dress well, but his sartorial splendour left a little to be desired.

He used to wear those artificial clip-on bow ties, and one day I said to him, "Harvey, I wouldn't wear one of those," and he told me it was none of my goddamned business. Now, I used to wear a regular bow tie, and one day I went into his office, and he pulled open his desk drawer and there were all these ties in there, and he says, "Okay, show me how to tie one."

—*Ernie Alderton*

Although he came to Malton from the United States, Smith was Canadian born. He was an orphan, and spent a good part of his life trying to find his birth certificate so he could locate his parents. When he brought his family to Toronto, he was provided with a company-owned house, which he refused to move into until the company had constructed a bomb shelter in the back yard.

Smith was an argumentive, self-centred sort. He'd argue with Jim Floyd over engineering; he'd argue with Ernie Alderton, A. V. Roe's new personnel director, over hiring practices; and he'd argue with Fred Smye over budgets. He even went head to head with Crawford Gordon's temporary assistant, Ron Adey. One day—Smith had been there about three months at the time—he was reporting in a meeting on the progress of the production department. Smye asked for Adey's opinion on the report. "It's a lot of bullshit!" said Adey. From that moment on the two locked horns.

As difficult as he was, Harvey Smith was a good thing for the CF-100 production program. Gordon and Smye had agreed on the goal of one aircraft per day, even though by October, 1952, only two had been produced. But by the following June, the build-up to the planned production peak of one a day had been achieved.

I give Harvey credit for the success of the CF-100. The first thing he did was to get in there and count all the parts of the plane—everyone refers to those "parts counts" meetings. Harvey would be there at seven in the morning and he wanted everyone working for him to be there at eight. He had a good sense of smell and was a hard-nosed production guy.

—*Fred Smye*

The new version of the CF-100, the Mk.4, appeared to be basically the same aircraft. But of the 15,000 or so parts that made up the Mk.4, 14,000 were brand new. The tools and dies for these new parts were manufactured in Detroit, and Smith's job was to make sure they arrived on schedule. He was known to say, "No matter how good a man is, he can't put a part into an airplane until you make the part and hand it to him." His efforts did not go unrewarded.

Another Gordon recruit arrived on the scene about this time as well, but quietly and almost unnoticed. So unpublic was his appointment that for years many people wondered who he was and what he did whenever he took one of his rare walks around the plant. Crawford Gordon called him his Grey Eminence but his real name was J. N. "Pat" Kelly. Kelly was lord chamberlain to Gordon's king. He decided what Crawford Gordon should pay attention to, whom he should see, and what documents or messages would land on his desk, whether for amusement or of necessity. And he did it all very unobtrusively.

Kelly was a "shadow man". He had some control over broad public relations policy. He had some responsibilities to do with government lobbying. He had influence in Ottawa, but most of all, he had influence with Gordon.

—*Jim Hornick*

Kelly was a well-known newspaperman in the thirties—financial editor of the *Vancouver Star* and founder in 1933 of the *Vancouver News-Herald*. He was also the first Canadian newspaperman to appear in *Time* magazine. In 1941, he joined the public relations firm of Cockfield, Brown and was immediately seconded as national public relations director for the Canadian Red Cross. He stayed in that position until war's end when he was offered senior positions with Coca-Cola, Seagrams, Brewers Association, and Cockfield, Brown. He chose Cockfield, Brown on the condition they let him set up his own public relations division (he didn't want to be involved with advertising, which was Cockfield, Brown's life blood in those days). His most important client was Crawford Gordon.

Bill Dickie had heard of Kelly largely because of his activities during the 1946 Hamilton Stelco strike and invited him to meet Crawford

Gordon for dinner one evening in early 1952. After dinner, Gordon opened up to Kelly complaining of the morale problems at the company and how it was becoming more and more a target for the Conservative Opposition.

Gordon wanted to borrow me for six months to clean out his publicity and P.R. people, so I took the job half-time, the idea being I would work at Malton mornings and back at my own office in the afternoons. The day after I started, I was appointed a member of the management committee, which didn't sit too well with some of them, including Fred Smye. I very seldom spoke at these meetings, but briefed Gordon before all of them. One of the very first suggestions I ever made to him was that it might be a good idea to start projecting the company as a Canadian company.

—*Pat Kelly*

Kelly decided very early on at A. V. Roe to conduct his business as discreetly as possible. He never participated in management decisions but always met with Gordon before any important meeting to go over the agenda, but once in the meeting, Gordon would do the talking.

It avoided conflicts. I had the full confidence of Crawford Gordon. Any decision I made had his approval.

—*Pat Kelly*

So taken was Gordon with Kelly that he'd only been on the job a few months before Gordon wanted him to join the company full time.

I was making $30,000 in those days, and Gordon offered me a five-year contract at three times what I was making, plus a pension. I refused. "You stupid bastard," he said, "why won't you take it?" "Loyalty," I said, "to Cockfield, Brown. They've been good to me." "Well, you're still a stupid bastard."

—*Pat Kelly*

About this same time Smye had been pressing Gordon about raising the level of public interest in the company and enhancing the prestige of both the company and its new president. What was needed, he reckoned, was someone with excellent public relations know-how, a real pro, and so they hired Ron Williams. Whereas Pat Kelly served as "personal" advisor to Crawford Gordon, Ron Williams was really Gordon's public relations advisor.

Williams was then with the Financial Post, *and I'd heard he wasn't too happy there and when I heard he'd been offered a job at the T. Eaton Co., I invited him to lunch and offered him the job but he ended up being a disaster.*

Williams was both dogmatic and argumentative. My whole approach was to function as a lawyer does; I would put before the President the possibilities he could do in a given situation but I made it clear to him that he made the decisions, his name goes on it and not mine. But Williams would end up going toe to toe with Gordon and argue with him until they nearly exchanged blows.

—Pat Kelly

Williams worked for Crawford, and I didn't get on well with him because he started to get his nose into things where it didn't belong.

—Fred Smye

If we had to talk business, we went to either the York or Toronto Clubs. If the business was personal, we'd meet at Briarcrest. One day at the Toronto Club, Gordon looked me in the eye and said, "I'm sick of that goddamned Williams. You got him here, you've got to fire him."

—Pat Kelly

Jim Hornick called it "a better kept secret than the C-102" but virtually everyone who worked at A. V. Roe Canada between 1951 and 1959 knew about Briarcrest. Many of them drove by it every day on their way to work.

When Walter Deisher came to A. V. Roe from Fleet Aircraft in 1946, he needed a place to live and paid $40,000, quite a sum in those days, for an 11-acre parcel of land at the corner of Islington Avenue and Dixon Road near Malton. On the estate was a beautiful Tudor-type mansion, described by one reporter in these words: "The builder had a taste for the theatrical. A Romeo and Juliet balcony overlooks the living room. A huge, ceiling-high window faces a meandering stream below. . . . Four theatrical faces are carved in wood over the main entrance." Briarcrest had a pool room which could only be reached by a stone staircase hidden behind a hinged panel. Walter Deisher had used this room for his electric trains.

When Deisher left the company in 1952, A. V. Roe paid him $80,000 for the estate. For the first few years, Roy Dobson used it as his home base whenever he came to Canada. Crawford Gordon's temporary assistant, Ron Adey, managed Briarcrest.

We had a housekeeper and chauffeur on full time, and it was their job to make sure the place was maintained and to satisfy all of Roy Dobson's needs.

—Ron Adey

Briarcrest was also used occasionally to host dinners and for executive committee meetings and other meetings. And whenever the company was going after a big deal, they very often billeted the potential customer in the estate and wined and dined him. Over the years, Prince Bernhard of the Netherlands, Viscount Montgomery, and even C. D. Howe made Briarcrest their stopping place. "The VIP's were royally treated," said the *Globe and Mail*, "but company officials using the place had to pay $25 a day."

11

HIGH FLIGHT

Crawford Gordon had by no means given up hope of someday finding a customer for the Jetliner. Over a drink with Bob Rummell, the head of Trans World Airlines (TWA), in early March, 1952, Gordon had raved about the Jetliner. Rummell's boss at the time, the owner of TWA, was the infamous Howard Hughes. A. V. Roe was already known to Hughes: the Hughes Aircraft Company of Culver City, California, had the contract to supply the fire-control system known as the MG-2 for the CF-100.

Rummell told Hughes about the Jetliner, and Hughes was curious enough to ask Gordon for a look at the plane. Knowing how touchy C. D. Howe was over the Jetliner at the time, Gordon ostensibly sent it to California as a useful development tool in testing the MG-2. It would be used as a camera platform since it could take off easily and fly at 30,000 or 35,000 feet in relative comfort, be pressurized, and was fast enough to keep up with the CF-100.

On April 7, 1952, the Jetliner left for California. The crew on the flight were pilot Don Rogers, co-pilot Syd Howland, flight engineer Bill Wildfong, and inspector John Thorne. Mario Pesando, Les Abbis, Jim Floyd, and Joe Morley were also aboard.

The day after we got there, Hughes came around and looked at the airplane with interest and wanted to have a flight in the airplane and have me check him out on it. We changed seats and he did about nine take-offs and landings. But when he landed, instead of taxiing back to the Hughes factory side of the landing strip, he taxied over to the other side, to the air strip. He put cars and guards around the plane and that was the last Hughes Aircraft ever got to see of the plane. They never did use it or even look at it as a flying test bed.

—Don Rogers

Fred Smye and Crawford Gordon had flown ahead of the Jetliner crew and took over an entire floor of the Beverly Hills Hotel in Los Angeles. At the time Smye had no idea that this would be his home for the next six months. Howard Hughes had himself a new toy.

I remember my first meeting with Hughes. I was told to go out of the back door of the hotel, cross the lawn to the side street, where I would find the green Chevy and Hughes. I drove with him to the Hughes plant, where an old Convair aircraft with a rusty undercart was parked. There was a mechanic standing by the plane with a fire extinguisher. We got in, although you could hear my knees shaking a mile away. Howard got the engines started but not the pressurization system, and fortunately, because of that, we could not fly. That was when he gave me a conducted tour of his properties and borrowed a dollar from me to buy some gas, as the tank of the Chevy was almost dry.

—Fred Smye

While Smye and Gordon lived at the Beverly Hills, the flight crew was billeted at the Hollywood Roosevelt Hotel. But, as the Hughes-Avro negotiations began to drag on, Hughes put the crew, their wives, and once school was out, their kids as well, in houses in Coldwater Canyon. Don Rogers spent six long months in California, but a mere thirteen and a half hours flying with Hughes.

He treated the Jetliner as his personal aircraft and the flight engineer and myself as his personal crew. I was never really free, you know, I was always on call. And that's the way he would work. His office would call in the morning and say Mr. Hughes is tied up today but he'd like to fly tomorrow so please stand by. So, I would sit and sit around, and finally the phone would ring again and his office would say Mr. Hughes is too busy today, etc. This went on for six months.

He kept very much to himself as far as any external contact was concerned. But with myself and my engineer he was most pleasant and hospitable and wanted to keep us entertained. The stories about his not having relatively conspicuous type clothes, and not having any money in his pocket, or any watch, are all quite true. The odd time we went to fly the airplane, we'd drive back into town and he'd say, "Oh, Don, what time is it?" I'd give him the time, and he'd say he was supposed to meet so-and-so, and he'd start looking along the side of the street for a service station with a phone in it. And he'd say, "Don, can you loan me a dime? I want to make a phone call." He never drove anything but a company Chevrolet. He was absolutely non-descript in every way. But one thing for sure, he was a good pilot.

—Don Rogers

In the Hollywood penthouse of Walter Kane, who was running the RKO studios for Hughes at the time, . . . Hughes had laid on a special dinner party for Gordon, Smye, two of the Hughes Aircraft executives, and myself. He had also invited two of the RKO starlets with the obvious intention of adding a little glamour to the occasion, which they certainly did. One of the girls was Margaret Sheridan, a beautiful and charming actress, and the other, whose name I can't remember, was a gorgeous model whom Al Capp apparently used for the character in the "Wolfgal" comic strip. Dolly Parton has nothing on this gal, and we discovered that she also knew something about the aviation business!

—Jim Floyd

Hughes was always asking us if we were interested in playing around, you know, wanting women . . . . And Jim [Floyd] would always say, "Gee whiz, Mr. Hughes, I'm so tired, I'd better go home."

—Joe Morley

The weeks turned into months and the negotiations began to get complicated. Rummell felt the Jetliner would be ideal for TWA's domestic routes, and TWA wanted to consider several versions of the plane: one with Derwent engines, one with Rolls-Royce Nenes, and one with Pratt & Whitney J-57's, as well as a redesigned version powered by Allison J-33 engines. The ideal solution for A. V. Roe was to have the Jetliner built under licence in the United States. The snag here, however, was that the American engine and aircraft industry was preoccupied with Korean War work. Hughes and Avro couldn't seem to work out a deal, and Crawford Gordon was losing patience.

The cloak and dagger atmosphere surrounding Hughes, and his elusive-

ness in both mental and physical terms, were completely alien to Gordon's own direct and positive approach.

—Jim Floyd

Hughes had, among other peculiarities, a habit of calling meetings with the Avro executives at all hours of the day and night and expecting everyone to be there. During one of these infamous meetings, Hughes had excused himself to go to the bathroom.

A few minutes passed with no sign of Hughes returning and after about an hour and a half had elapsed, Gordon became quite agitated and asked one of the Hughes people to go and find out whether Hughes had "disappeared down the goddamned hole." The man came back and said, "Mr. Hughes is on the telephone. Mr. Hughes has a number of telephones in the bathroom, especially for his use." I will not repeat the exact comment that this revelation brought from Crawford, but he left the penthouse almost immediately, muttering about "a bloody madhouse." I had a lot of sympathy for Crawford's reaction and would probably have reacted the same way in a similar circumstance, but Fred Smye was much more conciliatory on such matters and we stayed on until Hughes finally reappeared, obviously surprised and upset that Gordon had left.

—Jim Floyd

A few nights later, in another late-night meeting, a dismal incident occurred. Gordon usually smoked and drank his way through these meetings—to the endless irritation of Hughes—and was presently in need of a washroom.

"Howard," he demanded, "where's the can?"

"The washroom is down the hall," said Hughes.

"What's the matter with the can right here?" Gordon pointed to Hughes's special washroom adjacent to the suite.

"That's my special washroom to be used only by myself; you can use the one down the hall."

But before Hughes could stop him, Gordon was in the private bathroom with the door locked. No one quite recalls Hughes's reaction the next day when he discovered that, out of spite, Gordon had purposely urinated everywhere but the toilet.

Gordon returned to Malton soon afterwards, leaving any remaining negotiations with Hughes in the hands of the more patient Fred Smye. With Gordon gone, Hughes deputized Bob Rummell to attend the meetings for him. He was still determined to find a way to build the Jetliner under licence in the United States.

Back in Canada meanwhile, the Toronto-based *Financial Post* got wind of the negotiations. "New Home for Jetliner? Avro/Hughes Deal Likely" read the headline of August 9, 1952. The Jetliner was once again on the front page. Included in the article was a summary of the financial investment in the aircraft to the end of December, 1951. Over five years A. V. Roe had invested $2.264 million while the Canadian government had handed over $6.5 million.

Hughes finally made an offer. He wanted Smye to build, at Malton, thirty aircraft for TWA, all the financing coming from Hughes himself. When Howe heard of the Hughes offer, he was furious and wrote to Gordon:

> I have heard rumours recently that you are planning to use part of the space in the Avro plant for further work on the C-102 civilian airplane, or for other work for private customers. Having in mind the colossal investment of government funds in Avro at the present time, any such use of your floor space cannot be tolerated. I have instructed you before, and I repeat that instruction, the C-102 is to be moved out of any useful manufacturing space in your plant and put aside until such time as the Government investment in your facilities for Avro has been brought to a reasonable figure.

Hughes begged me to build his thirty Jetliners, but I had to tell him, sorry, we wouldn't do it. It wasn't an easy thing to do because he was going to finance the whole thing. I made this decision. Howe had nothing to do with it.

—Fred Smye

It was obvious, after this episode, that the Jetliner project was finished and that there was now no hope of rescuing what had promised to be an aircraft to put Canada ahead of any nation in the world in the development of inter-city jet transports.

—Jim Floyd

Hughes later tried to interest Floyd in a three-engined airplane, a delta-type configuration with a rear engine stuck on the tail. The proposal went through TWA's engineering department and was quickly rejected because TWA's engineers felt people wouldn't fly in a plane with one of the engines in the tail.

The Jetliner finally returned to Malton in the early fall of 1952. As for Gordon and Hughes, as antagonistic as their relationship had been in California, they nevertheless stayed in touch with each other for years. Long after the Jetliner was sent to the scrap heap, Hughes

(right)

The Anson assembly line at National Steel Car, Malton, 1942. More than 700 Ansons were produced at Malton.

(below)

Late summer, 1943. Roll-out of the first Canadian-made Lancaster at Victory Aircraft. Sitting at front row centre in dark suit is Jack Hilton, who was in charge of final assembly. When he saw the Lancaster for the first time a year earlier, Hilton remarked, "How are we going to build something that big!"

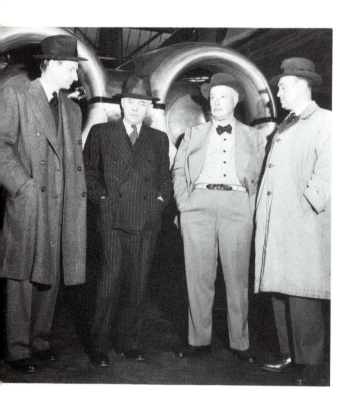

(*left*)

A. V. Roe Canada's first president, Walter Deisher (in pin stripes) with J. P. Bickell (in bow tie), flanked by two unidentified men, 1949. The Jetliner's engine nacelles can be seen in the background.

(*below*)

The Lancaster production line at Victory Aircraft during a shutdown due to parts shortages in the winter of 1944.

(*above*)

This view of Jim Floyd's Jetliner in flight shows its clean lines.

(*left*)

Jim Floyd with a model of the Jetliner in 1947. This was the first aircraft designed entirely by Floyd.

(*above*)

April 18, 1950. The crew and passengers on the Jetliner's historic flight into the United States. Left to right: Mario Pesando, Jim Floyd, Bill Baker, Don Rogers, Mike Cooper-Slipper, Fred Smye, and TCA president Gordon McGregor. Although no longer interested in the aircraft, McGregor was ordered on the flight by C. D. Howe.

(*left*)

April 18, 1950. The first jet-transport-delivered air mail in North America being loaded on the Jetliner.

(right)

April 18, 1950. The Jetliner arrives in New York. Toronto's Mayor Hiram McCallum and pilot Don Rogers are surrounded by women from the Canadian International Trade Fair who hold a scroll which was later presented to the mayor of New York.

(below)

C. D. Howe and Fred Smye with a model of the Jetliner.

(*above*)

Sir Roy Dobson, Harvey Smith,
Jim Floyd, and Fred Smye.

(*above right*)

Winnett Boyd and Paul Dilworth
standing in front of Boyd's Orenda,
one of the most successful engines
ever produced.

(*below*)

Four key players in the A. V. Roe
Canada story at the height of the
Arrow program. Left to right: Fred
Smye, Jim Floyd, Sir Roy Dobson,
and Crawford Gordon, Jr.

(*left*)

Sir Roy Dobson and A. V. Roe
president Crawford Gordon, Jr.

(*below*)

One of the two CF-100 prototypes
on the tarmac. The second prototype, 18102, crashed near London,
Ontario, on April 5, 1951, killing
both pilot and observer.

(*above*)

Three views of the CF-100's main spar showing Waclaw Czerwinski's pin joint, the dip in the upper boom, and the reinforcement plates. The author took these photos at Mountainview, Ontario, from CF-100's being dismantled for scrap.

(*below*)

Air Marshal Wilf Curtis, sitting in the observer's seat of a CF-100, chats with Don Rogers, head of flight test at Avro. From the air force side, Curtis was largely responsible for getting the CF-100 off the ground. Later he became a member of the board at A. V. Roe Canada.

(*above*)

CF-100 Mk.4B's, 18362 and 18387, with tip tanks, belonging to 428 (Ghost) Squadron, RCAF. Based at Ottawa, 428 Squadron flew CF-100's from 1954 to 1961.

(*left*)

Air Marshal Roy Slemon visits the Avro plant. Left to right: Slemon, Crawford Gordon, Jr., Fred Smye, Slemon's aide, and Harvey Smith.

(*left*)

CF-100's make a ceremonial fly-past at Cold Lake, September 12, 1958. In the foreground is 18663 of 433 (Porcupine) Squadron, with tubular rocket pods on wingtips.

(*below*)

Arrows on the assembly line; 17,000 drawings, 650 suppliers under contract, 38,000 parts, and 5,000 people were required to produce the Arrow.

(above)

CF-100 18554 of CEPE jettisons rocket pods prior to firing 2.75-inch rockets. A number of armament variations were tried on the CF-100's, including pods, a belly weapons pack, and slings.

(right)

George Pearkes, Minister of National Defence, receives a program from an Avro hostess for the Arrow's unveiling ceremony. With Pearkes is Fred Smye.

(left)

The Gordon family at the roll-out of the first Arrow, October 4, 1957. Left to right: Crawford Gordon III, Crawford Gordon, Jr., Avro lawyer and board member John Tory (in background), Mary Gordon, and an unidentified woman.

(below)

October 4, 1957. Pearkes is at the podium. Among those seated on the platform were four people who had growing fears over the Arrow program: fourth from left is Air Marshal Hugh Campbell (chin in hand); to Campbell's left is Sir Roy Dobson; eighth from left, seated beside Pearkes's empty chair, is Fred Smye; Crawford Gordon, Jr. (in hat and sunglasses), is at Pearkes's immediate right.

(*left*)

Test pilot Janusz Zurakowski.

(*below*)

The Arrow design team, left to right: Bob Lindley, Jim Floyd, Guest Hake, and Jim Chamberlin. When the Arrow program collapsed, Lindley went to McDonnell Douglas in California, Floyd returned to A. V. Roe in Manchester, Hake stayed on at Malton, and Chamberlin headed up NASA's Gemini program.

(*left*)

The Avro Arrow, RL-201, flying over Malton in 1958. The rear undercarriage had to rotate as it was raised in order to fit into the thin wing. Below the plane can be seen the Avro Aircraft facility.

(*below*)

The 34-ton flying triangle. Arrow RL-202 displays its clean lines. The weapons pack can be seen in mid-fuselage. This aircraft logged 23 hours, 40 minutes flying time.

(above)

Arrow RL-204 coming in for a
landing with air brakes deployed.
This aircraft logged a total of only 7
hours in the air.

(below)

Arrow RL-201 over Niagara Falls.

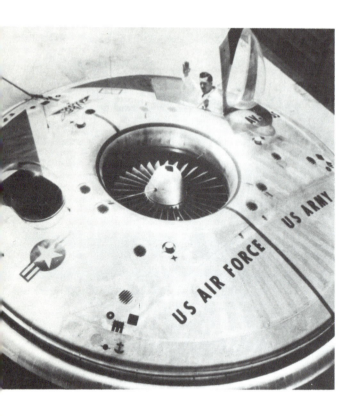

(*left*)

John Frost's Avrocar on the tarmac, piloted by Avro's Spud Potocki. After more than ten years of research and development, this project was finally abandoned in 1961.

(*below*)

Crawford Gordon, Jr. (at left), Gloria Collinson, and Bill Dickie at Briarcrest.

still persisted in calling Gordon at home at all hours of the day and night. So bothersome were his calls that Gordon refused to come to the phone, leaving the courtesies to his wife. To Howard Hughes, that aircraft was like a woman he always wanted but could never have.

In November, 1951, the RCAF, ironically, ordered two custom-built de Havilland Comets. The Jetliner, they said, "was still in the prototype stage and required further development." They were also choosing a long-range aircraft over the short-to-medium range Jetliner—the Comet had a range of 3,450 miles and a payload of 7,000 pounds compared with 2,000 miles and 10,000 pounds for the Jetliner.

The RCAF took delivery of the two Comets in the spring of 1953, but by that time the Comet was already in trouble. The first of two Comets ordered by Canadian Pacific Airlines in 1949, ready early in 1953 after some delay, was to be taken to CPA's base in Sydney via Karachi. As it was preparing for take-off at Karachi, it crashed off the runway, killing everyone on board. There were several more Comet crashes that year, and in January, 1954, both RCAF Comets were grounded. They did not go back into service until November, 1957, almost four years later, and only then after structural modifications. They were retired from service in 1963 and sold by the RCAF in 1965.

Aside from the landing gear malfunction on its second flight in August, 1949, the Jetliner performed perfectly, flying for Avro until the end of 1956, when the cost of maintenance and repair became impracticable for the one-of-a-kind C-102.

By 1951, A. V. Roe's gas turbine division had grown from two people (Ken Tupper and Paul Dilworth) to eight hundred engineers, technicians, draftsmen, designers, metallurgists, and support staff. Paul Dilworth no longer practised his engineering craft daily, but spent most of his day in meetings, listening to problems both technical and personal, and reviewing performance charts and tables. "It was a growing organization," he recalls, "and it had growing pains."

One of the problems was the friction between the experimental machine shop people—those who made the engine parts for the first Chinook and the Orendas—and Dilworth's design engineers, people like Boyd and Knowles.

The experimental machine shop people were basically tool room people whose experience was in jigs and fixtures. Aircraft production is a very

different art from engine production and they weren't accustomed to deal-
ing in tolerances of thousandths and ten-thousandths of an inch.

—*Paul Dilworth*

The situation produced a hotbed of hostility between the machine
shop and the designers. The shop people thought the designers were
unrealistic in their requests, almost asking for the world, whereas the
engine designers complained the shop people weren't really trying.
Needless to say, one of them had been Winn Boyd.

The average production person will take the attitude that, here is my
production machinery; we have to alter the design to make it with this
existing machinery; but a more enlightened production person will say,
is this what you want, and if so, I'll modify my existing machine in order
to make what you want.

—*Winnett Boyd*

Part of the problem was the fact that many of the machines in the
experimental machine shop went back to Victory Aircraft days. Harry
Keast had a more benevolent attitude:

I used a strategy with the production people. I used to tell them jet blades
had to be manufactured to a one-thousandth of an inch tolerance. And I
knew that nobody had made blades in Canada so the first ones we got
were one-thirty-second tolerance. So, I used to say, no, it has to be one-
thousandth. And they came back one-twentieth and then down to one-
tenth and then one-fifth and finally one-thousandth. And when they finally
did it, I would say, now that's what I wanted in the first place. Worked
every time.

—*Harry Keast*

Running the machine shop at the time was Earle Brownridge. Brownridge had been with the company since 1945 and had worked in the
time-study department. He was thirty in 1948 when Smye had asked
him how he thought an experimental shop for engines should be set
up. His written plan was so impressive that Smye pulled him out of
his obscure position in estimates and made him an assistant production
controller. Fred Smye liked Brownridge (Smye either liked you or he
didn't, he was never ambivalent or indifferent about his feelings) and
had recently made him an administrative assistant to the experimental
machine shop.

Earle and I got together one day and said we've got to stop the war between his people and my designers if we're ever going to get anywhere, so we made a pact. Basically I would agree to stop criticizing them if they would make an honest effort to produce what we designed . . . . From then on, the atmosphere changed dramatically.

—Paul Dilworth

At least for a while. Boyd had left the company by now, and Dilworth, recovering from a nervous breakdown, was stretched to the limit. Smye began looking for someone to take Dilworth's place, a general manager for the gas turbine division, someone who could take over the entire facility. He first offered the position to Ray Dorey, his old friend at Rolls-Royce; Dorey was ready to accept when Lord Hives persuaded him to take over Rolls' motor car division.

Smye then hired a Romanian named Carp who lasted about a week—Dilworth and Brownridge threatened to resign unless Smye got rid of him. Smye did, and then was sued by Carp for a million dollars for defamation of character. He claimed Smye had fired him because he was unable to work with Canadians. (Carp settled out of court for an undisclosed amount.)

Crawford Gordon, now in place as the company's new president, asked Smye to run the aircraft side while he would look after gas turbine himself until someone could be found to run it.

In a luckless move, Gordon hired Tom McCrae and Fred Luker to run gas turbine in November, 1951. McCrae, originally from Massachusetts, had worked for some time with the Curtiss Airplane and Motor Company of Buffalo. In 1931, he joined the research division of General Motors in Detroit, and rose to become director of engineering for their Allison Division. Luker, also American, and a graduate of the University of Kentucky, had spent seventeen years at Allison, six of them with jet engines.

It didn't take long for McCrae and Luker to make their presence felt. They alienated everyone and, far from commanding any respect, were made the brunt of many jokes. Gas turbine people quickly dubbed their new officers "Allison in Wonderland." They cost the company some good people.

I resigned from the company in July, 1952, and the two reasons I left were Tom McCrae and Fred Luker. They started imposing impractical policies, and I finally threw in the sponge. I went to Crawford one day and said, Look, you've got a choice to make here. You've either got to back me and get rid of these guys, or I've got to go. He said, "I'm sorry."

—Paul Dilworth

Dilworth was a guy with high principles, and he said to hell with it and walked out. Funny thing is, I didn't know about it until after he was gone.

—*Fred Smye*

With Dilworth out of the way, McCrae and Luker set their sights on Earl Brownridge, Dilworth's friend who was then running the experimental machine shop. They did not count on Fred Smye, however.

In conversation one day, I heard Gordon mention McCrae and Luker were going to fire Earl Brownridge for being crooked. And I said, "Say that again Crawford, I don't think I got you." He said, "Brownridge is playing games with Frigidaire around the manufacture of some of our jet engine blades." McCrae and Luker had been telling Gordon that Earl was crooked, getting kickbacks and so forth, and I said, "Crawford, you've got something mixed up here. You fire Brownridge and I walk out with him, so get that nice and clear." And that was the start of the end for McCrae and Luker.

—*Fred Smye*

John Frost was back in business. Persuading Fred Smye to loan him eight engineers, he put together what came to be known as the Special Projects Group and set up in a building everyone called the "penthouse" across the street from the Avro plant. He had come up with an idea for a vertical take-off device, a ground-cushion vehicle resembling a flying saucer. This kind of vehicle would obviate the need for an airport and would be especially useful on rough terrain like that in northern Canada.

At the time, several countries were experimenting with the ground-cushion concept. Frost discovered the ground cushion while studying the flat-rising, vertical-take-off airplane. Cockerell came upon it in England while making efforts to reduce the drag on ship hulls, and Carl Weiland in Switzerland had done research on the concept. As early as 1935, Toivo Kaario of Finland had built and tested what he called the ram wing, a first cousin to the ground cushion.

His idea seemed interesting, so I went along with him on the paperwork. Frost had a lot of inexpensive little trinkets and toys and out of that he proved the concept of the air cushion.

—*Fred Smye*

Des Earl had joined the company as an aerodynamicist in 1951, had worked on the CF-100, and was the first to go with Frost into this special projects group. Another was Waclaw Czerwinski, the hero of the CF-100. Czerwinski would stay with Frost in special projects for eighteen months before moving on to the Arrow program.

In the beginning, we wrote a little report on the possibility of a big-winged, possibly a circular-platformed, airplane. We started with a circular platform and then went to a spade-shape. The spade-shape was Czerwinski's idea. The spade-shaped vehicle was to be powered by a flat radial engine, which occupied most of the craft, and the pilot was to sit in the middle with a big flat disc rotating around him. The vehicle was designed to be supersonic.

—Des Earl

By July, 1952, this spade-shaped concept was given the name Project Y-1, and by the fall the group had constructed a wooden mock-up "smeared with patents" and were well on their way to securing a support contract from the Defence Research Board.

Jim Hornick was quick off the mark once again. "Avro design team working on flying saucer" shouted the headline on February 19, 1953. When C. D. Howe heard of the ground-cushion research, he was concerned that it would divert the company's attention from the more immediate problems with the CF-100 and the Orenda. In a letter to his co-ordinator of production, Howe made his position clear: he was "entirely opposed to any further work on this project with the Avro Plant . . . . Any further work should be administered by the National Research Council."

Nevertheless, by June, Frost and his group were in England with their spade-shaped model to talk to Sir Roy Dobson about the project. Dobson was excited about the saucer and organized a wind-tunnel test. The test showed promise enough that Dobson arranged for Frost and the others to meet with the British Ministry of Supply. It was decided to abandon the spade-shaped design and to go back to a circular design—the circle "was the best shape for an annular ground cushion jet and the optimum shape for structural simplicity and lightness." Project Y-1 now became Project Y-2.

Back at Malton, Project Y was attracting a good deal of attention, some good, some bad. Viscount Montgomery visited the plant as a guest of Roy Dobson, saw the saucer mock-up, and described it as "fantastic."

In Ottawa, however, Howe had been reading Hornick's articles on the "flying saucer" and fired off a letter to Crawford Gordon, reiterating his desire that the company give a hundred per cent of its efforts to the CF-100 and the Orenda: "If you are working on anything else, I should be advised in order that the matter be taken up with Cabinet and proper authorization be obtained."

However, the harshest criticism to Project Y came from Frost's own colleagues. Jim Floyd had no faith whatsoever in Frost's work and never once believed the saucer would fly let alone be built. And Jim Chamberlin, still smarting over his battles with Frost on the CF-100, circulated a report through engineering to management entitled "Project Y—Why *Not!*"

You never get something for nothing, and any time you bend air, you lose thrust. John seemed to think you gained energy.

—*Jim Floyd*

Not all was lost, however, for Dr. O. M. Solandt of the Defence Research Board had been able to interest General Putt, head of USAF Air Research and Development Command, on the project. At this time the Cold War was at its height, and both the Russians and the Americans were ready to jump at any new weapon that might give them the edge over the other guy. Frost's saucer might do just that. Putt envisioned a craft able to cruise at 300 mph at high ceiling, with a range of 1,000 miles. He wanted it to skim close to the ground, dart between trees, dip into small valleys, and hug the earth to confound radar. In short, he wanted an airborne cavalry.

A USAF contingent visited the company in September, 1953. They were impressed by Frost's presentation and promptly issued a contract for further development, which included subsonic and supersonic wind tunnel testing, static testing of the ground cushion, and configuration studies. The craft was to be supersonic and circular in shape, with a large, circular, radial-flow engine producing 30,000 pounds thrust, situated in the middle, the thrust proceeding through a series of stages to the outer edges to give the aircraft lift.

Now, for the first time we had money available to design a proper rig on which to start studying the ground cushion.

—*John Frost*

In the summer of 1952, A. V. Roe "redelivered" a new, improved Mk.3 version of the CF-100 to the RCAF, specifically to No.3 All Weather Operational Training Unit at North Bay, Ontario. This time there was no ceremony. The testing, put on hold since the previous October, resumed. And, even though, in a technical sense, the aircraft were redesigned versions of the earlier plane, they still had their bugs and quirks.

The nose gear sometimes failed to retract properly. Hydraulic pumps failed, fuel transfer valves stuck, and radios were unreliable. Pilots found the lack of nose wheel steering in the early versions a nuisance. An odd feature was the way the control column obscured the compass on the instrument panel. This had to be rectified by canting the control column to the right. Pilots joked that the complicated fuel management system, with dials all across the panel, made an engineering degree mandatory before checking out on the CF-100.

Needless to say, the RCAF was a little less enthusiastic about the plane than they had been the previous October. The CF-100, wrote Chick Childerhose in *Air Force*, "was slow, overweight and ponderous in movement. It looked like a pencil with two garbage cans tied on the sides. The stableboys [ground crews] referred to it as the CF-Clunk, the CF-Zilch or the Lead Sled."
Problems with the aircraft were persistent and regular enough to provide a degree of morbid humour.

We used to have a little joke that if the nose wheel retracted, that was the last transmission you'd hear. In other words, if the nose wheel clunked in, the radio would quit.

—S/L Joe Schultz

Bad radios they could live with. What bothered Schultz and the other pilots the most were "terrible fuel feed problems. A lot of accidents were the direct and indirect result of this." And with accidents, come losses.

At first, when we first got hold of the 100, we lost pilots and planes at the rate of one in ten. But then, as time went on, we realized we were losing them, not so much from the fact they weren't hat great an aircraft, but because we weren't training our pilots properly in their use.

—General A.C. Hull

To me it was insufficient knowledge of new airplanes and how they worked. Basically the air force after the war, on the operations side, were a lot of pilots who had not been in the development side of airplanes and who really didn't understand how long it takes to develop an airplane and what little tiny changes can cause you all kinds of problems. I remember sitting down at A. V. Roe and talking for an hour with a squadron leader who just plain didn't understand . . . . There was a lot of people unhappy because they thought they were going to get a perfect airplane.

—W/C Ray Foottit

Sure it had bugs and fixes were required. But our military were not prepared for this eventuality. They had always flown more or less tried and proven "old days." If you think the B-747's being delivered today are the same as Pan Am originally bought, you're off your rocker. The same can be said of the DC-4, the F-4, the F-15 Eagle. Any good airplane must have growth in it, otherwise it's a dud.

But there were those in the lower military ranks who just could not comprehend airplane development. [The CF-100] was mainly night and all weather, a real challenge for those who were used to clear skys day and night.

—Joe Morley

Escaping from the CF-100 should you ever run into trouble was something that bothered Avro designers and the RCAF from the very beginning.

Avro did not want to delay delivery of the CF-100, and in fact many aircraft were delivered to the air force in what was considered unsafe condition.

—Geoff Grossmith

The canopy, for instance, was a source of trouble from day one. The early canopies were manual, using a great big crank—you could start a Model T with it—and manual locks. Then the electrical ones came along and there were rigging problems. Then there was those removable explosive bolts . . . .

—S/L Joe Schultz

The canopy in the CF-100 was supposed to be blown away from the plane in flight by an explosive bolt similar to a shotgun shell. In front of these bolts, like long firing pins, were thin, rail-like bars held by springs. When a pilot wanted to blow the canopy, he pulled the jettison lever, the rails flew back and exploded the bolts, and the canopy was blown off the aircraft. What tended to happen much too often, however, was the canopy had a bad habit of jettisoning itself.

On Don Rogers first flight with me, there was a sudden, almighty bang followed by a violent gale of wind. I cut speed drastically ready for Don to bail out while I had a go at getting the plane down. But nothing followed the explosive crash, and we saw that the cockpit canopy had gone. Fortunately it had hurtled off without damaging the tail or anyone on the ground, and we landed without trouble. If nothing else, the episode provided us with a free canopy jettisoning trial.

—Bill Waterton

What had happened on this and subsequently on many other occasions was the shotgun-shell bolt had a tendency to corrode, much like the corrosion on a car battery, allowing the bolts to blow without much encouragement from the pilot or observer. In the event the bolts failed to blow, Avro engineer Geoff Grossmith remembers putting axes in the cockpit of all the early aircraft "so the pilot and navigator could chop their way out." On April 1, 1953, the CF-100 entered squadron service, a little over three years since its first flight.

When the Orenda was ordered into full-scale production, new production facilities became a priority. On August 28, 1950, the government had announced an immediate order for fifty Orendas and was providing $20 million to be spent on new facilities and the establishment of the engine plant. Deisher told Paul Dilworth that only "must" changes were to be incorporated on the Orenda, leaving other improvements and new developments for later stages in production.

Ground was broken in October, 1950, on a site very close to the aircraft plant on the other side of the highway. Construction on the building commenced in May of 1951, and by the following October the tool room had been set up, followed by manufacturing in April, 1952, assembly in May, and finally the office staff in July. The new plant contained six modern engine test cells and provided 400,000 square feet of floor space.

By the time the office staff had moved in, the executive face of the gas turbine division had changed. Dilworth and Boyd had gone. Crawford Gordon was president, and Tom McCrae was now general manager of gas turbine; Val Cronstedt, formerly of Pratt & Whitney, was director of engineering, Doug Knowles was chief engineer, Maurice Nix was experimental manager, and Earle Brownridge was works manager.

"The lack of adequate facilities has been our chief bottleneck," Crawford Gordon would tell the Toronto *Telegram*.

The Orenda, barring unforeseen difficulties, when the new gas turbine building is opened, we will be turning out at one per day. We would have turned out more CF-100's, but what's the use when we didn't have the engines to fly them.

The official opening of the plant was scheduled for September 29, 1952, and in late August, Gordon forwarded to Howe a press release and some remarks he hoped Howe might include in his speech. Gordon was somewhat disconcerted by Howe's lukewarm response. Howe wrote back that he "would hesitate to tell the world that we are making aircraft history. . . . I am also somewhat disturbed about stories circulating about the lack of co-operation between Avro and certain facilities that were established to support Avro."

Smarting from the daily criticism he was getting in Parliament over delays with the CF-100, despite an increasing government financial investment in the company, Howe felt he was being "conned." He reluctantly agreed to open the engine plant, but he had a few conditions. Everyone was to know that the plant was a "federal facility;" none of the "aircraft side" executives, apart from Fred Smye, were to take part; he couldn't very well bar the presence of Sir Roy Dobson, but Dobson was *not* to be invited to speak.

Dobson was more than a little surprised when he didn't see the likes of Edgar Atkin or Jim Floyd or John Frost at the ceremony, and even more astonished when he wasn't asked to speak.

Gordon kept the news of Howe's requests from him, but when he found out, he was furious, calling Gordon anti-British, anti-Group, and so forth.

—Pat Kelly

Howe's speech was followed by a twenty-minute air show, test pilot Jan Zurakowski flying a CF-100 upside-down above the podium and a demonstration flight of the Orenda in the Lancaster test bed.

By early 1952, A. V. Roe had orders on the books averaging $4 million a month, sometimes reaching as high as $9 million. By May the company payroll had reached 10,000 and the annual take-home pay of the 1,100 employees who lived in Brampton, just minutes from the plant, was a cool $5.5 million.

"You expect miracles in Canada in the way of production," Roy Dobson was to say in a speech to the Empire Club in Toronto that April, but it must be realized that the modern plane takes more than three times the number of man hours to produce than did its counterpart in the last war. Experience has proved that the development of a new aircraft or engine absorbs not less than five years and in many cases, even longer. In this respect, Canada is just about on schedule.

The speech did little to silence Avro's critics or calm C. D. Howe who was rapidly becoming one of them. In June he was once again under fire in Ottawa to justify government investment in A. V. Roe. To date over $120 million had been invested in A. V. Roe Canada. In July, the Hawker-Siddeley Group announced another $3 million would be invested in the Malton facilities, bringing their total investment to $10 million. At the same time share capital was increased to two million shares, of which half were issued to Hawker-Siddeley and the remainder held for future financing. The announcement also described A. V. Roe Canada as "essentially a private company engaged in development research and production of aircraft and jet engines." The phrase "private company" may have prompted Howe's insistence that the Orenda plant be announced as a federal facility and that Dobson be muzzled.

By November Crawford Gordon was able to announce that Avro Canada had joined the ranks of Canada's biggest employers. Hiring at a rate of thirty a day, the work force had now swelled to 12,000, with CF-100 production and the opening of the Orenda plant.

Nineteen fifty-three began with D. L. Thompson, who had taken over Crawford Gordon's position as defence production chief, defending A. V. Roe over the CF-100; the delays, he said, were caused by "hundreds of sub-contractors involved in the project." But a Conservative MP pointed out that de Havilland could produce aircraft for over forty different countries without delays. Was the delay at A. V. Roe really because of government interference, he asked.

In February, 1953, reports had reached the company that Curtiss-Wright's J-65 Sapphire engine was not living up to expectations, and Crawford Gordon suggested to Howe that A. V. Roe try to sell the Orenda in the United States. Howe immediately vetoed the idea:

Your full capacity is required for the Canadian aircraft program . . . . It would be a great comfort to me if you could give Parliament and the public the impression that all efforts of A. V. Roe are being devoted to carrying out the contracts you have in hand.

In April, Dobson came to Canada to formally buy the Orenda plant from the Canadian government. He granted a rare, lengthy interview to the *Globe and Mail* prior to meeting with Howe over the sale, in part to appease Howe and in part to set the record straight. His first words set the tone: "We came to stay and we are here to stay . . . . We are a private enterprise organization. But we are very useful to the government because of the planes and techniques we have developed."

In response to "the common notion that it has cost $100 million to develop the CF-100," Dobson answered,

> Nothing could be farther from the fact. Actually, the development of the CF-100 including armament and radar, cost something less than $10 million. That is much less than it usually costs to develop a new type . . . .
>
> We bought the plant and paid for it in cash . . . . We are not a government company. We are completely privately owned. But the government is our customer and it has been our job to supply it with what it wanted for the RCAF and to serve it to the best of our ability. Whatever they wanted us to produce, we would produce, and we are doing so now. We are right on schedule with all we had agreed to do.

In his pocket Dobson had $6 million as a down payment on the purchase of the Orenda engine plant. Although the original cost of the plant was close to $40 million, Howe let it go for $17.4 million, with the remaining $11.4 million to be paid over a ten-year period. The entire aircraft and engine operation was now privately owned by A. V. Roe Canada. The only thing Dobson didn't get was about 60 per cent of the machine tools which remained government property but on free loan to A. V. Roe as long as they were used exclusively on defence orders.

With the engine plant under the A. V. Roe umbrella, Fred Smye was now able to go after Tom McCrae, never having forgotten McCrae's role in the resignation of Smye's friend, Paul Dilworth, or his attempt to "frame" Earle Brownridge. He suggested to Gordon that the new company would need new blood; McCrae was fired, and in his place Gordon brought in Walter R. McLachlan, an old friend from the John Inglis Company who was now on loan to the Department of Defence Production. McLachlan quickly gave up his position in the DDP for the opportunity to work with Gordon at Malton, and on October 1, 1953, took over as head of the gas turbine division.

12

GODS OF THE AIR

Under the headline "New Canada Jets May Do 1000 MPH," Jim Hornick wrote: "The age of supersonics is knocking at Canada's door . . . . The projected new supersonic dart-shaped jet . . . will become the front-line fighter aircraft for the RCAF." It was January, 1952. Three days later, an angry Crawford Gordon criticized Hornick for speculating about a "delta-winged" fighter. "It so happens," he said, "we are not working on such a project." Hornick hadn't used the words "delta-winged fighter," and A. V. Roe Canada *was* working on such a project.

In the years immediately following the Second World War, the process of procuring a new plane for the RCAF, especially one designed and built in Canada, was long and complicated. The first step was the collection of domestic, British, and American intelligence estimates as to the immediate and long-range aerial threat to continental North America. Next the information was passed on to military planners within the RCAF and the Defence Research Board. Collectively they determined how Canada's forces could jointly meet the threat, planned a course of action, and identified the necessary hardware.

If the necessary hardware was not available, the RCAF Operational Requirements (OR) staff would draw up a set of preliminary specifications. For aircraft, this would include expected capabilities and performance. Canada's RCAF OR staff in those early post-war days consisted of two or three fellows with engineering degrees.

A typical OR was really in those days only two or three pages long. It was a scenario based on a defence plan, and the defence plan at that time was that Canada's focus was air defence. The threat is always defined in the plan, so you take the threat and the plan and ask what you need to complete the task . . . . Out of this comes the OR.

—*A/V/M John Easton*

The OR staff did not shop around for planes. That was left to the brass. Asking for the stars in the OR document is intentional, however, for the OR requirement is usually based on something within "the state of the art," not entirely in "never-never land."

—*General A. C. Hull*

The OR then went to the Air Council for approval, then to the Chiefs of Staff, then to the Department of National Defence for funding. At this point, military technicians at the Department of Supply and Services surveyed all foreign and domestic aircraft companies. If what was required was not available, tenders were put out to appropriate security-conscious companies containing the basic specifications for the aircraft.

If the aircraft manufacturer thought it could meet the specification, it submitted a design proposal to Supply and Services. When a bid was accepted (the RCAF can accept more than one), then a development contract was awarded for the production of one or two prototypes. The RCAF would monitor the project, and if things went well, and the air force was pleased with the prototypes, then the company received a production contract, subsidized by the Canadian taxpayer, to produce a specified number of aircraft, in so many months, at such a cost per plane.

Once the design and development contract was signed, the company would hire the necessary staff; obtain or manufacture the required jigs, tools, and fixtures; build a wooden mock-up of the plane; manufacture any new parts; assemble the prototype; and test the prototype. Once the prototype proved out, a production contract was awarded. Then tooling up would begin to produce the plane in quantity.

This analysis is all after the fact, of course. The development of the CF-100 and the CF-105, and the process of military procurement in general, was not nearly so orderly.

The story of the Arrow dates back to 1948 when the CF-100 program was well under way at A. V. Roe. Even though the CF-100 was still two years away from first flight, the RCAF, with Wilf Curtis in command, was already looking for its successor. John Easton was one of the RCAF officers involved in this long-range planning.

> *I put forward a program in 1945 that allowed a lot of fellows coming home from the war with university degrees to be encouraged by the RCAF to take upgrading in state-of-the-art technology. Consequently, we sent a number of young officers to school, guys like Paul Potter, Frank Foote and Deac Bray,. . . to study advanced aerodynamics, to study the next most likely configuration and general requirements for the future on defence aircraft to follow the CF-100.*
>
> *Bray went to the States, Britain, and France, and through all the industry, and put down his report. In it he outlined an airplane that had the configuration of a tailless delta-winged aircraft. Now this was 1948, and the general thinking of our boys in the back room. Bray's report let us know what the future airplane should look like.*
>
> *—A/V/M John Easton*

At Malton, A. V. Roe Canada was looking at a follow-up to the CF-100 as well, but more from an "adapt what we have" stance. Jim Chamberlin had worked with chief engineer Edgar Atkin to produce a number of configurations. The first effort of July, 1948, designated the C-100-S, was to be powered by two Turbo Research 9 (TR-9) engines; it resembled a swept-winged, swept-tailed CF-100. A second design in the summer of 1949, designated C-100-D and also powered by two TR-9 engines, was designed for supersonic flight. In the summer of 1950, a third design, powered by the same TR-9 engines, was designated C-104.

It wasn't until December, 1950, that A. V. Roe submitted to the RCAF a reworked version of the C-100-S (the swept-wing CF-100) which they called the C-103. Two prototypes were authorized by the government and work commenced in February, 1951, only to be shelved ten months later when wind-tunnel tests indicated that the C-103 would never reach supersonic flight. The full-scale mock-up of the C-103 bore a clear resemblance to the straight-winged CF-100 prototype of three years before.

Work continued on a number of other configurations until March 1952 when the All Weather Requirements Team (AWRT), formed by the RCAF to look at the new operational requirements for an advance fighter, issued their final report. By June, A. V. Roe had submitted two more proposals to the RCAF, C-104/1 and C-104/2, a single-engine and a twin-engine version of a delta-winged aircraft intended to meet the conditions laid down by the AWRT.

The proposal went back and forth between A. V. Roe and the RCAF and, although A. V. Roe was not the only firm hoping for the contract, one can imagine that the engineers at Malton had the inside track, owing to the presence of the RCAF liaison team (headed by W/C Ray Foottit) involved with the CF-100. Foottit had recently been put in charge of overseeing development of all new RCAF aircraft. Finally, in November, 1952, the RCAF issued Operational Requirement 1/1-63 Supersonic All Weather Interceptor Aircraft.

Public attention turned more and more to A. V. Roe: "A group of Canadian engineers at A. V. Roe in Malton," wrote Jim Hornick, "have completed specifications for the RCAF on a new delta-winged fighter that can exceed the speed of sound."

In January, 1952, Jim Floyd had taken over as chief engineer. With the CF-100 problems on the way to being corrected, Floyd and his team of engineers were spending more and more of their time in developing the necessary proposals for this new "supersonic" aircraft. By December optimism was high; they were very much in the running for the contract—except as far as C. D. Howe was concerned, who must have felt at this point that he had given birth to a monster. He wrote to Brooke Claxton, Minister of National Defence, who would have to approve funding for the project:

> I understand that your department is planning a substantial development programme for new supersonic jet engines and for a new fighter aircraft. Before authorizing these items, I think you should appreciate what has already been spent on the Orenda engine and on the CF-100 to date. I must say I am frightened for the first time in my defence production experience. I would argue that at least a year be allowed to pass before any further development work at Avro is undertaken . . . .
>
> I must tell you that the design staff at Avro is far from competent to undertake work of this importance. Their designing record to date is very bad indeed, measured by any standard. If we must have further development work, let us contract it with a British firm which has the personnel, equipment and experience that qualifies them to do work of this kind. Someone so equipped can do the work for a fraction of the cost involved in making the attempt at A. V. Roe.

I hope you will give serious consideration to the dangers inherent in worsening our financial position at A. V. Roe and issue a directive accordingly.

Early in 1953, A/M C. R. Slemon (who had succeeded Wilf Curtis as Chief of Air Staff on January 31) introduced recommendations for the development of a supersonic all-weather interceptor aircraft capable of meeting the new defence threat. In presenting the case to the Chiefs of Staff, Slemon produced figures to show that the cost of development and production would be comparable to similar projects in the United States. The F-86 interceptor aircraft produced from American specifications cost $250,000 each; the CF-100, a Canadian-designed aircraft, was currently being produced for $750,000 each.

The project would be limited to the development and production of an airframe. The power plant would be a fully developed jet engine of American or British make, and the armament and electronics control system were to be obtained from the United States.

The production order was to be based on equipping nine regular and eleven auxillary squadrons with 25 aircraft each by 1959. Allowing for about 100 for wastage, the total output would be around 600. The cost of producing two prototypes was estimated at $25 million; the annual cash requirements could be met from funds currently allotted for aircraft production.

The project was scrutinized most carefully by the Chiefs of Staff and the Department of Defence Production. The initial estimates for the first phase of the program seemed reasonable. The probable costs of the engine and the armament system, however, were only very roughly indicated. There was some hesitation in recommending a program of such complexity and magnitude that had so many unpredictable factors and hidden costs.

The Chiefs of Staff were concerned about the impact in future years of the additional requirements of funds for this aircraft project on the re-armament requirements of the other services. However, from the overall strategic standpoint, there was no doubt that the greatest and most immediate threat to Canada was from the Soviet long-range air force, which had at its disposal a growing stockpile of atomic bombs. It was therefore agreed that priority should be given to meeting this threat. As neither the United States nor England was developing a supersonic all-weather interceptor aircraft that would meet the particular Canadian requirements, the Chiefs of Staff agreed to recommend the project to the Minister of National Defence, Brooke Claxton, for urgent consideration.

Claxton approved the project for submission to the Cabinet Defence Committee; however, he pointed out, there might be some opposition to the project from C. D. Howe, the Minister of Defence Production, who was concerned about overloading A. V. Roe with a big development project when it was already deep in difficulties with production of the CF-100. The cabinet gave its approval to the development of an airframe for a supersonic interceptor aircraft to the extent of producing two prototypes at a cost of $25 million.

When the RCAF issued Specification Air-7-3, "Design Studies of a Prototype Supersonic All Weather Aircraft," in April, 1953, A. V. Roe Canada was able to produce most of the data required by the design study almost immediately. In fact, an RCAF team had visited the plant for three days that same month to discuss the effects the previous two A. V. Roe submissions would have on the study.

> *What the air staff were asking for was the moon. In short they required a two-place, twin-engined aircraft with all-weather reliability, long range, short take-off and landing, an internal weapons compartment as large as the bomb bay of a B-29, and a supersonic manoeuvrability of 2 G at Mach 1.5 at 50,000 feet, without any loss of speed or altitude—a requirement which has been met by few, if any, service aircraft even to this day. In addition, it was to be guided by the most sophisticated automatic flight and fire-control system ever envisaged. It was small wonder that Foottit's team had failed to find any such aircraft on the drawing boards anywhere in the world.*
>
> —Jim Floyd

> *The RCAF laid down such a complex and difficult specification that any engineering team in the world would have been hard pressed to meet that spec. At the time there were many American engineering teams who said they wouldn't even try to meet the spec and that we were off our rocker to even try it.*
>
> —Ron Adey

Rather than work up an entirely new specification, Floyd took another approach. The RCAF was still in possession of the two latest design studies, C-104/1 and C-104/2. Was it necessary to do another?

> *The C-104/1 was like the Arrow with a single engine and the C-104/2 was the Arrow, and the only reason we designated it C-105 was because it was the final submission for Air-7-4. Everyone called it Air-7-3 but it wasn't by the time we got it. Air-7-3 was just a statement of a requirement,*

Air-7-4 was our actual specification to which we designed C-104/1 and C-104/2. In truth C-105 was a fudged C-104 spec.

—Jim Floyd

The RCAF didn't need much time to conclude that the C-105 proposal fit their specification.

On June 6, 1953, the man Fred Smye called the father of the RCAF, Air Marshal Wilfred Austin Curtis, recently retired Chief of Air Staff, joined A. V. Roe Canada as a member of the board of directors.

Curtis had built the post-war air force. He had fought tooth and nail for the lion's share of the defence budget . . . . Those donkeys in the Chiefs of Staff Committee were anti-air force and were all former colleagues of Pearkes. Curtis had ridden all over them.

—Fred Smye

Curtis had had an intimate role in developing the CF-100 which went a long way in endearing him to the company, and to Fred Smye. Appointing him to the board was A. V. Roe's way of thanking him. In return for the benefit of his "experience" Curtis received $20,000 a year and a limousine and chauffeur.

Design work had already commenced on the C-105 by September, 1953, fuelled by a certain amount of excitement over the fact that, that very month at the Farnborough air show in England, a delta-winged aircraft stole the show. So much excitement was created, in fact, that the British government immediately put a ban on all data in Britain related to delta-winged aircraft, including a recent paper written by A. V. Roe's (Manchester) Stuart Davies entitled "The Family of Delta Aircraft."

In January, 1954, C. D. Howe announced that the Department of Defence Production had issued a design contract for a prototype of an advanced aircraft designated the C-105; he indicated the decision had been "delayed by the Cabinet for several months in order to consider the implications of supporting a vigorous domestic aircraft industry." The aircraft in question was expected to weigh more than 30 tons, fly at 1,200 mph, have a range of 1,500 miles, and fire guided missiles.

In the next few months the RCAF and A. V. Roe worked more closely than ever finalizing the design for the C-105. A. V. Roe was developing an engine that they eventually hoped to use in the C-105, but for now the specification called for the Rolls-Royce RB-106. At an advanced stage in the initial design of the plane, Rolls-Royce abandoned development of the RB-106. For Jim Floyd it was the Avon and the Jetliner all over again.

We quickly switched to the Curtiss-Wright J-67, only to have the U.S. government pull out support on that engine. The only suitable engine left was the Pratt & Whitney J-75, so we had to completely redesign the fuselage to take these engines since the power plants were integrated into the fuselage structure . . . . We finally came up with a design which would meet the demanding specifications, a tailless delta, an inevitable compromise between aerodynamic, structural and aeroelastic efficiency, with a very thin wing.

—Jim Floyd

The deal between A. V. Roe and the government was also "redesigned." The United States Air Force was consulted about ways and means of reducing the time lag in the development and the production of the CF-105. The RCAF was advised that to facilitate rapid production, new techniques in testing and proving component parts were required. The advanced procedure, called the Cook-Craigie method, involved the production of ten or more prototypes, so that testing and proving of several components could be accomplished simultaneously, and the risk of a long delay, in the event of the crash of one of the prototypes, eliminated. As a result it was decided in late 1954 that the original contract for two prototypes be amended to eleven "pre-production" aircraft.

Because of the tremendous urgency of the Arrow program, it was decided to eliminate the building of prototype aircraft and virtually go straight into production with "hard tooling" on the first aircraft. Only those who have been associated with the design of a new aircraft will even begin to appreciate the tremendous pressures put onto engineering by the combination of these decisions.

   Here we were dealing with an aircraft more complex in every way than any previous service project, and there were few reports or tests to substantiate the design features. We also had a brand new engine to develop at the same time (a combination avoided if at all possible by every aircraft designer since Icarus), and we were to issue full production drawings from scratch, from which permanent hard tools were made, well prior to even the basic testing program being completed.

   Because of this decision, we had to mount one of the most comprehensive series of wind tunnel, structural, equipment and systems testing programs ever undertaken. The full record of these tests alone would fill a book.

—Jim Floyd

From the time the basic configuration was established to the end of 1956, up to 460 engineers, technicians, and draftsmen worked on the design and development of the Arrow and its systems. "Aerodynamically, the Arrow was entering a new realm of science. Performance, stability, and control problems were difficult to evaluate, and data had to be obtained to establish airloads on the wing, fin, canopy and control surface." Analog computing equipment was installed at A. V. Roe to accelerate the solution of aerodynamic and stress problems. The company also obtained a new electronic digital computer of great speed and capacity, an IBM 704, a giant computer equivalent in calculating and problem-solving power to 3,000 perfectly organized and trained engineers.

Supersonic aircraft also involved problems not encountered in the past. Two such problems which required extensive investigation relate to structural weakness caused by heat and sound. The heat problem is caused by friction between air and aircraft skin. Temperatures attained while flying at supersonic speeds are high enough to weaken structure—the higher the speed, the greater the heat. There are two main types of detrimental sound—jet engine and aerodynamic. These can cause the skin panels of the aircraft to fracture and rivets to loosen. New materials and methods of construction that would withstand the rigours of supersonic flight had to be found or manufactured and tested. The hundreds of items of mechanical, hydraulic, electrical, and electronic equipment in the C-105 were all required to operate with the utmost reliability in a severe high-temperature, high-altitude environment. Such equipment did not exist in 1954.

Long before the first of 17,000 engineering drawings were released to the manufacturing division, preparations for production planning and tooling-up were already underway. The procurement department at A. V. Roe negotiated with more than 650 suppliers, and as the program progressed, more than 5,000 people were employed with sub-contractors in the manufacture of C-105 parts and tools. In the production shops, difficult machine and forming operations became the rule rather than the exception, while many major advances were made in tooling techniques and methods. The thousands of production shop personnel made and assembled some 38,000 parts for the first C-105. This was a major task in that CF-100 production was also going full tilt at the time. That the C-105 was fabricated and assembled in less than two and a half years from the date of the first design release is profound evidence of the successful pre-planning of the Arrow program.

Designers, especially those in the aircraft and engine business, are a funny breed. Misinterpreted most of the time by the outside world, and understood by few, they seek friendship and solace in the company of their peers. Generally an unemotional lot, their minds far outdistance their present surroundings, and once their design is on paper, they quickly move ahead to other things, leaving the nuts and bolts of their ideas to be cleaned up and fashioned into engines and aircraft by assistants and underlings.

Even before Winnett Boyd had left A. V. Roe Canada, he was tinkering with the future, with the next generation of engine beyond the Chinook and the Orenda.

In the last six months of 1950, the company had two successful engines and two successful aircraft and weren't about to spend time and money on anything else. But my attitude was we had to continue to look ahead so I secreted a couple of fellows and myself in a design office and worked on the Wakunda secretly. Basically, it was a design that added a couple of stages on the compressor, had 7,500 pounds thrust—we had another version of 10,000 pounds thrust—it was going to employ external combustion chambers but we'd given some thought to annular combustion chambers. This was as far as the Wakunda ever got because I left the company soon after.

—Winnett Boyd

By 1952 there was a need to upgrade the Orenda and there were two ways to do it. One was to make a modification, like designing a new front stage to it to bring it up to 8,000 pounds thrust. We tried to sell this 8,000-pound-thrust Orenda but we had two strikes against us. One was that the F-86 Sabre was pulling as much flow as it could through the inlet duct and the "straw it was drinking through" wouldn't take any more. This meant it was solely a CF-100 engine. The second strike against us was we couldn't put any extra thrust in the CF-100 because it was buffet-limited at high altitude. So we didn't manage to sell the 8,000-pound-thrust engine and after that it died . . . .

Afterburners are designed to give aircraft an extra burst of speed for brief periods, almost like having another engine. The principle is simple. The jet engine's tailpipe is lengthened and equipped with a perforated grid. When maximum power is needed, fuel is squirted into the stream of hot exhaust gas hurling through the tailpipe. The fuel is ignited and the plane gets added forward thrust.

—Harry Keast

Although the Orenda was a great success in its time, it was obvious that A. V. Roe would need something with much more power than a modified Orenda could be expected to achieve if the company hoped to compete with British and American engines to power the types of aircraft then being specified. There were some new faces at the gas turbine division by now: Val Cronstedt was vice-president of engineering, and Charles Grinyer had replaced Doug Knowles as chief development engineer. Harry Keast was Grinyer's assistant. Keast had done research on the new Pratt & Whitney J-75 engine, which was a two-spooled, cigar-shaped engine, and designed a computer program to calculate and project what performances might be achieved by two-spooled engines.

I did some parametric studies and decided we should look at the design specs. For the Arrow we had to optimize the engine to meet the spec. At that time the Arrow was expected to have the capability to do a 2G turn at Mach 1.5 at 50,000 feet. Our aircraft people had calculated the drag they expected from this type of airplane, so we worked backwards to see what it would be at ground level. . . . The idea was to look at engines ranging from a 10,000- to a 20,000-pound thrust. During this period I talked to Jim Chamberlin who was with the Arrow program and remember him telling me, "We've got a 42-inch-diameter hole. Think you can fill it?"

—Harry Keast

In the spring of 1953 a series of project studies—aerodynamic and performance studies and mechanical design lay-outs—were prepared for the Hawker-Siddeley Group Design Council. Cronstedt looked at the parametric studies, especially the PS-13 study, and at the Arrow specification; then he gave the go-ahead to turn the PS-13 study into an engine.

Charles Grinyer had been with gas turbine since March of 1952 having come from Bristol Aircraft in England where he had worked on the development of the Olympus and Phoebus jet engines. Before that he had put in ten years with the British Air Ministry. Although PS-13 had been influenced to some degree by the Arrow specification, in the beginning it was not a foregone conclusion that PS-13 would be *the* engine to power the Arrow. Grinyer, for one, believed the Arrow was not going to come to anything, so he designed the engine not only for the Arrow, but he had it in mind to meet American requirements also. Keast disagrees, saying it was the objective "right from the start that the engine would be in the Arrow." He does concede, however, that there was some resistance from the Arrow engineers.

They had a good J-75 there, and this was an untested engine. They had set up a production line and they'd have to make changes to accept the

Iroquois. Even though we were the poorer cousins, there was little difference in optimism between them and us.

—*Harry Keast*

There was no guarantee of success—it was a risky, speculative venture and in the initial stages would be funded by private capital—but in December, 1953, PS-13 was given approval by Hawker-Siddeley and the following January, just as C. D. Howe was announcing the C-105 contract, $3.5 million of Hawker-Siddeley funds were earmarked for PS-13.

Val Cronstedt gave PS-13 the name "Iroquois" in keeping with the Canadian Indian theme established by Winnett Boyd years before. Although they had no quarrel with following the Indian theme, few of Cronstedt's engineers liked the name Iroquois, especially Keast, who "figured the Americans would think it was a beer, after Iroquois beer in New York State." For Keast, there was only one name to give the engine: Wendigo, for evil spirit.

In August of 1954, Janusz Zurakowski, Bill Waterton's replacement on the CF-100 program, took a CF-100 Mk.4 for a test flight with a twenty-four-year-old engineer named John Hiebert in the observer's seat. The flight was scheduled to test a new heavy armament package, the ventral rocket pack, which would hold forty-eight rockets. It would be lowered to fire the rockets and then retracted immediately. The danger was that the aircraft would pitch upward and become unstable when the rocket pack was lowered. Zurakowski was skeptical of the plan and the test but, being the professional he was, went along with it. Hiebert, from the design office, went along to record the results.

The engineering division insisted on measurement of stability at all speed ranges with the pack up and down so that an automatic correction system to the controls could be designed to eliminate any change of trim occurring at the critical firing moment.

—*Janusz Zurakowski*

Suddenly, at 5,000 feet there was an explosion in the back of the aircraft and the controls to the aircraft locked; Zurakowski no longer had control of the aircraft.

I yelled to John to prepare to bail out . . . wait a few seconds and jettison the canopy. I then jettisoned the rocket pack and prepared to abandon the aircraft. A few seconds after jettisoning the canopy I heard a bang and assumed my observer had ejected. I was a bit surprised he had already gone. Now I ejected, and when my parachute opened I realized my left ankle was fractured. In attempting to force the controls I had forced my seat out and broke my ankle. I landed on my foot on a hard field near Ajax.

In the hospital I learned the second explosion was not the ejection of my observer but rather another explosion which probably damaged his ejection mechanism or incapacitated him. He was killed in the crash.

My impression was that the cause of the accident was probably ignition by electric spark of fuel spilled in the rear fuselage from fractured fuel lines due to excessive vibration of the aircraft with the rocket pack down.

Daily press stories that I was trying to save populated areas by directing the aircraft to open fields have no relation to facts. After the first explosion I was unable to move the controls even a fraction of an inch.

—*Janusz Zurakowski*

Hiebert's failure to get out of the aircraft brought up the disturbing possibility, to both A. V. Roe and the RCAF, that pilots and observers might not be able to escape from a disabled aircraft. Prior to Zurakowski's mishap, eight CF-100's had been lost. Of those, (including the first Warren/Ostrander crash) an abnormally high six pilots and six observers had lost their lives. John Hiebert was number thirteen.

In the flight test department at A. V. Roe was a young flight test observer named Geoff Grossmith who had been with the company since 1949. The CF-100 fatality list bothered the hell out of him.

In those days flight test engineers were into fuel consumption, aerodynamics, radios and things. I had ten in my group who flew in the aircraft occasionally; we were a hotshot bunch of guys. One day one of my guys came back from a flight that had lost a canopy and was complaining over having banged up his wrists during the flight. I got to talking to him and began to believe he wouldn't have been able to get out of the airplane. Prior to this I had heard rumors about what happened to young John Hiebert. He wasn't with my group but I had heard when they had found his body his hands were pretty cut up, damaged in flight; some said they had found him with his hands cut off at the wrists.

Well I kept yakking and yakking about it and finally convinced Don Rogers that there was a possibility you couldn't get out of the back of the aircraft, the back seat, if you lost a canopy.

To prove my point I went up as the observer in a CF-100 piloted by Peter Cope. All our aircraft were equipped with Martin-Baker ejection seats. To operate them, the pilot or observer had to reach up in front of him to a point just behind his head where he'd find a large ring device. To eject you had to pull this ring, much like reaching behind you in a shower to scrub your back with a large scrub brush.

At about 250 knots, I tried to reach up and pull the blind and I couldn't even reach the blind; my arms were waving all over the place. And when we landed it felt like I'd been hit by a couple of two-by-fours on each hand. Well, we tried it at 200 knots, same thing; at 129 knots, same thing; then, just above stall I was able to get my hands up to pull the ring. Next day I could hardly move my hands.

In the debriefing room afterwards I proved my point, that this kid had been killed because he couldn't pull the blind down. Shortly afterward they played the tape back of me during the flight and I was cursing and swearing and calling everyone a stupid bastard.

—Geoff Grossmith

After Grossmith's experiment A. V. Roe developed a windscreen for the observer's protection. This was installed on new CF-100's starting in February, 1955. It was adopted by the RCAF only after A. V. Roe observers were forbidden to fly in the plane for any further tests, at which point the air force tested it, and finding it a great improvement, issued a specification.

The first run of the Iroquois, scheduled for December 19, 1954, very nearly didn't happen.

The first run was terrible because we couldn't get the damn thing started. We originally felt the transonic compressor would have all the bugs but this was not the case. Every time we tried to start it and disengage the starter motor the engine would die. We worked until two in the morning, gave up, and came back the next day. Well, that very day Charles Grinyer [now vice-president, engineering, at Orenda Engines] had to go to Ottawa and report progress to the government. We had worked all morning trying to get the damn thing started. He had a four o'clock flight and he was very down in the dumps because it appeared he might have to go to Ottawa and report the engine wouldn't run.

The Arrow had a big requirement for air take-off, air conditioning, and so forth, and we didn't know where they wanted to take it off, so we put air take-off ports all around the outside of each compressor. I suggested we take off all the covers from the ports—leave them all wide open. Grinyer said okay, try it, but he had to go. So I got the guys to take them all off, and we had another go and the engine lit. It went up to 3,000 rpm—we cut the starter motor and it kept running between 3,000 and 3,100, self-sustained; this was the first time we'd had success.

I immediately got on the phone to Grinyer's secretary but he'd already gone to the airport. At that time you could page people at the airport, so she paged him: "THE IROQUOIS IS RUNNING SELF-SUSTAINED

AT 3000 RPM." Grinyer later told me he walked to his plane about two feet off the ground.

—Harry Keast

The Canadian government, through the Defence Research Board, had invested $409,000 in John Frost's saucer project since 1952, but C. D. Howe was eager to have the USAF take over the project entirely. "We decided it was not suitable to our purpose." He said "It didn't seem the sort of thing for Canada to be developing."

Fortunately for Frost the Americans thought otherwise. "These facilities are as modern and as well organized as any I have seen," wrote one senior USAF officer when the deal was closed. "And additionally you appear to have more expandibility than many of our U.S. concerns. Geographically we are all Americans and share the same security problem so I am more than happy that your capability is additive to that of U.S. industry."

They can have it, thought Howe. "The chances are five to one against it working out," he said. "We aren't pinning any hopes on it at all." By 1954, Frost's "special projects group" had grown to thirty. Now totally funded by U.S. dollars, Frost and his team, much to the relief of Jim Floyd as head of engineering, reported directly to Fred Smye.

The saucer's design had changed as well by this time. The single-power-plant idea had been abandoned in favour of having one large rotor powered by six off-the-shelf, annular jet engines. A model with six Viper test rigs was developed and the project was once again renamed, becoming System 606A.

On February 14, 1954, A. V. Roe Canada delivered its thousandth Orenda engine to the RCAF. "For a country that had never before designed and built even a piston engine," Crawford Gordon would say about the event, "this is an achievement of which we can be proud." And C. D. Howe, in a rare moment of praise for the company, called it an "excellent success."

For a company who's successes to date had been rare, Gordon searched for early indicators that one of them was making a profit. In Gordon's first year with the company, profits amounted to a modest $3 million, but by 1954 had jumped to $8 million, "and," said Roy Dobson, "we haven't taken a penny out of the country. It's all been ploughed back."

Because A. V. Roe Canada was a two-product company, engines and aircraft, and because the Canadian government was its only customer, many people, including most of the general public, still believed the company was government owned or at least a crown corporation. Not so, said Crawford Gordon. "The only government assistance we are receiving now is for certain machine tools and special test equipment. Of course, Ottawa makes security checks on all our employees."

A. V. Roe's being a two-product company bothered Gordon almost as much its being a one-customer company. For him the next natural step was diversification.

When you have a company that's built solely on government contracts, there's a certain amount of political interference. You're highly dependent on that one agency—the government. I mean it's only sensible to diversify if you can.

—Crawford Gordon III

The first step to diversification began on July 29, 1954, when the aircraft division of A. V. Roe Canada became incorporated as Avro Aircraft Limited and the gas turbine division became Orenda Engines Limited after their famous engine. A. V. Roe Canada Limited remained as a holding company controlled entirely by Hawker-Siddeley. Crawford Gordon remained president of A. V. Roe Canada as well as becoming chairman and president of both Avro Aircraft and Orenda Engines.

The second step, on December 4, 1954, was the purchase of Canadian Steel Improvement, a Hawker-Siddeley subsidiary in west Toronto that produced the blades of Orenda's engines and other light alloy products. "Each company," said Gordon, "will have its own board of directors, functions of finance, legal, industrial relations and public relations divisions. Each company will be free to develop its own products and customers regardless of the other's problems. At the same time each will enjoy the benefits of group association, notably financial and management strength of the group as a whole."

With diversification came some upward mobility appointments. Fred Smye was appointed vice-president and general manager of Avro Aircraft while Walter McLachlan was given the same title at Orenda. Vice-president, engineering, at Avro was Jim Floyd and at Orenda, Charles Grinyer. Earle Brownridge was appointed head of manufacturing at Orenda. Smye and McLachlan also became directors of the A. V. Roe Canada holding company. The average age of A. V. Roe Canada's executives was slightly over forty.

13

COMING OF AGE

As had been the case with Victory Aircraft and National Steel Car, Avro Aircraft and Orenda Engines had their fair share of labour problems. Most of them had to do with wages and unexpected layoffs due to parts shortages or changing production schedules. For the life of the company, all union personnel at Avro and Orenda were organized under the Machinists Union, at the time a no-nonsense outfit.

The first actual walkout at A. V. Roe Canada occurred in February, 1954, over the layoff of 55 workers. In January, 1955, 2,000 were laid off over CF-100 slowdowns while the company scoured Canadian universities in desperate need of 200 graduate engineers. Commenting on this layoff, a union representative at Avro said it was expected and charged that the company "should be turning out Jetliners" to keep the men working. "The prototype of our Jetliner," he added, "was flying slowly over head last week when the laid-off workers left. It was as if it were saying: Well boys its all over now."

In defence of the company, board member A/M Wilf Curtis remarked in a speech to the Toronto Branch of the Society of Automotive Engineers:

Our buildup to the present manufacturing and designing position was made possible to a great extent by inducing a goodly number of experienced men to emigrate to Canada from the UK and the US. There is a crying demand throughout the aircraft industry for young men with scientific training. It is a real national defence problem. Russia is training two and a half times as many engineering students as Canada.

So militant was the Machinists Union over the situation that C. D. Howe went out of his way to assure the Toronto Trade and Labour Congress that there would be no further layoffs at A. V. Roe. Nevertheless, two months later, in March, 1955, another 1,000 men were laid off with the dubious consolation that 300 would be called back to work on the CF-105 program. "Our aim is not to produce the maximum number of aircraft as quickly as possible," said Howe.

Rather it is to produce in the next few years enough of these instruments of warfare to bring our defences and those of our allies up to an adequate level; and to be ready in the event of an all-out war to produce at full blast. Since 1950, Canadian factories have manufactured more than 4,000 aircraft, including 2,200 jets, and 3,500 aircraft engines including 2,800 jet engines.

In April, 1955, the Machinists Union demanded fines for workers who put in overtime on the Arrow program, thinking the less overtime people worked, the more would be recalled. "We must get the CF-105 rolling in order to create employment on the production line," said industrial relations manager Bill Dickie, to which the union countered: Don't work overtime if you value your job. Howe was quick to blame the company's labour troubles on company management: "There is no lack of orders at the moment," he said. "Employment at the plant depends upon management."

Bill Dickie told a Toronto newspaper on May 12, 1955, that A. V. Roe Canada was now worth $65,057,725 including land, plant, and equipment, that contracts for the production of aircraft and engines were negotiated on the basis of a fixed fee plus incentive bonus, and that profits were limited to 10 per cent. Labour problems notwithstanding, Avro Aircraft and Orenda Engines were attractive employers. A. V. Roe had become recognized as a company that cared about its employees. One of its more "progressive" moves came in 1954 when the annual golf tournament at the Lakeview Golf Club was cancelled because the club refused to let Avro employee Jim Marshall on the course. Marshall was black.

Company benefits were good, and by 1955, the company's employment office was receiving over two thousand inquiries a month for jobs. Bill Dickie's staff was travelling 25,000 miles a year in the never ending search for skilled engineers and professionals. As well, constant recruiting was carried out through newspapers, magazines, professional journals, and university newspapers.

In many cases, new employees came from out of town or abroad, arriving at Malton with only luggage. Employee services kept a list of two hundred houses, apartments, flats, and rooms, furnished and unfurnished, for immediate occupancy until the new employee secured permanent residence.

The company's employment office also worked in close liaison with such organizations as the CNIB and other rehabilitation centres to help place disabled individuals in the company. By 1955 the company had employed six blind and over three hundred other physically disabled individuals in the company. "Employing handicapped persons can be good business for the community concerned and the community at large," said Crawford Gordon. "We're glad to have them."

Malton in the fifties was an exciting place. The Arrow, the Iroquois, and John Frost's flying saucer were all in the very forefront of research and development—and they were all top secret. A new employee joining Avro or Orenda in 1955 would be immediately obliged to take an oath of secrecy to reveal to no one any and all matters concerning the production of aircraft or engines. Employees were required to carry with them at all times photo-identification passes—colour-coded to indicate one of four levels of security clearance for entrance to certain departments. Security was crucial at Malton, and the company's security force numbered larger than many small cities in Canada. All of the company's security guards were duly sworn constables of the Peel County Police Force.

On any given day the chief of the air staff, or C. D. Howe, still arguably the single most powerful man in Canada, or highly placed American military personnel might be encountered. Successive incarnations of the CF-100 were constantly being tested to extend the plane's capabilities, and test-pilots flirted daily with death, sometimes with fatal results. In October, 1955, A. V. Roe test pilot Glen Lynes, while attempting, perhaps prematurely, some acrobatic manoeuvres, lost control of his new CF-100 Mk.5, which had flown for the first time only eight days previously. The Mk.5 had extended wingtips and tailplane tips and was 500 pounds lighter than the Mk.4 version. The Mk.5 was also subject to structural flaws which later became evident after it was taken on strength by the RCAF. It was not determined why Lynes lost control of his craft, but he did manage to get out;

however, officials said he had ejected too close to the ground for his parachute to open properly. The thirty-six-year-old Lynes did not survive.

Having a company the size of A. V. Roe next door changed the face of the village of Malton forever. In the 1850s, Toronto Township, in which the village of Malton then sat, boasted 31 blacksmiths, 4 clergymen, 16 school teachers, 4 doctors, 18 coopers, 615 farmers, 27 hotel keepers, 30 merchants, and 7 "gentlemen." A few years later, because the Grand Trunk Railway from Montreal to Sarnia passed through it, Malton became a shipping centre for much of the produce of the County of Peel. Things became so busy, in fact, that the railroad hired a full-time agent, night operator, and switch operator to keep pace with mile-long line-ups of farm wagons waiting to pick up goods at the station.

In 1867 Brampton was chosen over Malton as the county seat by the United Council of York and Peel. This sounded the village's temporary death knell, and its peak population of 500 soon slipped to 150, where it would remain for the next seventy years or so, until Toronto decided it needed an airport.

Pre-1938 Malton was little more than four corners, a scattering of houses and a drug store, when the city of Toronto set up a commission to find a place for an airport. The commission looked first within the city for the necessary space to operate an airfield. Centre Island was their first choice but it did not allow for much future expansion. Happily for Toronto, the commission looked farther afield. To the northwest of the city they found Malton and purchased 1,600 acres. The second Malton boom began.

The airport soon attracted other industries to Malton, the most prominent being National Steel Car which set up its aircraft division on 6 acres in 1938. By 1955 the population of the village had increased to 1,600. In terms of taxes, Avro represented over 90 per cent of the village's total assessment of nearly $1.2 million, of which only $100,000 returned directly to Malton. Feeling the pinch, the village made three attempts between 1946 and 1955 to incorporate as a town and secede from Toronto Township, a move totally supported by A. V. Roe president, Crawford Gordon, who said in 1954, "We can't hold a shield over Toronto Township forever. The people of the village are being crucified."

The village was happy to have the support of Crawford Gordon, but cohabiting with a monster the size of A. V. Roe produced its own special problems. One was traffic. The traffic jams during shift changes at A. V. Roe were called the worst in Canada. Another was housing. More than a thousand houses were being built by the company for A. V. Roe employees in Thistletown, Cooksville, Alderwood, Rexdale, Brampton, and Downsview, with another seven to eight hundred in the village of Malton itself. The terms were attractive if you worked for A. V. Roe—asking price was between $7,500 and $10,000, for as little as 10 per cent down and a 3 per cent mortgage. It was projected the population in the Malton area would reach fifteen to twenty-five thousand by 1960.

With the people and the houses came water shortages. On a number of occasions, the Avro plant had to be shut down, or workers would come to work showerless, because the village and the company relied on wells, which were incapable of keeping up with the increasing demand for water.

But the worst problem both for the village and for people living miles away, certainly the problem that A. V. Roe received the most complaints about, was the noise created by the jet engines. Jet engines, to be tested properly, need to be run, non-stop ("The Orenda ran for 784 hours without being taken off its test stand"). The noise not only easily penetrated the walls of every house in Malton, but the wail of the engines could be heard as far away as Weston and Mount Dennis, some 12 miles distant. "Teachers said pupils couldn't concentrate; Ministers resented the competition to their sermons, domestic discords were reported, and physicians said the noise frayed nerves." And housewives in Malton were complaining of headaches. The company received complaints daily, both written and telephone, about the jet engine noise until a sound-proofing system was eventually installed at a cost of over a million dollars.

Disaster struck Avro Aircraft when, in the early evening of March 23, 1955, a $5 million blaze swept through one of the hangars destroying the Lancaster-Orenda test bed, a Sabre, two CF-100's, and some test equipment.

I heard a funny noise and looked up to see a huge blue flash hop out of the fusebox. I ran for the fire extinguisher but by the time I got to the fire, the flames were already over the wall.

—*Ed McCormick*

Despite the loss of aircraft and equipment, company management breathed a sigh of relief because their "Big Engine," the Iroquois, wasn't there.

By June, Crawford Gordon was once again ready to add to the A. V. Roe family. Offering $30 a share, he acquired Canadian Car and Foundry. The head office was in Montreal and there were four divisions located in Montreal and Fort William. Dominion and Turcot Diesel and the engineering division in Longueuil produced freight and passenger railway equipment; the steel foundry division in Montreal was the largest foundry in the country and produced castings of all kinds; the Fort William plant, the automotive and aircraft division, made buses, transport trailers, and parts for military aircraft. It was the Fort William plant that had built the Hurricanes during the war, the same ones that Wilf Curtis had wanted for the western defence of Canada.

The assets of Canadian Car and Foundry totalled $36 million; Gordon paid $21 million, although A. V. Roe spent an additional $19 million to modernize and expand their latest acquisition. Canadian Car was then divided into two separate companies: Canadian Car and Foundry and Canadian Steel Foundries. "We consider that the products this company makes and the way it operates are basic to Canada," said Roy Dobson, "just as aircraft and engine design and development are also basic to Canada. I am quite confident that as time rolls by, we shall be seeing things rolling out of CanCar just as they have out of Avro and Orenda. And that to me will be another proud day."

"We did it to broaden our industrial base and diversify operations and interests," said Crawford Gordon. "With one stride we, as a country and company, stepped into what is unquestionably one of the toughest designing and manufacturing businesses in the world. And despite our late start we are doing all right." Even C. D. Howe was impressed, admitting that Avro Aircraft was in "the best position of any aircraft plant in Canada of receiving government contracts."

By 1955 John Frost's saucer design had moved along at a sufficient pace that wind tunnel tests were arranged at Wright Field in Ohio under the auspices of the Massachusetts Institute of Technology. A half-scale model—a 6-foot-diameter steel disc—was used in the tests which showed great promise until one of the group's engineers discovered an error in the work. In the words of Des Earl, it "really shot a hole in the line we'd been given on supersonic performance."

We very quickly learned that the annular jet cushion, although quite stable close to the ground, becomes progressively more unstable as the height is increased.

—*John Frost*

This was the trigger which forced us to subsonic. We felt this was a major disaster in the program because we realized our original hope for a Mach 3 airplane was not achievable.

—*Des Earl*

When Smye heard of the problem the group had encountered at Wright Field, he immediately got hold of Frost and asked if just looking at a subsonic vertical take-off vehicle was still worth it. When Frost said he felt it was, the group received their second reprieve. Work would continue.

"Do you really understand all we've been trying to do?" asked Des Earl of Fred Smye.

"Hell no!" was the reply. "But I can sell it!"

In December, 1955, A. V. Roe celebrated ten years as a company. There was a birthday bash at Toronto's most elegant hotel, the King Edward. Sir Roy Dobson made the last of the after-dinner speeches. In the boozy cameraderie of the moment, Sir Roy waxed almost sublime; in hindsight, his words seem almost tragic. Of Crawford Gordon, he said,

> When he sets his mind to do a job he'll do it in spite of hell and high water. And that is what he has done in A. V. Roe. If you compare A. V. Roe now to what it was just over four short years ago when Crawford came, you will realize some of the things he has done. You can rely on him. As long as he is at the helm of this company you haven't anything to worry about.

Of his "little empire in Canada," he said,

> What about the future, boys? Well, aircraft and engines are going to go higher and farther and faster. We have put the Jetliner to bed now but we shall probably have a go at another one, and it won't be anything like the one we have just done. It will be a truly supersonic job that will go across the Atlantic at, let us say, 1,500 miles an hour and do the Atlantic in two and a half hours with real regularity, and in comfort and safety. That is the sort of thing that is within our grasp. . . . You will get into electronic things . . . . You will get into missiles. You cannot avoid it. All kinds of fine engineering will have to be developed within our Group, whether it is in CanCar, Canadian Steel Improvement, Avro, or Orenda. Maybe the future will have some fancy gas turbine or diesel trains too. Those things have got to come . . . . The future will only belong to Canada if Canada—the people of Canada—have faith in the destiny of Canada and work like blazes to make that destiny come true.

By 1955, a revised proposal for the CF-105, at an estimated cost of $200 million, was approved by the cabinet. A. V. Roe now had a pre-production order of twenty-nine aircraft to facilitate full-scale production at a much earlier date. Further, the Iroquois commitment boosted the cost of development from the original $25 million of 1953 to $410 million estimated at the end of 1955.

Even this greatly augmented figure did not include the cost of the armament and electronic control systems. Initially the CF-105 was to take the Hughes MX-1179 weapons and fire-control system with Falcon missiles. The Falcon missile had been successfully developed by the USAF, but it was designed for a single-seat interceptor and required a very sophisticated ground environment for directing the pilot into the target; such a system would not meet the RCAF's requirements for operations well beyond the area of sophisticated ground control. The RCAF was following very closely the developments of air-to-air missiles by the USAF and the United States Navy. The United States Navy was developing a family of missiles known as Sparrow; the specifications of its Mark II version appeared to meet the requirements of the CF-105.

Switching to the Sparrow II missiles would entail finding a more sophisticated electronic weapons and fire-control system. The as yet undeveloped Astra system appeared to satisfy the RCAF specifications.

In mid-1955, the air force and the Defence Research Board came to the conclusion that the Sparrow Mark II air-to-air missile and Astra would provide the most suitable form of armament and weapons control for the CF-105. In December, 1955, the government approved the expenditure of $65 million to obtain a number of the Sparrow Mark II missiles for operational trials in the CF-100.

A modern fighter aircraft combines five separate, independent entities: airframe, engine, fire control, armament, and ground control. Sometimes the combination works; sometimes it doesn't. The case of the CF-105 was further complicated by A. V. Roe's decision to move straight from design to production, eliminating traditional pure prototypes.

When the Arrow program began accelerating in 1955, RCAF headquarters, as they had with the CF-100, began assigning officers with engineering and technical experience to Avro Aircraft to monitor as closely as possible the CF-105 program. In the beginning, for about a day a week, RCAF people monitored engine, air frame, and fire control developments and did liaison work with the various company subcontractors. Joe Schultz, for instance, one of the first to receive a preproduction CF-100 four years before, found himself assigned to Avro even before the mock-up was finished, because he "knew better than any man in the RCAF the problems they had with the CF-100." Besides their one day a week at the plant, the officers held formal regular meetings with Jim Floyd's engineers and kept in close touch with RCAF headquarters in Ottawa.

Progress, meanwhile, on the airframe and the engine for the CF-105 was slow. Wind tunnel tests were being carried out at Cornell University in Buffalo, and in August a scale model riding on a Nike missile broke the sound barrier. By the autumn of 1955, Fred Smye informed Defence Production officials that the sums already appropriated for the project were not sufficient for it to adhere to the timetable laid down earlier that year. The company requested an additional $60 million to keep the project on schedule. This acceleration of estimated costs shocked the government. A review of the entire project was ordered. A group of experts from the RCAF, the Defence Research Board, the Department of Defence Production, the Treasury, and the aeronautics establishment was formed to undertake the review and report to the Chiefs of Staff Committee.

The report, submitted in November, 1955, showed that much of the additional cost was occasioned by steady advances in the prices of materials, the rates paid for labour, and the heavier outlays for overhead, which were mainly charged to the CF-105 project. The experts concluded that the program would need additional funds if it was going to continue.

A major concern of the Chiefs of Staff was the effect of the increasing costs of the CF-105 project on the re-armament programs of the army and navy, especially in light of the current tendency of the government to reduce the defence appropriations. The allotment of $1.973 billion in 1953 declined to $1.858 billion in 1954 and to $1.688 billion in 1955. With this in mind, the Chiefs considered scrapping the CF-105 project altogether and substituting one of the United States supersonic interceptors, such as the F-101-B Voodoo or the F-102, which were in the last stages of development. The advantages in this course of action were obvious: the USAF would meet all the development charges, take all the risks, and sell to Canada at a reduced price made possible by tacking on the RCAF's requirement to the end of their production line. The RCAF would be able to make a realistic assessment of the cost of Canada's air defence commitment instead of having to face, every few months, the demands of A. V. Roe for more and more development funds.

In spite of these advantages, the RCAF was not satisfied that any of the American planes would meet the requirements for operations beyond the area of sophisticated ground control. Then there was the RCAF's insistence from its very beginnings, long-entrenched by now, that it be able to specify exactly what it required instead of having to shop around and settle for something that didn't quite come up to the mark. The thinking that pervaded the RCAF at this time had been expressed by Wilf Curtis in 1950 when he was Chief of the air force. It made no difference that he was talking about the CF-100, for as we now know, the design that would become the CF-105 had already been conceived.

> If you must have an Air Force, you must have an aircraft industry behind it, and, by encouraging a Canadian factory to build a Canadian type of aircraft, we were not only giving employment to engineers and setting up an engineering staff, but we were helping industry here to support the Air Force.

The government was concerned about going ahead with this costly, complicated, and highly technical project with which Canada had only limited experience. It had little to show for the $300 million already spent. Not one of the "prototypes" was ready to fly. After much discussion, the USAF was requested to send a team of experts to assess the whole project and to compare the technical details, and the progress being made, with that of comparable programs in the United States.

Two courses were open to the government: to continue the project at an increased cost of $60 million, with no firm estimates of the future funds required for the Sparrow missile system and the Astra electronic control system; or to cancel the whole project, and purchase from the United States, or manufacture in Canada, under American licence, an aircraft such as the Voodoo. This second course would require the establishment of sophisticated ground control and would limit tactical interceptor operations to the areas of ground control.

In December, 1955, the government decided to limit development to eleven aircraft, but to allow a start to be made on the production of the Astra electronic control system, with a limit on expenditures for all aspects of the project to $170 million a year until 1958, with the provision that the program would be reviewed after the first flight.

The project received a crushing blow late in 1956 when the United States Navy decided to discontinue development of the Sparrow II. For Canada to take over development and set up a production line for a relatively small number of missiles was bound to be expensive and uneconomical. One possibility was to revive the Canadian Velvet Glove missile project, cancelled earlier in 1956 mainly because the RCAF had chosen Sparrow II, but close examination showed that the Sparrow missile was in a more advanced stage of development, and from the RCAF's point of view, was far superior to Velvet Glove.

Another possibility was to abandon the concept of operating interceptor aircraft beyond the area of ground control and retreat to the earlier plan of the ground-controlled, air-to-air Falcon missile, which would be available shortly. However, the RCAF clung tenaciously to its original concept of an interceptor which would navigate and control the firing of missiles without the need of highly developed ground control. Anything less than Astra and Sparrow would be a waste of the CF-105's potential in terms of its ideal weapons platform. The government, with many other urgent matters to deal with, decided to shelve the Sparrow issue until such time as the CF-105 had made a successful flight.

Early in 1957—an election year—the CF-105 program was scrutinized by the Treasury Board and drastic cuts were ordered. The pre-production order was reduced from eleven to eight aircraft, and total expenditures for all elements of the project were limited to $216 million. Consequently the project was subjected to a further slow-down, and it was now forecast that the aircraft would not be available for squadron use until 1961 or 1962.

By October, 1957, a new formal RCAF management group was set up to monitor and co-ordinate development of the CF-105. The group, headed by W/C Ray Foottit, included people from the Department of Defence Production, the Department of Supply and Services, and the Defence Research Board. In all, seventy-five non-Avro personnel were involved with the Arrow project, fifteen of them RCAF officers.

Our senior air force people really didn't expect to get explanations for decisions from the company. They expected the explanations from the engineering people in the air force. Our job was to keep people informed and get decisions. And from the Avro people we got respect. There's nothing they wouldn't tell us. I've worked on other projects where I've been led astray but on the Arrow there was a very good rapport between the air force and the company. In fact, on a number of occasions before Smye and Gordon went to Ottawa for meetings, they would come down and tell me what they were going to talk about—they were seeking advice like "How do we put this over best with the air force or government."

—*W/C Ray Foottit*

From the beginning of the Arrow project, Avro Aircraft had the responsibility of coming up with the airframe and engine. The RCAF on the other hand took on the task of finding suitable fire control and armament, no small effort indeed, considering the technology at the time. "Canada's place in missile development is not yet clear," pronounced *Air Force* magazine in 1957.

The basic question is this: Can Canada afford to support a full-scale development program on one or more types of guided missiles specifically adapted to Canadian defence, or must we rely on American and British developments? We have tried both ways, with the Velvet Glove and the Sparrow II. If we attempt to manufacture foreign developments we must accept the delays which this approach entails. If we try to do our own research and development, we must be prepared to bear the costs.

We approached everybody about the fire control on the Arrow, and Hughes wasn't really interested since they were getting into the space program. We went down and discussed the whole program with Hughes—here's what we're thinking, etc.—and we got the greatest lecture in the world about not knowing a damn thing about fire control. We then went to Westinghouse and GE and to the USAF itself. Both the US Navy and USAF agreed with the general concept of an integrated fire control system.

—*A/V/M John Easton*

Throughout 1956 and 1957 Avro were sure the customer [the RCAF] had made a major error in trying to fit the CF-105 with a completely new fire-control and completely new missile, but were unable to bring any convincing arguments to bear. By 1958 the customer could see the difficulties for himself.

The new missile was called Sparrow 2. Though relying on Sparrow 1 aerodynamics and structure to a major degree, Sparrow 2 had totally new guidance and also differed greatly in flight control, propulsion, warhead, and in other ways. Prime contractor was Douglas Aircraft, but a complete team was built up in the US and Canada to create this new and sophisticated weapon which was hoped to be usable over long ranges in all environmental conditions, especially those that the Canadians were sure would defeat any missile that relied upon IR-homing. The CF-105 was to be capable of carrying Sparrow 2 both internally (the number depending on how many Falcons were also on board) and on four wing pylons. On any mission the big fighter was to carry not fewer than three of the radar-homing Sparrows, all of them capable of supersonic release at all heights up to 60,000 ft. In addition there were to be eight Falcons, four IR-homing, and four radar-guided, all capable of being fired on a single pass.

The new optimised fire control was called Astra I. Major contractors were RCA-Victor, the Montreal associate of the giant RCA, which unfortunately had little experience of avionics for fighters, Honeywell Controls and Computing Devices of Canada. Astra I was planned as an all-can-do system of extreme sophistication. One could even agree that it ought to be better than anything else, if it ever came to fruition, but from the very beginning Avro Aircraft were cast under a cloud of gloom. It was obvious that they could no longer control the programme costs, and the potential costs of Astra I were enormous (before long the CF-105 team wryly suggested that the system's name was short for "astronomically expensive").

We should have got rid of Astra as soon as we could. The project team was never really for Astra because you were getting too many developments in one single airplane.

—W/C Ray Foottit

From the day the CF-100 went into active service, C. D. Howe had hoped A. V. Roe Canada would be able to interest other countries, NATO countries, in purchasing the plane for their air forces. By 1955 the time seemed right to do some marketing, and the obvious place was Farnborough, England.

The annual air show at Farnborough, organized by the Society of British Aircraft Contractors, was the British aircraft industry's shopping market, as well as being, in the words of Bill Waterton, the test pilot, "the greatest display of its kind in the world." The show attracted a dazzling array of military and civil representatives from almost every nation; the public came in tens of thousands; millions more watched on television; the press and newsreels were present in force. The accent was on the spectacular; the test pilots dazzled and often baffled the audience with noise, speed, and breathtaking acrobatic displays.

Very early on in test flying the CF-100, Bill Waterton had wanted to take the aircraft overseas to Farnborough—some said to show off himself more than the plane—but the idea was nixed by Fred Smye, who felt it was too early in the test program. In September, 1955, however, the plane got another chance when A. V. Roe Canada test pilots Janusz Zurakowski and Glen Lynes took a couple of Mk.4's over for demonstration. Joe Morley promoted the visit and remembers that Zurakowski, much to his delight, "stole the show" with a series of aerial acrobatics that people still talk about.

I demonstrated the CF-100 in an attempt to sell the aircraft in Holland and Belgium. The Dutch Air Force had a rather poor fighter aircraft from the USA and needed a replacement, but they didn't want to upset their American friends. The Belgian Air Force had had bad experience with American aircraft, so they purchased the Hawker Hunter from England. The Hunter was in its early development, and the cost of essential modifications in the first year was higher than the original cost of the aircraft.

—*Janusz Zurakowski*

In night-fighter class, the Meteor NF-14 in the Royal Air Force was inferior to the CF-100 in range, speed, and armament, and Gloster was still solving low-speed instability of the Javelin by redesigning the wings, but the loss of two pilots and an aircraft was delaying development. A. V. Roe was in a favourable position.

But favourable positions don't necessarily mean sales, and after Farnborough things hadn't moved quickly enough for Joe Morley. He was about to play a key role in the only aircraft A. V. Roe Canada ever sold.

I probably know more about this than anyone, and take full responsibility for it. The secret of it was getting the "100" into Canadian Air Division in Europe, and it did a good job, a good night-fighter job patrolling; they were the only aircraft in the sky, many, many nights over there.

I had heard about the Belgians wanting to re-arm, so first I found an agent over there—there were four companies in the competition; the Gloster Javelin, the Trenkle Vautour, the Northrop Black Widow, and us. We were virtually unknown, so I got the Belgians to come over to Canada to fly it [the CF-100]. The competition was very severe for the contract, especially with our sister company, Glosters. So I went to see Roy Dobson and said, "Sir Roy, you have to make a decision. You can't show any favour." And he said, "Joe, I hope you win it. Glosters is going to have to make it on their own. You go. We'll help you."

So we started to work. Wilf Curtis went over for us a couple of times— the Brits and the Americans [manufacturers] didn't give us a chance— we set up possible subcontracts in Belgium; we agreed to have spare parts there before the aircraft arrived; the RCAF agreed to train the pilots; the USAF did all the rocket evaluations for us and so forth.

Roy Slemon [then Chief of the RCAF] and I—he used to get embarrassed because I'd call him in Paris or Rome and he used to say: "God Joe, you can't talk like that on the phone." He kept the file on the 100 in his desk drawer, and everytime I'd call him he'd say: "What have you committed me to now?" He was very, very co-operative but he was a military man.

We got down to the nitty-gritty when we went to see the Belgian minister of defence, and he said to our Canadian ambassador, "Mr. Ambassador, there's no way our country can buy your airplane because you won't release the latest model of the fire control system (the Hughes MG-2)" So I said, "Leave that to me, I'll deal with it."

—*Joe Morley*

Morley then quickly returned to Malton and explained the problem to his boss, Fred Smye. Like a runner in a team relay, Smye picked up the baton and ran with it.

I immediately went to Washington and took the matter up with Mr. Quarrells who was then the Secretary of the US Air Force. I explained the company position, and pointed out that our own air force had the same fire control system—and this equipment was being maintained in a depot in Rome which was heavily populated with communists, and if the deal fell through anyone could get hold of the system. He seemed to accept what I had said in principle and asked me to prepare a proposal which endeavoured to co-ordinate our system with the Belgian Air Force system. I wrote up the proposal, went back to Washington and submitted it. Quarrells looked at it briefly and he called a meeting with General Thomas White, who was Chief of Staff of USAF and a battery of intelligence people. The matter was debated and at the end Mr. Quarrells asked them to leave; then he turned to me and asked what he could do for me. Well, the US Mutual Aid Agreement was going to expire that very night, August 30, [1957], and I said I'd appreciate it if he'd cable his ambassador in Brussels to extend it or to defer it until the Belgians had made a decision, and, to confirm the release of the MG-2 by his government.

But before Quarrells did that he said to me, "Well, you're just an aircraft manufacturer; you're not the government of Canada." And he asked me what C. D. Howe would think of the whole affair, and I said I think he'll think it's a pretty good idea. He said, well, I better get him, so he asked his secretary to get Clarence Howe on the phone and I told him the House was in recess and Howe was in St. Andrews, New Brunswick.

"Get him there then," he said, but we couldn't get him. "Well then get me Ralph Kent" . . . couldn't get him. "Then get me Mike Pearson [then Canada's Minister of External Affairs]. Well he finally got Pearson on his way to London. Their was a man in Quarrells's office by the name of Dudley Sharpe, who was assistant secretary to the USAF at the time, and he was on his way to London also, so a meeting was arranged with Pearson at the Dorchester Hotel to go over the proposal and get the Canadian government's blessing on it.

But when I went back to Toronto I got a funny sort of feeling about the meeting, that every thing wasn't just hunky-dorey, so I hopped on an airplane from Montreal, and the next day I walked into the Dorchester and ran into a General Baker with the USAF who had attended the meeting with Pearson, Sharpe, and a Canadian Defence representative. Baker asked me what I was doing in London. I told him I really didn't know other than I just had a feeling I should be here. Baker said, "Well, you should be, but you're too late. Your government's just sold you down the river."

—Fred Smye

Joe Morley picks up the story:

It was about that time I made an appointment to see Howe and his assistant deputy minister, David Golden. I told them the Americans wouldn't release the MG-2 and that the Belgian defence minister had said there was no way he could accept anything that was less in performance than the fire-control system our allies were flying.

Howe agreed to help, and called his secretary in, and dictated a letter to Boss Wilson, a czar in American production circles and a friend of the minister [Howe].

A week later I was in Washington meeting with the Secretary of the USAF. I explained the situation to him, and he agreed with Howe that the situation was ridiculous. He said, "As of now, it's being made available to the Belgians. Now, how do you suggest I go about it?" And I said: "What I think you ought to do, Mr. Secretary, is write to our Mr. Pearson and send a copy to Claxton [Canada's Minister of National Defence] saying what you've done . . . and by the way, can I have a copy of the letter?"

He asked why, and I said I was leaving immediately for Belgium. He agreed, but on the condition I got our ambassador to talk to the American ambassador, because there was no way he could put the letter on the scrambler before I got to Belgium.

So I got to Brussels with the copy of the letter for Charles Hébèrt, our ambassador at the time. "What does this mean?" he asked, and I told him I got the fire-control released. He said "Goodness gracious! I must take this right over to the minister!" I said, "No, you can't do that because you don't have the letter and it has to go to the US ambassador first. We will both take it to the Belgian defence minister, and when we do I want you both to speak English in front of me so I know what you're saying." He said, "This is most unusual, I'll have to call Mike [Pearson]. But, oh, Mike's in London, and I can't call him because I don't know the letter exists do I? Would you call him?"

So I called Pearson at the Dorchester and spoke to Mary McIntosh, his secretary. She said it was "very kind of you" and she was sure when the minister got up he would talk with the ambassador. And he did.

—*Joe Morley*

Morley didn't know it at the time, but Smye was at the Dorchester as well, having just been told "your government's just sold you down the river." The next day, moments after Morley's phone call to Pearson, and as Smye was about to return to Canada, the Canadian External Affairs Minister re-convened the meeting and, with this new information, secured the release of the MG-2. "The British and Americans," recalls Morley, "where mad as hell at us."

For all their efforts, the Belgians eventually "purchased" a total of fifty-three aircraft and spares without paying a cent. Seventy-five per cent of the cost of the aircraft was paid for by the United States government. As NATO allies, the Americans had set aside some money under the Mutual Aid Agreement for the Belgians to re-arm, money which they put towards the purchase of the CF-100. The other 25 per cent was paid for by the Canadian government. A. V. Roe benefitted from the deal in two ways: it was their first "sale" which they hoped would be the first of many, and they made more than their traditional cost plus 5 per cent on the deal. Joe Turner negotiated with the Canadian government and played a large part in upping the ante. For his efforts in the Belgian sale, the company rewarded him with the position of vice-president of finance.

14

VISION OF THE NORTH

Crawford Gordon's acquisition of Canadian Steel Improvement and Canadian Car and Foundry for A.V. Roe Canada momentarily drew attention away from aircraft and engines and started some ripples of concern in the Canadian economic community. Nineteen fifty-six was the year Walter Gordon, a Canadian nationalist, chaired the Royal Commission on Canada's economic prospects which focused on foreign-owned interest in Canada and the idea of economic nationalism.

Many Canadians, writes Jim Dow,

were becoming increasingly concerned about the changing character of foreign investment from forms such as bonds that could ultimately be patriated to a situation of more or less permanent equity ownership. Through re-investment of earnings, a subsidiary was able to grow, either by improving its own facilities or simply by buying out other firms, in a process that was effectively closed to Canadian investors. When A. V. Roe began to diversify in 1955, it was to a great extent buying us out with our own money.

In April, 1956, Crawford Gordon was in New York addressing the Canadian Club. Pulling few punches, he said that American capital was heartily welcome in Canada "but Canadians feel that too often the investment has taken the form of an American-managed branch operation. There is a massive ignorance of Canada by a vast number of Americans."

And later, on receiving an honorary degree from St. Francis Xavier University: "It has been easier to import ideas, plans and money from our American friends rather than provide these ourselves. But in all this assistance there is a good measure of hazard."

Also in April a Toronto newspaper reported that Avro Aircraft was building an airplane that resembled "a 34-ton flying triangle" because the USAF had "handed Canada the job of stopping enemy bombers. Every plan, every photo, every blueprint is stamped 'SECRET' at the Avro plant." The article went on to say the plane would be ready in 1957, two years ahead of schedule, and added, somewhat prophetically, that the plane was "the biggest and the best and probably one of the last manned fighter planes in the world." The aircraft was the CF-105.

Then, on July 25, 1956, Fred Smye was appointed to the position he said he didn't want back in 1945: president and general manager of Avro Aircraft.

By the autumn, pressure was building against the company for more Canadian control. Crawford Gordon, after all, couldn't continue to tell the Americans what they could do with their money when Britain was telling him what to do with his. Knowing that close to 45 per cent of the business of the entire Hawker-Siddeley Group came from A. V. Roe Canada, T. O. M. Sopwith, now chairman of the Hawker-Siddeley Group, made an announcement on October 2: "Our Canadian Group has now become a vital part of the Canadian economy," he would tell *The Financial Post*,

in which every Canadian citizen is interested. At the same time, it has become a matter of concern to the Canadian people that so much of their industrial activity is in the hands of non-resident owners and, whilst they welcome the assistance which is being given in developing their vast potential resources, there is a growing feeling that they should be allowed to share in the ownership, as well as the operation, of these activities.

Since the inception of A. V. Roe Canada in 1945, said the prospectus issued by Wood, Gundy and Company of Toronto, "it has been the intention of the parent company, Hawker-Siddeley Group Ltd., to afford an opportunity to the Canadian public to invest in the company at a proper stage in the development of its business. After 10 years of growth and re-investment of earnings, it is considered that this stage has been reached." The stage involved an $8 million offering of 500,000 common shares of A. V. Roe Canada at $16 a share, which would allow Canadians to acquire 17 per cent of the company.

The selling of the share only relates to the multiple of earnings that is considered acceptable in the financial community at the time. If growth is anticipated, the company can demand an even higher price. A. V. Roe Canada went public to gain capital to acquire its subsidiaries. You can only go public when you show a reasonable success ratio over a five-year period.

—*Crawford Gordon III*

When A. V. Roe went public, Gordon phoned me at home one night and said, "I'm making out my 'special' list, so how many shares do you want?" I said that five hundred would be just fine and he said, "Oh, I'll put you down for ten thousand." And I said, "I can't do that. I can't afford it." "Well, put a mortgage on your house," he said, and I told him I couldn't do it, I was not that type, so I took five hundred shares courtesy of the Royal Bank.

—*Pat Kelly*

Crawford Gordon and A. V. Roe Canada now had an additional $8 million to play with, and it wasn't long before Gordon knew just what to do with it. John Tory, a director and the company's legal advisor, had been to Montreal to visit an ailing friend of his, C. B. Lang. During the visit, Lang spoke of his admiration for A. V. Roe and mentioned that his own company in Nova Scotia might soon be for sale. When Tory returned to Toronto he told Crawford Gordon of the conversation, and Gordon immediately asked what was the name of Lang's company.

"Dosco," was the reply.

Towards the middle of 1956 the Jetliner had accumulated a total of some 430 flying hours and had become "the most expensive laboratory in existence." Since a lot of systems on the Jetliner were "one-off" systems, that is, parts of the plane that had no spares, no tooling systems to make replacement parts, and no manpower to properly maintain the plane, it was only a matter of time before Avro executives had to face the inevitable. Besides, the mere presence of the Jetliner in the plant was an uncomfortable reminder of the many thwarted attempts to sell the plane.

"By late 1952," wrote Jim Floyd,

all funding on the Jetliner had ceased and no further certification, airline or military flying was authorized. It was, however, agreed that we could use the Jetliner as an observation and photographic platform during the continuous development flight trials of the CF-100. The speed and altitude development flight capability of the Jetliner made it possible to fly alongside the CF-100 during canopy-jettison trials, seat-ejection, and gun- and rocket-firing tests. The Jetliner was an ideal photographic platform and had ample space for all the sophisticated test and measuring equipment required to record the results of the tests at first hand.

The Jetliner was also included in the 1953 and '54 air shows at the Canadian National Exhibition waterfront, and Don Rogers put on spectacular demonstrations of its capability.

Even in the last years there was still the occasional comment coming out of Trans-Canada Air Lines. In October, 1953, TCA president Gordon McGregor, once again called upon to talk about the Jetliner, admitted that, although "TCA may have expressed an interest in the Avro Jetliner, there had been no formal contract." The reason, he said, that TCA didn't buy the plane was that the aircraft's "complexion was completely changed by the time a prototype was built." And then, three years later, the *Toronto Star* would report that Gordon McGregor told C. D. Howe that the reason TCA refused the Jetliner was that his "company would never get into the black if it purchased expensive jet airplanes." It was also intimated that because TCA would have been under severe criticism if it openly refused a Canadian product, the government used the Korean War as a "good excuse to get the government off the hook."

On November 23, 1956, Don Rogers took the Jetliner up with a crew of five for a short thirty-five minute flight. The plane would never fly again. On December 10, Jim Floyd received the following memorandum from Fred Smye:

PRIVATE AND CONFIDENTIAL: In accordance with our conversation of today, the Jetliner is to be grounded, effective immediately. In fact, with great regret I must say that the Jetliner is not to fly again, but rather be dismantled. In appropriate fashion, as quickly and quietly as can be done, every precaution being taken to attract as little attention as possible, with the avoidance of any fanfare.

Floyd made one desperate last attempt to get either the Smithsonian Institution in Washington or the National Research Council to take the aircraft as is, but both declined because of space limitations. At the next Avro executive meeting, Smye's memo was on the agenda for one last discussion. The meeting was a short one.

> *We were standing in the hangar when Jim Floyd walked up to us. He'd just left the management meeting on what to do with the Jetliner and he was visibly upset. He stared at us, then at the plane; then he paused and said quietly, "Chop her up."*
>
> *We were horrified. All along we had sort of expected it might come to this but we always hoped that maybe something would happen and production would start over again.*
>
> *I picked up a fire axe and took a swing—it didn't make a dent. We finally had to take her apart with power saws.*
>
> —Charlie Batchelor

The engines were sent to technical schools across Canada; the seats were sold to a local charter carrier; the gear boxes ended up on someone's power boat; the wings and fuselage went to Lax's scrap dealers in Hamilton for two cents a pound; and the wheels went into service on a farmer's utility wagon. The National Research Council, however, did want the nose section and this was removed as carefully as possible. It is now preserved in the National Aviation Museum.

Don Rogers refused to go into the hangar until the job was finished, and Jim Floyd, at times even today, finds it difficult to talk about the plane that he had put so much of himself into. When the job was finally finished, and the scrap removed from the hangar floor, Floyd did something he never did—he went out and got thoroughly drunk. "An aircraft," he would say later, "just born at the wrong time."

"Before I undertake the development of a civil aircraft again," lamented Roy Dobson, "they'll have to carve the contract in stone. That Jetliner broke my heart."

By February, 1957, the CF-105 had a name: the Arrow. It was chosen jointly by the RCAF and Avro Aircraft, said Fred Smye, "because it is symbolic of the missile concept of the aircraft and its general arrowhead configuration." Smye also went on to say that he expected the estimated cost to develop the Arrow would be in the $200-million range.

In the spring of 1957 it was made known to the House of Commons that the Department of National Defence had paid A. V. Roe Canada a total of $967,371,827 between January 1, 1949, and February 28, 1957; $704,396,228 was the cost of the CF-100 program, while $99,351,396 was the tab so far for the CF-105 airframe and engine.

On June 8, a CF-100 Mk.5 crashed at the London, Ontario, air show. Both RCAF crew members, F/O Les Sparrow and F/O C. A. Sheffield, were killed. The crash was the result "of both wings breaking;" although wing tests had been done on the Mk.4, they were never done on the lighter Mk.5 with its extended wingtips and tailplane tips; pilots did not always consider the difference in weight and balance. Subsequent investigations concluded that the aircraft had been overstressed and that the operating manual was not well understood by pilots. The CF-100 Mk.5 was the same plane that A. V. Roe test pilot Glen Lynes had crashed in two years earlier.

Without a doubt 1957 was A. V. Roe Canada's best year. It would be the year they blossomed into a complex of forty-four companies, with fifty thousand employees, and with sales in the $450 million a year range. They would find themselves on the list of the top one hundred companies in the world, the top eighty in North America, and one of the top in Canada after Canadian Pacific Railways and the Aluminum Company of Canada. The company's public relations people decided that A. V. Roe needed a motto. It was, appropriately enough, "The Next Big Step."

Nineteen fifty-seven would see Canadians gain 40 per cent control of the company, a company that was originally totally dependent on the military for contracts, but could now boast that 60 per cent of its business was civilian. It would also be the year they'd roll out the Arrow, the year they'd get a new president, and the year John George Diefenbaker would become prime minister of Canada.

Crawford Gordon was continuing on his trek away from aircraft and engines to broaden A. V. Roe's industrial base. In February he bought Canadian Applied Research, an aerial survey and electronics equipment company, and in May, he led A. V. Roe into the steel business, purchasing 11 per cent of the Algoma Steel Corporation for $18 million.

Gordon's forays in acquiring transportation and steel companies were calculated to complement A. V. Roe's primary business. "They guard against fluctuations in the aircraft industry or a sudden technological change," wrote John Harbron in *Business Week*. "They make it possible for Hawker-Siddeley, hard hit by Britain's recent defence cutbacks and emphasis on missiles, to pour its available capital into a relatively safe growth area."

Then, on August 7, the company put together what Jim Dow called "the biggest deal in Canada's industrial history" when it took control of the third largest steel producer in the country—the Dominion Steel and Coal Company of Nova Scotia. Dosco would be quite a prize for Gordon. With sales in the $210 million range, Dosco ran a $7 million annual profit and had book assets of $151 million. To top it all off, the company just recently completed a $100 million modernization program.

Rumours of Gordon's interest in the steel giant had been circulating through the country's financial community for months. In fact, A. V. Roe and Dosco stock had risen together during the spring while the rest of the market was in a slump. By mid-June, A. V. Roe stock had reached $25 a share, up from $17 in April, and analysts wondered why.

But Gordon's wasn't the only pair of interested eyes on Dosco. Phoenix-Rheinrohr and Mannesmann International, two German-based companies, were also interested. When word reached Dobson, he was quick to remark, "I don't want to see any German interests controlling steel manufacturing in Canada." With that he told Gordon to get cracking on a deal—and quickly.

Gordon wanted to offer Dosco stockholders cash and A. V. Roe stock, and one day he burst into my office and said to me, "Jesus, I'm in an awful jam. I've got to get $4 million dollars right away." So I sat there with him while he talked to the presidents of banks, and between calls he turns to me and says, "You've got some Roe stock don't you?" And I said "Yes, five hundred shares." And he said: "What are you going to do with them? Sell them to me." And I said: "Nothing doing. I bought them as an investment."

So he sold his own stock to raise money for the acquisition. Roe stocks had originally sold for $16 a share; he got them for $10 a share and sold them for $25.50 a share. Fancy, a man entrusted with running the company selling his own stock.

—Pat Kelly

On August 8, the offer to purchase was announced in the form of a letter of intent. "Reactions to the offer," said *Saturday Night* magazine, were swift and sometimes violent." Dosco directors were split down the middle; one faction "claimed the deal would take control of Dosco out of Canada because Roe control is held by the Hawker-Siddeley Group of Great Britain. They said Dosco would be dismembered and parts closed down with subsequent unemployment and economic distress for the Maritimes." R. A. Jodrey, a Dosco director, called Roe's offer "ridiculous." R. J. Bennet, mayor of New Glasgow, said it was a "pure steal. We're afraid they'll close down Eastern Car [a Dosco subsidiary] . . . . They have already spent $15 million on Canadian Car. They won't want Eastern Car too." Some A. V. Roe Canada people opposed the deal as well. Pat Kelly, Gordon's assistant, says he fought Gordon on the Dosco decision.

Dosco had been watered to death by Beaverbrook. It had only made money during the war . . . . It was too far from markets . . . . Gordon never bothered reading the history of the place.

—Pat Kelly

Pro-sell factions on the Dosco board said the campany needed new, efficient management and that Roe's money would be the making of Dosco. To meet the blast of opposition, Crawford Gordon sent a letter to every Dosco shareholder in which he indicated that A. V. Roe was prepared "to put up as much as $100 million in shares and cash because we are convinced the Dosco group of companies has tremendous growth and expansion potential. The idea being put forward in some areas, that we only want Dosco to close up part or all of it, is too ill-fetched to require a reply."

But Dosco opposition to the offer didn't cease. "How do we know what Roe stock will be worth," said R. A. Jodrey.

The market for it is so thin, and so much of it is held outside Canada, nobody can say what it will be worth. And what does Roe know about the steel business anyway? They've never run anything on a competitive basis. I say Roe's just seen the handwriting on the wall. The aircraft business is on the skids and they just want to save their skins with Dosco.

Dosco's products included iron ore, coal, coke pig-iron, ingots, forgings, nails, ships, railroad freight cars, and bridges. It had fifty-five subsidiary companies including Dominion Iron & Steel, Dominion Wabana Ore, Dominion Shipping, Halifax Shipyards, Canadian Bridge, Canadian Tube & Steel Products, and Dominion Coal. Through its subsidiaries, the company employed more than thirty thousand people, more than any other single organization at the time. On August 10, 1957, Roe took over 77 per cent control and Dosco, kicking and screaming, joined the A. V. Roe Canada family.

In addition to being president of A. V. Roe Canada, Crawford Gordon now assumed the presidency of Dosco. "Avro is now in the three basic areas we set out to get into," he would boast, "defence, transportation, and steel. We've come a long way and we're going a lot further—a whole lot further. To me the future is unlimited."

No one expected a Conservative victory. Despite the fact that the Tories had a new leader in John Diefenbaker, the polls indicated, even as late as January, 1957, that the Liberals were leading the Conservatives in popular support 48 per cent to 31 per cent. On the eve of the election, the *New York Times* said "it would take a political miracle" to defeat the Liberals and "there is no reason to expect such a spectacular overturn."

However, when the returns were in that night of June 10, 1957, the voters of Canada had elected a minority government of 112 Conservative, 105 Liberal, 25 Co-operative Commonwealth Federation (CCF), and 19 Social Credit members. C. D. Howe had lost his seat in Port Arthur, and John George Diefenbaker was Prime Minister of Canada after two decades of Liberal rule.

"He was described by an opponent as a 'small-time Prairie lawyer'," wrote Bill Gunston in his excellent work, *Early Supersonic Fighters of the West*, "and while this is unkind it does give a fair idea of his background.

"Dief" neither knew nor cared much about semi-active guidance and air-cooled turbine blading. He had swept into office on a tide of electoral promises, most of which were aimed at his homeland where you can fly a light plane over rolling golden wheat for an hour and still not reach the edge of the field. How could Dief make good on his battle-cry that his administration would give the farmers more dough? There seemed to be only one simple way and that was to cancel a major existing project. Long before he came to office the Arrow had been standing out like a sore thumb. Dief had spent a lot of time from 1956 trying to find out how vital it was to the RCAF. The fairly sudden emergence of the missile as a sort of "replacement" was manna from Heaven, and when Britain's Duncan Sandys published his Defence White Paper in April 1957 Dief's joy knew no bounds. All he needed now was for something to go sour in the Arrow programme.

With the Liberals so suddenly and unexpectedly out of office, A. V. Roe's link to power was severed. C. D. Howe, mainly because of his stand on the Trans-Canada pipeline, was unquestionably the prime scapegoat. Diefenbaker had been trying for years to get the lowdown on the Arrow, but in Opposition he got no co-operation from the RCAF or any of the Liberal government members. The civil service and the RCAF were still thick with the Liberals, and Diefenbaker plainly did not trust them.

Diefenbaker's first "military" decision was to join with the United States in the North American Air Defence Command (NORAD). The possibility had been long pondered by the previous administration, but they had not felt prepared to undertake it at the time. The surprising thing about it was that Diefenbaker made the decision largely on his own, without consulting the Chiefs of Staff. Clearly, there was now only one chief.

When the Liberals found out that Diefenbaker had acted independently of the Cabinet Defence Committee, indeed, had not yet even formed a Cabinet Defence Committee, Parliament was wracked by a long and bitter debate over the NORAD agreement. This only served to make Diefenbaker even more wary in his future dealings on defence issues. And the next issue was the Arrow.

In the wake of the election results, with the future of the Arrow on the line, some of A. V. Roe's employees began to look for other jobs. Fred Smye planned strategy. He formed the Long Range Planning Committee (LRPC), made up of key management personnel, in August of 1957. The committee was entrusted with looking at any and all new products and markets Avro Aircraft might want to get into. A. V. Roe Canada, the parent company, might no longer be a one-product company, but Avro Aircraft was, and with a new government in power, that one product was threatened.

How far and thoroughly the LRPC looked is evident in the number and variety of potential products they considered: commercial transports, bush transports, VTOL aircraft, private aircraft, a potential Mach 2.5 Arrow, high-energy fuels, nuclear power, anti-tank missiles, electro-gravitics, space flight, individual flying apparatus, metal curtains, anti-ICBM missiles, and P15, a combination helicopter–fixed-wing aircraft.

One of the more interesting possibilities was a monorail transportation system. "A study is being made," the committee reported,

> of the possibilities of a gas-driven vehicle operating on an overhead monorail to serve the Hamilton/Toronto/Oshawa area—an area selected because its rapid growth may with reasonable expectation lead to traffic congestion on a scale compelling the travelling public to depend on some such alternative mode of transportation. The skills, techniques and industrial potential of the A. V. Roe Canada Group may lend themselves to the designing of such a system.

Alluding to a potential problem with the Arrow program, the committee concluded in its first report that it was "essential to the continuity of the company's operations that a new major project be brought to a stage of readiness for manufacture to start by mid 1962 latest, and that to meet this schedule initial project engineering should proceed now, with design engineering commencing during 1958 at the latest." The committee also recommended a "stop-gap" program to alleviate the inevitable impact on the labour force in the event of the cancellation of current projects. The stop-gap program never got beyond this point. Instead the company elected to press the Department of Defence Production for a statement of policy on the future development of the CF-105.

Every company has an LRPC, somebody to look five years down the road. But nothing, nothing would have replaced the Arrow.
                                                            —*Fred Smye*

The Department of Defence Production recommended that an order of eight prototypes and twenty-nine pre-production planes be placed immediately to facilitate full-scale production within the next two years. This would put the Arrow in service in 1961 or 1962. This proposal called for $200 million for 1957/58 and did not include additional sums for the Sparrow missile and the Astra electronic control system. The government was taken aback. For Smye it was a king's gambit. If he could secure this contract while the new administration was still getting its bearings, the future of the Arrow would be assured. But while he waited for the government's next move, world attention was drawn to Russia. On August 27, 1957, the Soviets launched the first ICBM.

Diefenbaker's minority government was vulnerable to being defeated if it took too rash a step, and the NORAD issue had raised a few eyebrows already. The government decided to follow the previous administration's path on the Arrow at this time, and in October, 1957, authorized continuance of the project to the extent of $175 million for one year only. Public opinion was not the least consideration in this decision—the magnificent Arrow had already made its debut.

One measure of A. V. Roe's success was its ability to grab headlines, and the bigger the headline, the bigger the grin on Fred Smye's face. From the summer of 1957 through to February 1959, not a day passed without at least one of Toronto's three major newspapers carrying a story on A. V. Roe Canada, Avro Aircraft, or Orenda Engines. Company press releases were churned out at an almost hourly rate, and press conferences were called with such regularity that, by 1958, all three dailies had aviation writers on staff whose full-time beat was A. V. Roe Canada.

Everyone knew what the front-page stories would be that cool, sunny October fourth in 1957, the day they rolled out the Arrow for all the world to see. It was a typical A. V. Roe organized event, complete with speeches, military music, praise for what had been accomplished, and hopes for even better things ahead. Dignitaries present on the podium included Air Marshal Wilf Curtis (retired) and Air Chief Marshal Hugh Campbell, four air vice-marshals, George Pearkes, Minister of National Defence, three senior USAF personnel, J. A. D. McCurdy (who flew the *Silver Dart*, the first heavier-than-air machine to fly in Canada, in 1909), a handful of MPs, and of course Sir Roy Dobson, Crawford Gordon, and Fred Smye. The ceremony was planned for two in the afternoon, to be over at three-thirty, to allow the press boys time to file their stories for the evening editions of the newspapers.

A/M Hugh Campbell, recently appointed Chief of Air Staff (replacing Roy Slemon who had left to become deputy commander-in-chief of

NORAD) was a quiet, bashful man. He had been with the RCAF since 1931. During the war he had been posted to RCAF headquarters in England as Director of Air Staff until 1944 when he returned to Canada as Assistant Chief of the Air Staff. In 1949, he was appointed chairman of the Canadian Joint Staff in Washington and in that capacity had participated in the original work of the military committees of NATO. In 1952 Campbell was back in Europe commanding the RCAF Air Division during the time the air divisions were re-equipping with CF-100's. By August 1955 he had become Deputy Chief of Staff— Operations at Supreme Headquarters of the Allied Powers in Europe until replacing Slemon as head of the RCAF.

Although it was natural to have the Chief of the Air Staff present, Campbell was suspicious of "roll-outs" in general and agreed to come only if he could write his own speech. He said, in part:

> The planned performance of this aircraft is such that it can effectively meet and deal with any likely bomber threat to this continent over the next decade. We in the Air Force look upon this aircraft as one component of a complex and elaborate air defence system covering the whole of the North American continent. . . . The Arrow, including its missiles, flight trial and fire control systems, we believe will become a very important component of this overall defence . . . . Today we pass from one major phase to another in the growth of the Arrow. There are many difficult problems ahead— some can be foreseen, but some are hidden by the veil covering the unknown areas of aerodynamic science which has still to be explored . . . . There is still a great deal to be done before the aircraft we see today becomes the fighting machine which the Air Force requires for the air defence of Canada . . . . We shall follow your progress closely.

One of the last to speak that day was George Pearkes:

> Much has been said of late about the coming missile age, and there have been suggestions from well intentioned people that the era of the manned aeroplane is over and that we should not be wasting our time and energy producing an aircraft of the performance, complexity and cost of the Avro Arrow. They suggest that we should put our faith in missiles and launch straight into an era of push-button war. I do not feel that missile and manned aircraft have, as yet, reached the point where they should be considered as competitive. They will, in fact, become complementary . . . . However, the aircraft has this one great advantage over the missile. It can bring the judgement of a man into the battle and closer to the target where human judgement, combined with the technol-

ogy of the aircraft, will provide the most sophisticated and effective defence that human ingenuity can devise.

When Pearkes finished his speech he pulled a cord which symbolically opened a huge curtain stretched across one of the assembly bays. On cue, a fly-past of CF-100's swept overhead as the RCAF band struck up a fanfare and the Arrow was towed slowly out of the hangar to the applause of the twelve thousand assembled. Fred Smye said to Jim Hornick, "We'll have her in the air by the end of the year." Dobson, Gordon, and Smye returned to Briarcrest for cocktails to await the delivery of the late editions of the *Star* and *Telegram*. Wagers were taken as to how big the headlines would be. When the papers finally arrived, however, in place of ARROW splashed across the front page was the word SPUTNIK. October 4, 1957, was the day the Russians had chosen to launch Sputnik I. The missile age had begun in earnest.

The first flight of the Iroquois engine was to be in a test-bed, a B-47 bomber on loan from the USAF.

We used the B-47 because it was the biggest aircraft we could get our hands on, and the original idea was to take off a couple of the existing engines and hang the Iroquois engine pod under the wing. However, the USAF felt the engine would shake the wings off the plane, to say nothing of the decibel level, so that's why we put the pod on the back.

—Harry Keast

"On the back" meant mounting the cigar-shaped engine pod against the fuselage like a scope mounted on a rifle, but, whereas the scope is completely parallel to the rifle, the Iroquois engine pod was angled to 5 degrees.

The B-47 aircraft was not a supersonic aircraft and was limited in both its forward speed and its altitude. It carried six engines, but the single Iroquois could produce more thrust than all six B-47 engines combined. The single Iroquois with limited ratio of only 16,000 pounds thrust was more than sufficient for the aircraft; in fact, once airborne with the Iroquois started, it was necessary for the crew to throttle the plane's J-47 engines right back to idling.

Flying the aircraft was Avro test pilot Mike Cooper-Slipper; copiloting was Len Hobbs, who came from England to assist, and flight engineer was Johnny McLaughlin who had been on the Orenda program. The crew had trained on the B-47 at the USAF Strategic Air Command base in Kansas.

The B-47 just wasn't the right airplane for the job. The other big mistake was the engine nacelle pointed outboard 5 degrees which affected running so you had to keep two engines at full power to counteract this. You couldn't bring the Iroquois and the two B-47 engines to full power.

—*Mike Cooper-Slipper*

Charles Grinyer never saw the flight, having fallen victim to a nervous breakdown. It seemed to be an occupational hazard in the engine business. Harry Keast nearly didn't make it either; having taken over from Grinyer, he was now top man on the Iroquois program and was logging sixty to seventy hours a week at the plant.

Despite Cooper-Slipper's comments, the flight went effortlessly, so much so, that when the crew returned, there was only one person to greet them, Alex Muraszew, the chief experimental engineer. Burt Avery, the deputy chief engineer, and Harry Keast had gone to lunch.

"There were a few minor problems with the Iroquois and the B-47," according to the Arrowheads.

On one occasion, there was an explosion in flight with the engine. The trouble occurred about 50 miles north of Malton, near Barrie, Ontario. The B-47 was starting to climb with full Iroquois power on (this was the only recorded occasion that the Iroquois was put to full throttle while in flight test). Suddenly there was an enormous bang and the whole aircraft shook, followed by a deadly silence. The pilot's position was a long way from the Iroquois but dust flew up into the cockpit. The Iroquois was immediately shut down and its fire extinguishers pulled. The vibration diminished as the engine came to a stop.

The CF-100 chase pilot came close by to look at the pod and reported lots of smoke but no fire. It goes without saying that the B-47 returned to base rather quickly with a few anxious moments thrown in. What had happened upon inspection was that a blade had failed and pieces had penetrated the nacelle of the Iroquois and entered the rear fuselage of the B-47. Fortunately there was no major damage to the aircraft. The problem was later rectified by a change in blade design and manufacture.

Charles Grinyer saw the Iroquois as a power plant he might someday be able to sell to the Americans, the British, the French, or whomever. If Avro Aircraft wanted the engine for their Arrow, well, that was fine too, but first and foremost the Iroquois was an independent product up for sale.

> *When it came to the Iroquois and Arrow, the engine could have been more marketable than the airframe.*
>
> —Murray Willer

Grinyer knew this, and from day one he tailored and measured the performance of the Iroquois as the Americans would. The first step was the official 50-hour Pre-Flight Rating Test (P.F.R.T.) carried out on June 24, 1956.

> *We looked at 50 hours on the P.F.R.T. Then to a 50-hour flight rating test, and then the final 150-hour type test before the engine was cleared for production. The 50-hour P.F.R.T. test says this is an experimental engine; the 150 tests acceleration, cut-backs, and idling. The RCAF used this rating system based on US test program standards.*
>
> —Harry Keast

Grinyer's priority in promoting the marketability of the Iroquois rather than tailoring it to the Arrow disturbed a lot of the Arrow engineers and technicians, some going so far as to suggest that Grinyer purposely doctored Iroquois performance reports in the hope of making the engine unsuitable for the Arrow. Harry Keast is happy to clear Grinyer's name:

> *The performance of the engine had to be lowered because of the performance of the second-stage turbine blade which was very safe at 7,650 rpm. We wanted it at 7,800 rpm but I issued a directive that in flight, engines had to be down-graded to 7,650 rpm till such time as we got what we called new "toothpick" blades installed.*
>
> —Harry Keast

Efforts to market the engine abroad began to pay off in September, 1957, when Curtiss-Wright paid A. V. Roe for the rights to manufacture the Iroquois under licence in the United States.

> *This was ill-conceived in a sense, because there was no way the Pentagon was going to allow Curtiss-Wright to build another air-breathing engine. They were restricted to building rockets, and what's more, they were just about the worst company we could have chosen to pick up the option, because it blocked us from offering it to anybody else. The French at one time negotiated for two hundred Iroquois for their Mirage IV at a cost of $200,000 per engine.*
>
> —Harry Keast

Towards the end of 1957, Crawford Gordon relinquished his title of chairman of the board at Avro Aircraft to his close friend Fred Smye. Retaining his position as resident chairman of the board of the parent A. V. Roe Canada, Gordon had enough on his plate with Dosco and CanCar to feel more than comfortable in entrusting the aeronautical division to Smye. Gordon's annual salary was now $75,000—he was making more money than the president of the United States.

It was Wilf Curtis who first suggested John L. Plant to succeed Smye as president of Avro Aircraft. Plant, like Curtis, was a retired RCAF officer. He had a graduate degree in engineering from the University of British Columbia and had joined the RCAF in 1931. Wartime found him in England commanding two RCAF squadrons. In 1951, he was with NATO as Deputy Chief of Staff—Logistics under General Norstad and two years later was promoted to the rank of air marshal and made Chief of Staff for all Allied air forces in central Europe, retiring in 1956. In December, 1957, Smye asked him to join Avro Aircraft as executive vice-president and general manager. Four months later he was made president and general manager.

By the time of the Arrow roll-out, Avro Aircraft consisted of seven divisions: engineering under Jim Floyd, manufacturing under Harvey Smith, sales and service under Joe Morley, quality control and inspection under J. Fairbairn, finance under Joe Turner, the special projects group under John Frost, and flight operations under Don Rogers. It was flight operations that captured the imagination of the public, the press, and the Avro employees—flight operations was where the test pilots worked.

"Hollywood and novels portray the test pilot as a nerveless daredevil who has little or no regard for authority, convention, or his own neck," we find written in an old Avro brochure.

> But, in real life, he is seldom the glamorous superman of fiction. Rather, the proving of a modern high performance aeroplane demands a man with a serious approach to scientific research and some of the qualifications of an aeronautical engineer and an aircraft inspector, as well as being a competent and experienced pilot.

Test pilots had been part of the scene at Malton since National Steel Car days when the likes of Ernie Taylor, Leigh Capreol, and Don Rogers made sure the Lysanders and Ansons produced in those days were at least airworthy. The most famous of the original three, and not for longevity alone, was Don Rogers. In January, 1942, he joined National Steel Car, staying on during Victory Aircraft and the Lancaster development, and becoming A. V. Roe Canada's chief test pilot in 1946. In 1948, he flew jets for the first time, eventually piloting the C-102 Jetliner, some CF-100's, and doing some development testing of the Orenda engine. During the Arrow program he became manager of flight operations.

The first new pilot to join A. V. Roe after the war was twenty-six-year-old Mike Cooper-Slipper. Cooper-Slipper had flown Spitfires during the war and had won the Distinguished Flying Cross. Once, after the war, while on a visit to Birmingham, he saw a sign that said, "Come to Sunny Ontario." So he did just that.

I came on the Drew Scheme with two letters of introduction in my pocket. One was addressed to de Havillands in Downsview, and the other to Walter Deisher [then A. V. Roe's general manager]. I couldn't find de Havillands so I ended up in Malton. They put me to work nights filing jet blades for the Chinook at $2.50 an hour. I was scared to death of [Roy Dobson] when I first met him. He always referred to me as a "young bugger" because I was always doing something wrong and he was always catching me at it. I remember visiting the factory in England once. He'd grab me wherever I was and pour these enormous whiskeys for you until your heart stopped!

—*Mike Cooper-Slipper*

He did some flying on the Jetliner after its appearance, then became chief pilot on the Orenda-Lancaster test bed starting with its first flight in July, 1950. He spent hundreds of hours aboard this aircraft until its loss in the hangar fire in 1955. At the same time he also flew test-bed Sabres powered by Orendas. He was also one of the first CF-100 pilots and spent many hours flying that plane on engine development flights. On the odd weekend the Lancaster test-bed was used for a bit of joy riding over nearby New York State. The plane would be taken across Lake Ontario very low and would then pop up to appear on USAF radar scopes. The P-47 Thunderbolts based with the Air National Guard at Niagara Falls would scramble towards the radar blip, but were never able to catch the fast-climbing, jet-propelled Lancaster.

Cooper-Slipper's last project at Avro was flying the Boeing B-47 borrowed from the USAF as a test bed for the Iroquois engine.

Another long-time Avro pilot was Peter Cope, who had pin-pointed the CF-100's ejection problem. He joined the RAF in 1941 and learned to fly with the Army Air Corps in the United States, graduating as an Air Corps lieutenant. After the war he flew at Armstrong-Whitworth as a test pilot on aircraft such as the Meteor and the Lincoln. There he met Fred Smye who later offered him a flying job at A. V. Roe Canada. He joined A. V. Roe in May, 1951.

Cope spent over 1,600 hours on the CF-100, making some 1,900 experimental flights on over 200 different CF-100's, including the first and the last aircraft built. Because of his combat experience and his work in gunnery training, Peter Cope did much armament development work at Avro. A lot of this was routine flying involving the gun pack, wingtip rocket pods, and the fuselage rocket pack, but there were a few exciting moments. Firing .50s one day, he noticed a bullet hole appear in an engine cowling—he had overrun a round, probably one with a deficient charge.

Peter Cope remained at Avro until 1961. During the CF-105 test program, he made five flights in the Arrow and on July 6, 1961, he made his final flight in a CF-100. After leaving Avro he joined Boeing for a long career associated with the 747.

Chris Pike and Stan Haswell joined the company as production test pilots in 1952. Their job was to test out the CF-100's as they came off the production line. They flew nearly all of the CF-100's built.

By far the most famous A. V. Roe test pilot was Janusz Zurakowski. Quiet, unassuming, balding, diminutive, Polish-born—in looks the antithesis of the glamorous Bill Waterton, Zurakowski literally cartwheeled to fame when he performed the first completely new aerobatic manoeuver in twenty years. The now famous wing-over-wing "Zurabatic cartwheel" was first demonstrated at Farnborough, England, in 1951 to settle a discussion among some of the participating pilots. Peter Cope and Zurakowski tried to repeat the manoeuvre in a CF-100. The Meteor was an ideal plane for the cartwheel as its engines were far out on the wings, but the CF-100's engines hugged the fuselage. To move some weight farther out onto the wings to facilitate rotation, Cope and Zurakowski flew a CF-100 with tip tanks and under-wing bombs. In spite of their efforts the CF-100 would not comply. Its most exotic manoeuvre became the falling leaf, done with alternately idling engines.

Zurakowski first became interested in aviation as a youth, and the building of model airplanes was his prime spare-time occupation. He was fifteen when he won first prize in a national competition in Poland in 1929. The prize was his first ride in an airplane—a Lublin LKL-5. Poland's Military Officers School was the source of his education, and he began his flying career in 1935.

When the Second World War broke out and Poland was invaded, Zurakowski joined the RAF. He took part in the Battle of Britain, after which he joined the Polish Air Force Squadron of the RAF. Altogether he served with four squadrons, and became a squadron leader in 1942. Six enemy aircraft fell to Zurakowski's guns, and twice he had to bail out of a burning fighter. A distinguished fighter pilot, he was decorated with the polish *Virtuti Militari* for gallantry in action. In 1944 he was posted to the Empire Test Pilots School.

"Let me begin before that period," he said in a rare speech to the Canadian Aviation Historical Society.

Close to the end of the war, when victory was only a question of time, and my superiors were trying to push me from operational flying into a staff job in London, I discovered that there was a place for one Polish pilot in the Empire Test Pilot's School. I put my application in, was accepted, and started to learn to be a test pilot. After a year's course I was posted to the Aircraft and Armament Experimental Establishment in Boscombe Down where I had the opportunity to test most of the Royal Air Force fighters, Fleet Air Arm aircraft and American Navy fighters.

Two years later I left the Royal Air Force and accepted the position of experimental test pilot in Gloster Aircraft Company in England, dealing mainly with the development of the Meteor twin-jet interceptor aircraft. The Meteor was first flown in 1943.

Five years of experimental testing taught me not to accept much at its face value, to doubt nearly everything until proven, and to respect evidence and the importance of collecting flight-test information by special instrumentation.

Bill Waterton was my boss at Glosters and I was acting chief test pilot. I never really wanted to be chief test pilot because I didn't like the bureaucracy and all the sales stuff—I was quite happy doing experimental things— but eventually Waterton felt I was trying to take his job and started acting against me. I didn't want to fight about it and since my wife was unhappy in England, I sent letters to de Havillands and A. V. Roe in Canada. And Roe accepted . . . .

On April 21, 1952, I landed in Canada and the next day I started work as experimental pilot for A. V. Roe at Malton.

—*Janusz Zurakowski*

In December, 1952, Zurakowski flew the CF-100 MK.4 prototype supersonically for the first time. In the mid-1950s, Zurakowski became closely involved with development of the CF-105 Arrow, and on March 25, 1958, took it into the air for the first time. He, Peter Cope, Spud Potocki, and F/L Jack Woodman of the RCAF's Central Experimental and Proving Establishment spent the following months testing the exciting new aircraft. Zurakowski retired as Avro's chief development test pilot in October, 1958, and was awarded the McKee Trans-Canada Trophy for that year "in recognition of his outstanding contribution to experimental test flying of jet aircraft in Canada, and for his outstanding contribution to world recognition of Canadian aeronautical achievements."

Soon after his arrival in Canada, Zurakowski was joined by another former Polish Air Force/RAF fighter pilot, W. O. ("Spud") Potocki whom Dobson had recruited from the Vulcan bomber project in Britain to assist "Zura" in the CF-100 program.

Spud was my junior in the RAF. He was a sergeant and I was a flight commander, and we had heard Don [Rogers] had hired him at 70 per cent higher pay than the rest of us, and we jokingly said we'd go on strike as soon as he arrived in Canada.

—*Janusz Zurakowski*

Only three of Avro's test pilots would fly the Arrow—Zurakowski, Potocki, and Cope, followed by the only RCAF pilot to fly it, Jack Woodman. Zurakowski said the Arrow was "easy to fly. It did have a high landing speed, which was not a problem from a handling point of view, but did have an effect on the length of the runway and braking."

The fastest the Arrow would ever fly in its short life was in the hands of Spud Potocki who took the aircraft at three-quarter throttle to 1.98 Mach or 1,320 mph—and this was with the adapted J-75 engines, engines with 20 per cent less thrust than the Iroquois.

Whenever Zurakowski took the Arrow up, the ground crew noticed he never flew the same route twice. He was not only testing out the aircraft, but looking for real estate that might be for sale.

Zura was legendary for the things he could get an aircraft to do, but it turned out it was the direct opposite of what he did on the ground with an automobile. Although fearless in the sky, many Avro workers repeatedly witnessed Zura driving home from work, knuckles white around the steering wheel of his car, with a terrified look on his face, as he hobbled along at barely 35 mph.

An experimental test pilot is not a popular person in a design department. Most of the designers are highly optimistic about their own design and it is not a pleasant task after a flight to explain or to prove that optimism is not justified. See, I don't believe a designer can be objective enough to assess his own work. Quite often the reaction of a designer is to say that everything is excellent, that the pilots are simply too fussy, or that they want to have their own way, or that they have the prima donna complex. It's unpleasant to tell a designer that his plane is not good . . . .

In a production department the experimental pilot again is not a popular person. Nearly every production manager would like to set up his assembly line, set up a schedule, and run the production smoothly without any interruption. He is furious when every week five or more modifications have to be incorporated somewhere on the assembly line; the worst case is when the aircraft is ready for acceptance flight.

Who is to blame? Of course the test pilot. Why did he not discover the trouble before? Is modification really necessary? Why did it take so long to prove modification in flight? And so on.

We, in the Flight Test Section, hoped that we would be part of the team and participate in the solution of problems which we would have to face sooner or later.

There was a rumour that the directional stability of our new aircraft was poor. At this time a number of American fighters disintegrated in the air, and some designs were quickly modified to provide a bigger fin area.

We asked the design office for aerodynamic reports. We met with refusal because there could be a wrong interpretation of the reports by the pilots.

—*Janusz Zurakowski*

Zura had already upset some of the people in the design office over the CF-100. The CF-100 had a maximum design speed of .85 Mach, or about 85 per cent of the speed of sound, but its level speed at high altitude was slightly faster. When Zura once asked Jim Chamberlin what would happen if a pilot accidentally exceeded this speed, he was told that wind tunnel tests indicated that the aircraft could be uncontrollable, and that besides, the pilot's notes clearly showed Mach .85 to be the limiting speed.

For me, this answer was not satisfactory. The CF-100 was an all-weather and night interceptor, and if the pilot was not careful, he could be past aircraft limitations in no time. I considered it my duty to investigate behaviour of the aircraft at higher speeds and if dangers were discovered, to recommend some action. With instrumented aircraft I ran a series of dives at high altitude, checking recorded results between flights. Finally I reached 1.08 Mach number indicated in a dive at full power. A sonic boom on the ground confirmed surpassing the speed of sound. Behaviour of the aircraft was satisfactory.

The flight test department, company management, and the air force were delighted, but to the design office, I discovered, I was enemy number one.

Previously, without the knowledge of either the flight test section or the pilots, the design office had prepared a proposal for the RCAF recommending extensive re-design of the CF-100 by decreasing the thickness of the wings, sweeping them slightly back, and increasing their area—all this mainly to obtain a maximum diving speed of .95 Mach.

—*Janusz Zurakowski*

The RCAF investigated the proposal, but when the MK.4 reached the speed of sound, and expensive improvements were expected to show lower performance, the proposal was rejected with some sharp remarks.

My title was chief development pilot, but, because the design people controlled Flight Test, they were not giving me any information about what they were doing. They sent lots of propaganda stuff to the RCAF without letting me know what they were . . . . Guys like Chamberlin and so forth were putting themselves in such a position that they couldn't be replaced—they controlled all the knowledge themselves . . . . Even Jim Floyd, the vice-president of engineering, couldn't get proper control of the section. So one day I went to Don Rogers and said, "Look, I cannot be a chief development pilot if I have no control of anything. I asked my boss, Don Rogers, for help, but when his efforts were stalled, I tendered my resignation as the chief development pilot.

—*Janusz Zurakowski*

At first Jim Floyd never questioned the fact he had to get the aerodynamic report from flight test rather than from his own section, although it seemed unusual. But what really brought it to a head was when the latest estimations of the landing speed of the Arrow showed higher than originally estimated. Floyd questioned Zurakowski on this. Zura said he didn't know why either, because his request for reports from Floyd's engineering group had always been refused to him. "It was a bit of a shock to him," recalls Zura, "because he had previously instructed that reports be made available to the flight test section." When the reports continued to be withheld, Floyd located the culprit and fired him on the spot. He was Jim Chamberlin's right-hand man. From then on flight test became independent from the design office.

As for Zurakowski, he gave up flying in October 1958, belatedly fulfilling a promise he had made to his wife to quit flying as soon as he turned forty. He was forty-four.

Work on John Frost's subsonic saucer continued uninterrupted until September, 1957, when representatives of the United States Army visited Avro to monitor the project's progress and refine their specification. "In general terms," said the requirement,

The U.S. Army desires to perform the traditional cavalry missions of reconnaissance, counter-reconnaissance, pursuit, harrassment, etc., by means suitable to modern warfare. More specifically they require a vehicle which will carry a payload of 1,000 lbs. consisting of a crew of 2, weapons and cargo. This payload must be carried under certain specified conditions. A minimum range of 25 miles is required. The vehicle must be capable of hovering both in the ground cushion and in free air and obtain a forward speed of at least 25 knots. An endurance in normal flight of not less than 30 minutes is required; in hover minimum endurance is specified as 10 minutes.

In response to this requirement for "flying jeeps," as Frost called them, the group put together a brochure. The United States Army ate it up, funded it, and thus gave life to what became known as the Avrocar. "It was 18 feet in diameter," wrote Frost,

> a circular wing with a 20% elliptical section and 2% camber, and it's gross weight with 2,000 lb. of useful load was estimated at 5,650 lbs. The power was supplied by 3 J-69-5-9 turbojet engines which were estimated would provide the following performance: maximum speed at sea level, 225 knots; rate of climb at sea level, 4,500 feet per minute; ceiling (limited by no oxygen for crew), 10,000 feet; range at sea level, 145 nautical miles with 1,679-pound payload; range at 10,000 feet, 180 nautical miles, [also with 1,679-pound payload].

Despite the continuous misgivings Avro Aircraft's engineering department had about the Avrocar, in the late spring of 1958, Joe Morley's sales and service department produced two brochures on the project. One was a slick, thirty-four-page effort entitled "Avromobile: A New Family of Air Vehicles." Although the aircraft's first flight was still three years in the future, the brochure highlighted the principles behind the air-cushion vehicle and provided artist's conceptions of not only the Avrocar, but Avrotrucks and Avrocoaches.

The second brochure was entitled "Review of Commercial VTOL Aircraft Development Possibilities." It took a tongue-in-cheek look at the commercial possibilities of the Avrocar family of vehicles. It estimated that a typical Avrocoach flight from Toronto to London for instance, would take only half an hour flying at a speed of 135 mph and would cost the customer a mere $10.80, whereas the traditional Viscount would take an hour and twenty minutes, travel at only 60 mph, and cost $9.25.

In November, 1958, a third brochure appeared, by far the most bizarre yet, entitled "A Review of Promising Future Avro Projects." In it, the company boasted that "the prospects on both the military and commercial fields appear to be very good. No fewer than thirteen different vehicles show promise of a good potential market and some of these represent only one of a family of possible vehicles which should also be marketable." The vehicles, all based on the VTOL principle, included the Avroangel, an ambulance and firefighting vehicle; the Avrotruck, a combat cargo vehicle; the Avrodrone, a surveillance aircraft for the army signal corps; the Avrowagon, a family-type station wagon; the

Avrocruiser, a larger family-type station wagon; and the Avropelican, a bomb-carrying anti-submarine aircraft.

John Frost found the money, $10 million in all, to build two Avrocars, but neither went beyond the status of test vehicles. The first flight of the Avrocar took place just outside one of Avro's then deserted hangars on December 5, 1959. At the controls was one of Avro's few remaining test pilots, Spud Potocki.

As Frost had earlier feared, the higher the flight, the greater the instability. All flights of the Avrocar were tethered. It was a problem he and his team were never able to solve. In a year of subsequent flight testing the Avrocar never left its 4-foot air cushion and never travelled farther than perhaps a half a mile. From supersonic to subsonic to barely 4 feet and half a mile. For all the difficulties, however, Frost at least had proven the principle of vertical take-off.

The guy who invented the zipper never made a cent. But the guy who invented the machine that made the zipper made a fortune—this was the story of the saucer. Our guy had the idea but he didn't have the materials.

—*Geoff Grossmith*

15

THE ICARUS FACTOR

The Sputnik launching of October 4, 1957, had led the North American military community to conclude that by 1961 or 1962 the major threat would be missile forces, against which fighter aircraft would be useless. Although the air forces of both the United States and Canada still considered manned interceptors vital to the defence of the continent, it would now be more difficult than ever to justify large anti-bomber defence costs; the threat could be dealt with by guided missiles and available aircraft at a lower cost. All this was fuel to the Arrow debate, a debate that continues even today.

General Guy Simonds was Army Chief of Staff and Chief of the General Staff in 1953 when the decision to undertake the CF-105 project had been made. He was among the earliest and most vocal opponents of the Arrow. His objection to the government's funding of the CF-105 project had been a factor when he had resigned as Army Chief of Staff in 1955. His arguments were the first rumblings of the impending storm.

"His view was simple," says Robert Bradford:

that except for a very short intervening period, which did not justify the development of a new aircraft, missiles would replace

232

bombers and all combat aircraft would be obsolete. That an enemy might retain both missiles *and* aircraft, or that the marginal period might be quite long, or that the complementary nature of aircraft and missile systems might be proved, and thus require the maintenance of both, were possibilities that the missile proponents never adequately considered.

By February, 1958, three more voices joined the debate. Dr. O. M. Solandt, the former chairman of the Defence Research Board, said the Arrow "might well be the last piloted airplane to be produced in this country." The RCAF at that time, however, was making an average of two interceptions a day—interceptions not always involving Russian bombers, but mostly straying airliners or private aircraft, giving support to the argument that, unlike a missile, you can always call back an aircraft.

"We have decided to go ahead with the program to develop the Arrow," said defence minister Pearkes. "We believe that it will give us the added weight and speed we will need to cope with the latest versions of Russian bombers." "The planned performance of this aircraft," echoed Air Chief Hugh Campbell, "is such that it can deal with any likely bomber threat to this country over the next decade." Campbell would remain steadfast in his opinion that the Arrow was a necessary part of Canada's air defence.

Even the aviation trade journals joined in.

The idea that missiles will quickly replace all manned aircraft in the defence picture is no longer given any serious consideration. . . . Missiles will assume their role in defence as an evolutionary, not revolutionary, process. Nor will they ever completely eliminate the necessity for manned aerial vehicles. Military situations will always require human thought as an essential ingredient for success.

That might be all very well; however, "from the point of view of manhours and money invested," wrote Jim Hornick, "the program will be comparable with the building of the St. Lawrence Seaway."

Seemingly oblivious to the debate, Avro Aircraft prepared for the Arrow's first flight. Minor development problems had disproven Fred Smye's prediction that the aircraft would fly before the end of 1957. By March 21, 1958, with the country in the final stretch of an election, Diefenbaker having dissolved Parliament on the well-founded hope of achieving a majority, the aircraft was ready, but a broken oil line delayed it another four days. Believing there would be few, if any, surprises during the Arrow's first flight, Don Rogers told the Airline Pilots Association: "We are able to predict with fair accuracy how an aircraft will behave. It is not until the aircraft is pushed up to its maximum that troubles develop."

Then, on March 25, with Jan Zurakowski at the controls of an aircraft loaded with more power than was necessary to drive the *Queen Mary*, Arrow RL-201 taxied to the foot of Malton Airport runway 32 and lifted into the air. Zurakowski's twenty-five minute flight was problem-free save for a malfunction in one small switch.

By the end of March the government had paid A. V. Roe more than $100 million for the development of the airframe alone. Meanwhile, estimated costs of Sparrow and Astra continued to spiral, and the army and navy chiefs became more and more concerned that the CF-105 would eat into their own defence appropriation allotments. "It wasn't the need for an interceptor that was challenged," wrote Jim Dow, "so much as the wisdom of paying so much for so few aircraft."

The Chiefs of Staff Committee did not necessarily agree that the project should be scrapped entirely. Salvage was highly desirable. Perhaps the thirty-seven aircraft in various stages of readiness could be completed. Maintenance and repair might be a problem for such a small number of the type, but was anyone prepared to brave the political backlash that would follow in the wake of cancellation? If A. V. Roe was permitted to complete the work in hand, the impact on the workers of discontinuing the program could be spread out over time.

The RCAF did not want to give up on the Arrow. In discussing the salvage proposal, they argued that, while guided missiles could shoot down intruding aircraft, they could not tell the difference between an enemy plane and a TCA jet transport which had drifted off course. The few Arrows salvaged could perform the necessary identification and reconnaissance role. But the RCAF also made the point that the Bomarc missile was only a complementary weapon of air defence, and was not designed to replace interceptor aircraft. It was vulnerable to counter attack and electronic jamming. Even the thirty-seven Arrows, in combination with the Bomarc, would not be able to provide the kind of defence that the air force thought necessary. The RCAF would not accept the salvage proposal. They did not want to retreat in any way.

The CSC could see two courses for the government to follow. One was to complete the project for about $871 million, at a final unit cost of about $12 million. The alternative was to cancel all the CF-105 programs immediately, and to negotiate with the United States for the two Bomarc installations, along with the necessary SAGE complement and about a hundred supersonic interceptor aircraft from the production end of a United States assembly line at an approximate unit cost of $2 million. The Minister of National Defence, George Pearkes, agreed to put the second proposal to the government. At this point, however, the Chief of the Air Staff, A/M Campbell, expressed some concern lest the government concur, and the Chiefs of Staff were then accused of not providing all the relevant information. It was alleged that information was being held back to cover up the shortcomings of the previous administration in allowing the project to get so completely out of hand. Prime Minister Diefenbaker then demanded that the chairman of the Chiefs of Staff Committee, General Charles Foulkes of the Army, immediately produce a dossier on the whole project from 1952 to date, showing complete documentation of all decisions, studies, reports, cut-backs, submissions, and yearly expenditures. The document was prepared without delay, but not without some misgivings about the propriety of furnishing the government with confidential information of the previous administration, as this was contrary to custom.

There was a brief respite (this had been Campbell's intention) while the government studied the dossier. It showed lucidly enough that the major causes of the abnormal costs were, first, the decision to develop an engine; second, the RCAF's insistence on completing the Sparrow and Astra programs; and third, the several stretch-outs and cut-backs due to insufficient funding. The unit cost was ridiculously high when spread over a small number of aircraft; in addition, the lack of other buyers shrunk the production potential to about a hundred aircraft, which were loaded with eight years' plant overhead and development costs.

There were numerous meetings of the CDC and many prolonged cabinet meetings. Still no decision was announced. In spite of Diefenbaker's warning to keep the content of the meetings secret, A. V. Roe seemed well informed of the nature and substance of the discussions; Diefenbaker suspected the military, particularly the RCAF, of leaking information to A. V. Roe and of urging them to exert pressure on the government. The company, the trade unions, and the press clamoured for news on the future of the CF-105. Diefenbaker, annoyed by the intense lobbying, summoned the Chiefs of Staff and gave them a dressing down for the alleged leaks, warning them of serious consequences if the indiscretions continued.

The government was not necessarily unjustified in its supicions. After all, there was not only a permanent CF-105–RCAF liaison team in residence at A. V. Roe, some of the company's top men, notably Curtis and Plant, were ex-RCAF air marshals. It was in the interests of both the RCAF and the company to appease the government as much as possible on the requirements for the Arrow. A. V. Roe management no doubt collected all the information they could, by whatever means necessary, and used it, in combination with the press, to try to get the Arrow into production.

The Chiefs of Staff realized that, because of the high deficit, there was very little chance of a substantial increase in defence appropriations. If the program proceeded, there would be little, if any, funds for the re-arming of the air division in Europe, for the replacement of worn-out RCN frigates, or for the new tanks and armoured carriers for the army. On the other hand, there was a strong possibility that the SAGE system would be extended to Canadian air defence sectors to accommodate the operation of Bomarc. It would then be feasible to accept a United States interceptor aircraft and some of those aircraft would be available two years earlier and at a completed cost of about $2 million each.

But this was all far removed from the happenings at Malton. On April 19, the headline in the *Toronto Star* read, "Arrow Exceeds 1,000 MPH." Four days later, Earle Brownridge was promoted to executive vice-president and general manager of Orenda Engines. A year earlier, Brownridge had been recognized by the Canadian Aeronautical Institute when he received the McCurdy Trophy. Walter McLachlan continued on as president of Orenda and acquired the new title of executive vice-president, administration and co-ordination, of A. V. Roe Canada.

In early May, General Guy Simonds continued his criticism of the aircraft. Interviewed on CBC radio, he said:

> I believe the Arrow to be obsolete as a defence weapon, because before it becomes operational, the airplane will have ceased to be the primary weapon of air power. That role is passing, if it has not already passed, to the missile—both in strategic attack and strategic defence. This could be foreseen at the time the Arrow program was instituted. I expect the program will probably cost more than the projected $200 million, and in my opinion cannot possibly be finished until it becomes clear to even the most stubborn that the missile is the principal weapon of attack and the most effective weapon of defence.

The other guest on the broadcast was Avro's John Plant, who was offered the opportunity to reply:

> Airmen are the authors of their own misfortune with regard to the word obsolete. Every airplane that has come out in the past— airmen have declared it obsolete. They say there is a better airplane on the drawing boards behind. The same applies to the Arrow. People will believe it is obsolete even though it has only just flown.

In Parliament, confusion surrounded the Arrow issue; it seemed that few members were apprised of enough information. Finally, in response to an MP's request, Secretary of State Henri Courtemanche supplied Parliament with the status of the government's involvement with A. V. Roe on the Arrow program as of May 1, 1958:

The government has placed orders for the design, development and tooling for the Arrow airframe, Iroquois engine and the integrated electronic flight and fire control system and the manufacture of thirty-seven pre-production aircraft.

The currently estimated production cost of each complete Arrow aircraft within the thirty-seven pre-production order is $6.1 million. Should the decision be taken to proceed with production, the cost per subsequent aircraft will be reduced considerably.

The total cost to the government of the complete Arrow aircraft project including design, development, tooling and pre-production costs of the Arrow airframe, the engine programs and the integrated electronic flight and fire control system, up to May 1, 1958, is $233,000,000. This cost figure also covers two completed aircraft, three in final assembly and thirty-two others, within the present order of thirty-seven aircraft, in various stages of manufacture and material procurement.

The present plans for the production and development of the Arrow call for the introduction of this aircraft into operational use in 1961.

Wilf Curtis carried the Arrow cause in a speech to the friendly members of the RCAF Benevolent Association of Ottawa. Beginning his remarks by denying that Arrow costs were running at $200 million and that the aircraft was obsolete, he went on to say:

The Russians are still building high-speed bombers and Canada still needs fast interceptors to thwart them. The Arrow is not more obsolete than a 1958 car being rendered obsolete just because a later model is already on the way.

Three days later, *The Financial Post* picked up the speech and ran it full page, including a picture of Curtis in uniform under the headline, "The Avro Arrow NOT Obsolete."

In England, word had it that Sir Frank Spriggs, a Dobson crony and partner to him on that first trip to Canada in the summer of 1943, was stepping down as chairman of the Hawker-Siddeley Group. Next in line for the position was Dobson himself, but he was not the favourite. Although his gamble in setting up A. V. Roe Canada had turned into one of the major money-makers for the Group, there were still those on the board that frowned upon his methods, didn't like the way he did business, and were determined to prevent him from becoming chairman. Dobson had other ideas.

So Dobson got on the phone to Gordon in Canada and asked for help. Gordon then called a quick board meeting and demanded and got the resignations of all A. V. Roe Canada's directors and threatened to submit them to England unless Dobson was made chairman. Needless to say, the ploy worked and Dobson got his reward.

—*Pat Kelly*

That same month, A. V. Roe Canada issued its annual report for the year ending in 1958. With the accounting firm of Price-Waterhouse certifying the contents of the document as sound and secure, the A. V. Roe group of companies increased in consolidated assets from $145,754,527 in 1957 to $310,400,714 in 1958 and sales rose from $234,811,024 in 1957 to $370,751,856 in 1958. Employment created had doubled over the year, rising to 41,000. A. V. Roe Canada now had thirty-nine different companies in its group, sixteen thousand shareholders, and were located in eighteen different communities. There were 6,300 suppliers dependent on the group for some of their business. Yet the number one agenda item at every A. V. Roe board meeting that summer of 1958 was the Avro Arrow.

By the middle of August, Minister of National Defence George Pearkes had met in Washington with the American Secretary of State for Defence, Neil McElroy, to see if by chance the American government was interested in sharing in the costs of the Arrow program. They weren't. The Americans had suspended development of aircraft similar to the Arrow, one strike against Pearkes's proposal. They also objected to the plane itself, saying it was not capable of sustaining great speed for long enough. Instead, McElroy suggested that the Americans would be prepared to sell to Canada off-the-shelf, proven aircraft to meet any interceptor requirements, at a much lower cost than would be required to finish the Arrow program.

The Chiefs of Staff, in the meantime, had reached the tentative conclusion that the military and economic considerations did not justify the continuation of the project. Air Chief Campbell, of course, did not agree, and succeeded in delaying the CSC's presentation to the government. In the interim, the Prime Minister was subjected to a barrage of questions in Parliament, much to the discomfort of the other Chiefs.

"May I say a word first about the CF-105," said the Leader of the Opposition, Lester Pearson, in the House.

The Minister has pointed out that this particular manned interceptor, which is, perhaps the last word in the world in aeroplanes of this type, is of no use whatever and was not meant to be of any use against missiles . . . . A decision now has to be taken as to whether or not to go ahead to the point where these planes will be introduced into our squadrons along, perhaps later, with the Bomarc missile, or do we abandon this project in the light of developments in the last two years, which seem to be emphasizing the importance of other forms of air defence, which may not replace but will certainly have to supplement the CF-105? Do we try to do both?

For the moment, at least, the Arrow was living on borrowed time.

A. V. Roe's quest for funds on the Arrow had never been smooth; the project had been subject to periodic review right from the beginning, and the company had had to justify each new request for continued government financing. But during the summer of 1958, the company got the first inklings that something was going drastically wrong. Jan Zurakowski and John Plant got the first clues. Having given up flying by this time, Zurakowski was now involved in the administrative side of the Arrow program. In early August, he and Plant were part of a contingent from Avro Aircraft making a presentation at RCAF headquarters in Ottawa, something they had done many times in the past.

There were about fifty air force officers present and when Plant asked if there were any questions, there was silence until one of the officers said he was under explicit instructions not to ask anything about the Arrow. Now this was a very, very unpleasant moment for me. It was then I realized something was wrong.

—*Janusz Zurakowski*

Fred Smye knew something was wrong as well, but the Conservatives now had the run of things, and he could no longer simply pick up the phone and speak to Ottawa directly. His access to information had changed so dramatically, that every time a major article on the Arrow appeared in a newspaper or magazine, Smye would immediately contact the writer to see if the writer might know something he didn't. Of the ten directors sitting on the board of A. V. Roe Canada, only John Tory, the company's legal advisor, could boast of being a Conservative. In late August, Tory had met with Diefenbaker and returned white-faced to Malton to tell Smye point blank that the project was in trouble.

At Smye's request, Tory quickly arranged a meeting between Avro and the cabinet members concerned: Pearkes (National Defence), Donald Fleming (Finance), and Raymond O'Hurley (Defence Production).

Smye prepared a brief for O'Hurley, which attempted to show that Avro Aircraft and Orenda Engines were not profit-motivated, but product motivated, and presented arguments for keeping the Arrow and the Iroquois alive. It also intimated that cancellation would be catastrophic.

> Some indication of the risk involved in making these expenditures is given by manpower forecasts of the two companies on the basis of existing contracts and including the thirty-seven Arrows and an appropriate number of Iroquois engines. Whereas the total employment of the two companies is now approximately 15,000, there will be a gradual reduction to some 12,000 employees at the end of 1959. As of the end of 1960, this number will be drastically reduced to some 3,500, a difference between now and then of some 11,500. With a total employment of some 9,500 people between both companies, it would not appear to be economically justifiable to continue the operation of these facilities which are the subject of this brief.

During the meeting, Pearkes asked Smye, "Suppose we cancel the Arrow, what would you do?" Smye replied, "What would we do? I'd turn the key in the door and walk away." Pearkes shot back, "Can't you build automobiles or something?" Smye then asked Minister of Finance Donald Fleming if a reduction of some $350 million in the project would make any difference in the government's considerations. Fleming's reply was: "Mr. Smye, 350 cents would make a difference!"

Smye told the ministers that he would not be able to authorize any further capital expenditures on the project beyond just keeping the respective companies functioning "in the present uncertain circumstances." It was an attempt to take the ball and go home. O'Hurley, who, throughout the "Arrow debates," seemed to support the project, said he was delighted to have the information. He would tell Diefenbaker what Smye had said about a slowdown, take him a copy of Smye's brief, and get back to Smye after the cabinet had reviewed this latest information.

Smye had hoped for a more definite response. When he briefed Crawford Gordon on the meeting, Gordon decided to go and see Diefenbaker himself. "Somebody's got to take on the son-of-a-bitch in Ottawa," he said to Smye, "and I'm just the one to do it."

Those who recall seeing Crawford Gordon during that fateful summer of 1958 have a picture in their minds that bears little resemblance to the man who took control of A. V. Roe seven years before. His face was puffier now, much puffier some thought, and his voice, once deep, clear, and defiant, now had the tendency to crack at times; he left sentences unfinished, as if he could no longer find the right words. Now in his mid-forties, Crawford Gordon had done just about all he had set out to do—build one of the largest industrial empires in Canadian history. There's an old saying that when you get it all today, there's nothing left for tomorrow.

When he had first taken over A. V. Roe, Gordon was living with his wife and three children in Toronto's exclusive Forest Hill Village. His early days with the company had been invigorating—new job, new responsibilities—and since things had always come easily to him, he had confronted difficulty with an easy grace. In 1955 he bought a 7-acre "estate" in the Bayview-Lawrence area of Toronto. To Gordon, by this time, it mattered little where he lived, for he had become a workaholic. When he did go home, he usually brought Fred Smye or a portfolio full of work with him.

A turning point in his life was the loss of his secretary/mistress, who one day packed her bags and moved out West. Despite the fact that Gordon was, in his own peculiar way, devoted to both his family and his mistress, he was a notorious womanizer. His secretary eventually realized that Gordon would not give up his family for her, so, in order to spare herself further distress, she left. Her sudden departure was a terrible blow for Gordon. Fred Smye urged him to forget her, but Gordon, like a man possessed, made many attempts to see her again; however, the distance between Victoria and Toronto, and her own insistence to be left in peace, finally put an end to the affair. Gordon had never been abstemious when it came to alcohol, and now, in his despair, he turned more and more to the bottle. He became an alcoholic.

It was around this time, the summer of 1958, that people began to notice a change in Crawford Gordon, subtle at first, but change nonetheless. His devoted wife, Mary, recalls that he found it increasingly tiresome to attend the obligatory dinner parties and other social functions. It might be expected that a man in his position would use such occasions as business opportunities, but Gordon seemed to revel in being obnoxious. Most of his wife's time during these events was spent in apologizing to all the people he had insulted.

Occasionally, late in the evening, usually after a particularly hard day, Gordon's son would find him slumped in a chair, tears in his eyes, listening to Judy Garland records.

My father was forty-one at the height of A. V. Roe and dealing with people who were largely fifteen years older than himself. He loved to play golf, squash, and tennis, and loved watching hockey and football. But when he became so wrapped up in his work, he gave them all up. He simply eliminated all his fun things. And as the stress factors increased, he might have had the physical but not the mental capacity to handle it.

—*Crawford Gordon III*

With the Arrow debate heating up during the summer of 1958, colleagues saw less and less of Gordon; when he did put in an appearance, he usually had a glass of Scotch in his hand. Wilf Curtis, now vice-chairman of the board at A. V. Roe Canada, found himself chairing more and more meetings with Gordon so often mysteriously indisposed. Gordon's new secretary, Gloria Collinson, became expert at making excuses for Gordon on an almost daily basis, and Fred Smye privately expressed his concern for his doomed friend. Then the inevitable happened. In the early summer of 1958, Gordon left his wife and children and moved into Briarcrest.

In Ottawa, the Prime Minister was quite mindful of what was happening in Malton. One of the reasons was his party whip, John C. Pallett, who happened to be the sitting member for Peel, which housed the Avro plant. Pallett was a war veteran and had been legal counsel to the Peel Board of Education until he was elected to Parliament in 1954. Rising quickly within the party, it wasn't long before he became a close friend of Diefenbaker, strengthening a relationship begun back in 1947.

Pallett's predecessor in the riding had talked on occasion with the Prime Minister about A. V. Roe, but it wasn't until Pallett was elected and the Conservatives formed the government, that the information really started to flow. Although Diefenbaker's "official" advisors on the Arrow were the Chiefs of Staff and the departments of National Defence and Defence Production, he welcomed the information coming from Pallett.

We didn't deal with company officials: the people I was interested in were the shop stewards and the guys on the floor. I knew many of them on a first-name basis more than I knew the top echelons. All the fellows on the airframe would tell me about the engine; all the fellows on the engines would tell me about the airframe. It was absolutely foolproof because it gave me the total picture. It wasn't what I wanted to hear, however; I wanted to hear this was a superb aircraft and I found it wasn't a superb aircraft and this was very disturbing to me.

What was wrong? They developed a new engine and a new airframe, the only time ever that's been tried. It's like wearing two left shoes; it looks distinctive, but it isn't too bright.

I will say one thing about Dobson, however; he was a realist. Once I was at a company dinner at the York Club, and Crawford Gordon was making a speech about how the Arrow would be airborne by January, 1958. "No it won't," Dobson whispered to me.

—*John Pallett*

At the A. V. Roe head office on University Avenue in Toronto, Gordon's secretary had made an appointment for the boss to see the Prime Minister on September 17. In preparation for the meeting, Smye prepared yet another brief for the Prime Minister and the cabinet that Gordon might take with him. Framed in eloquent but not particularly tactful language, Smye's brief claimed that termination of the Arrow/Iroquois project would:

1. Destroy one of the free world's most progressive and advanced technical organizations in the aeronautical field together with Canadian prestige, self-reliance and independence for which this organization has stood. Moreover, it will virtually eliminate any future opportunity for Canada to regain a position of leadership in this field.

2. Create a catastrophic unemployment problem. Taken together with consequent snowballing losses in revenues from sales taxes and corporate and personal income taxes, this could seriously aggravate the present uncertain economic conditions.

3. Deprive this country of an effective Canadian-created component of its national defence which cannot be more adequately replaced from non-Canadian sources.

Pat Kelly advised Gordon to fly to Ottawa so that he would arrive quietly and refreshed, and to neither drink nor smoke on the way up. Gordon refused, and with Kelly and Joe Morley in tow, he boarded a train for Ottawa, arriving many hours later at the Prime Minister's door, "bombed" and "in no shape for solid conversation." To add to the situation, he'd left Smye's briefs on the train so that Kelly had to rush back to the railway station to retrieve them. To further aggravate matters, the Prime Minister couldn't see Gordon right away, but left him cooling his heels for almost two hours.

In an office adjoining the Prime Minister's was John Pallett, who was about to witness a confrontation that he would remember years afterwards. When the Prime Minister was finally available, Gordon, still wearing his trench coat, got up, lit a cigar, and with something of his old, confident air, marched in to meet Mr. Diefenbaker.

I'm not going to comment on his disposition, but Gordon was rude, incoherent, like a person demented.

—*John Pallett*

Gordon refused to sit or to let the Prime Minister get a word in. One can only imagine the scene. On one side of the desk, the Prime Minister of Canada, with all the assurance of a majority government; on the other side, the powerful but decadent industrialist, cigar in mouth, smelling of Scotch, pounding on his adversary's desk, demanding a guarantee that the Arrow not be scrapped, to which the Prime Minister might have replied: "My stockholders, sir, are eighteen million Canadians!"

He [Gordon] was acting very childish over a problem that was quite serious, like a kid who was having his toy taken away from him.

—*John Pallett*

When Gordon failed to lower his voice or stop the pounding, the Prime Minister warned he would be forcibly removed if he didn't settle down. At this, Gordon turned and stomped out, his trench coat flaring like a cape behind him. The "meeting" had lasted less than twenty minutes. When Gordon met Morley in the hall, his only comment was, "We'll turn it around," but later, when he called Smye, he described the meeting as the most devastating experience of his life.

On September 23, 1958, the Prime Minister issued a press release on the whole air defence situation. The main points were that the lessening bomber threat required less bomber defence; that the Bomarc missile units which, it was stated, could "be used with either a conventional high explosive warhead or a nuclear warhead," would be installed in Canada; that SAGE would be installed in the Canadian air defence sectors; that the use of CF-100's would continue; that a decision on whether the CF-105 Arrow would go into production be postponed, but that limited development would continue; and that both the Sparrow and the Astra programs were to be cancelled, and modifications made in the Arrow airframe to permit the use of a fully developed United States missile and fire-control system (the Hughes MX-1179 and the Falcon missiles). The Prime Minister went on to announce that the Arrow program would come under a complete review in six months, that is, in March, 1959. "By March, 1959," said the Prime Minister, "six

Arrows will have been completed for $398 million, then the situation will be reviewed again. To cut the Arrow off now would immobilize the industry."

The original decision was to cancel the Arrow in November. We local MPs had some direct intervention at that time not to have it cancelled but to keep it going at least through Christmas.

—*John Pallett*

It was then Crawford Gordon's turn. The next day he told the *Globe and Mail*:

Our situation remains unchanged. The program calls for six Arrows to be test flown by next March, at which time, 7, 8, 9, and 10 [Arrows RL-207–10] will be in flight test or on the production line. I feel confident the Arrow will be ordered into production March 31 when the government reviews its defence expenditures. Although we are in a state of gloom over the government's announcement, nothing could be further from the truth than that Avro and Orenda will close down, throwing thousands out of work.

The employees at A. V. Roe reacted to the Diefenbaker announcement with confusion, shock, and incredulity: "It just doesn't make sense" . . . "I'm amazed they'd scrap a plane of this value" . . . "Too much money has been spent so far to just give it up" . . . "I'm taking the next boat home." But the assembly bays and the engine plant were surprisingly calm. Ray Foottit, heading the RCAF management group at the plant, detected absolutely no speed-up in the program whatsoever. For Fred Smye, it was almost business as usual.

After the September 1958 announcement, we had a number of meetings about what we were going to do. Firstly, we would find out the facts. Curtis and Plant would talk to the military people, I would try and tackle the politicians, and Ron Williams would try and soft-peddle the films the company was making on the plane.

—*Fred Smye*

In sales and service, Joe Morley and Murray Willer started looking around and came up with a list of other projects Avro might tackle should the Arrow be cancelled. Some of the possibilities were obtaining sub-contract work from the Boeing Airplane Company; production-sharing work with the USAF and the United States Army; production of commercial aircraft in co-operation with North American Aviation in Columbus, Ohio; and multi-weapons development with NATO. None of these initiatives got beyond the paper stage. Unlike Willer and Morley, the company, for the most part, continued to keep all its eggs in one basket.

Guest Hake, the company's quality control and production manager, wrote a long, confidential memo to John Plant, in which he stated his opinion that "the circumstances applying to missile defence are such as to require complementary manned interceptors for some time to come," and suggested that, with some cost-cutting, the Arrow could be offered to the Canadian government sooner and cheaper than the F-106, which was currently being developed in the States and being considered as an alternative to the Arrow. "It is very clear that this is no time for heroics," he went on,

> cold common sense must prevail . . . . It appears to me that the RCAF have completely misread the political atmosphere surrounding their operations on this occasion . . . . We once went for the best and nearly lost all, let us now decide what our target really is and attack it directly, ignoring all diversionary tactics and practicing maximum economics. *Le mieux, c'est l'ennemi du bien* [leave well enough alone].

He was referring, of course, to the RCAF's holding out on the armament specification. The spiralling costs of Astra and Sparrow development, which had precipitated their cancellation, had been pushing the cost of the Arrow into an impossible range. A. V. Roe had been trying to get the RCAF to back up on the armament and fire-control system for some time.

> *About September I took an advance party of engineers down to Hughes Aircraft with the intention of bringing an Arrow out of Canada and down to Los Angeles to introduce the Hughes fire-control system into the aircraft on site. . . . But for reasons which I really can't even now understand, the aircraft wasn't allowed out of the country, therefore, although the system was adaptable for the Arrow, we just couldn't take it down to Los Angeles. Ultimately we endeavoured to bring the technology from Hughes back to Malton and introduce the system there, but . . . we didn't have the system in before the Arrow was cancelled. It was quite compatible with the Arrow and would have produced marked reductions in the cost of the aircraft.*
>
> —Hugh Mackenzie

> *John Easton must hold himself as one of those more than somewhat responsible for the death of the Arrow. He was responsible for the armament*

spec, and this was way, way beyond the state of the art. The cost of his program (mainly RCA Montreal and USA) was about one-third of the total cost of the program. Even in the dying days, when I implored him to let off and go with a less sophisticated system, he wouldn't relent. It took Wilf Curtis to break him down, and both went to Wright Field to negotiate a supply of USAF systems for a limited number of aircraft, but it was too late.

—Joe Morley

On October 2, nine days after Diefenbaker's announcement, an RCAF team headed by A/V/M John Easton went down to Hughes Electronics in Culver City, California, to see what could be done. At the same time, Fred Smye headed for Washington to meet with the assistant secretary of the USAF.

We explained the circumstances, of which he was well aware, and I asked if the USAF would be prepared to make a contribution to the project in order to get costs down.

We had several conversations. He, in turn, spoke to Mr. Douglas, who was the secretary of the Air Force. We didn't see Douglas but his assistant authorized me on Douglas' behalf to inform the government that the USAF would be quite happy to provide the fire control system, missile and other components free. He authorized me to tell our government. So the next day, I went to Mr. O'Hurley with a letter to this effect, and I stood there while he read it, and that was the last I heard of that.

In order to get the costs down and to cut out the chatter about escalating costs and so on, we voluntarily stepped up an offer for a fixed price for one hundred airplanes. That involved gigantic risk, believe me, and in the price—which was $350 million, three million five hundred thousand dollars—in that price was $500,000 for the fire control system—fire control system [which the United States would supply at no cost], not the missile. So we could knock half a million off the price right there, which gets you down to $3 million for a fly-away operational airplane including fire control system, the whole thing.

—Fred Smye

Details of Avro's offer to the government were given in a letter from the company to the D.L. Thompson, director of the aircraft branch of DDP, on 30 December. The letter confirmed a *fixed price* offer of $346,282,015 for 100 aircraft (25221 to 25320), including Iroquois engines and the Hughes MA-1C electronics systems. Adding applicable sales tax of $28,717,985 brought the price per aircraft to an even $3.75 million. The contract proposals attached to the letter covered design and development, tooling and tool maintenance, manufacture of 20 development and 100 squadron aircraft... and technical support for the squadron aircraft....

Since the government had not obtained a security clearance for Avro personnel to visit Hughes, information on the MA-1C was coming out the back door for the Canadians. The Avro proposal made no reference to the American offer Smye had passed to O'Hurley and it included no amount for missiles.

By mid-October, Sir Roy Dobson was telling A. V. Roe shareholders that 1958 was the greatest growth period yet for the company, and while earnings were down slightly over 1957, the company still pumped over a third of a billion dollars into the Canadian economy every year.

On a more sentimental note, the last CF-100, number 692, rolled off the assembly line. Just weeks before the last Orenda engine, number 3794, had done the same. CF-100's were flying in both the RCAF and the Belgian Air Force, and Orenda-equipped F-86 Sabres were currently in the air forces of West Germany, South Africa, and Columbia. Commenting on the CF-100, Jim Hornick would say:

It was never tested in battle; its cannons never fired in anger. As modern aircraft go, the CF-100 is something of an ugly duckling. It has stubby wings and its engines protrude like gnarled joints. In an aerodynamic beauty contest, it would be no match for the graceful Arrow that followed it off the drawing board.

Between April, 1951, and October, 1973, 103 CF-100's (including prototype 18101)—one-eighth of the fleet—were lost in accidents. In all, forty-nine pilots and fifty observers were killed.

Pilot loss was higher than it should have been because of our inexperience with the aircraft. I bet Sabre figures would have been neck and neck. The first CF-100's were not really ready. They were introduced to the air force rather quickly.

—*S/L Joe Schultz*

The CF-100 entered squadron service on April 1, 1953, a little over three years since its first flight. The last CF-100 would retire in December, 1981, an incredible twenty-five years of useful squadron life. The last word belongs to Bill Waterton: "Canada can take credit for the CF-100. It had its setbacks, but no more than many others and less than most." In the end, Fred Smye's gamble in ignoring Stuart Davies' advice to "burn it" paid off.

In an article in the *Orenda News* in October, 1958, under the headline: "A. V. Roe Canada Confident of Arrow and Iroquois Future," Crawford Gordon's defence of the Arrow program was reiterated.

> Mr. Gordon put particular emphasis on the question of cost and suggested a more realistic public appraisal of what it would be. He said: "The change in the fire control system and armament has resulted in substantial reductions in the overall cost of the programme as indicated in the Prime Minister's statement" and added that analysis of the implication of these changes had "reflected further savings in the program." In addition, Mr. Gordon said the figure previously mentioned for 100 aircraft ($9 million each) included the whole basic development and tooling costs. These expenditures, he said, should be eliminated from a realistic appraisal of the possibility of continuing the program because they have "already substantially been incurred or committed" and could not be recovered whether the programme was continued or not.
>
> By considering only those costs which would be incurred from this point on in the actual production of Arrows for combat use and including the new savings, it is now estimated that "we can produce 100 Arrows, complete in every respect, including the cost of the engines and fire control system, and excluding the missile armament, for a cost of approximately $3,500,000 each." Mr. Gordon said [that] "we cannot rely on a Maginot Line of fixed missile installations" and that the inherent flexibility of the manned interceptor establishes it as a major role in the air defence system. He said that on the basis of these facts, Roe is confident of a favourable decision in March and "we are proceeding with the utmost dispatch on the Arrow and Iroquois programmes."

Gordon's same argument was repeated in *Maclean's* magazine the following December. Under the heading: "We Should and Will Go on Building Arrows," Gordon began with "various publications, individuals and self-appointed experts of many kinds have been conducting burial ceremonies for one of the most advanced military and scientific undertakings in the history of the Canadian nation." The article was almost a reprint of the one two months earlier in the *Orenda News*, but somewhat angrier in tone. With three months to go before the Arrow program review, the gloves were off.

Also in December, John Plant would say with confidence that the sixth Arrow, the one to be fitted with the Iroquois, would easily break the world speed record. The current record, 1,404 mph, held by a Lockheed F-104 Starfighter, had been established the previous summer.

In late 1958, the Chiefs of Staff were advised that the government was ready to deal with the final stage of the Arrow program and required a proposal from the Chiefs of Staff Committee. "It was indicated," writes James Eayrs,

> that the Prime Minister did not want to combine the straightforward decision to cancel the project with the contentious issue of substituting a United States aircraft. The question of augmenting the present air defences was a separate matter that could be dealt with later.

A submission was accordingly drawn up which recommended cancelling the Arrow but left open for further study the question of a replacement aircraft. A/M Hugh Campbell, suspecting the government might stall on the acquisition of substitute aircraft, refused to go along with the submission.

During the Arrow episode, the individuals who sat on the CSC included Vice Admiral H. D. DeWolf, Chief of Naval Staff; Lieutenant General H. D. Graham, Chief of General Staff; Air Marshal Hugh Campbell, Chief of Air Staff; Dr. A. Zimmerman from the Defence Research Board; A/V/M Frank Miller, Deputy Defence Minister; and General Charles Foulkes of the Army as chairman.

Campbell had good reason for refusing to go along with the proposal; it refused to address the issue of an immediate replacement aircraft, and he suspected that the government had decided to make do with the Bomarc and the CF-100, an arrangement he felt would leave the Canadian sector of the air defence of North America wide open to any supersonic attack.

Pearkes had a high code of ethics but had gone entirely missile. DeWolf and Graham had agreed on a replacement aircraft—I did not. I had tried to reconfirm the original CF-105 requirement and had confidence we were going to have a supersonic interceptor almost to the very end. We might have had to accept a lesser system, but nonetheless, at least a plane.

—A/M Hugh Campbell

During November and December, 1958, and January, 1959, discussion on the Arrow dominated the CSC meetings. Despite Campbell's feeling that "you couldn't work with two nicer men," (DeWolf and Graham), debate was heated at times, both among CSC members and between the CSC and Pearkes.

The CSC were concerned the Minister of Defence had made very little attempt to explain to the public why money should be spent on defence.

—*A/M Hugh Campbell*

Because the recommendation of the Chiefs of Staff Committee was not unanimous, Pearkes, in an attempt to cover up what might be interpreted as dissension among the Chiefs, decided to put forward the submission to cabinet without any recommendation. In this way the government could make a decision *without* the advice of the CSC rather than risk having to admit that a decision on Canada's air defence was being made by politicians, in direct defiance of the advice of the Chief of Air Staff. "The formal submission," said Campbell, "was made by Pearkes and Foulkes. We had rejected it so the government acted alone."

16

OVERTAKEN BY EVENTS

By early 1959, still a long way from being accepted as an operational engine, Iroquois engines no. 115 and no. 116 were being readied for Arrow RL-206. The marriage that people had been talking about for years was about to happen. With the Diefenbaker announcement of September 1958 looming over the company like Damocles' sword, Avro and Orenda accelerated their respective programs. Their objective was simple: get an Iroquois-equipped Arrow into the air in the shortest time possible. When the cancellation came a month earlier than expected, on February 20, 1959, there are disagreements as to how far away the Iroquois-equipped Arrow was from first flight. Most say two weeks, some say months.

The thrust limits of the first fitted Iroquois would have probably been 16,000 pounds and about 20,000 pounds with afterburner. And the engine wasn't completely up to performance. We had trouble with the second-stage turbine blades. I had worked out a new blade design which would have solved the vibration problem, but they were never used. At the time, the top rpm speed of the engine was 7,800 but we put a limit of 7,650 on for flight because of the blade vibrations. The engine was put in, taken out, the pipes were adjusted, then put in again, but the program was cancelled before we could put in new blades (we called them "toothpick" blades). On the day of the cancellation the blades for the engines were sitting on my desk.

—Harry Keast

Test pilots at Orenda were more of a luxury than a necessity, and flight test at Orenda differed from flight test at Avro in that they definitely didn't like anything being said about poor test results by us. We used to be encouraged to appear on TV and radio, but only under strict control.

Grinyer was a bit funny—he couldn't be wrong. He was a rude little man. I got the feeling that if anybody had doctored reports it would be him. The thing with the Iroquois is that it wasn't a good engine. They had oil problems, a weird new oil system that had never been tested, and I don't think it would have worked.

The engine just wasn't ready, and my reports said it wasn't ready. There was about a year's gap between the engine being ready to put in the Arrows . . . It was rushed, it was a mad scramble . . . We just didn't do enough flight testing . . . It would have been a catastrophe if the Arrow had flown with the Iroquois in it when it was supposed to.

—Mike Cooper-Slipper

Christmas and New Year's were not as festive as they would normally be for A. V. Roe executives as the year turned to 1959. A. V. Roe was the third largest company in Canada and had had a long continuous relationship with the government of Canada, yet nobody in the company, despite the constant assurances of director John Tory, knew what was going on. For Fred Smye, nurtured in an era of picking up the phone and calling "C.D." on any matter large or small, it was particularly difficult. As much as he admired Mr. Tory, doubt was beginning to set in.

Here was John Tory, the most important lawyer in Canada, a gold medalist at Osgoode, a brilliant man. And a salesman too. Tory was a great promoter of Tory, and I had always thought, based on what he had told me, that he was a great friend of John Diefenbaker. Tory used to always run around saying, "You don't have to worry—I'll get working on John." It turned out he was just an acquaintance, and Dief didn't have much time for him because he was part of the Bay Street clique and a bagman for the Tories in Toronto.

I'll say this though, he was committed to Avro. Once when we were in the soup in the pre-Gordon days, Tory was a good friend of Oakley

Dagliesh of the Globe and Mail *and Tory arranged to get the* Globe *off
our backs because Jim Hornick was tearing us apart.*

*During the Arrow shemozzle he set up meetings with Dagliesh and
Bassett (of the* Telegram*) so I could reply to their editorials. Tory was
an important guy, but not as important as he thought he was.*

—Fred Smye

But despite the fact that he might not have been as close to the Prime
Minister as he claimed, Tory did have good connections with certain
members of the government and was able to arrange meetings with a
number of them between October, 1958, and February, 1959. A total
of seven meetings were held at various times, and only one thing was
discussed—the Arrow. Five of the meetings were conducted between
Fred Smye and either Pearkes or O'Hurley, one was held with Dobson
and O'Hurley in England, and the seventh with John Tory and Pearkes
on February 5, 1959. Curtis and Plant were present at some of the
meetings.

On the day before New Year's Eve, 1958, Fred Smye sent a final pre-
cancellation letter to O'Hurley on costs related to the Arrow. The letter,
almost a re-write of earlier letters, indicated the company would deliver
to the government a fly-away Arrow, sans missiles, for $3.75 million
per copy including sales tax but excluding engineering, development,
flight-testing, pre-production costs, and aircraft and engine spares.

Lester Pearson, often in awe of what was happening at Avro on his
frequent visits to the plant, and a defender of the company and the
aircraft in the House of Commons, made the unusual move of asking
C. D. Howe for his view, as if seeking guidance.

"Would it be too much to ask you," wrote the Leader of the Opposition,

to send me a note of your views on the CF-105 question? So far,
although I have said a good deal about it, I have been completely
non-commital as to the decision which the Government should
make and have confined my remarks to attacking them for their
tactics and fumbling words.

The letter reached Howe in Montreal the following day. His response
was immediate and unequivocal.

There is no doubt in my mind that the CF-105 should be terminated. Costs are completely out of hand. The electronics equipment, which is an essential part of the project, has never been
ordered. . . .

It seems to me the proper line of attack should be directed to
the Government's temporizing and fumbling with this decision.

You will recall that when the matter was last discussed by our Defence Committee in 1957, it was decided to continue the project for the time being, and have a complete review of the matter in September 1957. I had then recommended that the project be terminated due to runaway costs, but there were obvious reasons then why the decision should be deferred until autumn. Since then, costs have continued to mount, and results of test flights have been far from conclusive, both as to the aircraft and its jet engine, which is also a development project.

Howe was convinced that when Diefenbaker dropped Astra and Sparrow from the project in September, 1958, he had then decided to cancel the aircraft and the engine. "Subsequent expenditures," he wrote, "on both aircraft and engine were definitely an unemployment relief measure, and an expensive one." Should the final decision be to terminate, advised Howe, the best political strategy would be to expose the cost of the Conservatives' delay by having expenditures on the project tabled on the order paper. This would give the Liberals a clear target for criticism.

As the Arrow debate gained momentum, few politicians, including the Minister of Transport, had a clear understanding of the aircraft, or of the air defence plan, they were so energetically condemning.

The main argument against the Arrow was that by the time we took over the government in 1957, the Avro Arrow had become obsolete. Now this plane was designed around 1952 for the previous Liberal government, but by 1957 and '58 it had become completely outdated, for this reason: it was designed to fly up and intercept Russian bombers flying at a maximum altitude of 25,000 feet. And so the plane was designed with a fuel capacity, and a missile capacity to fire into the Russian planes, that would get it up to 25,000 feet and allow the plane to return safely to its starting point. The trouble was that by '57/'58, when we took over, the Russians had developed a bomber that would fly at not 25,000 feet, but 50,000 feet.

—George Hees

As imminent as the possibility of cancellation was during those midwinter months, at the plant in Malton it was business as usual, although one did sense anxiety in the air. Things were now done in half the usual time. People came to work, ill or not. Lunch hours shortened, coffee breaks became non-existent, and the pace quickened. People no longer stopped to talk to each other like they used to, or if they did, they yelled. They had trouble sleeping at night, and showed up at work hung over with anxiety, as if somehow they knew they were in a race, a race where the harder they ran the farther they fell behind.

Despite pressure from some of the members of his own party, by February the Prime Minister was under the gun from his cabinet to make an early decision on the Arrow. The cost of completing the thirty-seven aircraft on contract, he was advised, would be about $260 million from March 31 on. Completion of this portion of the program plus a further eighty-three aircraft would amount to approximately $770 million. Not included in these estimates was the total development expenditure of about $340 million, excluding what had been devoured by Astra and Sparrow, anticipated by March 31.

In Toronto on February 13, the Labour Conference announced it was setting up a task force to study the effects of any possible layoffs at Avro; United Auto Workers representative Dennis McDermott was saying that "offers" had been made to a sizeable number of engineers (at Avro) and many were just waiting for the March announcement to apply for visas to move to the United States.

At Malton, Fred Smye, quiet since his last meeting with Raymond O'Hurley on January 9, attempted one last kick at the cat and put together his best plea yet to continue the Arrow program. In a note dated February 11, and addressed to O'Hurley, these words, more than any before, symbolize what the Arrow program was all about.

> While the Arrow and the other projects which the Company has under development are very important, nevertheless they are only particular illustrations of the issue which I believe to be basically at stake. This issue is whether or not Canada should participate, within its economic means, in the rapidly advanced technology of aeronautics and space. . . .
>
> I submit that Malton is a great national asset . . . one which should be preserved and perpetuated as an essential ingredient contributing to the destiny of our country. To fulfil the role and attain the stature which I know you envisage for Canada, I am convinced that the advanced creative scientific and engineering enterprise is an absolute necessity. It is only with this native, distinctly Canadian creative contribution to a rapidly advancing technology that Canada can preserve her national identity and be recognized as a power in her own right amongst the nations of the world. Our independence and, in fact our very sovereignty depend upon it. Surely on the basis of our economic growth and future we should assume some degree of responsibility towards making, in this way, a contribution to the welfare of the Western world. The establishment of a long-term national policy for research and development, sadly lacking in the past, is something which I believe to be a prime requisite of our time.
>
> I do not feel that Canada should embark on this course independently, for obviously competition with the United States is unthinkable, but rather that she should carve her own niche within

the framework of consultation and agreement with the United States and the United Kingdom, participating as an acknowledged partner in an agreed portion of the overall effort without loss of her national sovereignty. I really do not believe that we can take our rightful place in the future if we are not established with at least some degree of this recognition, or if we allow ourselves to become completely dependent upon others in this advanced technical field. . . .

In the interests of preserving and utilizing the scientific personnel and facilities at Malton, and also of maintaining some fair degree of employment there, I suggest the following specific alternatives for your consideration:

1. To put the Arrow into production in reasonable quantity for the R.C.A.F. If the Arrow is put into production, I am fairly confident that it will be used by other countries. As indicated previously, it is our understanding that the United Kingdom has a military requirement for an aircraft such as the Arrow, and I suggested to you the possibility that they should buy Arrows, to be offset by Canada's purchase of a British VTO (vertical take-off) aircraft for RCAF use in Europe, as a replacement for the Sabre. We believe also, based on the Company's discussions, that there are distinct possibilities for the purchase of the Arrow, at an appropriate time, by Germany and Belgium.

2. Should it be decided not to put the Arrow into full production, to continue the 37 aircraft at present under contract . . . and on which a considerable portion of the cost has already been incurred . . . in order to retain the nuclei of the organizations until such time as any one, or more, of these alternatives can be brought into being, and also as national insurance in the event that production quantities of the aircraft may be required in the future to meet international exigencies.

3. To produce the Sabre replacement and the appropriate engine therefore, inasmuch as the Company is the only Canadian company experienced in supersonic and vertical take-off aircraft.

4. To design and develop a jet transport for TCA which should also be suitable for export markets. This could be done by the same team which led the world in the creation of the jetliner.

5. To accelerate the development and production of the VTO family of so-called "flying saucers," in conjunction with the United States Army and Air Force, who are both sponsoring at Malton two versions of the project at the present time.

6. To enlarge upon the design engineering now being carried on in conjunction with Atomic Energy of Canada Limited in the research and development of nuclear power.

7. To initiate and participate in a Commonwealth pool for the exploration of space, or to participate to an appropriate degree in United States programmes. Already the Company has proposals which could put an object into orbit by very economical means with a relatively small expenditure.

The important point I am trying to make in this letter is that if the engineers, scientists and accumulated skills and know-how now gathered together in one place in Malton are allowed to be dispersed, this country will have lost one of its great national assets, present and future. In my opinion, this will preclude us as a country from playing that fully independent part in the Commonwealth and through the world which is part of your vision for Canada.

What I must underline is that if the Arrow is not ordered into full production, it is imperative in order to preserve this great instrument of technology that the 37 Arrows now on order be not cancelled but that they be continued to help bridge the gap and hold onto the key personnel. After all, most of the materials and bought-out parts have been paid for or committed for and would in any event be a cost of termination.

I think it would be most helpful if the appropriate departments of the Government could be directed to discuss with the Company the more specific implementation of one or more of the various alternatives which I have proposed . . . .

Randy Smye didn't hear the knock at the door that bought his father into his room that dark February night in 1959, but when he finally realized someone was there with him, his father was already sitting on the bed with his head in his hands, looking more tired than Randy had ever seen him. Randy, elder of Fred's two sons, was just beginning his second term at Appleby College in Oakville, and the last person he expected to see, especially on a week night, was his dad. Aside from the fatigue, perhaps seeing his father without the familiar batch of papers under his arm, and not reaching for the phone to call the office, made him look somewhat smaller than his 6-foot frame and more vulnerable than usual.

Finally, after the longest of times, Fred Smye lifted his head and said, cryptically, "I want you to know that, whatever happens, everything will be okay. The family will survive this and we'll all carry on. Everything will be fine." Sure Dad, Randy thought, not quite understanding what his father was talking about. But before he could say anything, his father slowly got up and walked out of the room.

Geez, thought Randy once again alone in his room, that's funny. He'd seen his father go through some tough times with the company before, but nothing had taken quite as much toll as the Arrow program. It was consuming him. Randy made a mental note to spend some time with his father during the coming weekend. As he climbed into bed he glanced at the calendar on the desk. Good, he thought, tomorrow's Friday. . .

For a mid-winter Canadian day, Friday, February 20, 1959, weather-wise, was rather pleasant: sunny periods with a projected high of 20 degrees. Any storms that day would take place inside and not out.

In the flight test hangar at Malton, the long-awaited first Arrow Mk.2, with its newly-fitted Iroquois engines, was just a few weeks away from first flight.

8 a.m. For Jim Floyd this Friday was like any other, beginning with a meeting with his engineers—Bob Lindley, Stan Harper, Jim Chamberlin, Jack Ames, and Frank Brame. There was a meeting every morning to avoid unnecessary interruptions during the day, to keep people from walking in and out of each other's offices all day long. This particular meeting centred around an undercarriage problem.

8:30 a.m. The Avro design office was humming with work, with consultations over drawings in progress at several tables, and the occasional trip to the records section for blueprints, or to the library for a technical report. From time to time, an engineer from the stress section or from technical design would walk in to confer with a group over some detailed design problem. There was an underlying atmosphere of both apprehension and expectation throughout the company. But then it had been there for months. Statements from politicians and media had been conflicting. And disturbing. But the first Mk.2 Arrow with its powerful Iroquois engines would soon roll out to begin test flights and it was expected to set new records which NATO and NORAD would not be able to ignore.

9 a.m. At Briarcrest, the company estate, Crawford Gordon was still asleep. The night before he had spent long hours on the phone trying, without success, to contact Michael Starr, Minister of Labour, and Donald Fleming, Minister of Finance, to seek out new information. At about half past one he had left orders with the housekeeping staff not to be wakened except for an emergency at home. Gordon, for once, would try to make it into work by noon.

In the assembly bays, Bob Johnson recalls that the tempo was a little different than usual, "as if everyone was expecting something." Since the Prime Minister's September announcement, Johnson had been saying, "Every one of you buggers that doesn't vote Liberal is voting for the cancellation of the Arrow!"

Out on the tarmac, test pilot Mike Cooper-Slipper was once again crawling into the cockpit of the B-47 for another Iroquois test flight.

9:15 a.m. Fred Smye had just called the board meeting to order at Canadian Applied Research when one of the secretaries called him to the phone. Ottawa was on the line. It was Gordon Hunter from the Department of Defence Production calling to inform Smye that the Prime Minister would have an announcement about the Arrow and the Iroquois later that day. He wasn't waiting until March 31 to make a decision; the Arrow and the Iroquois would be cancelled that very day. "Holy Christ!" said Smye.

At RCAF headquarters in Ottawa A/V/M John Easton was at his desk when he received his copy of a confidential memo from Raymond O'Hurley, Minister of Defence Production, to the Chief of the Air Council. Two words caught his eye: "cancel" and "destruct."

Easton then phoned Ray Foottit, head of the RCAF–Arrow team, at Malton.

> *I was in my office, and I was told just before it was announced in the House. The part I can't answer for are the dollars. Whether this would have made the country bankrupt I don't know. There had been a gyration of cost but we never really thought . . .*
>
> —W/C Ray Foottit

9:30 a.m. "Mr. Speaker," said the Prime Minister, "with the leave of the House, I should like to make a somewhat lengthy statement on the subject of one facet of the national defence of Canada.

"The announcement I wish to make has to do with the decision regarding our air defence, which was foreshadowed in the statement made by me to the press on September 23 last." The "foreshadowed" is carefully chosen. It implies a notice of termination written on a wall. It falls within the limits of the deliberately vague announcement made five months before. It rings of fair play. Diefenbaker continues his summation to the jury: "The government has carefully examined and re-examined the probable need for the Arrow aircraft and Iroquois engine known as the CF-105, the development of which has been continued pending a final decision." Again he implies notice of termination. Forgotten are the meetings and telephone calls in which his ministers reassured company executives that this was not the case. "The conclusion arrived at is that the development of the aircraft and Iroquois engine should be terminated now."

The Prime Minister praised the Arrow as he buried it. It showed promise but had been "overtaken by events." The bomber threat had diminished and "alternative means of meeting the threat developed much earlier than was expected." This was the Bomarc. Air Marshal Campbell wasn't going to get the interceptors he wanted. The CF-100, Parliament was told, was still an effective weapon, though against what, the Prime Minister did not say. Various alternatives for the improvement of Canadian defence were being studied, he said, being careful to leave open the avenue that would later lead to Voodoos, the American interceptor purchased in 1961.

"Although the range of the aircraft has been increased, it is still limited," Diefenbaker said. The seed of public doubt about the Arrow's performance was planted. Maybe the idea came from the National Research Council, maybe from the Defence Research Board, but it did not come from the air force, which had set the requirements. In this area the RCAF was confident that the CF-105 would exceed the radius of action set in specification AIR-7-4.

Diefenbaker then turned to the matter of cost. Reaching back to 1953 he found an estimate for "five or six hundred aircraft" at a cost of $1.5 to $2 million each, and contrasted this with a cost per aircraft of $7.8 million for a program of 100 Arrows "including weapons, spare parts and the completion of development, but not including any of the sum of $303 million spent on development prior to September last." It was a shrewd choice of figures designed for the most dramatic effect in support of the government. How they were derived would remain secret, unchallengeable, even though they were prepared by senior officials of a department that had long since decided against the Arrow. That the development costs incurred between September and the moment of cancellation were not mentioned artfully avoided revealing the price of indecision.

10:15 a.m. At Malton, Janusz Zurakowski was walking across the tarmac when a reporter from the *Telegram* ran up to him yelling: "Hey Zura, did you know they just cancelled the Arrow?" Zurakowski stumbled back to the design office in shock.

In the sales and service department, Joe Morley had barely finished his first coffee, when the teletype machine came to life with the first official notice from Gordon Hunter. He grabbed the telex and ran to Fred Smye's office.

All I remember are the words "cease and desist as of receipt of this telex on all government contracts and acknowledge that you are so proceeding."

—*Joe Morley*

10:45 a.m. Briarcrest. After hanging up on David Golden, Smye had rushed to Briarcrest to waken Gordon.

We both sat down and tried to figure what the hell we were gonna do. Gordon hadn't heard at this point. The last thing Golden had told me was the cancellation telegrams were on their way.

—Fred Smye

As Morley was running, telex in hand, to Smye's office, Jim Floyd was on his way to keep an appointment he had made with Smye the day before. Not finding Smye, Floyd walked into the next office to see John Plant. With Plant were Ernie Alderton, Bill Dickie, Earle Brown-ridge, and a few others discussing the scheduled upcoming set of contract negotiations with the Machinists Union. Just as Floyd arrived they all heard a commotion outside Plant's office.

Running down the corridor, very white in the face, was Joe Morley, followed by Alan Hore, who was the DDP representative in the company. And Morley said, "the Prime Minister has just announced in the House of Commons that the Arrow, the Iroquois have been cancelled!" Hore had been on the telephone to Golden and confirmed what Morley had said.

—John Plant

The news spread like wildfire. All over the Avro and Orenda plants, employees were being called to the phone to hear the same thing from wives, husbands, girlfriends, even stock brokers.

10.55 a.m. Fred Smye called John Plant from Briarcrest. Smye suggested Plant make some sort of announcement to the employees.

We talked about it and I said, well, we will have to lay everybody off, otherwise we will be letting off people without seniority. And he said "I agree," or words to that effect.

—John Plant

11:15 a.m. John Plant sat down in front of the company's public address system microphone in the little brick building opposite gate 9 to announce the Arrow cancellation; it was one of the toughest jobs he'd ever undertaken.

How do you tell some nine thousand people that the job they have been dedicated to for years has been cancelled? How do you tell them that the product of their minds and hands has been eliminated?

—John Plant

Nonetheless, he did it:

The radio has recently announced the Prime Minister has stated in the House of Commons this morning that the Avro Arrow and Iroquois programs have been terminated.

We, the management of the company, had no official information prior to this announcement being made. The cancellation of the Arrow and the Iroquois has, however, been confirmed as fact by a Mr. C. A. Hore, the representative here of the Department of Defence Production.

It is impossible at this stage to give you any further details until such time as I receive the official telegram from Ottawa. In the meantime I would ask that you continue with your work. Later on in the day you will be informed as to our future.

Smye had asked Plant to round up as many Avro and Orenda executives as he could and come to Briarcrest. Gordon then phoned Pat Kelly and told him to come to Briarcrest, that he needed him. He also called his son Crawford, asking him to do the same.

He was quite calm. Smye was there, Ron Williams, Pat Kelly, John Plant, and Gloria Collinson. When I arrived he was on the phone trying to reach Dief. He eventually got him but I don't know what was said. He did tell me later, however, he felt it was done as part of Dief's vendetta against him.

—Crawford Gordon III

Pat Kelly recalls a different scenario at Briarcrest that morning. Years later in a letter to Scott Young, Kelly wrote: "Gordon phoned me to come to Briarcrest. When I arrived, the executives were sitting around the bar—some were drunk."

We kicked around for a while what to do. I was the one who pressed the idea of giving notice to the whole works, not Gordon. We'd bring back as many as we could to finish up any work but the game was over.

—Fred Smye

11:42 a.m. On the teletype machines in the offices of John Plant at Avro Aircraft and Earle Brownridge at Orenda Engines, exactly the same message was received, from the Department of Defence Production:

> Take notice that your contracts bearing the reference numbers set out below including all amendments thereto are hereby terminated as regards all supplies and services which have not been completed and shipped or performed thereunder prior to the receipt by you of this notice. You shall cease all work immediately, terminate subcontracts and orders, place no further subcontracts or orders and instruct all your subcontractors and suppliers to take similar action. . .

Smye asked that the telex be read to him over the phone at Briarcrest and suggested to everyone present that they should all return to Malton and caucus there.

Noon When the news broke over the wire services that the Arrow and the Iroquois had been cancelled, Jim Hornick was ready. The political contacts he had established in Ottawa over the years had become suspiciously quiet the last few days, and any reporter worth his salt knows that when people don't talk, something big is about to happen.

> *Because of the timing, this was going to be a fantastic story. Now the* Globe and Mail *at that time was a very very inefficient news operation compared to the* Star *which operated twenty-four hours a day. When the enormity of the situation started to set in I knew I couldn't cover the whole story by myself. Now I don't know how the hell I got the money for it, but I called for volunteers, and the first thing we did was get together up at my house in Willowdale and sort through all sorts of crap on A. V. Roe. I even sent a guy to Nova Scotia to see what effect this was going to have on the Dosco operation.*
>
> *I then got on the phone and got as many of the Avro bigwigs as I could, and out of the* Globe *library and my own humble library I prepared a political history of Canadian aviation. Smye told me they were calling a large press conference for the Monday, so I got my guys ready for it and what became very evident to us all was that right under our noses a great octopus had grown.*

> —*Jim Hornick*

In Ottawa the Prime Minister's office was filling up with radio and television people. John Pallett, wary of the press because of the "substantial increase in company-sponsored news after the September 1958 announcement," fielded his fair share of the questions.

I had heard ahead of time of the cancellation, by a couple of days I think, and anyone I spoke to at Avro then—I told them the Arrow was ending and to start looking for another job. There was a series of Cabinet meetings to make the decision to cancel because, politically, there were lots of pro-Arrow people. In fact, I don't know of anyone in the caucus who was vigorously against the Arrow. "He" made the decision when it was necessary although I was unhappy he did not release the performance figures on the Arrow because of Western security. I wanted him to but he refused. Not one member of the Chiefs of Staff wanted that plane he told me. Not one, not Campbell, not one.

—John Pallett

1:10 p.m.
We were called to the board room, all the executives, the management committee—there were about thirty of us. Crawford read the telegram out loud saying the Arrow was cancelled as of five o'clock that night and that no further charges were to be made to the contract.

—Ron Adey

The meeting was a brief one. Joe Turner said that any costs incurred after the date of the telex would be for the account of the usual privilege of operating under normal cancellation procedures. Accordingly, management took the only way out. Fire everyone and rehire them next day under a yet-to-be-negotiated cancellation contract. Don't think Avro was wrong, inconsiderate, in firing everyone. Dief was out to kill the company and he did just that.

—Joe Morley

2:00 p.m. The afternoon edition of the *Toronto Star* hit the newstands. "Diefenbaker Decides: SCRAP ARROW—No other work for makers of Arrow or Engines."

By now Jim Floyd was back in his office. His first impulse was to call his wife but he couldn't get a line out. The switchboard was jammed. He decided instead to call his engineers.

I called them in and told them I would have to let them go. Then Lindley came into the meeting with John Plant and said, "What about the six aircraft? What about the one with the Iroquois in it—can we fly it? Then Plant said, "We can't fly it. We can't do anything." Then Jack Woodman, the RCAF test pilot, showed up and asked if he could take one of the Arrows and ditch it in Lake Ontario.

—Jim Floyd

Company president John Plant returned to the microphone, reiter-ated what he had said earlier, and added that there was no further work and that the employees should not return to work until they were sent for.

3:00 p.m. Mike Cooper-Slipper, up in the B-47, was radioed to "come home." At Orenda Engines Harry Keast was in a meeting. His new "toothpick" blades for the Iroquois had just arrived that morning.

We were sorting out the critical path planning when my secretary came in with a little note. She put it in front of me, and it said "Programme Cancelled." I screwed up the note into a little ball and threw it in the basket and said, "Well, meeting's over chaps, it's the end of the programme."

—Harry Keast

4:10 p.m. Crawford Gordon sat down in front of the microphone where John Plant had sat two hours before and declared:

Following the Prime Minister's statement, we have received news from the government instructing us to immediately cease all work on the Arrow and Iroquois programmes at Malton. . . . Notice of termination of employment is being given to all employees of Avro Aircraft and Orenda Engines pending a full assessment of the impact of the Prime Minister's statement on our operation.

We profoundly regret this action but have no alternative since the company received no prior notice of the decision and therefore we were unable to plan any orderly adjustments.

Gordon then sent word to the Prime Minister, saying that as a result of the termination of the Arrow and Iroquois programs, the company had "found it necessary to suspend all operations at Malton with the exception of essential plant protection." He also requested a meeting with Diefenbaker, Pearkes, and O'Hurley "to discuss future govern-ment wishes in connection with employment of Malton facilities, tech-nical personnel, and labour force."

People were walking around in a daze. After the PA announcement twenty-five of us were called into Earle Brownridge's office. He said, "Well, this is what's left of the organization—twenty-five of us. He said we had to get some negotiations going with the government so that we could keep a hundred of our engineers.

—Harry Keast

In Joe Morley's office most of his staff was waiting for him. "What do we do now, Joe?"

My only answer was, "Sorry, we're all on our own now. I'll write letters of reference and help in any way I can."
    We were all very young, newly married, young children, large mortgages, not too much time to plan or think about the future, except getting the job done—the Arrow. We were all possessed with one ideal—the Arrow. No one, even in junior management, ever punched a time clock; it would have been as much overtime as straight time.

—Joe Morley

4:30 p.m. The late afternoon edition of the *Star* hits the streets. "Everybody Out Until Avro's Position Clear" screeches the new headline. Peter Podger, the Machinists Union representative, calls the situation at Avro and Orenda tragic.

Diefenbaker has sold out the Canadian aircraft industry. There's no excuse for the ways it's been handled. This news will also affect 15,000 other workers employed by over 650 Arrow and Orenda sub-contractors.

Dennis McDermott of the United Auto Workers echoed the sentiments:

We will now lose the cream of our skilled aircraft technicians to the United States. You just don't open and shut an industry like a workhouse. History will prove this to be one of the most colossal blunders made by a prime minister in the history of Canada.

5:30 p.m. Only the maintenance staff was on duty. Apart from a few night-shift workers who had been refused entrance and were milling around the gates, all 14,528 Avro and Orenda employees had gone home to think about the future. A few would be called back Monday, but the vast majority would never set foot inside the plant again.
    Crawford Gordon went back to Briarcrest and poured himself a drink.

17

SCATTERED TO THE WIND

Over the weekend, Jim Floyd, with permission from Crawford Gordon, put together a list of men he would ask back to work. Like Fred Smye, he was mainly concerned about the dispersal of his highly skilled corp of engineers.

We had already set up a forward thinking group under Mario Pesando which looked at everything from shuttle aircraft to nuclear energy, and we wanted more than anything to keep that nucleus of engineers intact.

We contacted a lot of aviation VP's in the States to see if they could use any of them. Jim Chamberlin and a few others went to NASA on loan, in the hope that if conditions changed here they would come back. In all we placed about 150 to 200 engineers out of the 2,000 we had.

—Jim Floyd

Harry Keast wasn't as fortunate. He had come in on the weekend as well to make up a list of 100 engineers Orenda might call back.

We selected our 100 men, and when I got home I received a phone call to come in Sunday—those 100 engineers had now been cut to 50.

—Harry Keast

In total, 14,528 employees had been let go, amounting to a weekly payroll of $1,162,240, equal to the earning power of all the people of Oshawa or Kingston. Joe Turner came in as well to begin work on the severance packages for the employees.

I was still in shock because I honestly believed the Arrow would be ordered into production.

—*Joe Turner*

A poll conducted by the *Globe and Mail* within a week of the cancellation indicated that one out of every three Canadians was "unconcerned" about the Arrow decision. Still, there was plenty of reaction in the press, and most of the criticism was directed at Diefenbaker.

In the *Toronto Star* on the following Monday, under the headline "Sell-out Spite? Furious Storm Breaks Upon Diefenbaker," people who had said little during the Arrow debates were now speaking out. Ralph Campney, the Liberal defence critic, said the decision "makes Canada a satellite power and means practically the ruin of the RCAF as a fighting organization." Hazen Argue, the CCF leader, called it "callousness and cruelty." Leslie Frost, Premier of Ontario, claimed that Ottawa had a "responsibility" to salvage the Malton operation. The Machinists Union accused the Prime Minister of "economic treason, political servitude and moral prostitution."

At the company's operation at Nobel, where 188 men and women were laid off as well, one worker was quoted as saying: "I'd like to get hold of our fellow Canadian," and from Toronto Fred Smye said that "quite a few" highly skilled Avro employees had already gone to the United States. Many also went over to de Havilland Canada. Crawford Gordon accused the government of refusing to talk with Avro about alternative programs, (a reference to Fred Smye's memo of February 11), while the *Toronto Star* claimed that "Dief handled the Arrow decision the way he did because of his personal animosity towards Mr. Gordon."

In the Prime Minister's defence the voices were few. Maurice Hecht of *Executive Decision* magazine charged that A. V. Roe officials

knew very well the Arrow would be cancelled and yet sat around for months and did nothing . . . . If you had asked them prior to receipt of the news what would happen if the Arrow was discarded they would have talked about a cutback of about 3,000 people, but instead they made a gesture and fired everybody. If we could see it coming, then surely they could.

Crawford Gordon and Fred Smye had their say at a press conference in the board room of the downtown office on Monday, February 23. Also present on behalf of the company were Ron Williams, Walter McLachlan, and A. A. Baillie. The room was jammed with press, television, and radio people.

Gordon, looking flushed and strained, opened the conference by announcing that only twelve men were called back to work that day, saying that "the vice president of manufacturing may be asked to become a foreman tomorrow." He offered his sympathies to the men and women thrown out of work and reiterated the fact that the company was not warned of the cancellation.

Gordon also announced that he and Smye would be meeting with government officials the following day to talk about six proposals the company had put forth to bring the men back to work. These were the proposals Smye had made in his memo on February 11: continuation of the Arrow, replacing RCAF Orenda-powered Sabres with Canadian-produced aircraft, producing a jet transport, expanding the vertical take-off project (Avrocar, etc.), developing nuclear power for commercial use in conjunction with AECL, and participating in space exploration.

Commenting on the last proposal, Gordon said that "for a relatively small expenditure we could develop equipment for some object to be put in orbit around the earth." Then Smye made a comment on the all but forgotten Avro Jetliner: "It had exceeded every specification and if it had gone ahead would be selling around the world today." What about the completed and almost completed Arrows at the plant? "They're government property," said Smye. Any support coming from Britain? No answer. What about the lay-offs? Did you really have to do it? "We had no alternative," replied Smye. "We bloody well didn't do it for fun."

On February 24 John Diefenbaker broke his three-day silence. Admitting the Arrow was an "outstanding" success, he said it was an aircraft "overtaken by events" that "would have been obsolete by the time it was ready for squadron use. No one advocates building buggies in the age of motor cars."

Diefenbaker also said that the company would be reimbursed for the eleven Arrows completed or in various stages of assembly, but not for the other twenty-six, and that $50 million had been earmarked to ease the impact of the cancellation. Charging the company management with "precipitated, un-warranted and unjustifiable dismissal of its entire working force," Diefenbaker claimed the mass firing was done "for the purpose of embarrassing the government." He said the company knew the Arrow was going to be scrapped but kept its workers believing otherwise. "I will not say they knew the exact date, but they knew what the decision was and that it was unchangeable."

In England, Sir Roy Dobson, unusually silent on the situation, denied the layoffs were intended to embarrass the government. "Our company was told," he said, "that the decision whether or not to proceed with the project be taken to the end of March. Suddenly, out of the blue . . . in such circumstances what could the company do?"

Years later in the House of Commons, the Prime Minister would reflect on the Arrow. "Some people talk about courage," he would say. "Well, we took a stand in reference to the Arrow. No one wanted to take that stand . . . . As I look back on it, I think it was one of the decisions that was right. Here was an instrument beautiful in appearance, powerful, a tribute to Canadian production . . . . This instrument that contributed little, in the changing order of things, to our national defence."

Generally, the Toronto newspapers were kind to A. V. Roe Canada. The company had gone out of its way over the years to make friends in the press, and this was now evident. Across the country it was a different story. The *Calgary Herald* called it "a decision of political courage;" the *London Free Press* said "the Diefenbaker Government has acted wisely." And in the nation's capital, where the newshounds might be expected to have an inside track, the *Ottawa Gazette* intoned: "There are some who believe that the personality clash between Dief and Gordon may have had something to do with the decision. It made it impossible for the government and the company to co-operate fully."

On Tuesday Gordon and Smye met for the last time with members of the cabinet. The ministers of Finance, National Defence, Labour, Defence Production, and Transport had been delegated ostensibly to discuss the six proposals Gordon had outlined at the press conference to keep Avro and Orenda in operation. The minutes of the meeting, together with the government's response, are reproduced in full in the Appendix.

Smye and Gordon made the point time after time that the company could not remain in operation without government contracts or support. Most certainly they expected the government to do something, perhaps even reinstate the Arrow. But the Prime Minister had been quite unequivocal in his statement on "Black Friday" as to the status of A. V. Roe: "Frankness demands that I advise that at present there is no other work that the government can assign immediately to the companies that have been working on the Arrow and its engine."

The *Toronto Star* said that when Gordon left the meeting he "appeared highly upset."

While Smye and Gordon were meeting in Ottawa, 10,000 Avro and

Orenda workers were attending a rally at the CNE Coliseum to demand $100,000 compensation from the government and to be called back to complete the Arrows on the assembly line at Malton.

By the end of the week about 1,500 employees had been called back to work to repair and overhaul CF-100's and Orendas in NATO service in Europe and to work with John Frost on his flying saucer project. Unlike the Arrow and the Iroquois, Frost's project was funded with American money and therefore immune to the Canadian government. Finance Minister Fleming promised to pick up the tab for 750 of the 1,500 workers "for months. By that time," he said, "some company projects should be substantially advanced." There were reports that American aircraft manufacturers were picking through the ruins of A. V. Roe looking for design, structural, engine-test, mechanical, propulsion research, electrical, and digital engineers. Anticipating the worst, the City of Toronto's Welfare Commission boosted its 1959 relief budget by $2.26 million.

Sir Roy Dobson and John Tory got their chance to meet John Diefenbaker and other government representatives for the first time in early March. Officially they were there to talk about the six proposals put forth by Smye and Gordon on February 24, but really they were attempting to heal the breach between the government and the company.

For Dobson it was a difficult trip to Canada. He spent much time with Wilf Curtis, and for the first time privately admitted that his confidence in Crawford Gordon was waning. While in Canada, he took the opportunity to announce that Hawker-Siddeley would be more than happy to take any ex-Avro or ex-Orenda engineers back to England. "I'll take the lot," he said. He was especially anxious to retain Jim Floyd. "I sent him out here, and I'll be jolly glad to take him back."

Premier Frost was concerned with the great number of unemployed. He sensed that the Arrow was not politically salvageable, but the Iroquois might be.

On March 10, he instructed his aide, T. C. Clarke, to research the history of the Iroquois engine and find out what aircraft it could possibly be used in. Clarke looked at four aircraft currently on the drawing boards: Republic's F-105, Blackburn's B-109, Dassault's Mirage IV, and Lockheed's supersonic transport project. From his preliminary study Clarke reported to the Premier:

If some short-term assistance were given Orenda Engines to complete the testing and the company was prepared to make a maximum effort to sell it, perhaps this phase of the Avro operation could be salvaged and re-established on a firm economic basis.

This, of course, would not solve the entire employment problem, but would certainly make a sizeable reduction in the number of unemployed Avro workers.

Eight days later, Clarke followed up with another memo to Frost (see Appendix) which smacked of optimism over potential for the Iroquois. But his proposals were based on federal support, and the government just wasn't interested.

At the end of March, the end of the federal fiscal year, the government produced figures that showed its total investment in the Arrow and the Iroquois programs: $132,146,018 for the Iroquois and $197,630,720 for the Arrow.

By April 1, 2,500 laid-off workers had been recalled to Avro and Orenda, 500 others had found new jobs, 410 were expected to return to England, and 750 had applied for United States visas. Some workers had even formed their own companies, but there were still more than 10,000 unemployed. Jim Floyd had made good his promise to help his engineers get work. Jim Chamberlin and 24 others had been hired by NASA.

A week later, on April 8, the first of many executive resignations began with Walter McLachlan, executive vice-president of Orenda Engines.

On April 10 Guest Hake received a letter from Dobson. It said, in part,

I am glad that our chaps have been able to get hold of a few of your boys and bring them back here. I am very distressed about the whole affair, as you can well imagine, and I am sure that something could have happened to avoid such a catastrophe . . . .
I was told on quite high authority that the Canadian government would never again start to develop an aeroplane or an engine on their own, and that they would only do it in partnership with some other government.
I could not help telling them that this would never happen as no government would share with another its development of such projects. I think this is something with which you would agree.
Maybe we shall meet again before long . . .

When it came to the disposal of military material, the government agency responsible was Crown Assets. A. V. Roe was instructed to cut up the Arrow and destroy all blueprints, all material associated with it. Crown Assets has no record of a disposal or aircraft during that period. Mme Nadeau, director of Crown Assets in 1979, stated in a CBC interview that, after the cabinet decision, the firm who built the aircraft had to mutilate them under supervision by the Department of National Defence and that DND is always there to supply proof of destruction.

In Mr. Diefenbaker's memoirs I think he said that he was not aware of these instructions, but I was aware of them because I was the fellow that received them, and I [at first] refused to act on them.

Now whether it was O'Hurley who phoned me, or Gordon Hunter, I can't recall, I forget. If I had to bet on it, I think I would bet on O'Hurley. In any event, I refused to do it . . . . We would scrap the work in progress and the components, and so on and so forth, of course, but to scrap those airplanes and those engines, that was the most powerful, the most advanced engine in the world, and so was the airplane, and to destroy those things, to cut them to pieces with blow torches, well I just wouldn't do it. Later on he came back and said, "If you don't do it, we'll send the army in to do it." And, like an idiot, I folded, and so I'm the person that issued the instructions to destroy the airplane. And that's the worst mistake I ever made in my life.

—Fred Smye

Around ten o'clock on the morning of April 22, 1959, a crew of Avro workers appeared on the tarmac, and on Fred Smye's orders started to dismember the six Arrows standing side by side. (The workers were using blow torches until someone alerted them that the airframes were made of some highly flammable materials.)

Crown Assets moved in soon afterwards and put the destruction and sale of the aircraft up to tender. The job went to Lax Brothers of Hamilton, a regular customer of A. V. Roe over the years.

We won the tender because we were the high bid. We bid on it as a package; we got all the jigs and fixtures in the plant as well as five planes on the progress line and I think there was five finished.

Our workmen did it. We walked in there and took them apart. We used saws—you couldn't use torches because it was too dangerous. The fixtures in the plant were torched; the aircraft were sawed. And we paid $300,000 for the works . . . . We put them on trailers and took them down to the smelters where every one was smelted down. Nobody could purchase the material from us because we were under security. They were watching us all the time. We had three or four men watching us, and we had to do it as quickly as we could. War Assets came and took the vital parts out of the aircraft, but when that was done they wanted them out in a hurry, scrapped and out.

When we got to the smelter the weights had to coincide with delivery. No part escaped. In fact I had to guarantee that if any got out I was in trouble.

—*Sam Lax*

Sam Lax remembers five Arrows on the assembly line and five complete. But there had been eleven. The rumours persist that one might have been saved. Wilf Curtis III, grandson of the Air Marshal, remembers playing with scale models of the Arrow as a child. His grandfather used to bring them to him. He grew up with the story that his grandfather had hidden one of the Arrows in a barn somewhere.

All the aircraft were cut up, torched and taken away by Lax Brothers. A. V. Roe did the initial destruction. We were advised through Hore, and I was told by him that this was on Dief's orders. I never saw the actual order on paper, but I know it came through DND to DDP to Hore. I and others objected, of course. Certainly there was a great deal of resistance to the order within management, but at the same time the company was dependent on the same government that issued the orders . . . . So there was talk, but no active deviance. A phantom Arrow? It is possible that one escaped—people were trying to preserve something, but I wouldn't like to say where it is . . . . Number 206, I know that it did escape . . . but not in any official way. It was a tricky business. Then remember that a number of Avro people ended up moving to Ottawa into the civil service . . . . So the removal of number 206 had a lot to do with their interests.

—*Norm Lucas, procurement manager at Avro*

The nose section of Arrow 206 did escape—it is now housed in the National Aviation Museum in Ottawa, opened on June 17, 1988.

Company records? These were retained by the company up north in an area between Huntsville and Bracebridge. Duplicates were made of all drawings and placed in a safe spot for security reasons as the Americans might use it. I believe this cache was mostly technical material including correspondence and engineering drawings . . . . No material was sent to England.

—*John Ready of Hawker-Siddeley Canada*

The thing that always bothered me was the way it was done, the cold, callous, deliberate way it was cancelled. Not that it was cancelled, but the way it was cancelled . . . . We salvaged nothing. We scrapped everything. Five million dollars worth of parts—brand new instruments, equip-

*ment, laboratories, simulators—were just cut up and scrapped with nothing
salvaged. Even the drawings had to be burnt. There was no allowance.
They should have saved those drawings. Even the information itself could
have been used by the British aviation industry and the States, because,
let's face it, the Arrow was the most advanced aircraft of its day. Yet all
that knowledge, all that development, years and years of study, was wiped
out. Deliberately wiped out. No salvage.*

—*Bob Johnson*

On Thursday, April 25, Janusz Zurakowski was making his usual cautious way home from the plant in Malton, careful not to exceed the
60-mph speed limit on the 401. He noticed a flat-bed truck pull up
alongside of him carrying a load of jagged white metal that looked
somewhat familiar. Not quite recognizing what it was at first, he looked
again and was able to discern the numbers "2," "0," and "1," blue
against the white metal. Suddenly it wasn't just white metal anymore.
It was RL-201, his Arrow, on its way to Sam Lax's scrapyard.

The cutting up of the Arrows was carried out under the watchful eye
of the Department of Defence Production. Company personnel were
free to come out onto the tarmac and watch what was going on, but
no one was allowed to take pictures; however, Herb Nott, a reporter
from the *Star Weekly*, managed to photograph the scene. Flying overhead in a small hired aircraft, he recorded the destruction of the Arrows,
the only known pictures of the event.

Like the Arrows, the Iroquois engines were cut up for scrap. Jack
Hilton at Orenda, who was assigned the task, cut up five of the fourteen himself. One went to the National Museum of Science and Technology in Ottawa; there are rumours that one found its way to Bristol
Aircraft in England.

Harry Keast recalls that the National Research Council appropriated
all his spare Iroquois blades, including his new "toothpick" blades.

*I didn't like to watch the cutting up. I saw all the bins of blades and
everything . . . I just didn't care anymore.*

—*Harry Keast*

David Golden, Deputy Minister of Defence Production at the time
of the cancellation, would tell the CBC in 1978: "As a fighting instrument of war, which must include an aircraft, an engine, and a sophisticated fire control system, then of course there never was an Arrow."

By the end of April 1959, a total of 5,500 Avro and Orenda employees had returned to Malton to work mostly on overhaul projects for the CF-100 and the Orenda engines. They were the lucky ones.

Those first few weeks back were strange for the men. Gone was the excitement in the air, the sense of purpose that most of them would never forget. Something that puzzled them those first days back was a sound not heard at Malton in over twenty-one years. Birds singing. "Birds are nice," said one of the mechanics, "but I'd rather hear the sound of rivet guns."

Although still president of A. V. Roe Canada, Crawford Gordon seldom went to board meetings anymore, or even to Malton for that matter, preferring to hole up at Briarcrest with a bottle or a woman or both. So infrequent were his appearances that many Avro and Orenda workers thought he had resigned the day Diefenbaker cancelled the Arrow.

Life was no longer kind to Crawford Gordon. Since February he'd seen one executive after another resign from the company. First Walter McLachlan, then Jim Floyd and Charles Grinyer, and finally his friend Bill Dickie. Although Fred Smye, John Plant, Earle Brownridge, and a few others still hung on, the company, once the flagship of Canadian aviation, was listing so severely, there seemed little hope of ever saving her.

Despite the fact that the Arrow had been cut up and melted down by this time, Sir Roy Dobson who, according to Joe Morley, would have done anything to reinstate the Arrow program, had been trying to do just that. Since February Dobson had been playing a high stakes game of political poker with his new partner Wilf Curtis, the Prime Minister, and some members of Diefenbaker's cabinet.

On June 17, he was ready to up the ante and offer Crawford Gordon's head. "I have been very dissatisfied with his work and his actions," he wrote to the Prime Minister, "which have not been in the best interests of the Company and the Country." Two weeks later Gordon was gone. In announcing his resignation, Gordon said,

There was no alternative. There was a disagreement which we were unable to reconcile.

My association with A. V. Roe Canada has been most satisfying in that I believe the company has contributed and will continue to contribute something of real and lasting value to Canada's industrial progress. The credit for this must go to the many thousands of men and women with whom I have worked in the last 8 years. I thank them sincerely for the help, co-operation and friendship they have given me, for, in the final analysis, it is they who are responsible for what has been accomplished.

On the same occasion Roy Dobson said, "Crawford Gordon has always been one of my best personal friends and, I believe, one of the most competent young industrialists Canada has produced. He has made a valuable contribution to the growth of the company and, indeed, best wishes for his future from myself and all his colleagues." The two men never saw each other again. Jim Hornick, for one, was not convinced that it was an amicable separation. "The resignation of Mr. Gordon," he wrote, "was widely interpreted in Ottawa as being a concession to the Diefenbaker administration, some of whose members were said to have developed a deep personal animosity to him."

About a month after Gordon's departure, Ernie Alderton was at Briarcrest, cleaning up the place, when the front door opened, and in walked Sir Roy with Harvey Smith. A year earlier Smith had been transferred from Avro Aircraft to the Montreal head office of Dosco. Alderton left quietly by the back door, unseen by the visitors, and headed back to Malton where he met up with Smith a few hours later.

> When I arrived at the old airport coffee shop, Harvey says, "Well, I guess you're wondering what I'm doing here? I'm back to take charge of Avro Aircraft. Wilf Curtis will continue to be vice chairman of the board, and I'm going to be the head of A. V. Roe and all its subsidiaries. Apart from Sir Roy, you're the only one that knows anything about this. When I come back in two weeks Smye is gonna be fired." I said that I had heard from Sir Roy that John Plant was going too. . . . Now I didn't know what to do, so I took a week off so I wouldn't have to look at Fred Smye.
>
> —Ernie Alderton

> Somehow or other—that I'll probably never know—Harvey Smith was coming back as president, and Smye was under him. When we went into the office that day and heard Smith was the new president, Bob Lindley, Stan Harper, and myself synchronized our watches, to see how long it would take for us to get fired. It took two hours.
>
> —Ron Adey

When Alderton returned the first assignment Smith gave him was to get rid of all the people he had known for years, people like Murray Willer and Joe Morley. As Smith's "troubleshooter," he was also given the job of "getting rid of all the booze, no matter where it was—C.A.R.L., Briarcrest, Orenda, the executive dining room, wherever."

> *So I loaded it all in my station wagon and took it to the cottage and stored it under my ping-pong table. Then one day, Smith calls and asks if the booze was still there, and arranged with Wilf Curtis to take it all to the RCAF staff college in Toronto. They came and picked it up in an air force truck.*
>
> —Ernie Alderton

If ever there was a man who's days were numbered, it was Fred Smye. His surprise at Smith's appointment was compounded by his apparent loss of favour with Sir Roy Dobson. For months Smye had been pushing Dobson to appoint Earle Brownridge as president of A. V. Roe, and now there was only one thing to do. On the evening of July 31, 1959, along with John Plant, Fred Smye walked out of his office at Avro Aircraft, leaving behind fourteen years of his life and vowing never to return. He was just forty-three years old.

A. V. Roe Canada's sunset years after the cancellation of the Arrow were anything but glamorous, stark contrast to the glory of the 1950s. Harvey Smith presided over an operation hauntingly similar to the one under Walter Deisher in 1946, when the company accepted any kind of work just to get going. Only now its future lay behind it, not before it. Contracts, few as they were, ranged from producing pots and pans, to sub-contract work for a boat company.

When the company struggled along with little success under Smith, Dobson recruited T. J. (Ted) Emmert to become president and chief executive officer at A. V. Roe Canada. Emmert's career in the industry began on the production line at Boeing in 1935. He had held executive positions at Boeing, Canadair, and Ford of Canada. Most recently he had been vice-president of Massey-Ferguson.

Despite the company's hopes of moving into the diesel field and other areas of transportation, and of somehow rebuilding the dream, by December, 1961, Emmert was to declare, "I will not be happy with the final results of 1961." Lack of business in railway rolling stock and aeronautical operations, and poor results from shipbuilding, bridge construction, and pleasure boat building, resulted in a loss of $7.5 million that year.

EPILOGUE

He was there in the beginning alone, and he was there in the end alone. For Sir Roy Dobson April 30, 1962, was a day for memories, a day for reflection. He really didn't want to go to the meeting that night, but, after all, he was chairman of the Hawker-Siddeley Group. Who better suited to do the deed than himself?

The meeting began with the usual call to order, the tedious reading of minutes. From his seat at the head of the table, the old man's eyes searched the room for faces from the past. There weren't any. His mind drifted back to that wartime summer of '43, to his first look at those Canadian-built Lancs.

I didn't think the buggers could do it. And J. P. Bickell, John Tory, and Freddie Smye . . . ah, Freddie, what a brash young bugger you were, just like myself in a lot of ways . . . such a long time ago now . . .

The chairman of the meeting asked Mr. Ted Emmert, president and chief executive officer of A. V. Roe Canada, to review the past year's projects and earnings.

Lumme, those were difficult days. If ever there was a company built on hopes, built on dreams . . . Joe Morley, Edgar Atkin, Jimmy Floyd . . . at least I got Jimmy back to England . . . that bloody Jetliner . . .

Emmert finished his report and opened the floor for questions. Dobson's eyes cast around the room once more, looking for faces he knew weren't there.

Gordon . . . Damn, he was good. Too young maybe. Just about killed everything. I should've been here more. Why did I ever put the whole thing in the hands of those bloody Canadian upstarts. The Arrow would be flying today . . . I wouldn't have to be here now to do this if it wasn't for . . .

"Sir Roy," said the Chairman of the meeting, leaning over to Dobson. "Sir Roy," he said again, a little louder. "It's time." The old man got to his feet, searched the room one last time before speaking. "Mr. Chairman," said Sir Roy Dobson of the Hawker-Siddeley Group, in that familiar Yorkshire brogue, "I so move we change the name A. V. Roe Canada to Hawker-Siddeley Canada, and I move we do so immediately." The motion was seconded, passed unanimously in a matter of seconds, and A. V. Roe Canada slipped into history.

APPENDIX

Meeting regarding the Avro situation, Mr. Pearkes' office, February 24, 1959

In attendance: Honourable Donald Fleming, Honourable George R. Pearkes, Honourable Michael Starr, Honourable Raymond O'Hurley, Honourable George Hees, Mr. Crawford Gordon, Mr. Fred T. Smye.

The meeting was opened by Mr. Pearkes, who asked what matters would like to be discussed and in what order. Other Ministers asked for a report of the position at the Avro Plant as it existed at the present time.

Mr. Gordon suggested that he should start by outlining the history of the Avro and Orenda industrial complex, which he did, and stressed the specialized nature of the Company's set-up and equipment, which had been designed specifically to meet the government's requirements.

Mr. Starr asked whether Mr. Smye could say what was actually happening now and what was likely to happen in the immediate future.

Mr. Smye mentioned that telegrams had been received ordering stoppage of work. He knew there had been some debate regarding the method in which the Company had made this stoppage, but the Company had thought for some time that the government would soften the blow by an orderly revision of the programme. The Company had felt they had to stop at once because the immediate implications of the announcement had not been fully examined. He stressed that the Company must get the wishes of the government for the future of the Malton industrial complex as a whole before the Company re-engages any staff. In the meantime, seniority rights had to be determined which would lead to this re-engagement.

Mr. Starr asked Mr. Smye whether or not the lists of seniority were up to date; surely they would be as this was normal in all industry. Mr. Gordon agreed, but pointed out that this procedure had to be worked out for two plants and that this was not just a case of a progressive, small scale lay-off; they had to prepare plans for what proportion of their employees would be re-engaged for various over-all requirements.

Mr. Smye then brought up the question of whether or not the Company would carry on with their existing contracts. They had at first assumed this and called back a few people. He pointed out that he and Mr. Gordon were in Ottawa to find out exactly what the government's wishes were. Mr. Pearkes asked how many persons were being kept on in each type of work at the moment. Mr. Smye said that in the overall Avro picture there were some 700 persons being employed, mainly in the categories of firemen, watchmen, security guards, etc. In the Orenda engine division they were keeping a few men working on their spare parts orders. There were none working on the Iroquois. They had seventeen professional engineers only, the rest were ancillary persons.

Mr. Gordon pointed out that the Company must consider the overall picture before accepting other orders, such as the order from West Germany for six million dollars worth of spare parts. In this regard he would point out that the acceptance of such an order would depend on the overhead position of the operation. Mr. Smye continued by saying that the Company must know what the government's wishes were regarding whether the Company shut down the whole works or not. He would stress that this was an industrial complex designed specifically for the production of aircraft and could not produce other items. He drew a parallel with the position of the Boeing Aircraft Company which, immediately after the end of World War 2, had geared up for the production of non-consumable household items, such as washing machines, and had nearly gone bankrupt in doing so. Mr. Gordon supported Mr. Smye, pointing out that this facility was set up at the end of the war for the government's use, virtually as an arsenal.

Mr. O'Hurley asked whether or not the overheads could not be cut to keep the plant going. Mr. Gordon said of course this could be done, had been done and was being done. However, he would point out once again that this was a specialized plant for aviation and aero-engine production and that this was very special and expensive equipment which was provided for this work. Mr. Smye added that everything in this type of operation was extremely expensive and that there existed a state of mind in the employees and management about the type of work which they were doing which was highly skilled and technical.

Mr. Pearkes asked whether he was correct in assuming that the work that they had on hand now after cancellation of the Arrow development was the Orenda engine spare parts and associated equipment, the repair of the CF-100 aircraft and the vertical take-off development programme, which was sometimes referred to as the "Flying Saucer." He then asked what of the repair of the CF-100 aircraft for the R.C.A.F.

Mr. Smye answered that Mr. Pearkes' assumption was correct, that of course only a small number of persons could be employed on the production of spare parts and repair work and that the VTO programme was a comparatively small one at the present time. With regard to the R.C.A.F. CF-100 aircraft, those in eastern Canada went to Avro, those in western Canada went to MacDonald Brothers in Winnipeg, and the European ones were repaired by Scottish Aviation at Renfrew in Scotland.

Mr. Starr asked whether he was correct in assuming that the contracts that they now held could not go on unless other work was obtained. Mr. Gordon said that this was in essence correct, as they would have to re-negotiate their contracts because they would perhaps have four-fifths of a plant idle and only one-fifth working. Mr. Smye again asked whether the government wanted to keep the facilities as a whole. The

Company had to decide if they could operate the Company under certain circumstances. Naturally, they wanted to keep as much as possible in operation, not only from the Company's point of view, but from the national point of view as well. They wanted to try to keep the nucleus of the engineering department to work on the projects that have already been mentioned. Mr. Starr asked whether it was correct to say that the Company had no alternative work that they had obtained on their own. Mr. Gordon took some exception to this, pointing out that it was not quite right as the Company had been talking to Trans-Canada Air Lines, the Department of Transport and the Royal Canadian Air Force regarding their future requirements and that they had not received any firm requirements from any of these organizations. He pointed out that the Company were developing, and had high hopes for this family of vertical take-off vehicles. So far no great interest had been shown except by the United States Air Force and Army. Trans-Canada Air Lines had a declared requirement for replacement aircraft for the Viscount in some five years, although they had not specifically stated what form of aircraft this should take. The Company would very much like to build another jetliner, having already built a prototype which had taken to the air some thirteen days after the first Comet aircraft in 1949, but which was later scrapped owing to lack of support.

Mr. Starr then asked how many people such a scheme would employ if it was immediately ascertained that there was a requirement for a jetliner of this type. Mr. Smye pointed out in some detail the requirements for such a programme, which would extend over some period of time, starting with a limited number of engineering and design consultants, maybe thirty to forty people, for a nine-month period, then after the requirements had been fully laid down and some design work done, there would be a gradual increase in the design staff and later in the preliminary engineering staff. Mr. Pearkes then said that this would apparently be very small at this stage. Mr. Gordon agreed, but said that it would build up quite sharply from that point on.

Mr. Starr then asked when this build-up would commence. Mr. Smye answered that it would be expected that in about eighteen months to two years there would be production.

Mr. Pearkes then asked whether or not a firm replacement programme for the Viscount would be unable to keep the plant and contracts going. Mr. Gordon gave an emphatic negative answer, stating that they would still have to cover other overheads on contracts by other work.

Mr. Smye then brought up another question, namely a replacement aircraft for the F-86 Sabres now employed by the Air Division of the R.C.A.F. in Europe. He made the statement that if such a programme was initiated in the Avro plant, there could be some considerable rehiring started in nine months' time. He pointed out that he knew that the Air Force had been considering two types of aircraft, namely the Grumman Super Tiger and a development of the Blackburn NA-39, known as the B-109, and that they favoured the former. Mr. Pearkes asked whether Mr. Smye felt that Avro could compete, on competitive tenders, with the big overheads that they would undoubtedly have. This would seem difficult. Mr. Smye stated that this was correct. Mr. Pearkes went on to say that if we replaced the aircraft at the Air Division, there would be a comparatively small number required—some 120 to 150 over a number of years. Mr. Smye stated at this time that if the government contracted for this aircraft with Avro and added the other contracts, the company could continue to operate. Mr. Fleming asked whether or not it was not correct to assume that the immediate problem which still existed, and that the so-called rot in the dispersal of their work force, would not continue. Mr. Hees asked what talks Avro and the company had had with Trans-Canada Airlines. He pointed out that Mr. Gordon McGregor would welcome a Canadian-built plane if it fulfilled the requirements of his company, and if it was built at a reasonable cost. He had had some experience of this problem prior to the purchase of the Viscount aircraft when he had suggested to Canadair Limited, of Montreal, that they build a somewhat similar aircraft, a project that they had not wished to undertake. Mr. Gordon mentioned that the company had talked to the T.C.A. officials and that they knew the company's view. Mr. Smye pointed out that it would take some months to reach the stage of talks of actual cost. Mr. Gordon said he felt that what was needed in this case was for the government to instruct the airlines and the companies to get together and to submit a definite proposal which the government would then consider and rule upon. This was being done in the United Kingdom. Mr. Fleming wanted to know if the company had enough in hand or in mind to carry on their operation at all. Mr. Gordon said that what the company was looking for was whether or not they could get enough work for the future to plan to build up the company to a healthy industrial unit in five to six years' time. Mr. Hees said he would then try to get Mr. McGregor to come to Ottawa today or tomorrow. At this point, Mr. Fleming suggested that the meeting should go through six proposals as made by the company in Mr. Gordon's press statement. Mr. Pearkes asked Mr. Gordon if he was right in assuming that the company were in doubt as to whether they could go with the small projects at the present time—Orenda repairs and vertical take-off, and whether they might not have to close down unless they knew more work was in view. Mr. Starr asked whether the German order could then be proceeded with if other work was provided. Mr. Gordon said this would depend on what contractual position was arranged between the company and the Department of Defence Production. Mr. O'Hurley stated that the main problem was the overhead factor, and that it would be difficult to avoid giving the impression of a straight subsidy from the government. Mr. Gordon pointed out the problem that for those employing Avro-made aircraft, at the present time the Company were the only ones who had facilities to manufacture spare parts and certain repair items, that no one else in Canada or outside had ability to build the items required. Mr. Pearkes then asked had not the R.C.A.F. got at least lifetime spares for all their CF-100s. Mr. Gordon replied that they would undoubtedly have lifetime spares of some parts, although others would be a continuing requirement purchased periodically from the Company.

Mr. Fleming then suggested that the meeting consider the statement. Mr. Pearkes started by reading the first point regarding the Arrow. Obviously this point did not have to be considered in the light of the Prime Minister's statement of Friday last. The second point dealt with re-equipping of the Air Division, and Mr. Pearkes outlined briefly the government and departmental postion in this matter. It was necessary to consider the future role of this military component, and the government had to decide whether they would replace some or all of the aircraft in Europe or would withdraw this force. The Supreme Allied Commander in Europe, General Norstad, had indicated that Canadian aircraft might be required to carry out three different roles. It would not be useful to attempt to operate three different types of aircraft for these roles, and it was considered by the government to be unnecessary. It was quite probable that the major role for the Air Division would be strike-attack. In particular, he stressed the point that it would be useful to have an aircraft that did not have too complex fixed facilities. Unfortunately, there was nothing quite suitable available at present or in the planning stage to meet the time factor involved. The R.C.A.F. had investigated at least twenty to thirty types. As Mr. Smye had pointed out, the most suitable ones in which the Air Force were interested were the Grumman and the Blackburn, (the latter re-engineered,) and the R.C.A.F. did consider the Grumman to be the better of these two, as a prototype had already been flown, and the Blackburn would require extensive re-engineering work, additional costs and a time lag. He mentioned that the British were concentrating on the "Lightning" as their last manned aircraft. Unless something appeared in the very near future that had a vertical take-off capacity, then we would have to go into something like the Grumman. Mr. Gordon intimated that the company well understood the requirements of the R.C.A.F., and that they could either supply an advance vertical take-off type at a later date, or could produce the Grumman. Mr. Pearkes pointed out that even if the family of VTO aircraft now being proceeded with by Avro was entirely successful, there would be a time lag of some six years before there was any chance of this aircraft being in production. Mr. Fleming agreed with Mr. Pearkes and pointed out that the Grumman would be available more rapidly. Mr. Hees then asked the company officials how long it would be before they would be ready for the Grumman aircraft if an order could be placed, and Mr. Smye said he thought it would be some eighteen months to two years if they could get engineering approval and clearance to start immediately on consultations with the Grumman company. Mr. Pearkes stated that the main requirement really was to get a few new aircraft into Europe to satisfy our allies that we were doing everything we could do to keep our Forces as modern as possible. There would be about 120 aircraft, he expected, and the peak years of production would be from 1961 to 1963, and he had been advised that the R.C.A.F. considered that they could meet the expenditures involved within the continuing limit of the defence budget as indicated by the government. Mr. Smye said that the action to provide such a programme would be the most speedy of providing help and that the company would expect to fly the first aircraft if they produced them in 1961. Mr. Pearkes then pointed out that this aircraft could, of course, be manufactured by other Canadian firms, and whether it was allocated or put to tender would have to be a government decision. Mr. Fleming then mentioned that while the Blackburn did not seem to be a likely starter, it was certain that the position regarding the Grumman should be investigated as soon as possible.

How would this fit in with the company's overall employment picture? Mr. Gordon stated that the company's planning was on the basis of trying to stabilize employment. Mr. Fleming asked whether it was right that if the company were given orders for the Grumman and a civil jet transport, this would keep all their staff. Mr. Smye said no, it would be a reduction of some 4,000 to a total of 5,000, rather than 9,000 in the aircraft plant. Mr. O'Hurley then enquired regarding the engine of the Grumman aircraft. Mr. Gordon said that it was General Electric J-59 made in the United States. Mr. Hees enquired whether this engine could be made in Canada, to which Mr. Gordon replied yes, under arrangement. Mr. Hees then asked what employment this would give in the Orenda Engine Works. Mr. Smye replied that he thought some 2,000 or 3,000 perhaps. Mr. Hees said it then looked as if there would be an overall work force of some 8,000 or so instead of 14,500 to which Mr. Gordon agreed. Mr. O'Hurley then turned to the question of an engine for a jetliner. He asked whether it would be necessary to make an entirely new engine for this project. Mr. Smye thought that this would depend upon the specific requirements, but it was most likely that an engine manufactured by Rolls-Royce or by Pratt-Whitney, both of whom had a wide range of engines both immediately available and in the planning and development stages. Mr. Gordon then stated again that this came back to the question as to whether or not the government wishes the Orenda Engine Company to stay as a facility.

Mr. Smye said that the company must endeavour to keep the key technical people and whether or not this was done, an announcement should be made at the soonest opportunity. He would point out that even the highest placed key personnel would naturally want to make new opportunities for themselves if they knew that there was no hope of the Avro company continuing as a manufacturer of aircraft.

Mr. Gordon said at this point that what he had really been trying to get last September, when he submitted his brief to the Prime Minister, was a sub-committee of officials to discuss the matters that were now being discussed at a ministerial level. He did not think that he had made his point very clear.

Mr. Pearkes then said that he would immediately phone the Chief of the Air Staff regarding the possibility of Avro engineers visiting the Grumman Company. This he did, and in the meantime Mr. Hees and Mr. Gordon discussed the question of further meetings to be held between the company and top officials of Trans-Canada Airlines.

Mr. Smye pointed out that the company were already trying to make other arrangements and had already sent a team of officials down to the Douglas Aircraft Company in the United States to see if any work could be obtained.

The meeting then turned to the consideration of Point 4, and Mr. Pearkes mentioned that this was the proposal for the development of a family of VTO vehicles, one of which was the so-called saucer. He understood that there were two types, the subsonic Avrocar or flying jeep which he understood the United States army were interested in, and the Mach 3 plane in which the United States Air Force had indicated some interest. He could not say what requirements we might have. At the best, he thought they would be very small indeed. In any case he did not see how the government or the department could commit themselves until this aircraft had flown.

Mr. Gordon then asked whether or not the R.C.A.F. or the U.S.A.F. could not report to the Minister regarding the advanced Mach 3 VTO strike attack bomber. To this Mr. Pearkes replied that he had as recently as last Friday received a full report on this matter from the Vice Chief of the Air Staff.

Mr. Smye then asked whether or not the government could or would make representations to the United States government and, through them, to the United States Air Force and Army to accelerate their support on this VTO project. He realized, naturally, that any such support would depend on the technical position. He pointed out that the feasibility of the project would be apparent in a very few months when the first flight was planned.

Mr. Pearkes then pointed out that of course the government had to find a tactical requirement for everything it bought. The U.S. Army and the Canadian Army visualized a large-scale, somewhat static, nuclear battle in Europe. He personally did not know whether this would happen. In addition, he pointed out that the United States had world-wide commitments of a various nature such as they had fulfilled last year in Lebanon. The Canadian concept was for the use of smaller peace-preserving forces under the United Nations.

Mr. Fleming said that undoubtedly the government would see what help might be given towards representations in Washington.

Mr. Smye pointed out that certainly an acceleration of this programme would help in keeping some more of their engineering staff.

There were two points that remained in the programme, Nos. 5 and 6.

No. 5 was the question of engineering for the provision of nuclear power on a commercial basis. Mr. Gordon pointed out that the company felt that the engineering work that they were doing for Atomic Energy Limited could be expanded. The company had received a call over the weekend from Mr. Gray of this company in which he asked specifically that the company maintain the facilities in Orenda Engines which were being used for work in the atomic field as his company had some $300,000 worth of engineering work which they needed to be done.

Mr. Fleming asked Mr. Pearkes if he would speak to Mr. Churchill in this regard, and Mr. O'Hurley confirmed that he understood that Mr. Churchill was well acquainted with the problem.

Mr. Pearkes then drew attention to Item 6 which was a suggestion for a Commonwealth pool for co-operation in space exploration.

Mr. Fleming asked whether this project could in any way be considered as an immediate solution to the implementable but that the company felt that they had technical personnel who could assist in such a programme. Mr. Fleming said surely the costs of a programme of this nature would be astronomical. Would this in any way be connected with the Bomarc programme? Mr. Pearkes said no, this was not the case; it would be more connected with the rocket vehicles, such as the NIKE.

Mr. Gordon said that the main point that the company wished to know was whether or not any of their technical scientific personnel could be of use in government scientific work. Mr. Pearkes said that he would look into this question right away and would get in touch with the Defence Research Board and the National Research Council.

Mr. Smye said that the company had wondered if Canada had any interest in putting a satellite into space and that the company had a theoretical project to shoot a satellite from an Arrow aircraft.

Mr. Gordon confidentially mentioned to the group that the talks which he had mentioned which were proceeding with Douglas were related to work on the NIKE family of weapons. He hoped that there might be some contract work of a highly specialized technical nature which the company could most certainly do.

Mr. Pearkes said that he welcomed this information as there was no doubt that this continent needed an elaborate NIKE-ZEUS anti-ICBM programme for defence and that we should be into this very soon.

Mr. Fleming drew the meeting to a close by saying that they had been over all the points mentioned in the statement, that some had promise and others looked somewhat doubtful. The Grumman looked like the major hope and some others would probably keep engineering personnel. The T.C.A. proposal might fit in very nicely.

Mr. Gordon then asked whether or not with the termination procedures and cancellation costs, the company could carry on the technical nucleus until the various proposals had been fully examined by the company. Mr. Pearkes asked whether he had the idea of a sort of educational course. Mr. Fleming said no, this would be a proposal to keep the key men until the government could see whether the company is to continue at all. He suggested that Mr. Smye put this proposal and the costs involved on to paper and this afternoon it would be considered by officials of D.D.P. and the Treasury Board. Mr. O'Hurley agreed that this was a wise procedure, one which was followed in the Astra and Sparrow programme.

Mr. Smye pointed out that there was more of a problem with the Orenda Engine Company than with the Avro Aircraft.

Mr. Fleming said that last Sunday he and Mr. Starr had met with officials, who had indicated to them that they had assumed that there was no future for the company at all. From these talks they wanted to know if there was any place for even their key personnel.

The government had not expected the company to close down and they wanted to see the technical skills stay. The main problem was to find out what could be done at once to save dispersal. We want to know what they are going to do and how much it is going to cost for these exploratory proposals.

Mr. Pearkes mentioned that if the decision was made to proceed with the Grumman, the R.C.A.F. would be quite willing to co-operate.

Mr. Fleming closed the meeting by saying that a report would be made to the Prime Minister later today and that there would be another meeting this evening.

In respect to Avro's six proposals, wrote a government official:

1. Diefenbaker definitely ruled out continuation of the Arrow plan.

2. It seems very unlikely that the replacement of Orenda-equipped Sabre planes in NATO could be anything more than a minor stop gap, but might provide some useful relief if practicable.

3. Diefenbaker is reported as stating that the company wanted a guarantee of a T.C.A. order of 25 aircraft at about $2.5 million each plus $30 million of federal funds for development and engineering. It was pointed out that T.C.A. is buying Viscounts for only a little more than $1 million each.

   This suggestion by Avro would appear to offer more possibilities of lasting value, · but whether it would prove to be a practical suggestion would depend upon how much taxpayers' money would be required not only at the outset but through the years. Canadians should not be required to pay exorbitant subsidies toward the maintenance of any product that can be obtained from another company.

   A more satisfactory arrangement would be to work out a division of responsibility in these Defence programmes in which Canada would have a fair share in producing military equipment. This was sought and achieved in some measure under the Hyde Park Agreements with President Roosevelt.

4. This proposal for the acceleration of production of a vertical take-off plane is another possibility that would depend upon the financial arrangements and its prospects of success.

5. The Fifth proposal, that Avro might be converted to the making of equipment to be utilized in the development of atomic energy, involves highly technical considerations. Only those associated with atomic energy experiments—Ontario Hydro, Mr. Smith and officials of Atomic Energy of Canada—could speak with any authority on this.

   It might be pointed out that some of the other companies, such as C.G.E. and Westinghouse, might well complain of the use of the taxpayers' money to subsidize products in which they themselves are experimenting and no doubt as qualified as any other company to produce.

6. The sixth proposal to initiate and participate in Commonwealth/U.S. research would appear to offer good prospects for expansion if the co-operation of other countries can be obtained and the information put to practical purposes.

Memo from T. C. Clarke; subject: Orenda's Iroquois engine (part); to: Honourable Leslie M. Frost, Prime Minister. March 18, 1959.

I have had further discussions with the A. V. Roe Company, including Mr. Crawford Gordon, on this matter of the Iroquois engine.

   The following is a summary of the information that I have obtained as a result of several inquiries. It should be pointed out here that Crawford Gordon stated that he planned to discuss similar material with you the next time you met.

   In my memo of March 10, you recall that I pointed out four possible markets for the Iroquois Engine. One of these was for the French Aircraft Mirage IV. It is interesting to observe, that an official of the Dassault Aircraft Company was in Canada last week, to endeavour to find out where the "Arrow" cancellation leaves his firm, and their proposal to use the Iroquois Engine in his Company's machine.

   It seems reasonable, in the light of this information, that if something is to be salvaged from this Iroquois operation, some concrete action should be taken shortly.

Consideration should be given to the fact that the Canadian Government has already spent $100 million on the Iroquois, which is already cleared for flying, but another $4 million is required for development to take it to the final type test. This $100 million has paid for (a) all design and development to date, (b) $12 million worth of tooling, (c) 11 development engines, (d) 3 production engines, (e) parts for another 40 engines, of construction. All this can be classified as wasted if there is no effort to salvage the Iroquois operations.

Two possible suggestions for the rehabilitation of the Iroquois programme have been suggested.

1. Orenda to confirm the deal with the Dassault Company and the French Government, regarding the use of the Iroquois in "the Mirage IV," on the basis of 300 engines. If these were produced at Malton, it would mean approximately $100 million worth of business and keep some 3,000 workers employed for three years. This is assuming production of 10 engines per month. However, to be competitive some financial support would be required on plant overhead, so that the delivered price of the Iroquois would be equal to, or below that of the competitive Pratt-Whitney J-75 engine. The present overhead rate is approximately 450%, based on repair and overhaul contracts on other Orenda engines now in use.

   Another item to be considered, is the possibility of the Iroquois being used in the machine that will replace the F-86 Sabre in the NATO Nations. This would reduce overhead costs to 250% because of the increase volume of work passing through the plant. The production of the Iroquois for the French, combined with these other factors, would produce an even lower overhead cost.

   It has also been suggested that the Federal Government not include the $100 million already spent in the computation of unit costs. If this were the case, it would virtually guarantee Orenda the French contract. Since this money is lost if the Iroquois is scrapped, it would seem logical that the Federal authorities would not object to this proposal. Particularly if it meant giving employment to 3,000 people over the next 3 years.

2. The Canadian Government might offer to the French Government, for $1, all the finished Iroquois engines and all the bits and pieces, along with the tooling, in order that this engine could be produced in France; in return for an agreement, whereby Orenda would supply the engineering and technical support for an annual fee. This seems to be, as well, a preferable alternative to scrapping the entire project. By doing this the Canadian Government would be making a substantial contribution to NATO and, at the same time, providing useful work for a nucleus of Orenda engineering talent.

These are not to be considered firm proposals, but could be taken as a solid base upon which the Minister of Defence production, Mr. O'Hurley, and Orenda's Executive Vice-President and General Manager, Mr. Brownridge, might carry out negotiations.

The foregoing proposals, indeed have a good deal of merit, but in my estimation do not deviate from the A. V. Roe basic problem of tieing their operations too closely to defence contracts. There is a great deal of mention of what the Federal Government should do or could do, but I fail to see any suggestion that the Company is willing to contribute any financial backing to the development and marketing of this engine. Perhaps, as a layman I am on the wrong track, but unless the A. V. Roe interests are prepared to help themselves, why should the Canadian people be expected to foot the bills.

Any of these suggestions might be a satisfactory temporary measure, for perhaps three years, but are certainly not a final long-term answer. The Federal Government would be wise, if they were to consider the proposals, to obtain an iron-clad guarantee from the Company that during the three years term of this Iroquois programme that they would be prepared to do everything within their power to seek new lines for production and wider diversification of their operations.

If I might be allowed a suggestion, would it be feasible for the Federal people to release their rights to the Iroquois engine, and saying to Orenda, there it is, produce and market it. Perhaps if necessary give the Company some financial assistance (perhaps the $4 million mentioned earlier for additional development) in the form of a long-term, low-interest loan. Surely a firm of this size has some sizeable financial resources that would make such a proposal feasible.

Also mentioned, during my discussions, was the possibility of the Company entering into the field of building turbines for steam-generated hydro plants. Also the question was raised whether the Hydro Electric Power Commission of Ontario would be interested in buying such an item. This is, of course, a possible alternative to the company, but again it is a situation in which the firm is looking, in an indirect way, to a particular market. A market that falls in the general area of Government contracts. Furthermore, it appears that it would be difficult for this Company, if it entered the field, to compete satisfactorily with U.K. manufacturers. As a matter of fact, I understand, Canadian General Electric and Westinghouse, firms that have been in this business for many years, are in the same position. Their bids in the past have been approximately 50% higher than those secured from the U.K. Another factor to be considered, is the trend towards nuclear power generation in future. The Honourable Mr. Macaulay suggests that this will be the area in which Hydro will be most interested in the coming years. He further advised that if A. V. Roe considered entering this field, they should have serious discussions with Mr. H. A. Smith of Hydro—their nuclear authority—regarding the myriad engineering and technical problems involved.

All these various proposals are worthy of consideration and perhaps they should be discussed by officials of the Province and the Company. If any of these suggestions are considered feasible, then they might be passed on to the Federal Government for their consideration.

                                                                        T. C. Clarke

NOTES

A. V. Roe Canada company documents have been placed in the archives of the National Museum of Science and Technology, National Aviation Museum (formerly the National Aeronautical Collection, Air and Space Division, National Museum of Science and Technology), Rockcliffe Airport, Ottawa. Many of the A. V. Roe Canada and Avro Aircraft documents cited were accessed through the privately held personal papers of former employees. Other documents and publications were found in the Canadian Institute of International Affairs, University of Toronto; the Royal Military Institute, Toronto; the Public Archives of Canada, Ottawa; the Peel County Library, Brampton; and the "morgue" of the Toronto *Globe and Mail*.

Citations in the notes are in abbreviated form. Full references are given in the bibliography. Interviews with approximately 150 people associated with A.V. Roe Canada, including most of the key players, formed an important part of the initial research for this book; listed below are the names and dates of those quoted.

INTERVIEWS
Ron Adey   *August 27, 1979*
Ernie Alderton   *August 2, 1979*
Jim Bain   *September 16, 1978*
Mrs. Ken Barnes   *October 6, 1978*
Winnett Boyd   *January 1, 1978; November 9, 1978*
Air Marshal Hugh Campbell   *August 28, 1979*
Mike Cooper-Slipper   *July 30, 1978*
Joe Cribar   *July 28, 1980*
Waclaw Czerwinski   *May 5, 1978*

Paul Dilworth   *Februrary 13, 1978*
Des Earl   *May 20, 1980*
Air Vice Marshal John Easton   *November 25, 1978*
Jim Floyd   *June 10, 1979*
Wing Commander Ray Foottit   *November 27, 1978*
Crawford Gordon III   *April 4, 1980*
Mary Gordon   *April 4, 1980*
Geoff Grossmith   *May 30, 1977; February 27, 1978*
Guest Hake   *July 28, 1979*
Jack Hilton   *January 2, 1978*
Jim Hornick   *February 12, 1978*
General A.C. (Chester) Hull   *November 21, 1978*
Bob Johnson   *May 10, 1978*
Harry Keast   *June 16, 1978*
J.N. (Pat) Kelly   *April 14, 1978*
Sam Lax   *September 12, 1979*
Hugh Mackenzie   *December 3, 1978*
Jack Millie   *March 8, 1979*
Ken Molson   *March 8, 1979*
Joe Morley   *May 2, 1978*
John Pallett   *July 9, 1979*
Mario Pesando   *March 8, 1978*
John Ready   *February 20, 1979*
Robert R. (Bob) Robinson   *January 6, 1977*
Don Rogers   *October 30, 1978*
Squadron Leader Joe Schultz   *November 26, 1978*
Fred Smye   *April 24, 1979*
Randy Smye   *April 24, 1979*
Joe Turner   *July 9, 1979*
W. A. (Bill) Waterton   *May 22, 1978*
Murray Willer   *April 11, 1978*
Janusz Zurakowski   *November 28, 1979*

PROLOGUE

Page Line
2   15   General Lauris Norstad quoted in Gunston, *Early Supersonic Fighters of the West*, p. 122; and Floyd, "The Avro Canada Story."
2   32   Hornick, "The CF-100: Canada's Boldest, Costliest Aircraft Venture."
4   21   Grossmith interview.
4   42   Hornick, "The CF-100: Canada's Boldest, Costliest Aircraft Venture."

CHAPTER 1: THE BUSINESS OF WAR

Page Line
7   11   Quoted in Earl, "How Roy Dobson Pushed Us into the Jet Age."
8   6   Quoted in Stanley, *Canada's Soldiers 1604–1954: The Military History of an Unmilitary People*, p. 340.
8   24   Quoted in Eayrs, *In Defence of Canada: Peacemaking and Deterrence*, p. 55.
9   17   Quoted in Eayrs, *In Defence of Canada: Appeasement and Rearmament*, p. 177.
9   40   Howe to King, June 25, 1940. Howe Papers, Public Archives Canada.
10   9   Newman, *The Canadian Establishment*, vol. 1, pp. 324, 325–26.
11   1   Ibid., p. 327.

11	16	Regehr, *Making a Killing: Canada's Arms Industry*, p. 16. See also Stacey, *Arms, Men and Governments: The War Policies of Canada*, p. 502.
11	24	Newman, p. 326.
11	41	Bothwell and Kilbourn, *C. D. Howe: A Biography*, p. 137.
12	6	Newman, pp. 315–16, 321.
13	11	Quoted in Roberts, *C. D.: The Life and Times of Clarence Decatur Howe*, p. 121.

CHAPTER 2: BATTLESHIPS OF THE AIR
Page Line

14	6	The Toronto *Globe and Mail*, August 10, 1943.
14	8	Ibid.
14	17	Ibid.
16	1	Gordon, "The Aviation Industry in Canada."
17	1	Grant in the *Canadian Geographical Journal*, August 1938.
20	9	Fred Smye interview.
20	12	Most of the biographical material on Sir Roy Dobson and the quoted passages in this section are taken from the article cited above by Marjorie Earl.
22	8	One visitor to A.V. Roe and Company in England during the war observed that Dobson ran the place like a "prison farm."
24	29	Quoted in Earl, "How Roy Dobson Pushed Us into the Jet Age."
24	38	Quoted in Garbett and Goulding, *The Lancaster at War*, p. 14.
25	11	When J. P. Bickell died in 1951 at the age of sixty-seven, he was reported to be worth $20 million.
25	15	Ferry Command Traffic Notice, November 1, 1941. Courtesy Paul Dilworth.
26	25	Hilton interview. It was originally thought that Victory Aircraft might get the contract to build British Sterlings.
27	19	Adey interview.
27	21	Hilton interview.
28	20	Molson interview.
28	34	Ibid.
29	3	Quoted in Earl, "How Roy Dobson Pushed Us into the Jet Age."
29	25	Fred Smye interview.
29	37	Ibid.

CHAPTER 3: TAKEOVER
Page Line

31	15	Fred Smye interview.
33	22	Floyd interview.
33	30	Ibid.
34	9	Ibid.
34	20	Ibid.
36	32	The *Toronto Star*, February 15, 1944.
37	19	Newman, p. 327.
38	4	Quoted in Earl, "How Roy Dobson Pushed Us into the Jet Age."
38	6	Fred Smye interview.
38	16	Ibid.
38	29	The *Globe and Mail*, November 16, 1945.
38	36	The *Toronto Star*, April 11, 1945.
39	13	Quoted in *Air Canada: The First Forty, 1937–77*.

39	23	*Avro Newsmagazine*, December 9, 1955.
39	34	The *Globe and Mail*, July 24, 1945.
40	2	Dobson to Symington, May 19, 1945. Howe Papers.
41	29	Fred Smye interview.
42	6	Ibid.
42	17	Ibid.
	32	The *Globe and Mail*, July 27, 1945.
42	38	Quoted in Earl, "How Roy Dobson Pushed Us into the Jet Age."
43	17	Fred Smye interview.
43	32	Ibid.
44	20	The *Globe and Mail*, October 11, 1945.
45	3	Ibid., November 30, 1945.

CHAPTER 4: A GATHER OF AERONAUTICAL MEN

Page Line

46	7	Floyd interview.
47	22	Quoted in Earl, "How Roy Dobson Pushed Us into the Jet Age."
47	35	Fred Smye interview.
47	40	Cribar interview.
48	41	On the choice of Walter Deisher, Fred Smye said: "I was not the man for the job. I lacked experience and qualifications."—Interview.
49	19	Jim Hornick remarked that Deisher "worried terribly about meeting people. He'd sit behind that desk of his and he'd sign things and somebody would wind him up and he'd walk to the window."—Interview.
53	35	Floyd interview.

CHAPTER 5: GETTING OFF THE GROUND

Page Line

56	19	See Eayrs, *In Defence of Canada: Peacemaking and Deterrence*, and Warnock, *Partner to Behemoth: The Defence Policy of a Satellite* Canada, p. 141.
57	7	Quoted in White, *The Making of the President 1972*, p. *xvii*.
57	21	Quoted in Eayrs, *In Defence of Canada: Peacemaking and Deterrence*, p. 320.
57	23	Quoted in Eayrs, "To Set the Record Straight."
58	9	Eayrs, *In Defence of Canada: Great War to Great Drepression*.
58	17	Ibid.
58	30	See Dow, *The Arrow*, pp. 72–73.
59	2	Quoted in Eayrs, "To Set the Record Straight."
59	8	Quoted in Pickersgill and Forster, *The Mackenzie Record*, vol. 4: *1947–1948*.
59	18	Quoted in *Saturday Night*, "Developing Canada's Air Defences."
60	6	Fred Smye interview.
60	32	Boyd interview.
62	22	Quoted in Young, *Jet Age*.
63	41	Canada, Department of National Defence, Specifications for Jet Fighter Aeroplane Type XC-100, AIR-7-1 Issue 2. See also Avro Aircraft, Historical Record of the CF-100.
64	14	Quoted in *Saturday Night*, "Developing Canada's Air Defences."
65	24	Bain interview.
65	32	Floyd interview.
66	30	Ibid.
66	35	Fred Smye interview.

67	6	Jim Bain remembers: "I was not only under the assumption we would get the Avon, I was under the promise of it."—Interview.
69	12	Glenn, "My First 35 Years in the Airline".
69	19	Quoted in *Saturday Night*, "Developing Canada's Air Defences."
70	14	Quoted from Milberry, *The Avro CF-100*, p. 13.
70	18	Chorley, "The Clunk: Canada's World Beating All-Weather Jet Fighter." See also Waterton, *The Quick and the Dead*, p. 163.
71	12	Dow, p. 38.
71	30	Brown to Howe, April 9, 1946. Howe Papers.
72	13	Symington to "All Senior Staff," April 10, 1946. Howe Papers.
72	17	Howe to Symington, April 14, 1946. Howe Papers.
72	35	Smye to Bain, April 16, 1946. Courtesy Jim Bain.

CHAPTER 6: JETS IN THEIR EYES
Page Line

74	2	Bothwell and Kilbourn, p. 275.
74	7	Howe to Dobson, August 12, 1948. Howe Papers.
75	9	Frank Whittle formed a company called Power Jets in 1936 to promote his turbojet engine. Power Jets was largely a design company, at first subcontracting work to other companies with turbine experience. With the construction of experimental engines, Power Jets took over their own testing in an old foundry in Lutterworth. Power Jets was nationalized by the British government during the war under the aegis of the Royal Aeronautical Establishment.
75	27	Parkin to Tupper and Dilworth, January 13, 1943. Courtesy Paul Dilworth.
76	38	Dilworth interview.
77	10	"Banks Report," June 6, 1943. Courtesy Paul Dilworth.
77	41	Dilworth interview.
78	17	Boyd interview.
81	1	Gordon to Howe, November 10, 1945. Howe Papers.
81	33	Howe to Gordon, November 14, 1945. Howe Papers.
81	40	Quoted in Earl, "How Roy Dobson Pushed Us into the Jet Age."
82	11	Wallace to Scully, February 28, 1946. Courtesy Paul Dilworth.
83	3	Deisher to Dilworth, May 4, 1946. Courtesy Paul Dilworth.
85	10	Fred Smye interview.

CHAPTER 7: STORM CLOUDS GATHERING
Page Line

88	16	Floyd interview.
89	6	Bain to Symington, October 9, 1946. Howe Papers.
89	34	Smye to Symington, February 12, 1947. Howe Papers.
90	1	Symington to Smye, February 24, 1947. Howe Papers.
90	16	See Dow, p. 39.
90	19	Deisher to Symington, March 6, 1947. Howe Papers.
90	25	Howe to Symington, March 11, 1947. Howe Papers.
91	3	Symington to Smye, March 12, 1947. Howe Papers.
91	13	Symington to Howe, April 8, 1947. Howe Papers.
91	27	Howe to Symington, May 1, 1947. Howe Papers.
91	29	Dobson to Howe, May 13, 1947. Howe Papers.
92	6	Howe to Symington, May 3, 1947. Howe Papers.
92	14	Howe to Symington, June 6, 1947. Howe Papers.
94	7	Quoted in Milberry, *The Avro CF-100*, p. 13.

94	21	I am indebted to Desmond M. Chorley for much of the information on John Frost. Chorley recorded one of the rare interviews with Frost for his work on the CF-100. See also W. R. Richardson in the *Canadian Aviation Historical Society Journal*, Fall 1980.
97	35	Floyd interview.
97	38	Fred Smye interview.
98	30	Howe to Symington, October 2, 1947. Howe Papers.
98	36	Floyd, *The Avro Canada C.102 Jetliner*, p. 50.
99	9	Dobson to Symington, October 27, 1947. Howe Papers.
99	30	Bain interview.
100	6	Floyd interview; see also Floyd, *The Avro Canada C.102 Jetliner.*
101	3	Quoted from Floyd, *The Avro Canada C.102 Jetliner*, p. 221.
101	8	See Dow, p. 46.

CHAPTER 8: STEALING THE THUNDER
Page Line

103	33	Frost interview with Chorley.
105	6	*Aviation Week*, "Details on Canada's New Jet Fighter."
105	20	The Toronto *Telegram*, November 12, 1948.
105	27	Fred Smye interview.
106	4	The memo, dated March 23, 1948, was sent by J. L. Brisley, head of the engine test section. Smye Papers, courtesy Randy Smye.
106	39	The *Toronto Star*, March 28, 1948.
108	20	The *Globe and Mail*, Februrary 11, 1949.
110	4	Quoted in Young, *Jet Age*.
111	4	The *Globe and Mail*, February 22, 1949.
111	16	The *Globe and Mail*, July 28, 1949.
111	17	Ibid.
113	10	Ibid. The Comet took to the air on July 27, 1949.
115	30	The *Globe and Mail*, August 18, 1949.
116	6	Fred Smye interview.
117	17	Floyd, "The Avro Canada Story."
117	30	Dobson to Howe, March 29, 1950. Howe Papers.
118	1	Howe to Dobson, April 6, 1950. Howe Papers.
118	7	McGregor, *Adolescence of an Airline*.
118	24	The photograph of the Jetliner and accompanying caption were run in numerous American newspapers, e.g., the Rochester *Democrat and Chronicle*.
119	12	Quoted in *Avro Newsmagazine*, June 1956 ("As Others See Us").
119	14	Ibid.
119	40	Howe to Smye, December 30, 1950. Howe Papers.
120	14	Fred Smye interview. A. V. Roe was in fact working on a second prototype jet airliner. By November, 1951, the fuselage mock-up was almost complete. "We had planned to use it as a test for pressurization," recalls Jim Floyd. As for other schemes in the works, Guest Hake, an Avro engineer, actually come up with a stretch version of the C-102 intended to be powered by four Nene engines.—Floyd interview.

CHAPTER 9: THE QUICK AND THE DEAD
Page Line

122	1	Long quoted passages in this section (pp. 122–29) are taken from *The Quick and the Dead*, the autobiography of W. A. (Bill) Waterton, p. 112, 162–79. Other quotes come from the interview with Waterton.

122 31   Rogers interview.
122 37   Cooper-Slipper interview.
123 21   Chorley, "Canada's World Beating All-Weather Jet Fighter."
123 29   Frost interview with Chorley.
127 12   Frost interview with Chorley.
127 28   Ibid.
137 9   The Montreal *Gazette*, October 11, 1951.
137 20   Mrs. Ken Barnes interview.
137 31   Fred Smye interview.

CHAPTER 10: THE COMING OF CRAWFORD GORDON
Page Line
140 17   Young, *Jet Age*.
140 27   Howe to Gordon, December 13, 1945. Gordon Papers, courtesy Crawford Gordon III.
141 4   Howe to Gordon, February 5, 1951.
141 8   *Saturday Night*, April 17, 1951.
141 33   July 11, 1951. Gordon Papers, courtesy Crawford Gordon III.
141 39   Fred Smye interview.
142 3   The *Globe and Mail*, October 12, 1951.
142 8   The *Toronto Star*, October 10, 1951.
142 34   Ibid., October 17, 1951. See also A. V. Roe Canada, Spearhead of Defence.
142 38   The *Globe and Mail*, October 15, 1951.
143 3   Ibid.
143 8   A. V. Roe Canada, Analysis of Major Projects at A. V. Roe Canada; Avro Aircraft, Historical Record of the CF-100.
143 10   Boyd interview.
144 9   Hornick, "The CF-100: Canada's Boldest, Costliest Aircraft Venture."
144 15   Ibid. See also Keith, "I Flew in Our New Jet Fighter."
144 31   Howe to A. V. Roe Canada Ltd., November 12, 1951. Howe Papers.
145 28   House of Commons, *Debates*, April 4, 1942.
146 20   Howe to Crawford Gordon, January 25, 1952. Howe Papers.
146 26   Fred Smye interview.
148 26   Ibid. Smye repeated exactly the same story to journalist John D. Harbron at the Toronto Press Club in 1968. Courtesy John D. Harbron. Fred Smye confirmed the story in a letter to the author, January 29, 1977.
149 3   Floyd interview.
149 8   Adey interview.
150 12   A. V. Roe Canada, Historical Record of the CF-100.
151 17   Fred Smye interview; Earl interview.
152 2   Adey interview.
152 20   Gordon Papers, courtesy Crawford Gordon III.
153 30   Adey interview.
154 11   Floyd interview.
156 20   Hornick interview.

CHAPTER 11: HIGH FLIGHT
Page Line
161 21   Kelly interview.
162 2   *The Financial Post*, August 9, 1952.
162 12   Howe to Gordon, November 15, 1952. Howe Papers.

163   7   Maxwell W. Mackenzie, Minister of Defence Production, the *Globe and Mail*, December 11, 1951.

163   31   Dilworth interview.

167   16   Earl interview.

167   18   The *Globe and Mail*, February 19, 1953.

167   24   Howe to G. M. Grant (co-ordinator of production, Department of Defence Production), February 13, 1953, Howe Papers.

167   33   Earl interview.

168   2   Howe to Gordon, March 4, 1953. Howe Papers.

169   4   Milberry, *The Avro CF-100*, p. 34.

169   15   Childerhose, "The Stable." Childerhose also said: "You've got to give it to those CF-100 pilots. They're ordered to fly the plane and they do."

171   14   Grossmith interview.

171   38   The Toronto *Telegram*, April 23, 1952.

172   9   Howe to Gordon, August 23, 1952.

172   15   Fred Smye interview.

172   35   The *Globe and Mail*, April 25, 1952.

173   16   Avro news release, July 24, 1952.

173   26   The *Globe and Mail*, January 15, 1953.

173   35   Howe to Gordon, February 28, 1953. Howe Papers.

CHAPTER 12: GODS OF THE AIR

Page Line

175   1   The *Globe and Mail*, January 4, 1952.

175   6   Ibid., January 5, 1952.

177   25   For discussion of the design evolution of the CF-105 Arrow, see Gunston, *Early Supersonic Fighters of the West*, pp. 122–25. For drawings of the various proposals, from the CF-100 to the Arrow Mk.2 with Iroquois engines, see Arrowheads, *Arrow*, p. 12.

178   4   See Arrowheads, p.13.

178   16   Ibid., January 4, 1952.

178   29   Howe to Claxton, December 19, 1952. Howe Papers. Quoted in Dow, p. 85.

179   4   The author is indebted to Professor James Eayrs for providing a paper he wrote in 1967 with General Charles Foulkes on the Arrow story, "To Set the Record Straight." Most references to the government, the Chiefs of Staff Committee, and the Cabinet Defence Committee are drawn from the paper. See also "The Arrow: The Untold Story of Canada's CF-105," by James Eayrs.

181   25   Stuart Davies, "The Family of Delta Aircraft." Courtesy Jim Floyd.

183   3   Arrowheads, p.17.

183   16   Ibid., p.21.

184   9   In September, 1950, Frank Whittle, Keast's former employer, who had pioneered in British jet engine technology, visited A. V. Roe Canada's gas turbine division. Keast took Whittle through the engine test cell where the Orenda was running full tilt. Whittle watched the engine running for some time, then turned to Keast and said, "Axial?" Keast said, "Yes sir." Without batting an eye Whittle whispered, "Traitor!"—Keast interview.

185   21   See Arrowheads, p. 121.

185   27   See Peden, *Fall of an Arrow*, p. 31.

188	15	The order that observers were forbidden to fly without a windscreen was issued by Mario Pesando, head of the flight test department at this time. Personal communication, August 23, 1988.
189	6	The *Globe and Mail*, April 23, 1953.
189	7	General O. P. Weyland to Gordon, August 21, 1954. Howe Papers.
189	14	The *Globe and Mail*, April 23, 1953.
189	25	Ibid., February 14, 1954.
189	29	Ibid.
189	33	Ibid., March 24, 1953.
190	2	Ibid., February 14, 1954.
190	23	Ibid., December 4, 1954.

CHAPTER 13: COMING OF AGE
Page Line

191	13	The *Globe and Mail*, January 16, 1955.
191	14	Ibid.
192	1	Ibid., January 20, 1955.
192	13	Ibid., April 14, 1955.
192	23	Ibid., April 18, 1955.
192	27	Ibid.
192	30	Ibid.
193	17	Ibid., April 17, 1954.
194	3	Peel Country Library was the source of the historical information on Malton.
194	34	The Toronto *Telegram*, January 6, 1954.
195	18	The *Toronto Star*, March 23, 1955.
196	12	A. V. Roe Canada. Tenth Anniversary Souvenir Programme.
196	18	The *Globe and Mail*, June 9, 1955.
196	23	Ibid., July 16, 1955.
196	30	Earl interview.
197	6	Ibid.
197	14	A. V. Roe Canada. Tenth Anniversary Souvenir Programme.
197	21	Ibid.
197	37	See Eayrs, "To Set the Record Straight."
198	40	Schultz interview.
199	14	See Eayrs, "To Set the Record Straight."
200	3	Quoted in Milberry, *Sixty Years: The RCAF and CF Air Command 1924–1984*, p. 256.
201	35	*Aircraft*, October 1957. See also the *Globe and Mail*, February 25, 1958 ("Missiles Program Lacks Definition").
202	12	Gunston, p. 129.
203	11	Waterton, p. 155.
204	37	Fred Smye interview with CBC for the film "There Never Was an Arrow," outcuts, 1979.

CHAPTER 14: VISION OF THE NORTH
Page Line

208	10	Dow, p. 100.
209	3	April 24, 1956. Gordon Papers, courtesy Crawford Gordon III.
209	8	May 29, 1956. Gordon Papers, courtesy Crawford III.
209	12	The Toronto *Telegram*, April 30, 1956.
209	29	*The Financial Post*, October 2, 1956.

209 40   Wood, Gundy & Company. "500,000 Shares, A. V. Roe Canada Prospectus," 1956.

210 32   The *Toronto Star*, June 30, 1958.

211 1   Floyd, *The Avro C.102 Jetliner*, p. 119.

211 18   The *Globe and Mail*, October 16, 1953.

211 24   The *Toronto Star*, June 30, 1956.

211 27   Ibid.

211 33   Quoted in Floyd, *The Avro C.102 Jetliner*, p. 119.

212 26   Floyd interview.

212 27   Quoted in Earl, "How Roy Dobson Pushed Us into the Jet Age." See also the *Globe and Mail*, June 10, 1956.

212 31   The *Globe and Mail*, February 19, 1957.

213 3   Avro Aircraft. Report No. C100/AERO/655: Mk.5 Accident at RCAF Station London, Ontario, 8 June 1957.

213 32   Harbron, "Young Company on the Way Up."

213 39   Dow, p. 102

214 9   The *Globe and Mail*, August 10, 1957.

214 26   Quoted in Baiden, "A. V. Roe's Bid for Dosco Control." See also the *Globe and Mail*, August 10, 1957; Harbron, "Young Company on the Way Up."

215 5   Ibid.

215 10   Ibid.

215 28   Quoted in Harbron, "Young Company on the Way Up."

215 36   Quoted in McInnis, *Canada: A Political and Social History*, p. 630.

216 5   Gunston, p. 133.

217 18   Avro Aircraft. Long Range Planning Committee Report No. 1.

217 27   Ibid.

219 15   Quoted in *Avro Newsmagazine*, Summer 1958.

219 31   Ibid.; see also Arrowheads, p. 37.

220 8   Hornick interview.

221 17   Arrowheads, p. 127.

223 27   *Avro Newsmagazine*, 1956. Stories of the Avro test pilots are found in Milberry, *The Avro CF-100*, pp. 39–47.

224 6   Cooper-Slipper fought in the Battle of Britain and fought the Japanese over Singapore where he was briefly captured in the jungle and escaped by Chinese riverboat to India. He received his DFC for ramming a German bomber. The impact sent both planes screaming down in flames; Cooper-Slipper recovered consciousness hanging from his parachute with some of his fingernails ripped away. When asked why he rammed the German plane, he said, "I was out of ammunition. Everyone was doing that sort of thing at the time. It seemed, well, stylish." Taken from Callwood, "The Day the Iroquois Flew."

226 1   March 1, 1978. Courtesy Janusz Zurakowski.

226 37   Quoted in Milberry, *The Avro CF-100*, p. 47.

227 10   Zurakowski interview.

229 19   Ibid.

229 23   Chamberlin's "right-hand man" was Walter Dubishinski.

229 31   Avro Aircraft. U.S. Army Requirement for a New Family of Air Vehicles.

230 6   Frost, "The Canadian Contribution to the Ground Cushion Story." (The Turnbull Lecture, May 25, 1961.) Courtesy Des Earl.

230	19	Avro Aircraft Avromobile: A New Family of Air Vehicles.
230	24	Avro Aircraft. Review of Commercial VTOL Aircraft Development Possibilities.
230	33	Avro Aircraft. A Review of Promising Future Avro Projects.
231	9	See Milberry, *Aviation in Canada*, p. 137.

CHAPTER 15: THE ICARUS FACTOR

Page Line

232	17	Bradford, "Avro's Fallen Arrow."
233	9	The *Globe and Mail*, February 21, 1958.
233	15	Ibid.
233	18	Ibid.
233	24	Quoted in the *Globe and Mail*, February 21, 1958.
233	31	The *Globe and Mail*, February 21, 1958.
234	1	Ibid., March 21, 1958.
234	13	Dow, p. 116.
234	16	See Eayrs, "To Set the Record Straight," and "The Arrow: The Untold Story."
236	13	The *Toronto Star*, April 19, 1958.
236	22	CBC Radio, referred to in the *Globe and Mail*, May 9, 1958.
236	34	Ibid.
237	3	House of Commons, *Debates*, May 1, 1958.
237	26	Curtis speech, May 13, 1958, printed in *The Financial Post*, May 16, 1958. "Once an official Soviet delegation visited the Orenda plant. There was a large model of the Arrow on the conference table and one of the Russians calmly walked over to it and ran his finger down the trailing edge [wing] and remarked casually: "Oh, do you people still use this technique?" Bob Robinson to the author, December 6, 1987.
238	38	House of Commons, *Debates*, August 8, 1958.
240	6	"The Arrow Program," August 1958. Smye Papers, courtesy Randy Smye.
240	18	Fred Smye interview.
240	36	Ibid.
243	13	September 1958. Smye Papers, courtesy Randy Smye.
243	30	Pallett interview.
244	10	From Harbron, *"I Never Say Anything Provocative"*, p. 2.
244	22	Diefenbaker, press release on Canada's air defence, September 23, 1958. See Eayrs, "To Set the Record Straight."
244	36	Ibid.
245	10	The *Globe and Mail*, September 25, 1958.
245	19	The Toronto *Telegram*, September 27, 1958.
246	7	Hake to Plant, September 25, 1958. Courtesy Guest Hake.
247	35	Morley to Thompson, December 30, 1958. Sessional Paper 198, 1959, pp. 24–27. Public Archives Canada. Quoted from Dow, p. 124.
248	18	The *Globe and Mail*, December 5, 1958.
248	34	Waterton, p. 179, and interview.
249	4	*Orenda News*.
249	32	*Maclean's*, December 20, 1958.
250	5	Eayrs, "To Set the Record Straight."
250	33	Campbell was right; replacement aircraft were not ordered until 1961 when off-the-shelf F-101-B Voodoos were purchased from the United States.

250   37   Campbell interview.
251   11   Ibid.

CHAPTER 16: OVERTAKEN BY EVENTS
Page Line
254   27   Pearson to Howe, January 21, 1959. Howe Papers.
254   35   Howe to Pearson, January 25, 1959. Howe Papers. See also Bothwell and Kilbourn, pp. 301, 340; Dow, p. 126. Howe told friends that he was losing sleep over the Arrow program.
255   12   Howe to Pearson, January 25, 1959. Howe Papers.
255   32   Quote by George Hees taken from CBC Radio's "Morningside," "The A. V. Roe Story," February 20, 1979; and CBC film "There Never Was an Arrow," March 1979. Hees went on in the same vein, his total lack of information and understanding becoming, if possible, more evident as he continued. "Our interceptor, the Arrow, would have to fly 50,000 feet into the air, discharge its missiles into the Russian bomber, destroy the atomic bombs coming across at the time, and be able to return to earth. But with the design that had been put into the plane, it would not have been possible for the plane to fly up and fly back. It would be able to fly up to the 50,000 feet, then it would have expended all of its fuel, and the plane would of course crash when it returned to earth to land. And that was of course not a practical idea at all, and so, instead of going ahead with the plane which would have cost the Canadian people three quarters of a billion dollars because each plane cost $7 million to build, it was decided to scrap the whole plan because it was ridiculous to put $700 million into a plane that was obsolete and produce a plane that simply wouldn't do the job, and couldn't do the job, for which it had been originally designed; therefore it would have been a complete waste of money to go ahead.... The Arrow wouldn't do the job.... Now the plane was obsolete and there's no question about it, it was obsolete, it couldn't do the job. Not one of those planes could ever have taken off to do the job they were supposed to do because you can't send a plane up to intercept a bomber, and then know that the plane and pilot are going to crash on return to earth."
256   21   Smye to O'Hurley, February 11, 1959. Smye Papers, courtesy Randy Smye.
258   28   Randy Smye interview.
259   22   Adapted from Shaw, *There Never Was an Arrow*, p. 79.
260   3   Johnson interview.
260   14   Fred Smye interview.
260   18   Easton interview.
260   26   House of Commons, *Debates*, February 20, 1959.
261   31   Zurakowski interview.
263   6   *Avro Newsmagazine*, March 1959.
263   29   Kelly to Young, 1978. Kelly Papers, courtesy Pat Kelly.
264   4   D.L. Thompson, Department of Defence Production, to J. L. Plant, President, Avro Aircraft, 11:42 a.m., February 20, 1959.
264   37   Pallett inverview.
265   27   The *Toronto Star*, February 20, 1959.
266   5   Cooper-Slipper interview.
266   26   *Avro Newsmagazine*, March 1959.

267	1	Morley to the author, September 19, 1979.
267	12	The *Toronto Star*, February 20, 1959.
267	15	Ibid.
267	20	Ibid.

CHAPTER 17: SCATTERED TO THE WIND

Page Line

269	8	The *Globe and Mail*, February 23, 1959.
269	13	The *Toronto Star*, February 23, 1959.
269	23	CBC Radio's "Morningside," "The A. V. Roe Story," February 20, 1979.
269	26	That many A.V. Roe people went over to de Havilland Canada is stated by Fred Hotson in *The de Havilland Canada Story*, p. 205. Hotson tells the story (pp. 204–6) of the last years of A.V. Roe Canada before its eventual purchase by de Havilland Canada at the direction of Sir Roy Dobson after de Havilland was swallowed up by Hawker-Siddeley.
269	29	The *Toronto Star*, February 23, 1959.
269	34	Ibid.
270	8	Ibid.
270	21	Ibid.
270	24	Ibid.
270	26	Ibid.
270	31	The *Globe and Mail*, February 24, 1959.
271	4	Ibid.
271	9	From the CBC film "There Never Was an Arrow," March 1979.
271	38	House of Commons, *Debates*, February 20, 1959.
271	41	The *Toronto Star*, February 24, 1959.
272	10	Ibid., February 27, 1959.
272	27	The *Globe and Mail*, March 4, 1959.
272	38	T.C. Clarke to Leslie Frost, March 10, 1959. Smye Papers, courtesy Randy Smye.
273	26	Dobson to Hake, April 10, 1959. Courtesy Guest Hake.
274	1	CBC interview, March 3, 1979.
275	7	Wilf Curtis III, personal communication, June 27, 1988.
275	27	The National Aviation Museum was originally opened on October 25, 1960, at Uplands Airport, Ottawa. New facilities were built and opened in June 1988.
276	35	From the CBC film "There Never Was an Arrow," March 1979.
277	8	The Toronto *Telegram*, April 28, 1959.
277	30	Dobson to Diefenbaker, June 17, 1959. Courtsy Gloria Collinson.
277	34	The *Globe and Mail*, July 2, 1959.
278	3	Ibid.
278	9	Ibid., August 1, 1959.
279	1	Alderton interview.
279	32	The *Globe and Mail*, December 30, 1961.

APPENDIX

Page Line

283	1	Smye Papers, courtesy Randy Smye.
289	46	Ibid.
290	29	Ibid.

BIBLIOGRAPHY

Air Canada: The First Forty, 1937–1977. Montreal: Air Canada, 1977.

(Richard Organ, Ron Page, Don Watson, and Les Wilkinson) Arrowheads. *Arrow.* Cheltenham, Ontario: Boston Mills Press, 1980.

Aviation Week. "Details on Canada's Jet Fighter," November 8, 1948.

Avro Aircraft. Twin Engine Supersonic All Weather Fighter CF-105, n.d.

———. Armament and Electronic Equipment Installations, Falcon/Sparrow II, n.d.

———. Design Study of Supersonic All Weather Interceptor Aircraft, May 1953.

———. CF-105 Supersonic Project, Februrary 1954.

———. CF-105 Twin Engine Supersonic All Weather Fighter, September 1955.

———. Presentation of the CF-100 Aircraft, January 1956.

———. Historical Record of the CF-100, April 1957.

———. Report No. C100/AERO/655: Mk.5 Accident at RCAF Station London, Ontario, 8 June 1957.

———. U.S. Army Requirement for a New Family of Air Vehicles. Development Programme Report No. 4, November 26, 1957.

———. Long Range Planning Committee Report No. 1, January 30, 1958.

———. Arrow II—Twin Engine Supersonic All Weather Fighter, March 1958.

———. Brief Summary of Progress of First Arrow (Aircraft 25201), May 1958.

———. Avromobile: A New Family of Air Vehicles, June 1958.

———. Review of Commercial VTOL Aircraft Development Possibilities. Development Programme Report No. 8, June 26, 1958.

———. A Review of Promising Future Avro Projects. Development Programme Report No. 9, November 1958.

————. Model Specification for Arrow II—Airframe and GSM Installations, January 1959.

————. A. V. Roe Canada. Spearhead of Defence, October 17, 1951.

————. Analysis of Major Projects at A. V. Roe Canada Ltd., 1952.

————. Tenth Anniversary Souvenir Programme, December 1955.

————. *Avro Newsmagazine.* 1955, 1956, 1958, 1959.

Baiden, R. M. "A. V. Roe's Bid for Dosco Control." *Saturday Night*, September 14, 1957.

Bothwell, Robert, and William Kilbourn. *C. D. Howe: A Biography.* Toronto: McClelland and Stewart, 1979.

Bradford, Robert, "Avro's Fallen Arrow." *Air Enthusiast Quarterly.*

Callwood, June. "The Day the Iroquois Flew." *Maclean's*, February 1, 1958.

Canada, Department of Defence Production. Arrow Cost Estimates, February 1959.

Canada, Department of National Defence. *The Post War Canadian Defence Relationship with the United States: General Considerations. Report of the Working Committee on Post-Hostilities Problems.* Ottawa: King's Printer, 1946.

————. *Canada's Defence.* Ottawa: King's Printer, 1947.

————. Specifications for Jet Fighter Aeroplane Type XC-100, AIR-7-1 Issue 2, September 1, 1948.

————. Design Studies of a Prototype Supersonic All Weather Aircraft, AIR-7-3, April 1953.

Childerhose, Chick. "The Stable." *Airforce*, April 1978.

Chorley, Desmond M. "The Clunk: Canada's World Beating All-Weather Jet Fighter." Unpublished.

Cowan, J. S. *See No Evil: A Study of Chaos in Defence Policy.* Toronto: Annex Press, 1963.

Dow, James. *The Arrow.* Toronto: James Lorimer and Co., 1979.

Earl, Marjorie. "How Roy Dobson Pushed Us into the Jet Age." *Maclean's*, July 20, 1957.

Eayrs, James G. *In Defence of Canada: Great War to Great Depression.* Toronto: University of Toronto Press, 1964.

————. *In Defence of Canada: Appeasement and Rearmament.* Toronto: University of Toronto Press, 1965.

————. *In Defence of Canada: Peacemaking and Deterrence.* Toronto: University of Toronto Press, 1972.

————. "The Arrow: The Untold Story of Canada's CF-105." The *Toronto Star* (1977).

Eayrs, James G., and Charles Foulkes. "To Set the Record Straight." Unpublished paper written in 1967.

Floyd, James C. "The Canadian Approach to All-Weather Interceptor Development." *Journal of the Royal Aeronautical Society*, vol. 62, no. 576, December 1958.

————. "The Avro Canada Story." *Canada Aviation*, June 1978.

————. *The Avro Canada C.102 Jetliner.* Erin, Ontario: Boston Mills Press, 1986.

Frost, J. C. M. "The Canadian Contribution to the Ground Cushion Story." (The Turnbull Lecture.) *Canadian Aeronautical Institute Journal*, May 25, 1961.

Fuller, G. A.; J. A. Griffin; and K. M. Molson. *125 Years of Canadian Aeronautics: A Chronology, 1840–1965.* Toronto: Canadian Aviation Historical Society, 1983.

Garbett, Michael, and Brian Goulding. *The Lancaster at War.* Shepperton, Surrey: Ian Allen Ltd., 1971.

Glenn, Clayton. "My First 35 Years in the Airline." May 3, 1978. Air Canada Archives.

Gordon, Crawford, Jr. "The Aviation Industry in Canada." *Canadian Banker,* Autumn 1954.

Granatstein, J. L. *Canada's War: The Politics of the Mackenzie King Government, 1939–45.* Toronto: Oxford University Press, 1975.

Grant, J. F., in the *Canadian Geographical Journal,* August 1938.

Gunston, Bill. *Early Supersonic Fighters of the West.* Shepperton, Surrey: Ian Allen Ltd., 1976.

Hanna, Donald. "Avro: Quality and Quantity," in *Flypast.* Manchester England Library. Stamford, Lincolnshire: Key Publications, 1983.

Harbron, John D. "Young Company on the Way Up." *Business Week,* November 16, 1957.

———. Edited by Margaret Wente. *"I Never Say Anything Provocative."* Toronto: Peter Martin Associates, 1975.

———. *C. D. Howe.* Toronto: Fitzhenry and Whiteside, 1980.

Hornick, James. "The CF-100: Canada's Boldest, Costliest Aircraft Venture." *Saturday Night,* January 18, 1958.

Hotson, Fred W. *The de Havilland Canada Story.* Toronto: Canav Books, 1983.

Keith, Ronald. "I Flew in Our New Jetliner." *Maclean's,* November 1, 1950.

Jet Age. December, 1955. Written and edited by Scott Young with insert written by Crawford Gordon, Jr.

McGregor, Gordon R. *Adolescence of an Airline.* Montreal: Air Canada, 1970.

McInnis, Edgar. *Canada: A Political and Social History,* 3rd. edition. Toronto: Holt, Rinehart and Winston, 1969.

McLin, J. *Canada's Changing Defence Policy 1957–63.* Baltimore: Johns Hopkins Press, 1967.

Massey, H. J. *The Canadian Military Profile.* Copp-Clarke, 1972.

Minifie, J. M. *Peacemaker or Powdermonkey: Canada's Role in a Revolutionary World.* Winnipeg: McClelland and Stewart, 1960.

Milberry, Larry. *Aviation in Canada.* Toronto: McGraw-Hill Ryerson, 1979.

———. *The Avro CF-100.* Toronto: Canav Books/McGraw-Hill Ryerson, 1981.

———. *The Canadair North Star.* Toronto: Canav Books, 1982.

Milberry, Larry, general editor. *Sixty Years: The RCAF and CF Air Command, 1924–1984.* Toronto: Canav Books/McGraw-Hill Ryerson, 1984.

Newman, Peter C. *The Canadian Establishment,* vol. 1. Toronto: McClelland and Stewart, 1975.

Orenda News. October 1958.

Peden, Murray. *Fall of an Arrow.* Toronto: Stoddart Publishing, 1987. (First published in 1978 by Canada's Wings.)

Pickersgill, J. W., and D. F. Forster, eds. *The Mackenzie King Record,* vol. 4, 1947–1948. Toronto: University of Toronto Press, 1970.

Porter, John. *The Vertical Mosaic: An Analysis of Social Class and Power in Canada.* Toronto: University of Toronto Press, 1965.

Public Archives Canada. C. D. Howe Papers. When the research for this book was done, the Howe Papers were not yet organized into volumes and files, as they are now.

Regehr, E. *Making a Killing: Canada's Arms Industry.* Toronto: McClelland and Stewart, 1975.

Roberts, Leslie. *C. D.: The Life and Times of Clarence Decatur Howe.* Toronto: Clarke, Irwin, 1957.

Robinson, Robert R. *Scrap Arrow.* Toronto: General Publishing, 1975.

Royal Canadian Air Force. The Defence of North America Against Air Attack from the North. December 1955.

Saturday Night. "Developing Canada's Air Defences," May 2, 1953.

Shaw, E. K. *There Never Was an Arrow.* Toronto: Steel Rail Publishing, 1979.

Stacey, C. P. *Arms, Men and Governments: The War Policies of Canada, 1939–45.* Ottawa: Queen's Printer, 1970.

Stanley, G. F. G. *Canada's Soldiers 1604–1954: The Military History of an Unmilitary People,* revised edition. Toronto: Macmillan of Canada, 1960.

Warnock, V. W. *Partner to Behemoth: The Defence Policy of a Satellite Canada.* Toronto: New Press, 1970.

Waterton, W. A. *The Quick and the Dead.* London: Frederick Muller, 1956.

White, T. H. *The Making of the President, 1972.* Newark, New Jersey: Atheneum, 1973.

Young, Scott. *Jet Age.* Winter 1955. This issue of *Jet Age* was written and edited by Scott Young for A. V. Roe Canada's tenth anniversary.

INDEX